PAPERS DELIVERED AT THE SMITHSONIAN INSTITUTION ANNUAL SYMPO-
SIUM, 14–16 MAY 1969

Marvin Bressler
John H. Crook
Irven DeVore
Robin Fox
Louis J. Halle
William D. Hamilton
Julian Jaynes
Hans Kummer
Susanne K. Langer
Glen McBride
Margaret Mead
Detlev Ploog
Edward O. Wilson
Robert B. Zajonc

Smithsonian Annual III

MAN AND BEAST: COMPARATIVE SOCIAL BEHAVIOR

Edited by J. F. Eisenberg
and Wilton S. Dillon
Preface by S. Dillon Ripley

SMITHSONIAN INSTITUTION PRESS
CITY OF WASHINGTON

The Smithsonian Institution acknowledges with apprecia-
tion contributions in support of the Symposium by
Alfred P. Sloan Foundation; Capital Cities Broadcasting
Corporation; Charles Pfizer and Co.; Columbia Broad-
casting System, Inc.; The Commonwealth Fund; Eli
Lilly and Company; Geigy Chemical Corporation; The
Grant Foundation, Inc.; Harcourt, Brace and World,
Inc.; Hoffman-LaRoche Foundation; International
Business Machines Corporation; Litton Industries, Inc.;
Louwana Fund, Inc.; The Merck Company Foundation;
Olympic Airways; The Population Council; Reader's
Digest Foundation; Russell Sage Foundation; The
Washington Post; Westinghouse Electric Corporation;
Xerox Corporation.

Smithsonian Annual I, *Knowledge Among Men*,
published by Simon and Schuster, 1966.
Smithsonian Annual II, *The Fitness of Man's Environment*, published by the Smithsonian Institution Press,
1968.

PREFACE

S. DILLON RIPLEY

SECRETARY OF THE SMITHSONIAN INSTITUTION

What is man? Is the study of animals, including insects, fish and birds, also the study of man? Should the study of man be based on man alone? If we are not yet the end product of evolution and can still change within ten generations, do genes control how we hunt, protect our young, affiliate, compete, cooperate, fight, or claim territory? Is man unique because of his toolmaking, brain-body ratio, all-season mating, upright posture, digital dexterity, and the use of language and symbols with which to build and purposefully transmit civilization? Can man learn to control himself and his environment and make habitable this small planet?

These are only a few of the age-old and new questions examined during the Smithsonian Institution's third international symposium held in May 1969 as part of our broad and continuing mandate calling for "the increase and diffusion of knowledge among men."

The contributors to this volume have provided for us a feast of reason. Our own Smithsonian scientists and scholars, with their distinguished contributions to the study of ecology, animal behavior, and human evolution enjoyed the opportunity to carry on dialogs with those who came from so far to be with us. The objective of this symposium, as well as the earlier two, was to bring into the open knowledge intrinsic within a subject but not readily available to the layman or educator because of the usual fragmentary division among disciplines and reliance upon specialist jargon. Particularly appropriate to the "Man and Beast" theme, the intersections of humanities, social biology, psycho-history, anthropology, sociology, pediatrics, psychiatry, public health, law, and international relations have begun to indicate an emerging pattern whose significance transcends purely internal aspects of these disciplines.

There is probably no area of human inquiry where premature conclusions can be more harmful to social values than in appraising the relevance for man of his growing knowledge of the factors underlying the social behavior of animals. The workings of social systems inviting comparison to human societies have been demonstrated for virtually all of the higher animals, especially those living in groups or colonies. Man's biological inheritance is gaining widespread attention as the counterpart, for our generation, of the Freudians' discovery of the unconscious. As with the work of Freud, premature conclusions are being drawn in every important realm of social thought. Comparisons most often made to human societies from the findings of behavioral biology have been the intriguing ones, not necessarily those that are valid. The breadth of the implications of discoveries of animal behavior is recognized by all, but the manner of applying them to specific human situations is contested everywhere. It was in just this way that social Darwinism accumulated destructive legacies for our century.

Even with the glorious advent of men on the moon, future intellectual and social historians analyzing the late 1960s may be struck by evidence, such as in this volume, of an enormous awakening of public and scholarly interest in what one anthropologist has called "the humanity of animals and the bestiality of men."[1] Alongside the outpouring of curiosity about lunar rocks, the historians might note the organized and capricious human violence--as manifested in Vietnam, wars between people along the Jordan, the Nile, and Niger rivers; assassinations of leaders in Dallas, Memphis, Los Angeles, Lomé, Dar es Salaam, Camire, and Nairobi; armed invasions of small countries by big ones; the mixing of student and police blood on the campuses, in Chicago, and at the Pentagon; and the Christian barricades of Belfast—which is part of the current stimulus to widespread questioning about how we humans compare with other creatures and animals.

As Louis Halle pointed out last year, books advancing the thesis that man is a predatory aggressor by nature are welcomed and acclaimed by the intellectual community. "If I should write a book," he observed, "showing that man, like the great carnivores, is predatory by his unchangeable nature, I could be sure that it would be widely read and acclaimed. But if I wrote a book that took an optimistic and teleological view of man's evolution, regarding it as an ascent from the level of beasts to something ethically and spiritually higher, it would hardly be well received and few would read it. The burden of living up to a high stand-

---

[1] David G. Mandelbaum, "Violence in America: An Anthropological Perspective," *Economic and Political Weekly* (India), III (43, 26 October 1968).

6

ard is something men can do without."[2] Marvin Bressler, also a participant in our symposium, has commented, in conversation, that pessimism and "telling it like it is" have affected the academic community to the extent that scholars are "rewarded" or "punished" by colleagues and students, according to whether or not they are filled with forebodings about man's dark future, and that generally means that we should admit our "animal" natures, and learn to live with them. On the other hand, we have not yet heard from portions of our younger generation who celebrate hair and nudity, who might identify "lower" animals with honesty and integrity—even relevance.

This book represents a Smithsonian response to public demand for critical interpretation of ideas and hunches found in the growing popular literature on ethology. In the wake of Julian Huxley's earlier essays, *The Uniqueness of Man,* we can refer to those recent stimulating mixtures of scientific and popular writing which include: Niko Tinbergen's *The Herring Gull's World,* Konrad Lorenz' *King Solomon's Ring* and *On Aggression,* Robert Ardrey's *African Genesis* and *The Territorial Imperative,* Desmond Morris' *The Naked Ape* and *The Human Zoo,* John Bleibtreu's *The Parable of the Beast,* Arthur Koestler's *The Ghost in the Machine,* Ashley Montagu's *Man and Aggression,* Anthony Storr's *Human Aggression,* Lionel Tiger's *Men in Groups,* John Napier's *Roots of Mankind,* Gerald Durrell's *Birds, Beasts and Relatives,* and John Pfeiffer's *The Emergence of Man;* I should also mention such film documentaries as Japan's prize-winning *The Monkeys and the Scholars,* NBC's *Man, Beast, and the Land,* involving Smithsonian scientists, and the National Geographic Society's films on Jane van Lawick-Goodall's toolmaking chimpanzee friends—all contributing to the growth of a worldwide public constituency for comparative behavioral studies of humans and other animals.

The papers, and the discussions and commentaries hopefully have already started to provoke new syntheses, new research, and new speculation and debate. Of one thing I can be immediately certain—my own personal gleaning of much of great interest from the participants. I was careful to note, for example, as Hans Kummer had reminded me to do in his chapter on spacing mechanisms, that during a reception at the symposium the women present seemed to stand closer to each other than did the men. I was able to speculate, too, about the advantage or disadvantage of sending one's child to a school with students of a single sex

---

[2] Louis J. Halle, "The Student Drive to Destruction," *New Republic,* 159 (part 2, 19 October 1968): 12.

7

rather than to a coeducational one, as a result of comments by Margaret Mead who lamented the onset of puberty as a detriment to learning, and felt that latency was a great asset in education. Presumably coeducational schooling at certain ages is a handicap, or is it? I confess to being unable to carry comparisons any further than to note that the assumption of social roles within the societies of mice and of baboons is perhaps reflected by human adolescent reactions which make them appear more neatly dressed in a coeducational classroom.

My own interest in animal behavior commenced with my hobby of keeping waterfowl in captivity and reading the works of Oskar Heinroth and Konrad Lorenz. Later, silent upon an unknown peak in New Guinea, I pondered in awe, the proportionately huge, six-foot, tepee-like structure made by the gardener bowerbird, a strong, single-minded creature the size of an American robin or thrush. Day after day I would be drawn back to one or other of the bowers near my camp, to watch the placing of particular fruits, berries, or flowers in neat, foot-square beds, as I called them, on the scrupulously tidy front stoop of the house.

Although Susanne Langer does not seem quite to believe it in her chapter on the great shift from instinct to intuition, I found that these bowers are virtually a year-round preoccupation with the male birds rather than an extra-long seasonal one, and that the female may come and visit the bower during the nonbreeding season as well. Furthermore, the young males watch the adult birds and so, during the several years of their maturation period, may have a chance to profit by the example of their elders. By this process a transfer of training as well as an enhancement of innate instincts is taking place. I say this because I was able to observe critical selections for color and tone of objects. In one case a flower that I had picked, which was not being used to make up one of the flower beds, was rejected out of hand by the male bird presumably for reasons of color. In another case a flower, not otherwise picked by a male bird, was accepted and, after being slightly rearranged, was included in the bed, even though the flower was of a different species. The color, a pinkish red of this orchid, matched very well the pinkish red of the bed flowers from a vine.

Finally I was able to create a new vogue among two of the bowerbirds. Small shotgun shells with bright-red cardboard casings and brass ends were left about the jungle track as a result of my collecting efforts. One bowerbird began collecting these used shells and finally after several days made a great heap of them on his terrace, twenty-nine in all. Obviously he had ranged widely to gather them. I could not find that his territory was contested, or that he was chased by others during his foraging.

At last a second bowerbird began a smaller collection. This was a new object, and presumably the young maturing males were learning about these shells as a desirable collecting item. These observations, as raw data, are some of the stuff of ethology. I find this sort of material suggestive, as I have found other observations of my own. For example, rhinoceroses vary their behavior by species; some solitary, some living in pairs, some relatively gregarious, they can shift their behavior from strictly territorial to a wandering phase without territory, presumably controlled by a sexual response. I find great interest in reading such field data of ethologists and students of comparative behavior, and I wish that sociologists and anthropologists would do likewise. It is not likely that field behavior studies will lead students into a trap of unreasonable deductions or florid grammatic misnomers, but rather that they will provide future clues.

Out of data such as this may come important experiments on principles of behavior as well as principles of population dynamics influenced by conditions of proximity, spacing, and stages of territorial assumption. In any case that is the purpose of our Smithsonian seminars, as I have already said, to bring together specialists in differing fields who then can derive benefit from interactions with each other, and potentially give great benefit to the audience drawn from what is Washington, that melange of public and government.

I liked Edward O. Wilson's phrase, "anthropological genetics," in his discussion of competition and aggression. The study of the inheritance of traits which affect culture is much needed. As John H. Crook shows in his chapter on cooperative behavior, higher primates can inherit not only traits like speculation or curiosity, but also traits of constraint or caution. In the repertoire of human instinctive reactions there must be a series of such partial antonyms as curiosity-caution, boldness-timidity, and competition-cooperation.

Almost all the contributors were agreed that culture was not an appropriate word to use in regard to animal societies. I am inclined to agree in that culture is a human word drawn from our own vocabulary. It was similarly assumed that overtly at least humans differ from other animals in the possession of language and in the evolution through language with social dynamics, introspective thinking, and patterns of behavior which having long since evolved through language, now overlie and subordinate instinctive behavior. Again this may all be true or it may be somewhat too subjective, too overlain with our own prejudices.

I feel that our definitions are in danger of breaking down as we stand on the threshold of still further discoveries in the language of animal

9

species, and in the degree to which certain animal species may some day be demonstrated to possess their own patterns of response to stimuli about them, from the environment or from their own troops or aggregations of relatives. Experimental work like that of our own Smithsonian Regent, Crawford Greenewalt, on bird song, shows totally unexpected realms of vocal dynamics and range and variety of song, most of which humans cannot hear, so that, like the vocalizations of porpoises, we may be in the presence of a kind of language for which our own experience and habits of thought may not be prepared.

One of the most important things that a number of the contributors referred to was the ability of man to shift a pattern of behavior, either genetically, or through a rapid response of some sort to the environment. Some patterns are persistent, and may persist in a relict state as Irven DeVore pointed out. A highly significant one is the hunter-gatherer way of life as practiced by certain aboriginal groups. To the consternation of modern economists like John Kenneth Galbraith, such people are not clinging to some miserable subsistence way of life, but are amply fed, and, what is most important, beautifully adjusted to an ecological niche. The persistence of such atypical patterns of behavior—atypical that is for most of the rest of us—should be encouraged, for they provide a reservoir of examples of human adaptability which should be a model to economists, psychologists, and, I might add, politicians.

Part of the final problem of all of this was ably demonstrated by Professor Halle, following in the footsteps of Glen McBride and Robin Fox. If we can husband our behavioral repertoire so as to be able to maintain flexibility, we may be all right. Failing this, if training and traditions continue to smother responses or to slow necessary reactions, we may be in trouble.

For Professor Halle the specter is violence—the two classes: the good guys and bad guys syndrome—which is so inculcated in us by tradition, by early school training, and now by the instant communication of television. I am inclined to think that the evidence which he himself helped to bring forth shows that violence has its own countervailing force in constraint, and that the history of the world demonstrates that humans can respond with self-discipline in the face of very real emergencies. If we cannot love other people and if they do not love us, as Americans are discovering to their disappointment, we can at least substitute the imposition of manners.

What no one mentioned in the symposium, however, was conservation. It seems to me that the human being is not in harmony with his environ-

10

ment once he has perfected the technology to conquer nature. And this is what we have now done. We are brought up to be at war with nature. Nature is endlessly hostile, threatening, and is a generous provider of sustenance which can be cropped or raped at will. Man may well have inherited culture traits which, if needed, can suppress violence on his fellow man, but he seems singularly ill-equipped with genetic responses or cultural antonyms to counteract the responses or thoughts implied by the words crop, develop, exploit, manage, and, I might add, pollute.

Can there be shown to be natural, innate, programed patterns of behavior which imply constraint where nature is concerned? I think not, for it is virtually if not actually instinctive in us to fear nature. If we fear nature and we have no innate constraints, then we will destroy nature.

Recent archeological work has shown that a very considerable number of Pleistocene species of animals have become extinct in recent times.[3] Evidence is not conclusive, but it is at least suggestive that the moas, a good source of food, became extinct after the arrival in New Zealand of the first wave of Polynesian hunters. Similarly the large ground lemurs became extinct in Madagascar after the arrival of humans. Ice Age camels and sloths became extinct in North America in hunting man's time. Again, the giant orangutan, the giant pangolin, tapirs, rhinos, and small elephants became extinct in South Asia and the Indonesian islands about the time of arrival of the hunting proto-Malays from southern China. Except for domestic animals and plants, man has a poor record of conservation. Indians in North America were largely limited from exterminating the buffalo by lack of technology rather than strong cultural traditions. Why otherwise massacre them in such vast drives over the cliffs?

The greatest problem today is human population growth. The next greatest problem is our lack of innate or learned constraints in regard to our biosphere—that thin envelope of water, land, and air within which we live. If religion fails us in imposing constraint, if our culture encourages waste and destruction in the name of the expanding economy, then we need a new morality. Let there be a new print-out on the programmer before it is too late and let it start somewhere in the mother's womb or just thereafter—and let it say, "Nature is my friend."

[3] Martin, P. S., and H. E. Wright, editors, "Pleistocene Extinctions: The Search for a Cause," volume 6. *Proceeding VII, Congress International Association of Quaternary Research,* Yale University, 1967.

ACKNOWLEDGMENTS

J. F. EISENBERG

Αἱ ἰδιοφυεῖς δυνάμεις ἅς κέκτηται ὁ ἄνζρωπος συχνάκις δύνανται νά ἐκφρασζοῦν ἤ ἀνευρεζοῦν μόνον ἐντός ἑνός καταλλήλου κοινωνικοῦ περιβάλλοντος. Πόσον σημαντικόν εἶναι ὅταν ἡ πίστις καί ὁ σεβασμός ἑνός ἀτόμου διά τόν ἄλλον, δύνανται κάλλιστα ν' ἀποτελοῦν τήν λιδίαν λίζον δι' ὅλας τάς δημιουργικάς προσπαζείας. Θά ἡδυνάμην ν' ἀνταποδώσω πίστιν καί ἐμπιστοσύνην μαζί εἰς σέ Ντέμπορα, ἡ ὁποία δίς ἐταξείδευσες μετ' ἐμοῦ εἰς νέας χώρας.

Following the translation of Konrad Lorenz' *On Aggression*, the general public evinced a great deal of interest in the relevancy of the ethologist's findings to the understanding of human behavior problems. In the fall of 1966, Secretary Ripley asked me to give an informal address to the Smithsonian Advisory Council. I presented a brief summary of Lorenz' theories at their evening banquet and was mildly surprised at the heated discussions which were generated. At this same banquet, Mr. Ripley suggested that the public colloquium for 1969 be concerned with the question of the relevance to human affairs that studies on the social behavior of animals seemed to offer.

In 1967, Matthew Huxley, John Napier, Philip Ritterbush, and myself began to discuss the organization of such a symposium and the possible speakers. Our desire was to select a dozen or so people from such diverse fields as zoology, anthropology, psychology, philosophy, and sociology. The selection—an agonizing one—was finally accomplished, and the early organizational efforts fell to Huxley. With his departure for the National Institutes of Mental Health, however, the symposium became the responsibility of Wilton S. Dillon, who began the difficult task of assembling and editing the manuscripts.

Dillon and I have attempted to share the load of editing within the spheres of our professional competency, yet we both owe a great debt to those who lent their efforts to such manifold tasks as coordinating publicity, arranging receptions, and making the conference memorable in many ways. These include the Ladies' Committee of the Smithsonian Associates, Ellen Godwin, Louisa Barker, and Meredith Johnson who served as chiefs of special events. We gratefully acknowledge the unique reception staged at the National Zoological Park which was organized by Dr. Theodore H. Reed and Mr. Warren Iliff.

We are grateful to session chairmen, Richard S. Cowan, the Honorable Fred R. Harris, Caryl P. Haskins, Henry W. Riecken, Saul H. Riesenberg, and the Honorable Hugh Scott; to round table chairmen Martin Moynihan, John Napier, and Henry Owen; to Lionel Tiger for his participation as a discussion panel member; and to Timothy Asch of Brandeis University for making available his fine motion picture "The Feast."

The Russell Sage Foundation, which pioneered in linking the social sciences to genetics and other disciplines, provided not only critical financial support but valuable help in planning the program. Paul MacLean, Kenneth Goodall, Neil Cheeck, David L. Sills, and Rhoda Métraux made useful editorial suggestions. Ruth Frazier not only helped to manage the entire symposium but contributed greatly to the early phase of editing the manuscript. The professional staffs of the Grant Foundation, the Sloan Foundation, and the Commonwealth Fund contributed, moreover, to the interdisciplinary nature of the symposium by sharing their knowledge about persons at the crossroads of medicine, biology, and the behavioral sciences.

In recognition that man and his fellow creatures are caught up in a common world environment, the Smithsonian used the occasion to invite Dr. Lee A. DuBridge, science adviser to the President, to present Hodgkins' medals to Professor Arie Haagen-Smit of California Institute of Technology, Pasadena, California, and Dr. Jule Gregory Charney—MIT, Cambridge, Massachusetts, for their contributions to basic research.

We are especially appreciative of the keen interest of the Honorable J. William Fullbright in the Man and Beast Symposium which led to an informal session on the subject for his Congressional colleagues.

PROLOG

WILTON S. DILLON

The chapters of this book are grouped arbitrarily around four interrelated questions. These questions are elicited by the many raised at the symposium and those mentioned in the preface: What are the physiological and behavioral mechanisms underlying social behavior? Is man unique? Are creatures similar? Can man endure? That is, can man tame his aggression, increase his cooperation, and tailor his reproduction rate to fit living space and food supply?

On the assumption that human beings will be the only readers of this fascinating material, and that we are indeed interested in ourselves, the first group of chapters touches upon the evolutionary processes which we humans share with other life forms. The second grouping deals with the functional classes of behavioral mechanisms which make up what is conventionally known as "social behavior." The third grouping is of authors who deal with the common denominators of the whole range of creatures —men and other animals—but focus on the unique characteristics which set us apart. Finally, the contributors to the last part—about human self-control—emphasize some of the conditions for survival of all the species in an age of violence, pollution, and population explosion.

Inspired by Roger Sessions' *The Musical Experience*—a book about the composer, the performer, and the listener—I find that music provides some useful analogs for understanding the symposium and the composition of this book. All the players (contributors) are highly trained, accomplished musicians playing on different instruments (academic disciplines). Some play their own compositions. Some interpret the work of others. A few of the players make their music out of totally different musical traditions and notation systems. For example, the geneticist (William Hamilton) performs with mathematical models and game theory. He provides a strophe to the stanza of the biologist (Edward O. Wilson), but is memorable for his solo part and, from the perspective of the uninitiated, the mystery of his melody. By standards of conventional occidental music, the players from neurophysiology, social psychology, and philosophy—to name a few—may never harmonize. Hearing them play on the same platform is comparable to mixing, say, Bach, Wagner, and Cage with a sample of Japanese court music and the recordings of the mating songs of humpback whales.[1]

At times, cacophony and diversity may prevent the listener-reader from easy discovery of the themes and contrapuntals which run through this collection. But the themes can be discovered. Being a series of slightly overlapping soloists, all members of this particular orchestra have never before played together. Unlike jazz musicians, they do not improvise; instead they arrive and depart with their own set pieces. Yet some pick up the tunes of others and give signs of wanting to assemble again for another full-scale rehearsal.

As an editor, I appear on the stage only after the performance, and am left with the sheet music—some of it still being composed—and some lingering resonances, dissonances, and echoes which I now, in this overture, try to capture for you. If there is a leitmotif or single theme, it is that learning about the behavior of all creatures is pertinent to finding out about man's continuing evolution. The finale is that knowledge about ourselves as part of nature can help keep us alive and help us decide where we want to go in the future. Such a simple theme and final flourish, however, are deceptive. They should not take one's attention away from the complicated undergirding, the hard work of discovery, the grace notes, and minor keys vital to the right synchrony of evidence and hunch.

Music is not the only analogy by which to explicate—apart from substance or content—a symposium and its publication; science, some of its practitioners forget, is a human institution and a piece of a larger social system. It is interesting for me, a veteran of international conferences, to think of these gatherings as temporary social structures. An international symposium, functioning as the intellectual equivalent of a world fair—on a modest scale to be sure—ideally might produce in the way of new knowledge what, for example, the Chicago World Columbian Exposition of 1893 stimulated in the way of architectural influences long after the prototypes were dismantled or converted. Similarly, in the history of literature or philosophy, it is important to remember the coffeehouse gathering—also a temporary social structure—of such movements as the Pre-Raphaelites of London, or the logical positivists of Vienna. Scholars and their publics, assemble by design and chance, come together and depart. The encounters establish or strengthen the interpersonal networks through

---

[1] Such as found in the current research on whale vocalizations by R. S. Payne of the Rockefeller University.

16

which important data, insight, hypotheses, bibliography, and gossip about ongoing research, continue to be exchanged long after the face-to-face event. This book is a partial record of such an encounter. For academia, this is a phenomenon not unlike the processes by which architectural, literary, and philosophical modes are diffused.[2]

Participants in such gatherings may not be aware, at the time, of the potential consequences of their discourses. A formal paragraph in a paper, or a chance remark, may in time have detonating effects. In her commentary at the end of this book, Margaret Mead, for example, refers to the work of the late Helen Blauvelt on comparisons between human children and infant goats. Dr. Mead participated with Dr. Blauvelt in the Cornell and Princeton conferences of the Josiah Macy, Jr. Foundation in 1954 and 1955. Tucked away in published proceedings and the personal memory bank of participants, these conferences develop a kind of immortality once they get into the stream of scientific communication. Materials may lie dormant for years, and then pop up in a new context, giving surprise and perhaps fresh insight.

Historians of Freud date the start of his impact on the American scene from his Clark University lectures. Similarly, historians of the spread of ethological studies might choose the participation of Konrad Lorenz in the 1954 Cornell conference as a significant stimulus to the present link-up between new and old world studies of animal behavior,[3] symbolized in the 1969 Smithsonian symposium by the frequent references of debt to Dr. Lorenz, and the presence of his collaborator, Detlev Ploog. Even without the benefit of sociometrics, the study of the processes of science absorbs anyone who gets in its web and who keeps a penchant for detective stories.

Apropos future intellectual work which ought to spring from the gaps

---

[2] Three significant contributions to the sociology of science, though not so intended, are John Ziman's *Public Knowledge, The Dimension of Science,* Cambridge: Cambridge University Press, 1968; Margaret Mead and Paul Byers, *The Small Conference,* Paris and The Hague: Mouton & Co., 1968. See also my article "Museums: Fossils No More," in *Perspectives on Education,* New York: Teachers College, spring 1970.

[3] See Bertram Schaffner ("Animal Studies and Human Behavior," *Human Organization,* 15(1):195) for an interpretation of these many conferences by the editor of their proceedings. Other milestones in the growth of ethology, to name a few, are the symposia organized by the Russell Sage Foundation, the American Association for the Advancement of Science, the American Sociological Society, Stanford University, the Wenner-Gren Foundation, the University of Virginia, and, of course, the international ethology conferences, the most recent of which was held in Rennes, France.

in this book, I should like to see gurus, scholars, scientists, and humanists deal with the implications of studying animal behavior for a sharper understanding of the concepts of race and culture.[4] The new understanding might lead to some shifts of emphasis within such academic disciplines as anthropology, and—for modern Americans preoccupied with the "black power" movement—some badly needed new framework for analyzing social reality. If nothing else can be said for a zoological perspective on human behavior, it is the blessed relief—even if temporary—to be found in the intellectual exercise of extrapolating from beasts to humans. From that perspective, the category "human being" consists in differences in skin color, hair texture, and the infinite variety of human manners and customs. I do not seek to deny the *social* reality of race and cultural differences, which, after all, is the stuff of my own subject matter. Rather, I want to convert academic heathen—those uniquely focused on *Homo sapiens*—to the pleasures of mind-stretching which come when you drop conventional tools of analysis, have a new vision, and pick up the old tools again. They never cut again in quite the same way.

A species-wide view of the family of man need never reduce our new dependence on the value of animal behavior studies. Even if one agrees with Susanne Langer that we can learn little of sociological value directly from animals, that animal communities are not human societies—what with our possession of religion, morality, law, and government—I no longer can imagine how we can look at human laughter, play, reciprocity, love, and learning without questioning, if or how, our fellow creatures do these things. I suspect that, after reading what is ahead, you will face the same liberation of outlook.

---

[4] A splendid start for yet another symposium would be "The Chimera of Race," in Paul Bohannan, *Social Anthropology,* New York: Holt, Rinehart & Winston, 1963.

18

CONTENTS

		Page
Preface *S. Dillon Ripley*		5
Acknowledgments *J. F. Eisenberg*		13
Prolog *Wilton S. Dillon*		15

PART I WHAT ARE THE BIOLOGICAL BASES FOR SOCIAL BEHAVIOR?

Introduction *J. F. Eisenberg*	25
Chapter 1. The Nature-Nurture Problem in Social Evolution *Glen McBride*	35
Chapter 2. Selection of Selfish and Altruistic Behavior in Some Extreme Models *William D. Hamilton*	57
Chapter 3. Neurological Aspects in Social Behavior *Detlev Ploog*	93

PART II WHAT ARE THE BASIC MECHANISMS OF SOCIAL BEHAVIOR IN ANIMALS AND MAN?

Introduction *J. F. Eisenberg*	129
Chapter 4. Attraction, Affiliation, and Attachment *Robert B. Zajonc*	141
Chapter 5. Competitive and Aggressive Behavior *Edward O. Wilson*	181
Chapter 6. Spacing Mechanisms in Social Behavior *Hans Kummer*	219

CONTENTS

Page

Chapter 7. Sources of Cooperation in Animals and Man
        John H. Crook   235

PART III IS MAN UNIQUE?

Introduction J. F. Eisenberg   263

Chapter 8. The Cultural Animal
        Robin Fox   273

Chapter 9. The Evolution of Human Society
        Irven DeVore   297

Chapter 10. The Great Shift: Instinct to Intuition
        Susanne K. Langer   313

Chapter 11. Evolutionary Universals, Continuities, and Alternatives
        Julian Jaynes and Marvin Bressler   333

PART IV CAN MAN CONTROL HIMSELF?

Introduction J. F. Eisenberg   347

Chapter 12. International Behavior and the Prospects for Human
        Survival
        Louis J. Halle   353

Chapter 13. Innate Behavior and Building New Cultures:
        A Commentary
        Margaret Mead   369

Epilog Alex A. Kwapong   383

Author Index   391

Subject Index   399

MAN AND BEAST: COMPARATIVE SOCIAL BEHAVIOR

PART I

WHAT ARE THE BIOLOGICAL BASES FOR SOCIAL BEHAVIOR?

INTRODUCTION

J. F. EISENBERG

Part I considers some aspects of the genetic and physiological bases for social behavior. Such an excursion into the biological mechanisms underlying the overt behavior patterns is a most necessary first step, since any general theory of observable behavior must be consistent with the existing data from the study of genetics and physiology. Hamilton's contribution deals specifically with genetic models, whereas McBride's discussion spans the gaps among genetics, physiology, and overt behavior. Professor Ploog's incisive essay pinpoints several neural mechanisms and their role in the integration of behavioral responses.

The nature-nurture question really should not be posed in the form "Is this behavior pattern heritable?" but rather to what extent does the genetic background of the individual influence the expression of the observed behavior pattern when the environment of the individual is controlled? It is this problem, the nature-nurture question, to which McBride so ably addresses himself. McBride rightly points out, however, that the relative heritability of a trait is quite different from the question of whether the trait is innate. McBride attempts to debunk the innate-learn dichotomy by focusing on the interrelated factors (i.e., genetic, physiological, experiential, external, and internal) responsible for behavioral expression.

McBride, in attempting to show the multiplicity of factors contributing to the overt behavior patterns which we study and measure, develops a novel conceptual framework in which physiological and modifying environmental variables may be grouped.

The behavior of individual organisms is regulated by time-dependent factors. Organisms mature and as they mature they often have successively different behavioral repertoires. Some behavior repertoires are related to phases of maturation (e.g., infant, juvenile, and adult) whereas others are related to temporal changes on an annual basis (e.g., reproductive phase versus non-reproductive phase). In the latter case, environmental variables (day length, temperature, etc.) often modulate endogenous rhythms of response to produce successive behavioral "castes" within the life cycle of an individual. Here we see an interplay of extrinsic and intrinsic factors.

Behavior patterns are organized in time and space into functional sequences or blocks and the controlled expression of such sequences is subject to two general physiological systems: the chemical system and the electrical system. These systems, although interrelated, are roughly equivalent to the hormonal and neuronal substrates of behavior. McBride develops a computer analogy to show how the same subsystems of overt behavior patterns may be differentially integrated by discrete master sets of higher regulatory control systems. In all cases, the master regulating systems are somewhat subservient to the external factors, although the response level of different control systems may vary temporally by endogenous rhythms.

Returning to questions of trait heritability, McBride states that the ability to form conditioned responses is partially heritable; hence, mankind has the inherited capacity to learn and transmit learned responses through teaching or culturally determined instruction. Man utilizes the same principles of information storage and retrieval in a cultural sense that are operative in a physiological sense within himself and other animals.

The contribution by Hamilton explores the fundamental question concerning the heritability of social behavior patterns. Unless we can establish the fact that social tendencies indeed share a heritable basis, then it is impossible to go on and ask the question: "Does behavior indeed evolve?" and, in particular, social behavior. Hamilton's examples are drawn in the main from animal studies. The extent to which heritable tendencies influence the culturally shaped patterns of human behavior, although discussed by the author, will be deferred for a thorough consideration in Parts II and III.

That behavior patterns have in part a heritable basis is no longer doubted. Pioneer work by Fuller and Thompson (1960) and Scott and Fuller (1965) has firmly established that for a variety of organisms, including mammals, social traits are heritable although shaped within limits by the environment in which the animal develops. Indeed, the capacity to learn is in itself heritable and the capacity to be influenced by varying forms of early experience is to some extent determined by the genetic constitution of the individual.

In order to fully appreciate Hamilton's contribution, some background material is necessary. Fisher (1930) based his theoretical model of natural selection upon a consideration of life tables. For any given breeding population, a life table can be constructed yielding information concerning life expectancy, the probability of reproducing, and the resultant reproductive rate of the population. A population is stable if the individuals comprising

28

it leave at least one offspring on the average to replace them at their death in the future, reproducing generation. If the reproductive rate is less than one, the population is declining and, if the rate be greater than one, the population increases. Genes affect survival and reproduction; hence, any advantage gained by an organism with a given genotype "will be conserved in the form of an increase in population . . ." or extending this thought —fitter individuals leave the most progeny. In short, the relative fitness of an individual was defined in terms of the individual's contribution in numbers to succeeding generations.

The preceding model works quite well for predicting the spread of gene frequencies responsible for a variety of traits but the model runs into obvious difficulties when the trait in question is a behavioral mechanism which actually decreases the "fitness" of the bearer. For example, how does one explain the evolution of neuter castes (non-reproducing progeny) in social insects? How does one account for behavioral traits which decrease the life expectancy of the receiver? This is not hard if the recipient is the immediate offspring of the donor since such "altruistic" behavior contributes directly to individual fitness as previously defined. Nevertheless, altruistic behavior is not necessarily confined to offspring as recipients.

In 1964 Hamilton redefined fitness to include cases of gene-frequency survival rather than progeny survival and, in addition, proposed that behavioral mechanisms which preserve gene frequencies "identical by descent" in related individuals could of themselves be selected for. As a result, the new model accounted for an increase in average "inclusive" fitness for a population of partially related individuals and this newly defined concept of fitness would obey the same rules applied to the old classical definition of fitness.

Altruism in Hamilton's sense could evolve in populations composed of small, inbreeding units. Recent studies of population dynamics indicate that temporary family group formation may be more common than was heretofore supposed (Anderson 1965). Still more important Ehrlich and Raven (1969) propose that the basic units of evolution may no longer be the classical "species," but rather may turn out to be smaller more inbred populations which collectively comprise the more broadly defined classical species. That the basic unit in mammalian social groupings is a female and her progeny can no longer be doubted (Eisenberg 1966). Altruism as defined by Hamilton involves the recognition of near relatives in order to be selected for. This question, that is, "How are relatives recognized?" is considered by Crook and Zajonc. As Hamilton rightly points out, cultural mechanisms for keeping track of genealogy are part and parcel of human

29

J. F. EISENBERG

behavior, although one effect of modern cosmopolitan civilization is a de-emphasis of such considerations.

Not content to deal only with the evolution of altruistic behavioral mechanisms, Hamilton deals with the fixation of behavioral traits which may be considered selfish or in extreme cases "spiteful." Utilizing the simplest models, he rightly shows how extreme forms of "spiteful" behavior, if genetically controlled, would soon lead to the extinction of small populations. Nevertheless, mildly selfish behavioral traits may be genetically fixed and over the long run may be of benefit to individuals when buffered with alternative behavioral mechanisms of an altruistic nature. He raises the intriguing question that gregarious behavior in its simplest form may be an expression of mildly selfish behavior.

He closes with a warning to students of human behavior. The theories derived from a consideration of natural selection do not tell man how to act when conflicts of interest occur. A value system constructed on the possible goals of competitive breeding does not permit the humanistic goals of tolerance and humane involvement with other cultures and nations. What is needed is a set of values which permit constraints on those residues of our "animal heritage" which we may carry within us.

Leaving aside questions of human communication and heritable tendencies, we turn to the fact that overt behavior patterns have a physiological basis. One could approach the physiological substrates of behavior from many different disciplines. The perception of the external world through the major sensory modalities: vision, hearing, taste, smell, and touch, as well as from the internal sensory modalities, giving awareness of the states of the digestive system, reproductive system, etc., are to be found in all higher organisms. Acting on internal and external inputs to sensory organs, the organism takes action. The perception of change in the internal and external environment is not only related to the physical environment but also to changes brought about by the action of members of one's own species. When information is exchanged among animals or men, it can be analyzed from the standpoint of perception or from the standpoint of the energy exchanged in the form of signals. Indeed, the analysis of animal perception and the various modes of information exchanged have been the topic of many recent reviews (Marler and Hamilton 1966, Busnel 1963). The study of perception leads into social behavior through the analysis of communications systems and information exchange processes, some elements of which are common to animals and men, although man's language appears to be a unique expansion of certain latent heritable tendencies (Cherry 1957).

30

Once social signals have been perceived, they are processed and integrated by the action of the central nervous system. To an extent the way in which an animal integrates is a function of past experience; hence, learning can modify the mode of integration, yet at the same time certain response pathways and mediation centers of the central nervous system are determined and place limits on the way in which an organism can respond. Hence, we run up against a basic dichotomy. To what extent does the form and function of the central nervous system and the receptor organs determine the expressed behavior? Further, to what extent are such structures maleable or subject to alternative forms of expression which are generally subsumed under the rather vague concept of learned behavior? The comparison of the action of different central nervous systems is a consideration of differences in capacity to respond. Given a specific nervous system, one can determine how a behavior pattern is initiated and, once initiated, how it is terminated. The readiness to respond to certain stimuli changes with time and, in essence, this leads us to a consideration of both exogenous factors and endogenous processes which can potentiate, initiate, or terminate the expression of behavior. The whole problem of the perception of signals and the correlation between the signal system and the receptor system has been untouched in this section. Furthermore, the basic questions of motivation, learning, reinforcement, and the extent to which behavior is mediated by endogenous mechanisms and modulated by exogenous factors have not received special treatment. (For a review of physiological mechanisms, see Delafresnaye 1961).

In the essay by Ploog, the basic neural structures mediating social behavior and integrating social behavior patterns have been brought into focus. Ploog considers the evolution of the vertebrate brain and shows that in higher mammals the brain consists of three parts derived structurally from their forerunners in their reptile, old mammalian, and finally new mammalian ancestors. Taking the squirrel monkey as his example, Ploog examines a "higher" brain and discerns brain mechanisms underlying auditory communication and display. He further demonstrates how such potential communication mechanisms are involved in the control of social behavior. Motor units related to aggressive acts and sexual acts are analyzed and related to discrete loci within the brain which control the expression of these behaviors.

Ploog demonstrates very well that there is, within certain parts of the brain, considerable overlap between the areas responsible for aggression and sex, and that many elements are shared in common between the two master control systems. Refer again to McBride's article for a similar suggestion. Ploog emphasizes that species of animals have stereotyped components in their communications systems which may be elicited from direct stimulation of the brain. He infers that there are many similar "species specific" components composing human communications systems. Although pointing out the uniqueness of human speech, he nevertheless relates the phenomenon of human speech to forerunners in primate communication but states that the motor control necessary to effect human speech is unique to man. Ploog closes with some very interesting speculations concerning the impairment of speech in autistic children.

In the past, lists of human behavior patterns and, in particular, cultural patterns of human societies have been attributed largely to early experience factors and the processes of learning. Nevertheless, it may well be that a set of limits is placed on what can be learned and these limits may be determined by the genetic background of the individual. This question has not been adequately explored, although such constraints surely do exist. Furthermore, the extent to which nonverbal communication is involved in human social interactions is a new and fruitful area of research which has only been pioneered by a few investigators (Birdwhistell 1963).

Recent work by Eibl-Eibesfeldt (1966) has amply demonstrated that a number of nonverbal communication patterns are universal for all human cultures and seem to function in a similar fashion with respect to the transmission of information concerning the motivational state and probable subsequent behavior patterns of the sender. Hence, the very fundaments of social interaction, namely, the communication processes, at least at the nonverbal level, are to an extent acultural. This concept actually increases our scope of appreciation for the uniqueness of the human animal and establishes the feeling of community since such gestures as have been described as universals indicate that the basis for human understanding at a nonverbal level is present and that all men are indeed brothers.

REFERENCES

Anderson, P. K.
    1965. "The Role of Breeding Structure in Evolutionary Processes of *Mus musculus* Populations." *Proceedings of the Symposium on Mutational Processes* (Prague), pages 17–21.
Birdwhistell, R. L.
    1963. "The Kinesis Level in the Investigations of the Emotions," in *Expressions of the Emotions in Man*, P. H. Knapp, editor. New York City: International Universities Press.

Busnel, R. G., editor.
   1963. *Acoustic Behaviour of Animals.* Amsterdam: Elsevier.
Cherry, C.
   1957. *On Human Communication.* Boston: Massachusetts Institute of Technology Press.
Delafresnaye, J. F., editor.
   1961. *Brain Mechanisms and Learning.* Oxford: Blackwell.
Ehrlich, P. R., and P. H. Raven.
   1969. "Differentiation of Populations." *Science,* 165:1228–1232.
Eibl-Eibesfeldt, I.
   1966. "Zur Ethologie des Menschen," pages 514–525, in *Ethologie.* Frankfurt: Athenaion.
Eisenberg, J. F.
   1966. "The Social Organizations of Mammals." *Handbuch der Zoologie,* VIII (10/7), Lieferung 39, 92 pages.
Fisher, R. A.
   1930. *The Genetical Theory of Natural Selection.* Oxford: Clarendon Press.
Fuller, J. L., and W. R. Thompson.
   1960. *Behavior Genetics.* New York City: John Wiley.
Hamilton, W. D.
   1964. "The Genetical Evolution of Social Behavior," Parts I and II. *Journal of Theoretical Biology,* 7:1–16 and 17–52.
Marler, P. R., and W. J. Hamilton.
   1966. *Mechanisms of Animal Behavior.* New York City: John Wiley.
Scott, J. P., and J. L. Fuller.
   1965. *Genetics and the Social Behavior of the Dog.* Chicago: University of Chicago Press.

CHAPTER 1

THE NATURE-NURTURE PROBLEM IN SOCIAL EVOLUTION

GLEN McBRIDE

UNIVERSITY OF QUEENSLAND

NATURE-NURTURE: A DICHOTOMY   That old lemon, that mystical dichotomy, the nature-nurture problem, needs to be reconsidered. It seems to have more reality in the minds of men than in the world they see around them. We conceptualize what we see in nature, and then impose our ideational structure on the world in an attempt to create order. When the structure fits what we see, then we have a good working hypothesis about how the world may be organized. But when the information does not fit comfortably into the taxa we erect, we usually discard them and seek better ones.

The things we see in the biological world have *never* fit into a nature-nurture dichotomy. Yet we have not discarded the dichotomy but maintain it in as many forms as there are fields, calling it not only nature-nurture, but genotype-environment, biological-cultural, innate-acquired, or instinct-learning. It seems that controversy has emerged as a substitute for study, and arises because of a failure to analyze the organization of behavior to find units suitable for meaningful study. Much of the problem has concerned man, and here it arises from a failure to recognize the nature of the differences between man and other species.

We can turn first to geneticists for information about the dichotomy called genotype-environment. Geneticists have long since discarded any controversy here, and have set about the task of measuring the relative importance of these two processes and their interactions in contributing to the variability they see in the characteristics of animals and plants.

Their approach is to locate characters or traits which can be measured in some way. These measurements are then subjected to statistical analysis which produces numbers, which indicate the proportion of the variation due to differences between animals in (a) their genotypes, (b) the inter-actions between their genotypes and environmental fluctuations, and (c) the differences in tangible and intangible factors in their environments. All of these calculations are based upon measures of the similarity between relatives, and some understanding of the genetic basis of similarity between different types of relatives.

The techniques are reasonable, and are justified by the utility of the estimates of *heritability* obtained, for these are used in the planning of selection programs for improving commercial traits in domestic animals or plants. Studies such as these have given us an idea of the genetic behavior of measurable quantitative characters during inbreeding, crossbreeding, and selection. These are processes involved in evolution and the characters affected are of the same type. We are now able to make some generalizations. Low heritability traits are slow to respond to selection, deteriorate with inbreeding, and show hybrid vigor in crosses, while high heritability characters respond well to selection and generally show little hybrid vigor or inbreeding depression. We also know that the analytic techniques are useful for a wide range of traits, such as growth and reproductive processes, morphology and behavior. All types of characters give essentially similar results when selected.

Many arguments may be raised against the heritability approach to the nature-nurture problem. Two arguments concern us here. First, the analytic techniques are statistical only. They allow us to say what proportion of the variability is genetic, or environmental, but nothing about the way these processes contribute to variability. The second is more serious. To anyone thinking about biological systems, it is difficult to see how one can separate out a single character for study. One can certainly choose a measurable trait which has interest, but on analysis, it always turns out to have many component subsystems, each related to other parts of the whole system in various ways. We can consider some examples.

Body weight is a good general character, often studied. Yet its variability may reflect age, sex, appetite, availability of food, efficiency of conversion of food to tissue, social dominance within a group, resistance to disease, presence of infective agents—bacterial, parasitic, or viral—environmental temperature, and so on. Yet body weight is a sensible unit character at a high level of organization.

Falconer and Latyzewski (1952) showed that selection for body weight in mice gave different results in body composition if carried out separately on a full and a restricted diet. On an adequate diet, variation in rate of fat deposition was selected, but this character was absent in the mice on a restricted diet. James and Foenander (1961) found that a line of fowls selected for egg production early in their laying year were more aggressive than the control line. It was shown that dominant birds reached sexual maturity earlier than subordinates, and early sexual maturity was responsible for much variability in the character selected.

On the whole, these problems do not create serious difficulties to animal breeders. The dangers of unexpected component characters are well recognized, and the desired characters are selected. Selection for such conglomerate characters may be useful, but it is not likely to yield any real understanding of the processes by which characters are built up. We may be able to define unit characters, but we always recognize component characters at lower levels of organization, or arising from interrelations with other parts of the animal system of organization. We do not usually see the nature of the organization which welds the components into higher units.

When we come to consider behavioral characters, the problems of measurement for this type of analysis are usually great. This is particularly true of social behavior. One can make up a wide range of units which are measurable, but we must look at the way societies are organized to see the types of units which have meaning in social behavior. There has been much attention given to aggressiveness measured in the speed of initiating fights and in the ability to win them or to the rate of learning various tasks. I have never seen any discrete category of behavior called "aggressive" or learning. I have seen fights in organized interactions, incorporating feeding, nesting, and sexual behavior with fighting responses. The fights occur in many separate types of situations such as at the breaking of bonds, (pair or parent-offspring), against strangers, or against rivals. Animals organize behavior within their societies, and any units we find correspond with structures in the societies. The units are seldom all aggressive or sexual, rather they are functional groupings, as in the mixture of behavior in fights.

Animal societies can be thought of as structures in space, with individuals as the building blocks, and the behavior of the animals providing the architecture. It is within these societies that I shall now look for units of behavior. To do this, I will first discuss some features of the organization of the societies; I shall then deal with the way behavior seems to be organized to create and maintain societies, raising again the question of nature and nurture in the development and evolution of the behavioral units.

SOCIETAL ORGANIZATION The simplest definition of a society (McBride 1966) is a nonrandom distribution of animals in space, arising from the spacing behavior of animals to neighbors rather than from discontinuities in the physical environment. The two main types of nonrandom spatial distributions are overdispersion and aggregation. Overdispersion describes situations where the distances between neighbors are uniform, like soldiers on parade, or animals on territories of equal size. Aggregation refers to the tendency of animals to come together in discrete groups. There may be, nevertheless overdispersion of the groups, and usually also of the animals within the group. Spacing is a very important criterion of social organization. Whatever else we have in mind when we discuss animal societies, spacing concepts are always involved.

The societies we see are presumably all functional systems of animal organization, in some way adaptive. We see their structures, speculate about their functions, and assume that they are adaptive, for indeed we have no other explanation than that of evolution by natural selection. All societies arise from the organized behavior of animals. The societies are present even in the so-called solitary animals, on territories or home ranges, for these show regular spacing behavior to neighbors and engage in interactions of various types when they meet. They also engage in a range of locating behavior usually communicating caste,[1] identity, and location, for this provides the basis for spacing responses. To remain solitary involves social behavior and organization.

Societies also vary with time, often changing with seasons as well as diurnally. This is seen both in their spatial organization and in the activities of the animals in each social situation. When there is variation in the societies in time, this arises in turn from the organization of the behavior of the animals in time. Animals are not uniform within a species; they vary in age and sex, and even these patterns of behavioral organization vary cyclically throughout each day and year. The grouping pattern is also variable in the societies of animals. All societal structures can change with the systematic cycles of animal behavior. Finally animals vary in the way they space relatively one to the other, or between groups.

Earlier I have suggested that there are four main subsystems in the organization of animal societies: (1) the organization of societies in time, (2) the grouping patterns, (3) the patterns of dispersion, and (4) the organization of the animals responsible for these three types of societal variations (McBride 1966). Here we are concerned with only two of them, the organization of societies and animals in time. We may deal now with these two components of social behavior, keeping in mind that the object of the study is to see the nature of the units in the organization of social behavior of animals. From this point we may be able to see something of the difficulties inherent in attempts to create nature-nurture dichotomies.

---

[1] *Editor's note:* He gives a more extended explanation on page 42, and in his article, "A General Theory of Social Organization and Behavior," *Faculty of Veterinary Sciences Publication,* volume 1. St. Lucia, Brisbane, Australia: University of Queensland Press, 1964. (W.D.)

Time Factors—In this section, we are interested in three social systems or phases. The first concerns the regular major seasonal changes in organization, particularly for the mating season and the nonbreeding season. The second is the coordinated behavior of solitary animals in diurnal rhythms, and the third is the distinctive patterns of *social subphases* of animal groups, associated with coordinated activities of the members. The subphases generally follow each other in a regular diurnal cycle.

Territories are common in the breeding phases of many species, while in the nonbreeding season a different territorial pattern may be found or the animals may change their group structures. Thus the English robin takes up pair territories in the breeding phase and individual territories for the winter phase. There are often separate social phases for migration between the two main phases.

The social-phase system is also found in solitary animals but, within phases, the societies vary with the activities of the animals on a diurnal cycle. The emission of each type of behavior appears to be dependent upon the time of day, forming the circadian rhythms of activities. The effect is to coordinate activities throughout the day; social contacts with neighbors, for example, as in territorial defense, occur daily at the same time. Here it seems clear that in evolution by natural selection, not only is behavior shaped, but also the time of day and season of its emission is determined. This may occur by including the physical features of the time component among the stimuli which release behavior; the releasing stimuli probably include the physiological cycle. Such cycles seem to be a normal feature of the biochemical organization of animals.

The diurnal cycle takes on additional properties of coordination in gregarious species. Changes in activity are communicated throughout the group so that the group reorganizes structurally for feeding, resting, moving, sleeping, body care, and alarm. *Social subphases* are changed by social facilitation or by such mood-indicating and mood-transferring signals as alarm calls. Natural selection has presumably shaped the behavior of animals to produce group structures which provide a suitable social context for each of these activities.

Organization of Animal Behavior—Here we are interested in the behavior responsible for the arrangement of societies in time. Here it seems that animals are all like werewolves (though perhaps the morphological changes are less drastic), reorganizing their behavior periodically to specialize themselves for the activities of each of the social situations they enter. We see three main levels of organization of social behavior: the caste, the role, and the interaction.

When we look at the animals of a species, we see all types—males, females, and juveniles—of various ages. All of these animals are organized differently in some way, to specialize them in morphology and behavior for different (and presumably complementary) ways of life within their societies. At different times of the year we see the animals again reorganized, perhaps the deer have grown antlers, or the birds have molted into their breeding plumage. This major form of behavioral organization we call caste. (The word caste is used to denote organic organization of behavior and often morphology, as it is in the social insects, but differently from its normal use in human sociolgy.) The main types of caste are based upon age, sex, and season.

Animals do not grow up in a smooth continuous sequence behaviorally; rather they pass through a series of relatively discrete stages or castes. Within each caste, the behavior is organized appropriately to the way of life at that age. The most common age castes are infant, juvenile, subadult, and adult. These are organized in insects into a series of instars. In birds there is usually a sequence of feather molts changing the appearance of the birds for each caste. The primates generally change color as they develop from infants to juveniles, and puberty marks the change to the subadult caste.

There may also be a division of labor among adults into sex castes. Where the division of labor between the sexes is equal, then the sexes are not separate castes. Here sexual behavior is generally restricted to a single mating interaction, as in the spawning of shoaling fish. In the great-crested grebe, both parents take up a territory together, either for nesting or for feeding and nesting. Both incubate the eggs, care for the young, together at first and later by dividing the brood between them. The sexes are not separate castes in such cases.

More frequently the sexes lead different but complementary ways of life as sex castes, representing an important division of social labor. This is seen in different behavior and often morphology.

The adults of any species are generally organized differently in their behavior to mark each social phase. Thus the sexes could be separate castes in the breeding season but a single caste in the nonbreeding season, as with the California quail. The behavioral differences associated with seasonal caste changes are often combined with major morphological modifications, such as the breeding plumage of birds or the antlers in deer.

The organization of castes always provides major units of behavior at the social level. Natural selection operates on the behavior of animals, but normally only within the caste system. Caste is dependent upon the endocrine system which is the major organizer of behavior in animals. It seems that all behavior restricted to castes is dependent upon the caste-hormone status of the animal, perhaps as a part of the stimulus-response mechanism. The same animal in different castes responds differently to the same stimulus, and responds also to different sets of stimuli. Thus a predator may release a broken-wing display in a breeding passerine bird, but the response is only flight in the nonbreeding season.

The next level of organization of behavior occurs in a diurnal cycle. This is the circadian rhythm in solitary animals. In groups the diurnal cycle is divided into a series of discrete activity subphases. The role is the repertoire of behavior of each animal within the group for the length of the subphase. Roles differ among animals of different castes and within castes, and there are differences associated with social rank. Usually the alpha animals have the most distinctive roles. Social dominance can be understood only in terms of roles, for rank is expressed as a set of roles, one in each subphase. The ability to dominate others in the immediate vicinity is part of the behavior in some roles, but rank may be compounded with interactions concerned with leadership, sentry duties, or group defense, to give a characteristic role repertoire in each subphase.

There appear to be two main components of role behavior. The first is concerned with the maintenance of spacing patterns with neighbors of each caste and rank (i.e, role) to give the distinctive spatial architecture of the social subphase. This is maintenance behavior concerned with the observance of personal distances, which vary with roles. The second component of role behavior is the repertoire of interactions which can occur within each activity subphase. For example, one seldom sees mating, aggressive, or affiliative interactions in movement or alarm subphases.

I think the term strategy is a better description of these two components of role behavior. Thus a sheep may graze with its head down, keeping its nearest neighbor at an angle of 60° from its body axis, and within a social distance (Hediger 1962). Attention is divided between food and neighbors. Yet when food is scarce, the attention to food increases relative to neighbors, and the group disperses more widely. Animals maintain their spacing and carry out their activities, and can draw upon a range of interactions to maintain the organization of their subphases.

It appears that natural selection shapes the behavior appropriate to each role, so that the role emerges as an important unit of behavior in gregarious animals. The effect is to determine both the spacing and interaction components of each role. Caste thus refers to a repertoire of roles in group-living species. The next level of organization of behavior involves

43

sequences between two or more animals, or between an animal and an object.

An interaction is always initiated with an alerting or orienting response as animals move within each other's personal areas. This is followed by a sequence of responses until a terminating response occurs. This is generally the separation of the interactants beyond the personal distance. Thus the initiation of an interaction always specifies some minimum sequence of responses. There may be a limited range of alternatives at each step of the interaction, and this was best illustrated by Grant (1963). What seems clear is that the initiation of the interaction "uncovers" a range of available responses while "covering" all other behavior. The available responses may be drawn upon, but only when assembled together in permissible or syntactic blocks. Yet there is an almost infinite range of sequences possible in an interaction, a fight for example. At every juncture each animal "assembles" the next block of responses to be emitted, using information from its whole context, but more specifically in the form of feedback from the behavior of the other interactant.

It sometimes appears as though inappropriate responses occur in interactions. For example, when two cocks come together at the beginning of an agonistic interaction, they first take up the male fighting postures, with necks outstretched and hackles raised. Yet at a later stage one male may stop to tidbit to the other. This is a feeding sequence used by hens to chicks and cocks to hens, but here it is modified by raising the tail, which converts the sequence to a threat. Later a male may waltz. We do not understand the significance of the waltz, but it is used in both threat and precopulatory courtship situations. Thus in a fighting interaction we see fighting behavior and also sequences borrowed from feeding and perhaps sexual situations. Yet all of these sequences are now appropriate parts of the fighting interaction.

Thus it seems that any interaction has a program during which any of a number of responses and subsequences may be "called." Many of these may have originated in quite different interactions, yet have now been recombined, and generally modified, to fit them into appropriate places in new interactions.

We have divided, then, three main levels of behavioral specialization into units in time, the caste, the role, and the interaction. There are, of course, smaller units, the subroutines mentioned above and even the various single responses which are combined to form the interactions and subsequences already described. The organization of behavior at lower levels has been reviewed recently by Barlow (1968). The picture he describes shows units of behavior nested within larger units, with the blocks of units assembled on syntactic principles, but largely under feedback control. Stereotypy is present at each level, contributing to the syntactic sequences, but even here, there is some feedback guidance from the animal's context.

There is spacing control in both interactions and in roles. Small-movement responses are involved here in a continuing maintenance operation. Both responses and subsequences are amalgamated according to rules, to form new interactions and to add variety to old ones. The spacing responses plus the repertoire of interactions are federated and become available to animals occupying certain roles. Variety can still occur when different animals use different sets of interactions from those available in a role. Sets of roles combine to form the basic behavioral repertoire of castes.

At this stage we may turn aside to speculate on the way animals may be organized to generate such a hierarchy of behavioral units. For the expression of a single response may occur only in a particular interaction which in turn is limited to one or a few roles, in the repertoire of a single caste. As with all such systems, all levels operate together. If we specify small units, there is a chance that they may be found in many or only a few higher units, not necessarily always amalgamated in the same way or combination. The larger units are always conglomerates, containing large samples of behavior, but all organized in specific ways down to the mission of the smallest units. The large units are, in fact, contextual for the smaller ones.

The intermediate role system is absent in solitary animals, but the hierarchy of control is still present. The caste is usually the large unit, with the time of day, probably acting through a circadian rhythm, as the intermediate level.

THE CONTROL OF BEHAVIOR: A HYPOTHESIS: Two separate but mutually interdependent systems must be postulated to explain the organization of these main units. The evidence suggests that we could call these the chemical and electrical systems.

The chemical system—This might be more appropriately called the endocrine system, but we do not know whether the latter encompasses the full range of chemical control of behavior.

Animals sense changes in their environment by their electrical or neuronal system. They respond to these changes in various ways, but

45

usually by altering their internal environment by chemical changes. These changes in turn specialize the animals behaviorally for various periods of time. Some examples may be helpful.

Changes in day length are sometimes sensed, and the animals respond by secretions from the endocrine system. The effect of the hormones is to cause dramatic effects on behavior, perhaps the animals become very aggressive as they enter the breeding season. The animals adapt by changing their spacing behavior by taking up territories, so that a new equilibrium is established between animals in their new seasonal castes. We tend to use the term sex hormones to describe all of the chemical substances associated with the onset of sexual maturity and with the breeding season. Yet we know that these substances affect a wide range of behavior. They are, of course, social organizers which are concerned with the whole phenomenon of sex caste. The behavior emitted by these castes in turn organizes the society to form a total context in which the sexual activity takes place. Yet sexual behavior is only a tiny part of the behavior which is organized by these endocrine changes.

We do not know how caste behavior depends upon the hormonal state. There is an analogy in the phenomenon of drug-dependent learning. A rat, trained to give a set of responses while under the influence of a drug, is next tested when free of the drug and appears quite untrained. Yet when the drug is administered again, the animal clearly shows knowledge of the behavior learned. This type of study may provide one of the essential keys to the understanding of the chemical organization of behavior.

We know that animals acquire a wide range of behavior in their first breeding season. Most of this is new to them, some obviously available to them with minimum opportunities for learning. Much more is acquired from experience, and skills develop in parental or mateship behavior, or in the role of defenders of territory. During the next social phase, there is no evidence of any of this behavior, nor of the skills acquired. There may not even be a recognition of an ex-mate. Yet all of the behavior and skills reappear when they change caste for the next breeding season. Seldom do we find that animals have not improved as parents and mates in their second and later breeding seasons. The phenomenon seems very close to that of drug-dependent learning, and one awaits studies on hormone-dependent learning with great interest.

Moving down one level, we have the role which organizes behavior during a subphase in gregarious animals. We might expect that the behavioral organization of the role derives in part from a diurnal physiological rhythm, but a high degree of coordination has been achieved within a subphase context. We have no clear indication of a chemical control of roles because subphases are short-term structures, and the techniques for the study of biochemical changes in group-living animals are only just emerging. Yet we are aware of diurnal physiological rhythms, and of endocrine changes associated with alarm subphases. More biochemical changes are certainly associated with sleep and feeding. In man at least, we know that behavior during sleep is reasonably well organized, but not even remembered later, perhaps again equivalent to drug-dependent learning. Some of the activity subphases in the social insects seem to be dependent upon the spread of external hormones, the pheromones.

We need to know two things about the role organization of behavior. Firstly, are there coordinated biochemical changes associated with the subphase system; and second, do these chemical changes have regulating effects on behavior, both learned and unlearned? Here we have moved by extrapolation from the caste situation, where there is clear organization of behavior by the hormone environment to the smaller behavioral unit of roles. Only in some roles do we know that there are biochemical changes, but in all we see the regulation of behavior. The model for the alarm phase seems to be as follows. The animals sense the presence of a predator, respond by endocrine secretions, producing what we might call by analogy the "emotion" of fear. As a result they emit behavior expressing this feeling, perhaps an alarm call. The emotion is transferred to other animals who also respond by the alarm call. The deviation in external context has produced an internal state expressing the deviation, and the animals move to reduce their internal deviation by removing the external disturbance. The common strategy is for the group to gather tightly or flee.

The extrapolation must proceed to the next step, to the interaction unit. Here we know that they are initiated by an alerting response (as are roles), and attention now remains high within the interaction until it is terminated. We know that many physiological changes accompany the alerting or orienting response, and that the rate of learning increases. What we do not know is whether there is some chemical system of control of the behavior available within an interaction. There is certainly endocrine involvement in some types of interactions such as fighting or nursing.

We tend to think of interactions as electrically programed, as indeed they seem to be. For readers familiar with computers, the following analogy may be helpful. When an interaction is initiated, it is as though the "computer" is given a series of instructions such as:

a. List "n" (a finite quantity of patterns of behavior available for use) of responses and subroutines is now ready.

b. Assemble the small units (behavior with communications value, such as a muscular twitch or visual signal) according to syntactic rules, but continuously check feedback to see what unit is appropriate, and what is blocked.

c. When conflict exists about appropriate response at any stage, draw on list of displacement behavior (alternate courses of action open to animal when thwarted from goal-directed behavior, such as scratching head).

d. Only behavior on lists labelled "n" and "displacement" may be used. The restrictions on lists are defined by caste, role, interaction, and context.

What I am suggesting, or speculating about, is that there is a chemical basis for the organization of behavior units in these three main social levels. In all cases, the initiation and termination of the chemical state is under control of the electrical system, as probably are even the intensity and concentration of the chemical organizers. Within this system all behavior flows in interactions or maintenance responses (such as spacing maintenance within groups).

I think we can make another step, mainly by analogy with our own experience of the organization of behavior, though there is evidence that the same mechanisms are present in other species. We respond to deviations in our social context by internal states which express these deviations. We sense these internal conditions and name them as the emotions of fear, anger, anxiety, guilt, and so on. We know very little about the organization of emotions, yet we have methods of reducing their intensity: negative feedback mechanisms which restore the equilibrium state. Firstly, we can engage in behavior in the form of interactions, according to some strategy, perhaps flight, avoidance of the situation, or fighting though the habitual use of this strategy leads to negative feedback at the social level, or social control by others. Alternative behavioral strategies may include withdrawal by "cut-off" of sensory input (Chance 1962) or by some intelligent behavior aimed to reduce the deviant social situation without harming others. The second line of defense seems to be in the habituating mechanism, so that we learn to ignore or forget the potential stressor. Failing these, there may be physiological mechanisms of adaptation (the general adaptation syndrome), but should these break down, a positive feedback situation results and a neurosis develops.

We know that we can generate experimental neuroses in animals when we place them in some deviant context, and remove the possibility of behavioral adaptation by avoidance. It seems that the internal expression of deviations in the outside world provides the motivation or drive which leads us to avoid deviant behavior ourselves, and to reduce deviations when they occur around us. Such situations may operate to activate many types of behavioral interactions.

We are aware also of responses to favorable situations which also activate behavior, the positive reinforcers. These we also reduce by acquiring new behavior which ensures the continuation of these states as a new equilibrium. Animals sometimes acquire appropriate social responses by negative social reinforcement, when they express deviant behavior and are punished for it. They learn some appropriate feeding behavior by the positive reinforcement of food, and they also develop strong bonds and affiliations as a result of strong positive reinforcers. Man alone uses these bonds to provide positive social reinforcers for the shaping of appropriate behavior of all types in young children, though he also uses negative reinforcement in the form of punishment to shape appropriate responses to social rules.

Though I have included these emotional regulators of behavior under the heading of the chemical system, naturally I have no idea whether this classification is appropriate. We know that there is a definite cognitive component of human emotions, but we have no real understanding of the underlying physiological organization.

The electrical system—All movements, programed sequences, responses, activities, and behavior appear to be operated through the electrical or neuronal system. All sensory input is in this digital form, all is processed, and the processing leads to responses or modification of responses, or to changes in the endocrine system.

I do not wish to create a dichotomy in this behavioral system, but the behavior emitted is both in the maintenance category and in the larger units of interactions. By maintenance I refer to the minor movements which maintain spacing, allow avoidance of obstacles when moving, or control the head movements of grazing animals. These are hardly conscious, yet they allow animals to regulate their environment to some habituated model of normality. All of this appears to occur without any obvious alerting responses.

Deviations in day length are sensed, again without apparent alerting, while they also control the period of the circadian clock as a zeitgeber. Indeed the model proposed here suggests that the sensory input operates to control a physiological state, setting up patterns of normality for that state. Then deviations, or specific stimuli alert the animal, which moves, either to change a role, or to initiate an interaction made available by the chemical system.

We know that behavior is ordered, so that responses can occur in certain places but not others. Yet displacement activities can occur from time to time, injecting seemingly inappropriate behavior into sequences. Yet when the same type of displacement subroutine appears regularly in some interaction, one should probably assume that it is a part of the program, however inappropriate it may appear. The tidbitting routine of cocks during a fight has been commonly described as displacement sequence. Yet it is clear that the bird's tail is down in normal feeding, but tail-up tidbitting is a regular threat behavior. Thus tail-up tidbitting is quite appropriate in a fight.

The important lesson here is that it is often difficult to classify behavior without reference to its context. Female sexual behavior is a common form of submissive gesture, which operates to terminate an aggressive sequence. Sexual presentation is used in this way by domestic hens and many primates. Infantile behavior is another common form of submission. Thus we have sequences which evolved first in one context in well-programed interactions. Yet they have been transferred to a completely different type of interaction. This is very important, because it suggests that interactions are built up of smaller sequences which are brought together and arranged according to the rules of behavior programing. The subunits are then part of the array of behavior available to an animal when it enters upon a certain type of interaction.

Thus an interaction may be concerned with fighting, but may be compounded of components borrowed from sexual, nest-building, infantile, or feeding interaction. All of these components are available when the fighting control system is operating, rather like calling up subroutines in a computer program. The subunits may appear first in a new interaction by displacement, or small units may be shaped by learning. It is fairly clear that we have too little understanding of either the chemical or electrical systems of behavioral organization. No one doubts that both systems are operating, and that they constitute a complex feedback control of behavior. The only contribution offered here is the suggestion that the system is organized around these three units of social behavior. There is clear evidence of chemical control of the caste units, the alarm roles, and the fighting interactions. The units do seem to provide a model around which some attempts at the experimental study of behavior may develop.

THE CODING AND INHERITANCE OF BEHAVIOR Evolution by natural selection has produced the genetic mechanism itself, as well as the multitude of other characters we see. Behavior may be coded genetically, and in this form is transmitted automatically from generation to generation. With the evolution of learning, a new system of coding behavior appeared, but this is no simple mechanism, for it involved a selective coding process, retaining only behavior reinforced positively, avoiding that reinforced negatively, and leaving the other possible responses unlearned. Yet the ability to code behavior could not become a new genetic system until the routine transmission of behavior in regular patterns could evolve. Once this developed, the processes of selective coding and uniform transmission became a new inheritance system itself coded in the genotype and evolved by natural selection. This new system we call cultural genetics, and it takes many forms. For example, some behavior can spread widely within a generation by imitation, and later to descendants by the same process. More commonly in animals the society develops teaching properties, by which each succeeding crop of youngsters is trained to observe a range of social rules and behavior. The parent-offspring bond is the frame in which most of this teaching occurs. Let me give some examples.

When a sow first stands after farrowing, she does so slowly, rocking herself from her side, with gentle movements. Throughout, she gives a series of snorts, rather similar to the threat snorts of adults. The piglets respond by moving away to huddle together, about one meter from her. Regularly one leaves the group and walks to the sow, who nudges it back, gently at first, but with increasing roughness, until she finally grasps the squealing piglet in her mouth, shakes it violently, then throws it back into the group. The avoidance behavior of the piglets was coded genetically, but the sow supplemented this with an effective teaching routine.

When young chicks are about six weeks old, the young males repeatedly go through a mating routine with their dam. This is eliminated within a few days by the dam's behavior. A few days after sexual behavior is suppressed, the young males approach and threaten the hen, who returns the threat. The expression of aggressive responses to the hen is suppressed within a few days. The dam breaks the parent-offspring bond by attacks on her young, a system common also in mammals. Over a period of a few weeks the juveniles learn to keep away from their dam by continued negative reinforcement. Later they approach other adults but are driven off; they soon learn the appropriate spacing behavior toward adults.

In these cases we are aware that the social system has teaching properties, but we do not know how these are coded. It could be learned anew by each generation of animals, or the teaching behaviors may be coded genetically. If the latter, then the separation of instinct and learning becomes almost impossible. We know that nature and nurture correspond roughly with inter- and intra-generational processes of behavior acquisition, but the existence of the cultural genetic system prevents learning processes from being restricted to either category. It does seem important in evolution that the full range of behavior of a species be acquired. It seems irrelevant from an evolutionary point of view how this is achieved, for the evolutionary process has produced a number of ways to acquire behavior: genetic coding, selective learning by reinforcement, and the use of this in social teaching systems. None of these systems is likely to be completely independent, nor is there any reason why they should be.

The processes of behavior acquisition seemingly lead to the building of the main behavioral units from smaller units. There is much stereotypy in the system, but there is also scope for innovation, particularly by recombination of the smaller units. Interaction sequences commonly include subsequences "borrowed" from other interactions in which they are largely genetically coded. Yet there are mechanisms for retaining them in their new programs, and these probably involve reinforcement learning. Similarly, learned sequences may be built up and also transferred to other interactions, also by learning. One sees sequences moved between interactions where they are attached to new releaser or stimulus context, interactions are moved between roles, and roles between castes. I believe that many of the interactions and roles used by the cock and his hens in feral chickens evolved first in the dam-brood group (though many small modifications are now present).

When we look at the organization of behavior into units in this way, we can see why it is so difficult to make meaningful categories of behavior which ignore the structuring of behavior. I have mentioned that a fighting interaction may contain feeding, sexual, nesting, as well as fighting behavior. Yet no one doubts that this is a fight. But if we make categories of behavior called aggressive, sexual, or nesting these categories simply cannot be shown when we deal with the conglomerate interactions. Even aggressive interactions vary systematically with castes, in male-male, male-female (at the end of a mating bond), female-offspring (at the end of the parent-offspring bond) situations, and with group structure, so that inter- and intra-group fights may show different programs.

ADAPTATION AND GENETIC ASSIMILATION   Animals have the ability to adapt to a wide range of conditions, to heat and cold, to noise, to some pollution of the environment, and so on. Much adaptation is physiological, but much more is also behavioral, by learning of behavior appropriate to the situation. Waddington (1953) first demonstrated that animals able to adapt tended to survive and breed, so that selection could operate on the ability to adapt. The adapted characters could be subject to selection and eventually become genetically assimilated.

The ability to learn, to develop interactions, regulatory behavior, and roles seems to be one of the most flexible adaptive processes in animal evolution. Adaptive behavior may be learned, and even shaped to develop the most adaptive form, *within a single individual and generation.* When such behavior is then subjected to natural selection, one has the most potent system imaginable *to guide the forces of natural selection at the genetic level*—genetic assimilation. Effectively it means that the most appropriate behavior shaped within a generation enables the adapted individuals to survive and leave offspring. *Thus the behavior to be assimilated has already been tested by intra-generation selection.*

From an evolutionary point of view, the mechanism of acquisition is irrelevant. It could be the development of a cultural inheritance system, by direct genetic coding of all details, by the coding of a teaching process within the society, or by developing a high intelligence or learning rate and capacity. The important feature is that the behavior be organized and available in every generation in its appropriate place.

The new behavior may be developed by any of the processes already described which build and modify large units from existing smaller ones. It is clear that the selective process can and has operated on behavior—whether or not it was genetically coded—sometimes to assimilate the code genetically and at other times to develop a cultural inheritance system.

The behavioral units are the units selected, the interactions, roles, and castes. Thus selection operates between individuals on variations in the caste repertoire of each caste, within each role on the variations between individuals in their role behavior, and within and between interactions on variations between individuals at this level. Interactions which gain more effective responses and lose less effective ones tend to spread throughout the population because of the success they give to the individuals carrying them. Individuals with role repertoires which have gained more advantageous interactions and responses than they lose are also more successful, and the process operates also at the caste level.

Thus the units of behavior, the castes, roles, and interactions have a sort of existence of their own in evolution as characters of selective development. Further, *this is not dependent upon their being genetically coded.* In fact, one would expect that the ability to learn, and the syntactic rules of behavioral coding are the basic genetic elements. The components of the main units are always likely to be a mixture of nature and nurture.

One characteristic likely to be selected in a chemical-electrical control system is the degree of integration between the two. Variation here would be seen in the relative freedom of coded characters to appear independently of their chemical control, i.e, their sensitivity to the chemical. The amount of chemical control produced is also likely to be genetically selected. Both characters are likely to determine the freedom of behavior to move between units. Presumably learning processes can operate here to control the rates of secretion, and to condition the appearance of behavior independently of the chemical system. Many animals have acquired the ability to breed throughout the year, and under domestic conditions it appears to be possible to evoke a wide range of behavior out of its normal context. This seems to imply a change in chemical dependence.

BEHAVIOR IN MAN   In man, it seems that the same general principles of behavioral organization operate. We have age and sex but not seasonal castes. We have roles within groups but, whereas animals tend to live in one group and change subphases with activity, man has become a group-forming animal with special groups for many specialized activities. Thus man changes roles when the activity of his group changes, but he also moves between groups to change roles. Yet he attempts to restrict the role repertories of his castes, particularly the adoption of "male" roles by females, and the interaction repertoires of many of his specialized roles (as in professions). He affiliates within each of the groups he normally enters, and may even have difficulty remembering individuals when he sees them outside their accustomed roles. Man develops interactions consciously to fit his activities, but always maintains their syntactic structure, and learns them by a built-in reinforcement learning system as old as the species.

Man is unique in his acquisition of a superb system of cultural genetics, which has almost replaced the genetic system as the mechanism of coding and transmission of behavior. The mechanism here is the use of human speech and language for the coding of all of the behavior which makes cultures, and its transmission from generation to generation by societal teaching or socialization. The cultural-genetic system has created a better system for adaptation but all of the necessary modifications in the mechanisms have been coded genetically.

All animals use positive reinforcement to form bonds, but only man seems to use these bonds to produce positive social reinforcers which actively foster the teaching and learning of behavior, mostly coded in speech. Naturally man also learns the rules of his societies by punishment, but he can also learn to accept the rules in the form of a reason or rationalization. He can then attach a powerful guilt response to the failure to observe rules. Because we can affiliate in many groups, we have an extensive repertoire of affiliative reinforcers, smiles, humor, laughter, or even agreement and the reduction of cognitive dissonance or the susceptibility to group pressures.

I have suggested elsewhere that human language evolved by the incorporation of an actonic message interaction within a social regulating interaction concerned only with the here-and-now of the interaction itself (McBride 1968). The suggestion is more attractive in view of the fact that much of the culture transmitted is in the form of interactions. Much of the significance of language lies in its use in the transmission of behavior by teaching. Yet the ability to acquire this language is itself coded genetically.

When we look at the operation of the new genetic system we see that it works with behavior still organized into the role and interaction units. Each of these units is still built up from smaller units. Interactions and roles still spread by selection, or are lost and become extinct.

Most of the behavior of man may well be coded in speech and imitation, both learned. Yet these learning systems and every other aspect of the cultural genetic mechanisms are coded genetically. Natural selection has produced a new genetic system, allowing evolution by natural selection at high speed, or the coding of any culture and society. Genetic evolution has shaped man into the carrier of this new genetic system. The two are complementary and interactive. There seems to be no room for a dichotomy.

REFERENCES

Barlow, G. W.
    1968. "Ethological Units of Behavior." In *The Central Nervous System and Fish Behavior,* David Ingle, editor. Chicago: University of Chicago Press.
Chance, M. R. A.
    1962. "An Interpretation of Some Agonistic Postures. The Role of 'Cut-off' Acts and Postures." *Symposia of the Zoological Society of London,* 8:71–89.

Falconer, D. S., and M. Latyszewski.
  1952. "The Environment in Relation to Selection for Size in Mice." *Journal of Genetics,* 51:67–80.
Grant, E. C.
  1963. "An Analysis of the Social Behavior of the Male Laboratory Rat." *Behaviour,* 23:260–281.
Hediger, H. P.
  1962. "The Evolution of Territorial Behavior." In *The Social Life of Early Man.* S. L. Washburn, editor. London: Methuen.
James, J. W., and F. Foenander.
  1961. "Social Behaviour Studies in Domestic Animals, 1: Hens in Laying Cages." *Australian Journal of Agricultural Research,* 12:1239–1252.
McBride, G.
  1966. "Society Evolution." *Proceedings of the Ecological Society of Australia,* 1:1–13.
  1968. "On the Evolution of Human Language." *Social Science Information,* 7(5):81–85.
Waddington, C. H.
  1953. "Epigenetics and Evolution." *Symposium for the Society of Experimental Biology,* London, number 7:186.

CHAPTER 2

SELECTION OF SELFISH AND ALTRUISTIC BEHAVIOR IN SOME EXTREME MODELS

WILLIAM D. HAMILTON

UNIVERSITY OF LONDON

> *Anti-Darwin.* As for the famous "struggle for exist-
> ence," so far it seems to me to be asserted rather than
> proved. It occurs, but as an exception; the total ap-
> pearance of life is not the extremity, not starvation, but
> rather riches, profusion, even absurd squandering—
> and where there is struggle, it is a struggle for *power.*
> One should not mistake Malthus for nature.
>
> *Nietzsche 1889*

It seems certain that both selfish and altruistic adaptations exist. That
is, there are situations in which animals increase personal fitness by harming their fellows, and there are others in which they regularly take risks
in order to benefit their fellows. It is always very difficult to know what
particular traits, especially behavioral traits, do for biological fitness, and
it may be, therefore, difficult to convince a skeptic of this by means of one
or two examples. Nevertheless I think that careful consideration of a
typical animal fight will reveal evidence of both selfish and altruistic
adaptation.

Apart from loss of status or territory by the loser, fights do sometimes
cause injury or death. The armor on the shoulders of boars would not
have evolved unless injury were fairly frequent in this species (E. Darwin
1796, C. Darwin 1871, Geist 1966). Usually, however, as soon as it
becomes obvious which combatant is likely to win, and thus just when
serious wounding might be expected to occur, the fight stops and after a
brief pause in which the loser shows submission in some way, he is
allowed to retire. Although it is not quite what we mean by altruism in a
human sense, the restraint of the victor in this context is altrusim:
because the loser has not been killed he may have to be fought again in
the distant future. Although the loser may have been ousted from the
immediate neighborhood, the winner may shortly suffer a slightly
increased territorial pressure because the loser reinserts himself elsewhere in the colony, and so on. Yet, according to Lorenz, the inhibition
of the winner when the loser submits is instinctive and therefore of

genetic rather than cultural origin. In particular, the inhibition against inflicting a fatal wound when this has become easily possible, seems to be so strong and reliable that the loser's submissive posture can actually exploit it so as to make any further hurt less likely (Lorenz 1966, Eibl-Eibesfeldt 1961, Kummer 1968). Such "ritualized" ending of fights plus the existence of armor evolved for intraspecific fighting is a combination of facts which will be very hard to explain in any single version of a "group selection" theory, and also equally hard to explain with the assumption that all adaptation is concerned with individual fitness.

Selfishness creates less difficulty than altruism for the classical models of natural selection; therefore, I propose to consider first the possible extremes of selfishness. It must be remembered, however, that if one trait is treated as "selfish," the alternative traits must be relatively altruistic, so that circumstances that are found to be unfavorable to selfishness must be at least relatively favorable to altruism. The classical models were based on the concept of individual reproduction and so it is not surprising to find that selfishness has an easy field. The simplest model, that of random mating in a single very large population, allows free play to a rather unrealistic ferocity of selfishness. The individual will do all the injuries of which he is capable if he gains thereby even the slightest increase to his personal fitness. The only limit to selection of this kind is set by the extinction of the population. This could occur quickly if the selfishness is severe. For example, consider a recessive type which has a slight advantage over other types in the number (n) of offspring which it rears, but gets this advantage through the killing of more than n other adults. Clearly at some point during the spread of such a genotype the number killed will reach the total of the current generation. Yet such a type certainly has a selective advantage, as can be seen directly when we consider that the killings are subtractions made from the gene pool at random. They involve a set of genes having the characteristic ratio of the gene pool, and their removal, therefore, does not alter the frequencies in that pool, whereas the selfish gains are additions to the gene pool coming from the particular selfish genotype: the additions change gene frequency and this is natural selection.

Even more destructive behavior can be selected if the random mating population is not "very large." Let us call an action which harms others without benefitting the self "spiteful," and if a spiteful action involves harm also to the self, let us call it "strongly spiteful." The condition for the selection of a strongly spiteful trait is that the total of harm (in units of fitness) done to others shall exceed the harm done to the self by a factor

60

almost as large as the size of the population (exactly, by a factor greater than $N - 1$). A population which is small enough, and sufficiently bunches together, to make possible the distribution of such extensive harm must be in danger already, and the spreading of any strongly spiteful mutation is very likely to cause its extinction. Such trends of selection in small populations, if they occur at all, must act like a final infection that kills failing twigs of the evolutionary tree. The word "adaptation" seems to imply at least a little complexity in the achievement of some end, and complexity is unlikely to be based upon a single mutation. Accepting this, it seems unlikely that a multigenic spiteful adaptation could evolve.

No selective trend of any of the kinds yet discussed has ever been observed. Probably this is not only because of the practical difficulty of expressing murderous selfishness and pervasive spite; it is probably partly owing to the unrealistic "panmixia" of the classical model. Panmixia is usually used to imply random mating; I intend it here to imply that the distribution of social effects to other members of the population is also random. If mating is not random, then presumably it is also likely that harms and benefits will not be distributed randomly. If they are not, or if harms are somehow moderated when directed at like genotypes, then the evolution of spitefulness is a more realistic possibility, in that selection will be less likely to bring demographic disaster.

I propose to leave aside for the present the question of whether mating is random. Indeed I propose to start by avoiding it altogether, by letting a model of competing asexual strains do duty for a model of Mendelian population. This may seem to confine me to the evolution of protozoa and bacteria for which the social possibilities seem rather limited; but the analysis is much simpler, and, so far as I can see, using reasonable assumptions, the main features of the sexual model can be predicted from it. Moreover, the two models do really approximate very closely for the sexual case where the traits of heterozygotes are arithmetic means between the traits of their homozygotes.

INTERACTIONS IN PAIRS   As a further simplification it will be supposed that the social trait affects only one other individual. Again, in many contexts this may seem unrealistic, but once more, we may hope that the simplest model will illustrate the sorts of things that can happen in more complex models.

Inherited traits are supposed to be expressed when organisms meet in pairs. The pairing can either be of a type lasting a considerable time or a mere passing encounter. Suppose there are two types in the population, a "normal" N, and a "mutant" M, and their frequencies are p and q. The

61

outcome of the three possible types of encounter can be set out in a matrix:

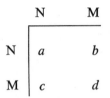

	N	M
N	a	b
M	c	d

By convention the values in the matrix are those received by the type at the left. Thus in an encounter of M with N, M gets c and N gets b.

If pairing is at random we have the average value obtained from a pair, which is $(pa + qb)$ for N and $(pc + qd)$ for M. If the values in the matrix are taken to be actual fitness and not merely parts of fitness, then selection proceeds in favor of the type having the greater average. The equation for change in strain frequency expresses this fact:

$$\Delta q = pq\{(pc + qd) - (pa + qd)\}/W$$

where W is the mean fitness.

If the mutant is of the strongly spiteful type, and if when paired together, two mutants harm each other as much as a mutant harms a normal, then $c < a$ and $d < b$ (and by equal amounts), so that the mutant can never progress.

If such a mutant could *discriminate* and moderate the harm which it causes to its own type to such an extent that $b < d$, then its prospects are slightly better in that it would come under positive selection if its frequency exceeds the value $\dfrac{(a - c)}{(d - b) + (a - c)}$.

This could happen through a chance concurrence of mutants in a small group founding a new population. Even so the case can be dismissed as very unrealistic; it is mentioned as showing the most extreme case for dysgenic natural selection in the case of pairs.

Returning to merely selfish traits, it is fair to assume that in all cases $c > a > b$; that is, when paired with a normal the selfish individual increases its own fitness at its partner's expense. These relations are in themselves sufficient to ensure that the mutant starts to progress in frequency. As selection proceeds mutant-mutant pairs become commoner (as q^2), and the finish depends on what is achieved in these pairs.

If $d > b$ the spread of the selfish strain continues to completion. In the reasonable case where the paired selfish mutants do not do so well as the paired normals we have the overall arrangement:

$$a \qquad b$$
$$\wedge \quad \diagdown \quad \wedge$$
$$c \qquad d$$

During selection of the selfish mutant the mean fitness of the population falls from a to d. In game theory a "payoff" matrix having this form is associated with a controversial problem known as "Prisoner's Dilemma" (Luce and Raiffa 1957, Rapoport 1966). On the basis of this parallel I propose to refer to a biological situation having the above pattern of fitnesses as a *"PD."* The question of whether the outcome in natural selection has any bearing on the controversy about the game will be briefly touched on later. Situations of the *PD* type are probably quite common in nature. I will cite two possible cases.

One is involved in the conditions of sex-ratio selection that sometimes occur in sperm-storing and readily incestuous arthropods. I have discussed these conditions at some length in another paper (Hamilton 1967). Although there is not much evidence directly relevant to the special case which involves the *PD,* the overall correspondence between fact and theory seems good. Since the competing strain model is not directly applicable to sexual organisms, a parallel study of a diploid model was carried out by computer simulation, and this gave an optimum sex ratio which differed only slightly from that predicted by the strain model. Both models confirm that the more selfish type wins in natural selection in a *PD* situation, so that mean fitness may fall; and, as stated, the data broadly confirms the models.

More tentatively, I suggest that a *PD* situation is involved during evolutionary trends to polygamy. Such trends seem to have been quite numerous, for example, in birds (Verner and Willson 1966). Successful polygamous males must have higher reproductive expectations than they would have if monogamous, and the increase in their fitness must come at the expense of males that are barred from breeding. The number of offspring reared per female is probably reduced relative to monogamy. Consider a generally monogamous species in which males become bigamous if they can capture the territory of a neighboring male. A mutant type whose increased pugnacity and skill in territorial encounters often enables it to oust one of its male neighbors would spread through the population in much the way predicted in our model for pairs. When mutants tried to oust each other it is easy to imagine that through real fighting and the probably reduced per-female fitness of the winner, they would end up with lower average fitness than a contentedly monogamous male. Yet their average fitness would certainly be greater than that of the ousted nonmutant males $(d > b)$ and this gives the condition for monogamists to be supplanted completely.

In other situations moderately relevant to the model for pairs it is clear that a genotypically controlled selfish tendency must reach an equilibrium because $b > d$. Consider, for example, tendencies to usurp nest burrows that are very widespread among solitary bees and wasps (Hamilton 1964), and tendencies to dump eggs in other nests of the same species in birds (Friedmann 1932, Hamilton and Orians 1965). These tendencies are selfish in a way that can be called *parasitical,* and it is obvious that the population cannot come to consist entirely of usurpers or dumpers who are unable to make nests for themselves. This kind of situation will be referred to as an *EP* (equilibrium of parasitism).

In considering the equilibrium frequencies in intraspecific situations of this kind caution is again necessary in generalizing to sexual organisms from the case of competing asexual strains. Nevertheless, if the heterozygous class behaves exactly like one of the homozygous classes (i.e., there is complete dominance) the equilibria at least remain unchanged.

Actually it is not known whether the not uncommon parasitical variants of nesting behavior are based on genetical polymorphism or whether these are merely built-in potentialities of which the realization depends on environmental factors. Females of the sand wasp *Mellinus arvensis* may be observed repeatedly trying to force entry into burrows occupied by other females, and going from one burrow to another in their attempts to do this. Fierce fights sometimes occur and these may lead to fatalities (Hobby 1930). Simultaneously other females in the same populations can be observed actively digging their burrows. There are various possibilities as to the nature of the parasitical variants. They may be genetically different from the others. If so, their parasitic inclination may be obligate, or it may be facultative in the sense that they would dig their own burrows after some initial trials have shown that opposition to parasitism is stiff, or that fellow parasites are numerous. On the other hand the females may be constitutionally no different from the others and may be merely behaving the way they are because some accident has destroyed their own burrows and thus caught them in the wrong physiological state or too late in the season to begin burrowing again. Some observations of Fabre (1879) show that this can happen in a mason bee, *Chalicodoma muraria*. In general, however, the truth is unknown, but there is a strong likelihood that something like the described *EP* either is now involved or has been involved in the evolutionary past.

When any such equilibrium occurs it is likely that selection of modifiers that cause a changed reaction when like meets like will eventually resolve it, that is, will allow the selfish gene to complete its spread. The various possibilities could not be discussed in detail for the case of *Mellinus* without reference to a far more complex model. But probably the evolutionary avenues that we see open in the elementary pair model correspond fairly well to avenues that are open in the more complex real cases.

DISCRIMINATION AND SELECTIVE PAIRING   If while held in equilibrium the selfish type evolves the ability in some way to moderate its selfishness or aggressiveness when paired with its own type, then d rises and we tend to return to the *PD* situation. As soon as d exceeds $b,$ the selfish type is able to supplant the other completely. Fairness returns, but each time this happens we expect slightly more the chafing litigious fairness of would-be thieves. Resolution of equilibria in this way is likely to be common with intelligent teachable species. With man, for example, I think it is clear that most selfishness and much criminality arises from evolved selfish potentialities which are latent in all of mankind and which come to be expressed either owing to lack of opposition, as through a "spoiled" upbringing, or under stress, as in poverty.

It is similarly adaptive for the more altruistic type to react selfishly where selfishness is expected in the partner. In theory such adaptation by both types tends to bring on a situation with an unstable equilibrium, but in practice the type which is slower in evolving discrimination is simply eliminated from the population.

Another course open to both types when held up in an *EP* involves nonrandom pairing. Rather than continue in a jangling partnership, the disillusioned cooperator can part quietly from a selfish companion at the first clear sign of unfairness and try his luck in another union. The result would be some degree of assortative pairing.

In accordance with the common aims of the "altruists," their assortative pairing would leave selfish individuals with no alternative but to injure each other. The selfish strain, however, would be evolving the opposite way, with its members tending to seek unlike pairings. For example in the *EP* situation, instead of moderating their selfish action when they find themselves paired together—the road we have already seen to lead to a kind of universal "equity of thieves"—the members of an early-formed selfish pair could part and seek contact with other unpaired individuals who might prove to be unselfish. Insofar as they are successful, dissortative pairing would result. Of course attempts by "parasitical" individuals to attach themselves *always* to suitable hosts have to fail when, through initial success, they have become too numerous. So in a sense this is a weaker course than that which leads to the "equity of thieves." Nevertheless if a dissorting selfish mutant is introduced into a random-pairing *EP* situation it is clear that it would replace the non-dissorting selfish type and end up equilibrated at a higher frequency (Appendix I.)

The biological literature has many examples of pairs of fairly closely related species of which one has become parasitical on the constructive labors of the other. Any species which makes or stores things for future use seems open to the possibility of such parasitism. Presumably in these cases sporadic traits like those evident in *Osmia* (Descy 1924), *Halictus* (Plateaux-Quénu 1960), *Mellinus* (Hobby 1930), *Psammochares* (Crevecoeur 1931), *Polistes* (Yoshikawa 1955)—to mention insect examples only—have evolved via dissortation into a much more permanent condition (Wheeler 1919, Scheven 1957). In such sexual species, however, assortative mating must at some stage have accompanied the dissortative pairing, and on this account it is difficult to imagine the sympatric speciation of a host-parasite sibling pair from a single species. Rejoining of allopatric subspecies or sibling species could provide suitable conditions in both respects. It was on this basis that Richards (1927) outlined a plausible course for the divergence of the nonsocial cuckoo bees, *Psithyrus,* from a social industrious group ancestral to their present bumblebee hosts, *Bombus,* using as illustration the sporadic parasitism practiced by the more southerly *Bombus terrestis* on its more northerly sibling *B. lucorum* in Britain. A striking parallel to this illustration has since been documented in a different subgenus of *Bombus* (Milliron and Oliver 1966). The fact that the less specialized nest parasites are usually found parasitizing closely related species suggests that this was the usual beginning even for the highly specialized examples which are now found imposing on distant genera.

As is shown in detail in Appendix I, whereas dissortation is favorable in only a limited way to selfish traits, assortation is very definitely unfavorable to them, which means, of course, that it is favorable to altruistic traits. Full assortation eliminates all equilibria; it eliminates unlike pairs completely and selection proceeds in favor of the type with the fitter "homopair." Thus in the case of a *PD* situation, in going from no assortation to full assortation the direction of selection must completely reverse.

Assortation makes altruists enjoy the benefits of their altruism, and this obviously applies to assortation of any kind, not just to that which can occur among pairs. From here on I will be concerned mainly with the various ways in which assortation can occur and the degrees of altruism that can be supported. With my emphasis now shifting from the negative to the positive aspects of sociability, however, it seems an appropriate point for a brief digression on a conspicuous kind of animal sociability which I think ought to be left behind here as mildly selfish, although many writers seem to regard it as positively social.

GREGARIOUS BEHAVIOR   G. C. Williams (1964, 1966) has suggested that the schooling of fish is to be regarded as the outcome of cover-seeking instincts of the individual fish: each fish behaves as if trying to put other fish between itself and the potential predator. If a fish succeeds in this it is behaving selfishly: the school is more conspicuous and less maneuverable than a lone fish so presumably the predator gets his meal more easily. In other words mean fitness in the school is probably lower than it would be if the fishes did not school. The school may be the "many body" analog of the harm-exchanging pairs that we have seen to be selected under *PD* conditions.

I think that Williams' experiments demonstrate that seeking cover is certainly an important element in schooling behavior and I am less cautious than he about generalizing the idea to cover most occurrences of massive animal aggregations, including relatively static ones like nest aggregations of birds, and even, by further extrapolation, aggregations in timing such as those shown in the sudden mass emergence of bats from caves (Moore 1948, Pryer 1884). There is evidence in most of such cases that predators do tend to take peripheral individuals and that in the actual presence of these predators, the individuals of an aggregation react in the way the hypothesis leads us to expect (Darling 1937, Baerends and Baerends-van Roon 1950, Hostmann 1952, Tinbergen 1953, Hudleston 1958, Crook 1960, Kruuk 1964, Coulson 1968, Lack 1968).

A hint of this idea with regard to gregarious behavior is recorded in an essay by Francis Galton (1871) on the behavior of half-wild cattle in South Africa. Reading this passage stimulated me to consider some geometrical models which should help to show how readily gregarious behavior could originate through predation if it was initially completely absent. I considered an edgeless distribution of cattle feeding in long grass which could conceal at any point a sleeping lion. If the cattle became aware of the presence of the lion, although completely unable to guess its position, and if each cow then moved in a way tending to reduce its chance of being the cow closest to the lion, it appeared that any initially random or spaced-out arrangement of the cattle would undergo progressive condensation into close-packed groups of ever-increasing size (Figure 1). Of course the perfect concealment of the lion combined with a sudden universal awareness of his existence is very unrealistic in this case. A slightly better example in which the enemy would be concealed almost anywhere up to the moment when it begins to move toward its prey would be that of oestrid flies attacking reindeer (Espmark 1968).

The suggestion that selfish cover-seeking has been an important factor in the evolution of gregarious instincts does not oppose the possibility that other forms of selection may also favor gregarious behavior either working alone or in conjunction with selection for seeking cover nor does it deny that social structure and cooperative relations may also exist in the aggregations. It does predict, however, that social structure should be less evident during phases of panic than at other times. Galton (1871) claimed that the cattle herds had leaders and attributed some altruism to them— this is implied, indeed, by their very willingness to move outside the herd.[1]

---

[1] Galton thought that leaders both of cattle and of men were hereditarily endowed, and he outlined, very vaguely, factors of selection that might stabilize a leaderlike disposition at low frequency. To judge from sheep (Scott 1945), he was probably wrong about leaders of ungulate herds. Regarding the usually male leaders of macaques, baboons, and men he may have been more nearly right. Various data are reviewed by Russell and Russell (1968) and also by Crook in this symposium (Chapter 7).

FIGURE 1. The *main diagram* shows part of a random dispersion of cattle, represented by black dots. A lion is imagined to be concealed somewhere among the cattle. It will suddenly attack the *nearest* cow. This situation specifies a danger domain for such cow as a convex polygon bounded by right bisectors between a cow and certain neighbors. It contains all points nearer to that cow than to any other.

If a cow becomes aware of the presence of the lion without being able to guess its position, it usually decreases its danger domain by approaching its nearest neighbor. For example movement from *a* to *b* changes the domain from *A* to *B*. Having reached the nearest neighbor in general a further decrease of domain can be achieved by moving to a particular side of the neighbor (position *c*). Thin arrowed lines indicate nearest neighbor relations for all the cattle and link primary groups that should form if all cattle are alerted simultaneously and move towards nearest neighbors.

In the rare case of a domain completely determined by three neighbors in an acute-angled triangle (frequency .009), as at *y*, movement to the nearest neighbor, or to any side of it, may not decrease the domain; the minimum domain is equal to the triangle of neighbors and is obtained from its orthocentre, as at *z*.

The *inset diagram* illustrates the two geometrical principles of minimum domains.

68

Fairly elaborate intrapopulation structure based on components of hierarchy, territory, and family groups is also often detectable in mammalian aggregations, especially when unmolested. Altruism, however, only becomes conspicuous in certain types of small groups. We have now to ask, what is it that makes musk oxen, for example, form outwardly facing mutually defensive stands against a predator when their near-relatives sheep, under similar threat, not only tend to face inward but may attempt to butt or jump themselves into the flock—inward from the perilous outside ranks? Here we return to the problem of conditions for altruism.

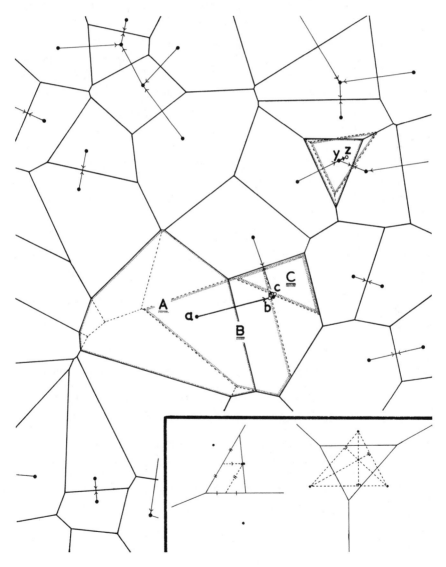

RECOGNITION OF RELATIVES   Galton (1871) stated that cows that have dropped out of a moving herd in order to calve will attempt to fight off predators, although a solitary condition is one which usually causes great terror. This phenomenon, of course, is well known with many normally timid species and as an aspect of parental care it is easily understood even in the classical models of natural selection. But the case can also be viewed as conditional altruism encouraged by a particular kind of assortation of like genotypes; the mother and offspring have half their genes in common by direct replication.

Other cases of relationship may be viewed in the same way. The relatives of an individual can be considered to carry his genes in a statistically diluted state with the dilution depending in a definite way on the structure of the relationship (Hamilton 1964, part I). Distant relationships are obviously more dilute. Indeed the required precise measure of relationship corresponds more or less to the vague popular notion of "blood" similarity.

These ideas are illustrated in Figure 2. In general, if we know all the paths that connect two relatives through their common ancestors, we can say what fraction of the genes carried by one can be expected to occur as replicas in the other. When we are concerned with selection at a particular locus it may be useful to think of this fraction, which is probabilistic for any particular pair of relatives, as being the expectation applying to a large set of relatives having like pedigree connections. The fraction can be called the *coefficient of relatedness*. For relationships which do not involve inbreeding it is the same as Sewall Wright's coefficient of relationship, which is the correlation between relatives on the basis of wholly additive gene effects.

Consider a relationship with coefficient b between two individuals A and B. If A knew the relationship and could intelligently consider the conse-

FIGURE 2.   Related individuals have genes in common due to common ancestry. The pedigree diagram shows certain near relations of individual A and the blackened fraction shows their probable content of genes which are replicas of those carried by A. Nonreplica genes can be supposed to derive from individuals unrelated to A and therefore to have a probable genetic constitution the same as that of the gene pool, as indicated by the level of horizontal shading in the unblackened fractions.

The diagram below represents an altruistic action by A that has null selection. The cousin B receives eight times as much reproductive potential as is sacrificed by A through his altruistic action. The expected additional replicas of A's genes through the additional potential of B exactly make up for A's loss. There is also a nonselective addition to the gene pool.

quences of a selfish or altruistic act toward *B*, he would see that a fraction *b* of the effect he caused to *B*'s fitness consisted, in a statistical sense, of pure loss or gain to genes which he himself carries. The remaining fraction of the effect he would see as a loss or gain to the undifferentiated fragment

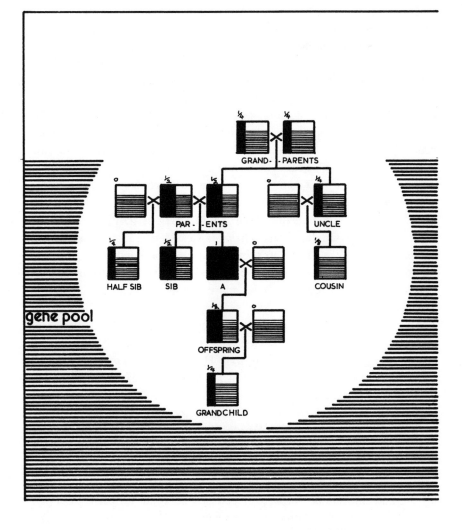

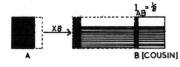

71

of the gene pool that makes up the rest of B's "expected genotype." If A was interested in the natural selection of the genes which he carries he would regard the effect which might be caused to this second part with indifference: it is merely an increment or decrement to the gene pool as it already stands. The effect which he might cause to the "related" (effectively identical) part of B's genotype he has to weigh against the magnitude of the effect his action has on his own fitness. In the case of a selfish act, for example, he has to consider whether the gain to personal fitness is going to be greater than a fraction b of the amount of fitness which he destroys in his relative. If it is greater, then the concentration of his own genes in the gene pool will be increased. The result will be either a contribution to selective advance or perhaps, if A is a heterozygote, a contribution to the maintenance of equilibrium.

Of course there is no need to suppose that individuals think intelligently about natural selection or about the genetic constitution of their relatives: this notion is brought in merely to aid explanation. The model we are concerned with here supposes that A's genotype causes him to act in a particular way toward B; if δ_A and δ_B are additive effects to fitness of A and B due to A's action, then A's genotype is positively selected if $(\delta_A + b\delta_B) > 0$. On this basis I have suggested that it may be useful in contexts of social evolution to replace the classical concept of individual fitness with a concept of "inclusive" fitness, consisting of A's own fitness plus the sum of all the effects he causes to the related parts of the fitnesses of his relatives.[2]

The evolutionary outcome of such selection might well be that A appeared in his social behavior to value his relatives' fitness against his own according to weightings given by b_{AB}. He would always value a unit of fitness in a relative less than a unit of his own fitness except in the special case in which the relative is clonal (as in the case of an identical twin): then $b_{AB} = 1$. In man, twinning is too rare for any special social adaptations to have arisen upon this relationship, but the idea that clonal groups should show almost perfect cooperation helps to explain other contrasts in nature—for example, the contrasting behavior in budded clones of sessile marine organisms and in sessile colonies derived from settling larvae; and the similar but weaker contrast between the perfect cooperation of cells within a multicellular organism and the imperfect coopera-

---

[2] Note that A's own fitness in this aggregate has to be taken not as the fitness A expects to express but as what he would expect to express were he not subject to the social effects that come from his relatives.

tion among the sexually produced individuals of the colonies of social insects.

Man has a great interest in his blood kin. Popular terminology reflects that interest. Human knowledge of human pedigrees is sometimes amazingly extensive, and it is so especially, considering the dependence on oral tradition, in primitive societies. There is no doubt that an appeal to kinship in general does tend to moderate selfishness and encourage generosity in human social interactions; but, at the same time, human sociability is certainly far from being regulated wholly in accordance with the above principle. Human generosity seems also to depend partly on idealism and partly on correspondences of personality that encourage friendship. Moreover, it is well known that enmities between relatives can be exceptionally bitter and destructive. Progressive human cultures seem to have been rather inclined to reject nepotism. The growing importance in human social life of what might be described as a symbiosis of aptitudes, based in part on training but also in part on genetical endowment; in other words, the growing importance of the civilized socioeconomic system, may play some part in this reaction. On the whole, if not in all details, the trend seems to be as one should wish.

It is certain that no other animal has any abstract conception of relationship. But many higher animals can recognize individuals by personal attributes, and this permits some discrimination toward very close relatives, possibly to the distance of nephews and grandchildren. In the Japanese macaque a male's position in the rather elaborate social hierarchy seems to depend partly on nepotism and partly on ability as a leader, much as with man. This and other cases are considered in Dr. Crook's chapter (see pages 241–245). Less intelligent animals, which would be unable to remember their siblings or offspring individually, may still be able to differentiate between relatives on the basis of physical similarity and nearness to the place of birth.

There is some evidence, but no proof, that some social insects are hostile to aliens on the basis of physically inherited traits (Ribbands 1965). Such a system would have the advantage of making enslavement and usurpation by parasite queens very difficult, but presumably would have disadvantages through the occasional occurrence of segregating colonies which would fight within themselves. An acquired colony odor homogenized by food exchanges seems to be a more common method by which social insects distinguish the closely related members of their own colony from aliens. Odor is evidently important as a means of group identification in many species of mammals, especially in rodents (Barnett

73

1967, Bowers and Alexander 1967, Lorenz 1966). The odors discriminated appear to be acquired rather than inherited.

The phenomenon of visual imprinting suggests how an individual could discriminate on a basis which would be largely genetic. Auditory imprinting could work the same way, but aptitude for vocal mimicry, such as exists in birds, would lessen the reliability of this method.

The simplest case where nearness to place of birth implies relationship is that of nestlings and litter mates. I think the evidence in general shows that agonistic behavior in groups of siblings is mild compared to what takes place after they leave the nest. There are various seemingly contrary cases where extensive cannibalism takes place among sibling groups, for example in the embryonic stages of some mollusks. I have suggested reasons for such exceptions elsewhere (Hamilton 1964). A point worth noting here is that *structural* adaptation for attack and defense in these situations has not evolved, whereas it has done so, for attack at least, in cases where competing young are unrelated (see Chapter 5 by E. O. Wilson, pages 189–190 for cases in parasitoid Hymenoptera; and Lack 1968 for cuckoo parasitism in birds).

POPULATION MODELS   If at maturity panmictic dispersal takes place, there is no further distinction to be made; the individuals can be reckoned never to encounter their more distant relatives. If, however, dispersal distances tend to be limited, then neighboring individuals will tend also to be relatives of varying degree. So also will mating pairs; some degree of inbreeding follows almost inevitably from limited dispersion.[3] Wright refers to models of this type as involving "isolation by distance"; more briefly, they can be referred to as "viscous." The population is a continuum but in terms of the gene flow of a few generations, distant parts are isolated from one another. Most generally realistic are the cases in which dispersal has something like a normal form with the mode at the place of birth.

Another type of model which allows only limited dispersal is the "stepping stone" model of Kimura and Weiss (1964). Here internally random-mating populations of finite size are arranged on a line or in a lattice and certain fractions of individuals migrate reciprocally between populations in each generation. This model suggests a very general and realistic one which would include both Wright's "isolation by distance" and his "island" models as special cases (see Figure 3). The effect of

---

[3] Panmictic dispersal by only one sex (or type of gamete) is sufficient to ensure random mating. Thus in theory it is possible to have a population structure in which neighboring individuals have non-inbred relationships through single common ancestors (half sibs, half cousins, and so on).

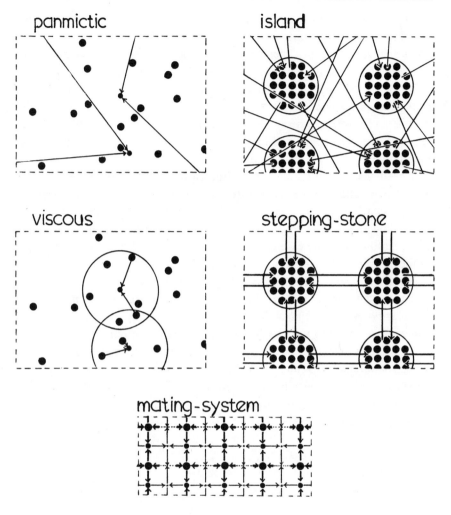

FIGURE 3. Examples of simple breeding structures. In the "panmictic" and "viscous" structures and the example of a "mating system," smaller dots indicate newly formed, or younger, zygotes; in the "island" and "stepping stone" structures newly formed zygotes are not shown. Arrows indicate particular parenthoods, particular migrations between subpopulations ("island"), or regular paths of migration ("stepping stone"). In the island and stepping stone structures most reproduction is supposed to occur through random unions within subpopulations. The mating system diagram illustrates a cycle of four generations. Most analyses of mating systems have concerned linear systems: to the author's knowledge the one shown has not been analyzed.

having a distribution of migration (instead of migration to the nearest population only) has not been analyzed in detail, although it is not beyond the scope of the methods used. The generalization required in abandoning the lattice arrangement has not been considered.

In all models which lack panmictic dispersal it appears that genetic drift reaches no equilibrium except for that holding in local patches of gene fixation, with the mean size of patches ever increasing. This is so, at least, so long as the factor of mutation is not considered. In the absence of mutation, ultimately each individual should become related with almost unit coefficient to all its neighbors. But during progress to the final state, after a population has been sown from a random mixture, and also subject to the occurrence of mutation (which, of course, an evolutionary model must allow), relationship can be expected to fall off with increasing distance, gradually in the case of the viscous models and stepwise in the case of the stepping-stone models.

No detailed study of social selection in such models has yet been made. There are various difficulties: the analytical complexity of the models, the complexity of the coefficient of inclusive relationship under inbreeding, and even doubt as to the validity of coefficients based purely on pedigrees when there is selection in the system. It seems worthwhile, however, to make some tentative remarks on the basis of a coefficient which is easily obtained from coefficients discussed in the pioneer accounts of the models, and which should certainly serve to point out the main social implications. This coefficient is

$$b_{AB} = \frac{2r_{AB}}{1 + F_A} \tag{1}$$

where r_{AB} is the probability of "identity by descent," or correlation, of random gametes drawn from the two individuals A and B, and F_A is the correlation of the homologous genes of A, whose social trait is being considered. To see a rough justification for this formula, it may help to imagine oneself standing in the place of one of the genes of A in the role of matchmaker and considering arranging a successful mating for either A or $B;$ the chances that genes passed on through such matings replicas of the "matchmaker" gene are $\frac{1}{2}(1 + F_A)$ and r_{AB} respectively. Alternatively b_{AB} can be considered as the *regression* coefficient of the additive genotypic value of B on that of A.

Unless A is specially inbred, F_A will be the mean coefficient of inbreeding (F). Sewall Wright's work has given much attention to coefficients like F and r. His papers of 1951 and 1965 review a form of analysis of population structure in terms of "*F*-statistics" which is particularly useful from the present point of view. This touches, however, a rather technical field and for further information the reader is referred to Appendix II. The most useful predictions to which the analyses give rise can be briefly summarized as follows:

1. Highly dispersive species (F_{IT} low)[4] will show little positive sociability, although they may be gregarious. They are more likely than indispersive species to be polygamous.

2. Within species, fights will be most damaging when combatants: (a) differ most in heritable characteristics perceptible to the opponent, (b) derive from distant regions or from different subpopulations.

3. Among species, fighting will be least damaging in species with the most viscous or the most subdivided populations.

4. Cooperative relations and weak social heirarchy within groups will correlate with the following interrelated factors: (a) small group size, (b) hostility to strangers, (c) endogamy, (d) high F_{ST}.

5. Conservation of local resources by populations will correlate with the factors cited in 4, subject to the requirement that a population remains in and defends a group territory for many generations.

6. The general level of aggressiveness in a population will rise during periods of increased dispersal and will *remain raised* until a higher average relationship between neighbors has been re-established. The persistence of aggressiveness after a population crash may be relevant here, but study of F_{IS} and F_{ST} over the whole period of a population cycle would be necessary to confirm this.

INTERGROUP HOSTILITY, WARS, AND CRUELTY In a recent study of biochemical polymorphism in farm populations of the house mouse, Petras (1967) found no evidence of other than random mating within local groups, but on the basis of gene-frequency differences between groups he estimated $F_{ST} = 0.18$. Substituting in (2) this gives $b = .305$, which shows that within groups mice should treat the average individual encountered as a relative closer than a grandchild (or half sib) but more distant than an offspring (or full sib), referring to an outbred population.

It is well known that mice and rats in the wild have unusually united social groups in which dominance behavior is very restrained and polygamy moderate. This mutualism is in strong contrast to the treatment of strangers which is rather vicious; in rats at least, aliens are often killed if they cannot escape (Lorenz 1966). The variability of aggressiveness in

[4] F-symbols used in this section are explained in Appendix II.

captive colonies of mice (Southwick 1955) perhaps depends partly on the extent to which the founding animals came from different wild groups.

Some birds seem to have gone further than rodents in evolving small cooperative groups (Crook 1965, Lack 1968). In some cases several females may contribute eggs to a common nest and take turns in brooding them, or offspring may help their parents to rear subsequent broods, so approaching the situation of some primitively social bees and wasps (Michener 1958, Sakagami 1960). But as with these bees and wasps the stage has not been reached without the appearance of signs of parasitic tendencies (Hamilton 1964, part II).

In all these cases group territories are defended. From what has been said it would not be surprising to find the demographically stronger groups pushing into the territories of their weaker neighbors. Fission could either precede or follow the taking over of territory. No doubt strong groups would also have higher rates of emission of long-range migrants looking for fresh land to colonize or seeking assimilation into other groups, but for the reasons already given I suspect that production of new colonies by budding is relatively more important in the most mutualistic species.

Similar rather closed and highly cooperative societies appear in primates. As would be expected, with increased intelligence, they are much more complex, but intergroup hostility in varying degrees still occurs (e.g., Kummer 1968; Southwick, Beg, and Siddiqi 1965).

With still further increase in intelligence, with increase in ability to communicate (and hence also to organize), with invention of new weapons (primarily for hunting)[5] and ability to transmit culturally the techniques acquired, and with increase in possessions that could be carried off or usurped and used in situ, I find no difficulty in imagining that it could become advantageous for groups to make organized forcible incursions into the territory of their weaker neighbors. In other words, I suggest that

---

[5] The origin of the sting in Hymenoptera provides an evolutionary precedent for Ardrey's (1961) suggestion that in hominids the use of tools for hunting was quickly followed by their use as weapons of combat. The sting was originally the ovipositer of a vegetarian sawfly (Malyshev 1966). It then became a paralyzer of insect prey. Finally in many species it has become a lethal weapon against conspecifics, used both in aggression and defense. The structure and use of the sting depends almost wholly on genotype. The human use of tools depends largely on intelligence; thus the parallel conversions of hand-plus-tool in hominids could be expected to occur much more rapidly. There are other examples of appendages converted as murderous weapons in arthropods (e.g., Corbet and Griffiths 1963, Woodring 1969). Among arthropods, however, mortal combats are more usual than among vertebrates.

warfare was a natural development from the evolutionary trends taking place in the hominid stock.

As mentioned by Wilson, something very like warfare occurs within many ant species. The human phenomenon of slavery also has a parallel in ants; and robbery, in various forms, occurs in bees, wasps, and ants, with examples both within and between species. Social insect colonies with multiple queens also parallel man in having a "tribalistic" breeding structure, and whether or not they have multiple queens they are certainly highly intra-related and show the expected marked contrast between inward cooperation and outward hostility.

The social insects also parallel man in two out of four of the extrinsic trends mentioned above as occurring in the hominids (communication and possessions). If we accept that the elaborate instinctive patterns involved in the "war," "slavery," and "robbery" of the social insects are evolved by natural selection, can we consider it unlikely that in man also the corresponding phenomena have a natural basis? In man certainly we are concerned with amorphous and variable inclinations rather than instincts; but, of course, considering what a newcomer man is to his present ecological situation; compared to any of the highly social ants, bees, or wasps, and how differently the ontogeny of his behavior is planned, this is what we expect.

I hope that by now the relevance to my theme of the quotation from Nietzsche will have become apparent. Populations are usually viscous and subdivided. On considerations of inclusive fitness we do not expect to find everywhere a Hobbesian war of all against all for the necessities of life—the "Malthus" of Nietzsche's phrase. There should be restraint in the struggle within groups and within local areas in the interest of maintaining strength for the intergroup struggle or for the united repression of outsiders. We now see at least one reason why the "struggle for existence" should often become restrained and conventional. I suspect that what Nietzsche meant by a "struggle for power" is what we would now refer to as striving for social dominance, for territory, or for a place in an "establishment." From his all-doubting eminence, relying on common observation, Nietzsche seems to have noticed an important discrepancy in Darwin's theory. At the same time, as appears from the rather muddled paragraph following the one quoted, he was probably far from being able himself to explain what he saw, and he offered no amendment to Darwin's argument. Neither for a biological nor for a human context did he indicate how Malthus is to be answered.

The evolutionary process certainly has no regard for humanitarian principles. Pain is itself evolved to teach the animal to avoid harmful stimuli. In the immediate situation pain warns of a threat to fitness; when a mortally threatened animal cannot extricate itself, it may be expected to experience pain until, approximately, its situation is such that further efforts could not possibly avail. Thus whatever the major agencies of natural selection happen to be—whatever kind of "struggle" occurs— pain must be a usual prelude to elimination, and, as determined by the birthrate, elimination has to go on. Darwin, of course, was aware of this and recently the point has been reemphasized by Williams (1966) and Lack (1969).

Unfortunately with man there may be additions to the basic toll of suffering which the nature of life exacts. Man is certainly able to learn to exploit the pain of others selfishly and seems even to have instincts acting in this direction. In the light of the evidence for a cruel streak in human nature, "natural" systems of ethics, including Nietzsche's own look less attractive. If as I believe, and as others have thought likely (Freeman 1964, Emlen 1966, Alexander and Tinkle 1968), vicious and warlike tendencies are natural in man and were formerly (at least) adaptive, Nietzsche's exhortation to follow one's instincts makes it not surprising that some of his admirers developed a cruel warlike ethos. Along with a seeming gloss over the Malthusian issue, Nietzsche's attraction to early Hellenic culture perhaps also helped him to overlook the worst aspects of human "nature." The Hellenes in Homer were readily warlike but not wantonly cruel. In the Iliad, for example, the pictures of two cities which Hephaestus the smith god wrought on Achilles' shield well represent the two aspects of tribalistic society that I have described: the inward harmony and the outward snarl. Yet as described by Homer, the warfare around the besieged city is clean: no captives are being tortured for information, no peace emissaries are being sent back blinded and mutilated into the town. In the siege of Troy likewise, revenge is ruthless but the killing of captives is mentioned with censure and there is no torture. There are none of the atrocities of conquest which a little later the Assyrians proudly perpetuated in their bas-reliefs. Hopefully, these traces of relatively humane conduct in the bloody dark-age tribes who fought against Troy may be connected with the marvelous contributions shortly to be made by their descendants to human culture; but less hopefully, the restraint may have been due to the fact that they were fighting against their not-very-distant kinsmen. In general, as Freeman has emphasized, the atrocities recorded in human history appear to bear witness to the existence of a spontaneous drive to imagine and carry out cruelty which, at least in some people, in some circumstances, has been given free play and public approval.

Bringing together evidence from social anthropology, from early historical literature, from the fossil record of hominid violence and cannibalism (Ardrey 1961), from studies of primate behavior, and from theoretical considerations of social evolution, I find it only too easy to imagine that the genes that reared cruelty out of the primate's aggressive drive have been favored by natural selection in the hominid line. For the selection of cruelty, indeed, it is unnecessary even to consider inclusive fitness, except insofar as this may have been involved in the speeding-up of progress in mental and linguistic ability. With animals able to communicate and intelligent enough to see distant objectives, there would be nothing surprising in one refusing to communicate some information useful to another; nor would it be unnatural for the other to try to obtain the information by force. With pleasure in cruelty as the motivation to punishment (Cazaly 1962), and with cruelty to create terror, an individualistic argument sounds less plausible; but considering inclusive fitness, or group selection (which may be a really appropriate term for many human situations), there is no theoretical difficulty. For example, a priori, terror seems as good a weapon as false promises in bringing about the early submission or removal of a threatened tribe.

Against the last-mentioned mode of selection, terror tends to unite otherwise dissident enemies. Also, against all modes of selection, the intrinsic resistance to cruelty must continually increase. As was pointed out in connection with simpler cases at the beginning of this presentation, evolution produces shields to its own weapons. Perhaps in a slow natural course of events we may become as unconcerned about cruelty and terror as we are now about lies, given and experienced—but this will be a long time to wait and in any case "natural" man will have invented fresh horrors by that time.

PRISONER'S DILEMMA   The increasing subtlety of the process of natural selection in the hominid line, which has been far from wholly eugenic if the above suggestions are right, and the corresponding subtlety of its product, bring me back to a topic touched on earlier, the theory of games. This theory lights up fascinating and disturbing problems in human biology. But in nonhuman biology, at least as regards preconsidered strategies, its relevance must be very limited. The theory presupposes beings able to think, and, potentially, to communicate. Regarding the first attribute, already the theory has provided problems insoluble to *Homo sapiens*. Regarding the second, I suspect that animals fall short not so much in ability to communicate as in ability to deceive; by our lofty standards animals are poor liars.

The implications of *game-like* situations in ecology are not so difficult to see as the implications of the corresponding "game" in game theory. For example, if "prisoner's dilemma" is played between individuals meeting at random and if the payoffs are fitnesses, we have seen that it "pays" in natural selection to take the selfish course consistently. This is because the type which does so gets greater-than-average fitness when associated with any other type, in no matter what ratio. If assortation occurs, however, this outcome is not certain; increasing correlation of partners must eventually reach a point where fitness in the "homopairs" dominates the mean fitnesses of the types. The concept of inclusive fitness provides a simple test for the resolution of games in this way. The test consists in adding to the expressed fitnesses a fraction b of the fitness of the partner where b is the coefficient of relatedness of the partner. The differences between the totals so formed are differences in inclusive fitness. For example, if the partners are sibs

2	4	gives rise to	3	4½
1	3		3	4½

showing that with this degree of relationship the incentive to "let the partner down" has become zero. If the partners were full sisters in a male-haploid species ($b = ¾$), the matrix would become

3½	4¾
4	5¼

and the altruistic course is then definitely favored.

The possibility that the real payoffs might be other than as they are represented in the matrix of a game is carefully precluded in the formal development of game theory: the payoffs must show what the players really prefer. Nevertheless the point from natural selection serves to emphasize that it is unrealistic to suppose that there exist real situations which present the same game to all pairs or groups of people. It is quite unrealistic, for example, to represent the payoffs of prisoner's dilemma in terms of years in prison, or as sums of money expected from a partnership, without making allowance for the degree of fellow feeling that exists between the "players."

I am doubtful whether the findings from natural selection throw any light on the problem of how it is rational to act when the desirabilities of outcomes are really in the pattern of prisoner's dilemma. But natural selection, the process which has made us almost all that we are, seems to give one clear warning about situations of this general kind. When payoffs are connected with fitness, the animal part of our nature is expected to be more concerned with getting "more than the average" than with getting "the maximum possible." Little encouragement, I think, can be drawn from the fact that this may, in some cases, imply less than maximum population densities; it implies concurrently a complete disregard for any values, either of individuals or of groups, which do not serve competitive breeding. This being so, the animal in our nature cannot be regarded as a fit custodian for the values of civilized man.

REFERENCES

Alexander, R. D., and D. W. Tinkle.
  1968. "A Comparative Review." *Bioscience,* 18:245–248.
Ardrey, R.
  1961. *African Genesis.* London: Collins.
Baerends, G. P., and J. M. Baerends-van Roon.
  1950. "An Introduction to the Ethology of Cichlid Fishes." *Behaviour,* Supplement 1:1–242.
Barnett, S. A.
  1967. "Rats." *Scientific American,* 216(1):79–85.
Bowers, J. M., and B. K. Alexander.
  1967. "Mice: Individual Recognition by Olfactory Cues." *Science,* 158: 1208–1210.
Buechner, H. K., J. A. Morrison, and W. Leuthold.
  1966. "Reproduction in Uganda Kob with Special Reference to Behavior." In *Comparative Biology of Reproduction in Mammals,* I. W. Rowlands, editor. Symposium of the Zoological Society of London, 15:69–88.
Cazaly, W. H.
  1962. "A Theory of Cruelty." In *The Scientist Speculates: An Anthology of Partly Baked Ideas,* I. J. Good, editor. London: Heinemann.
Corbet, P. S., and A. Griffiths.
  1963. "Observations on Aquatic Stages of Two Species of Toxorhynchites (Diptera: Culcidae) in Uganda." *Proceedings of the Royal Entomological Society of London,* Series A, 38:125–135.
Coulson, J. C.
  1968. "Differences in the Quality of Birds Nesting in the Centre and on the Edges of a Colony." *Nature* (London), 217:478–479.
Crèvecoeur, A.
  1931. "Le Maraudage Occasionel. Tendence au cleptoparasitisme chez

divers Psammocharidae." *Memoires de la Societe royal entomologique de Belgique,* 23:183–187.

Crook, J. H.
1960. "Studies on the Social Behaviour of *Quelea quelea* (Linn.) in French West Africa." *Behaviour,* 16:1–55.
1965. "The Adaptive Significance of Avian Social Organisation." *Symposium of the Zoological Society of London,* 14:181–218.

Darling, F. F.
1937. *A Herd of Red Deer.* Oxford, England: Oxford University Press.

Darwin, C.
1871. *The Descent of Man.* London: Murray.

Darwin, E.
1796. *Zoonomia.* London: Johnson.

Descy, A.
1924. "Recherches sur la sexualite et l'instinct chez les hymenoptères." *Bulletin biologique de la France et de la Belgique,* 58:1–37.

Eibl-Eibesfeldt, I.
1961. "The Fighting Behavior of Animals." *Scientific American,* 205(6): 112–122.

Emlen, J. M.
1966. "Natural Selection and Human Behaviour." *Journal of Theoretical Biology,* 12:410–418.

Espmark, Y.
1968. "Defence Reactions to Oestrid Flies by Forest Reindeer." *Zoologische Beitrage,* 14:155–167.

Fabre, J. H.
1879. *The Mason Bees.* Reprinted in translation by A. T. de Mattos, 1914. London: Hodder & Stoughton.

Foster, W. A.
1967. "Cooperation by Male Protection of Ovipositing Female in the Diptera." *Nature* (London), 214:1035–1036.

Freeman, D.
1964. "Human Aggression in Anthropological Perspective." *The Natural History of Aggression.* J. D. Carthy, and F. J. Ebling. Pages 109–110. New York: Academic Press.

Friedman, H.
1932. "The Parasitic Habit in the Ducks Theoretical Consideration." *Proceedings of the U.S. National Museum,* 80(18): 1–7.

Galton, F.
1871. "Gregariousness in Cattle and Men." *Macmillan's Magazine,* 23:353–357.

Geist, V.
1966. "The Evolution of Horn-like Organs." *Behaviour,* 27:175–214.

Haldane, J. B. S.
1932. *The Causes of Evolution.* New York City: Cornell University Press.

Hamilton, W. D.
1963. "The Evolution of Altruistic Behaviour." *American Naturalist,* 97: 354–356.

1964. "The Genetical Evolution of Social Behaviour," Parts I and II. *Journal of Theoretical Biology*, 7:1–16 and 17–52.
1967. "Extraordinary Sex Ratios." *Science*, 156:477–488.

Hamilton III, W. J., and G. H. Orians.
1965. "Evolution of Brood Parasitism in Altrical Birds." *Condor*, 67:361–382.

Hobby, B. M.
1930. "Evidence of Conflict Between Females of the Fossorial Wasp *Mellinus arvensis* L. at the Burrow." *Proceedings of the Royal Entomological Society of London*, 5:110.

Hostmann, E.
1952. "Form und Struktur von Starenschwarmen." *Verhandlungen der Deutschen Zoologischen Gesellschaft* (Freiburg), 153–159.

Hudleston, J. A.
1958. "Some Notes on the Effects of Bird Predators on Hopper Bands of the Desert Locust (*Schistocerca gregaria* Forskal). *Entomologist's Monthly Magazine*, 94:210–214.

Kimura, M., and G. H. Weiss.
1964. "The Stepping Stone Model of Population Structure and the Decrease of the Genetic Correlation with Distance." *Genetics*, 49:561–576.

Kruuk, H.
1964. "Predators and Anti-predator Behaviour in the Black-Headed Gull (*Larus ridibundus* L.)." *Behaviour Supplement*, 11:1–129.

Kummer, H.
1968. *Social Organization of Hamadryas Baboons*. Chicago: University of Chicago Press.

Labine, P. A.
1964. "Population Biology of the Butterfly *Euphydryas editha*, I: Barriers to Multiple Insemination." *Evolution* (Lancaster, Pennsylvania), 18.

Lack, D.
1968. *Ecological Adaptations for Breeding in Birds*. London: Metheun.
1969. "Of Birds and Men." *New Scientist*, 41:121–122.

Lorenz, K.
1966. *On Aggression*. London: Metheun.

Luce, R. D., and H. Raiffa.
1957. *Games and Decisions*. New York: J. Wiley and Sons.

Malyshev, S. I.
1966. *Genesis of the Hymenoptera and the Phases of Their Evolution*. Translated from the Russian. London: Metheun, 1969.

Michener, C. D.
1958. "The Evolution of Social Behaviour in Bees." *Proceedings of the Tenth International Congress of Entomology*, 2:441–447.

Milliron, H. E., and D. R. Oliver.
1966. "Bumblebees from North Ellesmere Island with Observations on Usurpation by *Megabombus hyperboreus* (Schonh.) (Hymenoptera: Apidae)." *Canadian Entomologist*, 98:207–213.

Moore, W. G.
1948. "Bat Caves and Bat Bombs." *Turtox News* (Chicago), 26:262–265.

WILLIAM D. HAMILTON

Nietzsche, F.
1889. *Twilight of the Idols: The Portable Nietzsche.* Reprinted in translation by W. Kaufmann. New York: Viking Press, 1954.

Petras, N. L.
1967. "Studies of Natural Populations of *Mus,* I: Biochemical Polymorphisms and Their Bearing on Breeding Structure." *Evolution* (Lancaster, Pennsylvania), 21:259–274.

Plateaux-Quénu, C.
1960. "Utilisation d'un nid de *Halictus marginatus* par une fondatrice de *Halictus malachurus.*" *Insectes sociaux,* 7:349–352.

Pryer, H.
1884. "An Account of a Visit to the Bird's-nest Caves of British North Borneo." *Proceedings of the Zoological Society of London,* 532–538.

Rapoport, A.
1966. *Two-person Game Theory.* Ann Arbor: The University of Michigan Press.

Ribbands, C. R.
1965. "The Role of Recognition of Comrades in the Defence of Social Insect Communities." *Symposium of the Zoological Society of London,* 14:159–168.

Richards, O. W.
1927. "The Specific Characters of the British Bumble-bees." *Transactions of the Entomological Society of London,* 75:233–268.

Russell, C., and W. M. S. Russell.
1968. *Violence, Monkeys and Man.* London: Macmillan.

Sakagami, S. R.
1960. "Ethological Peculiarities of the Primitive Social Bees *Allodape lepeletier,* and Allied Genera." *Insectes sociaux,* 7:231–249.

Scheven, J.
1957. "Beitrag zur Biologie der Schmarotzerfeldwespen *Sulcopolistes atrimandibularis* Zimm., *S. semenowi* F. Morawitz und *S. sulcifer* Zimm." *Insectes sociaux,* 4:409–437.

Scott, J. P.
1945. "Social Behaviour, Organisation and Leadership in a Small Flock of Domestic Sheep." *Comparative Psychology Monographs,* 18(96): 1–29.

Southwick, C. H.
1955. "The Population Dynamics of Confined House Mice Supplied with Unlimited Food." *Ecology,* 36:212–225.

Southwick, C. H., M. A. Beg, and M. R. Siddiqi.
1965. "Rhesus Monkeys in North India." In *Primate Behaviour: Field Studies of Monkeys and Apes.* I. DeVore, editor. New York: Holt, Rinehart & Winston.

Tinbergen, N.
1953. *Social Behaviour in Animals.* London: Metheun.

Verner, J., and M. F. Willson.
1966. "The Influence of Habitats on Mating Systems of North American Passerine Birds." *Ecology,* 47:143–147.

Wheeler, W. M.
  1919. "The Parasitic Aculeata: A Study in Evolution." *Proceedings of the American Philosophical Society,* 58:1–40.
Williams, G. C.
  1964. "Measurement of Consocation among Fishes and Comments on the Evolution of Schooling." *Michigan State University Museum Publications, Biological Series,* 2:351–383.
  1966. *Adaptation and Natural Selection: A Critique of Some Current Evolutionary Thought.* Princeton, New Jersey: Princeton University Press.
Woodring, J. P.
  1969. "Observation on the Biology of Six Species of Acarid Mites." *Annals of the Entomological Society of America,* 62:102–108.
Wright, S.
  1945. "Tempo and Mode in Evolution: A Critical Review," *Ecology,* 26:415–419.
  1951. "The Genetical Structure of Population." *Annals of Eugenics,* 15:323–354.
  1965. "The Interpretation of Population Structure by F-statistics with Special Regard to Systems of Mating." *Evolution* (Lancaster, Pennsylvania), 19:395–420.
Yoshikawa, K.
  1955. "A Polistine Colony Usurped by a Foreign Queen." *Insectes sociaux,* 2:255–260.

APPENDIXES

APPENDIX I. INTERACTIONS IN PAIRS WHEN PAIRING IS NONRANDOM

There is a close analogy between the model for paired asexual organisms and a model for selection in diploids: the asymmetry of the fitness matrix (see p. 62) can correspond to meiotic drive. Random pairing corresponds to random assortment of gametes. For nonrandom pairing the frequencies of normal-normal, normal-mutant, and mutant-mutant pairs may be represented

$$P^2 + pqA, \qquad 2\,pq\,(1{-}A), \qquad \text{and } q^2 + pqA,$$

where p and q are, as before, the frequencies of the normal and mutant strains, and A is a parameter exactly analogous to the inbreeding coefficient, F, used to measure departure from Hardy-Weinberg genotype distribution.

Association of like with like (assortation) is indicated by positive A. When $A = 1$, unlike pairs do not occur; this can happen at any frequency. Association of unlikes (dissortation) is indicated by negative A, but in this case the minimum value of A depends on the frequencies of the strains and can reach -1 only when they are equally frequent. In general the minimum is $\dfrac{q}{p}$ or $\dfrac{p}{q}$, whichever is the greater. Thus selection under "maximum dissortation" will imply selection under progressively changing negative values of A.

With fitness matrix as before, the change in strain frequency in one generation is

$$\Delta q = pq\,[(pc + qd) - (pa + qb) + A\,\{p\,(d - c) + q(b - a)\}]/W$$

The table below shows the effect of maximum dissortation, and of half and of full assortation, on examples of model situations. The four examples that have been chosen are ones discussed in the text; out of twelve possible significantly different situations these four seem to have the most biological meaning.

APPENDIX TABLE 1

Matrix	Type of behavior	Maximum dissortation	$A = 0$	$A = \frac{1}{2}$	$A = 1$
4 2 3 1	Spiteful, undiscriminating	$\check{q} = \frac{1}{3}, \hat{q} = \frac{2}{3}$	↖	↖	↖
4 1 3 2	Altruistic, discriminating Spiteful, discriminating	$\check{q} = \frac{1}{4}$	$\check{q} = \frac{1}{2}$	↖	↖
3 2 4 1	Selfish, undiscriminating	$\hat{q} = \frac{3}{4}$	$\hat{q} = \frac{1}{2}$	↖	↖
3 1 4 2	Altruistic, undiscriminating Selfish discriminating	↘	↘	$\cdot\,\Delta q = 0$	↖

Arrows show the direction of selection. $\wedge$ and $\vee$ symbolize stable and unstable equilibria, respectively.

APPENDIX II.   VISCOUS AND SUBDIVIDED POPULATION MODELS

An outline of this analysis can be introduced by quoting an identity, which Wright proves:

$$(1 - F_{IT}) = (1 - F_{ST})(1 - F_{IS})$$

In this identity F_{IT} is the correlation of uniting gametes relative to the array of gametes of the whole population, F_{IS} is the correlation of uniting gametes relative to the array of gametes of their own subdivision, and F_{ST} is the correlation of gametes drawn randomly from a subdivision relative to the array of gametes from the whole population.

For evaluation of b from (1), F_{IT} must be used in the calculation of both r_{AB} and F_{A}. If instead F_{IS} is used, an inclusive coefficient is obtained relevant only to selection within the subdivision. It could easily happen that an altruistic trait that was "too generous" to increase in frequency within its subdivision (except by drift), increases, nevertheless, in the population as a whole due to the more rapid expansion of those subdivisions which contain altruists in highest frequencies.

Consider, for example, the straightforward and often realistic case where the altruistic trait is expressed not toward particular relatives but in all social encounters. If there is free mixing within subdivisions an encounter concerns a randomly selected pair from the subdivision. The correlation of gametes from such a pair is zero with respect to their subdivision. Thus an altruistic trait expressed in random encounters is certainly counterselected within the subdivision. The correlation of gametes with respect to the whole population is F_{ST}, which is always greater than zero, depending on the degree to which the gene frequencies of the isolates have differentiated. Thus if there is a gain to inclusive fitness on the basis of the coefficient

$$\frac{2F_{\text{ST}}}{1 + F_{\text{IT}}}$$

the genes for the trait are positively selected in the population as a whole. If mating is random within subdivisions $F_{\text{IS}} = 0$, so that $F_{\text{ST}} = F_{\text{IT}} = F$ (say), and the coefficient is simply $2F/(1 + F)$.

The formulas, graphs, and tables of Wright's papers will permit the estimation of b on the above lines for a wide range of cases in his "island" and his "isolation by distance" models and in various "mating systems." How far the inclusive coefficients so estimated will give useful criteria for social selection is unfortunately not very clear. Wright's analysis is worked out for the case where there is no selection. He has used it as a basis for qualitative discussion of the implications of breeding structure for ordinary selection but we cannot follow with quite equal confidence using concepts of social selection and inclusive fitness. There are added doubts: first, about the validity and sufficiency of the single coefficient under selection and inbreeding, and, second, because social selection will tend much more than classical selection to change the breeding structure as it progresses. Nevertheless, I feel confident that by linking the concept of inclusive fitness to Wright's type of analysis we can come nearer to understanding genetical social evolution than we could do with no quantitative ideas at all.

The favoring of altruism in subdivided populations can be seen as due to the fact that drift tends to bring about assortation. Chance concentrations of altruists, due to drift, will tend to grow rapidly. Within subdivisions, apart from the influence of immigration, the frequency of altruists may be everywhere tending to decrease, but if the vigor of the altruistic groups can somehow counteract the backward drift and selection in other groups, positive selection may hold overall. How can such general enrichment take place? And how can it avoid altering too much the general structural situation?

In models with discrete subdivisions ("island" and "stepping-stone") there are two reasonable ways in which the vigor of altruistic groups could manifest without causing too much structural alteration.

1. The size of groups could be kept constant by different rates of emission of migrants; with the condition for an advantage in inclusive fitness satisfied, the population of migrants would be richer in altruists than the population of nonmigrants, and the random acceptance of migrants into groups would lead to general enrichment. Wright (1945) drew attention to the possibility that altruism could be established by a process of this kind.

2. Vigorous groups could grow in numbers and then divide when some critical size was reached. To keep the total population and the number of groups roughly constant, the smallest groups could be removed, or, in the "stepping-stone" model, the smallest neighboring group could be "overrun" and replaced by an emigrant portion of the vigorous neighbor. Groups which increase rapidly, due to fortunes of initial constitution, immigration, and drift also divide often and so spread the gene in spite of its *average* tendency to decrease within groups. This is the one type of selection process that can reasonably be called "group selection." Haldane (1932) discussed the selection of altruism with this sort of process in mind, but accompanied his verbal discussion by a strangely irrelevant mathematical analysis in which he considered numbers of genes rather than gene frequencies (Hamilton 1963).

For the "isolation by distance" model, parallel alternatives can be seen. Corresponding to (1), local regulation of density by more long-range migration out of areas of increasing density will have a powerful effect in limiting the relationship of neighbors and is correspondingly against altruism, especially its initial establishment. Corresponding to (2), regulation by local adjustments of the spatial distribution (for example, some sort of elastic slumping from high-density areas), together with random elimination to keep overall density constant, will be more favorable to altruism.

As in all cases the altruistic mutation still faces the initial difficulty that at its first occurrence it tends to waste its altruism on individuals unrelated at the locus in question. This difficulty is particularly severe, of course, for a dominant mutation. But even for a dominant, provided the altruism is not suicidal, the recurrence of a mutation plus the possibility of local increase by drift can overcome this barrier. Eventually there will occur a clump of altruists of such size and purity as to reverse the local counterselection, and with further growth increasingly determinate progress can take hold.

Social selection cannot occur in completely regular "mating systems." It may be noted here, however, that the most "system-like" version of an "isolation by distance" model, which is supposed to preclude long-range migration *and* elastic expansion from vigorous areas is rather hostile to altruism. Inside the patches which form the average, reproductive performance is the same whether the patch is of altruists or of egotists; on the margins altruism tends to benefit both types equally; and when, more rarely, altruists occur in isolation, they benefit mainly egotists.

The occurrence of negative F_{IS} in some mating systems, demonstrated by Wright (1965), raises the interesting point that with avoidance of consanguine mating within subdivisions, *negative b* for mates relative to their subdivision could arise in more natural systems. This implies that spite between mates could be positively selected within subdivisions. It could take the form of preventing a mate from having offspring by unions with other individuals.[6] For the population as a whole, however, such episodes would be transitory; as we found earlier when considering supposedly pervasive spite not connected with dissortation, the selection of spite will tend to cause the collapse and extinction of the groups in which it occurs.

---

[6] The only possible case of such spite known to me is the insemination reaction caused by some male *Drosophila* in their mates. This is but one of many examples of males attempting to prevent re-insemination (for example, Labine 1964; Buechner, Morrison, and Leuthold 1966; Foster 1967), but generally such action does not lower fertility of the mate and, considering the possibility that the last-given sperm will have precedence in fertilization, it has obvious adaptive value in terms of individual fitness.

CHAPTER 3

NEUROLOGICAL ASPECTS IN SOCIAL BEHAVIOR

DETLEV PLOOG

MAX PLANCK INSTITUTE FOR PSYCHIATRY
MUNICH

EVOLUTIONARY TRENDS OF SOCIAL BEHAVIOR Let us suppose that every 2000 years of natural history were one hour on television. Let us further assume that we watch the screen for sixteen hours each day. It would require about three days to view the evolution of man since he has obtained his present bodily form, which is a period of about 100,000 years. To observe the evolution of the human lineage since it diverged from that of the apes (perhaps about 10 million years) would require ten months. The evolutionary course of such families as those of the cat, dog, and horse (35 to 55 million years) would take 3½ to 5½ years. Whereas almost a lifetime would be necessary to follow a documentation of the entire fossil record, which represents a history of about 600 million years. Seeing the entire course of evolution on the screen would take us 250 to 400 years (Stebbins 1966). More than 500 million years ago the first vertebrates appeared, about 300 million years ago reptiles evolved, and 100 million years later, the first mammals emerged.

The enormous structural changes in the nervous systems which were necessary for each of these steps in evolution to have occurred from the early reptilian to the mammalian brain are striking. Even more impressive changes appear to have taken place in the primates and their ancestors over a period of about 60 million years, as shown in Figure 1. In 1a and 1b we see the so-called primary cortical projection areas (hatched) for the elaboration of movement, somatosensation, audition, and vision. Very little secondary cortex (white) also called association or integration cortex is evident. By far the most extensive part of the brain of these insectivores is the rhinencephalon (stippled), which will be dealt with later under the term limbic system. In Figure 1c, d, and e, the prosimian brain is represented. It is evident that the rhinencephalic area is covered to an increasing extent by the cortex; this trend continues in monkeys (Figure 1f and g) and man (Figure 1h). The figure does not reflect the astounding increase in the brain weights. The increase in volume capacity of the skull, which is indicative of brain size, progressed from about 30 cc to nearly 1500 cc relatively slowly over a period of about 50 million years; even during the most intensive phase of hominid evolution during the last million years the average increase per generation (of 25 years) was not more than 0.057 cc (Stebbins 1966). Do these figures bear on the evolution of social behavior? I think they do. There is no reason to doubt that the evolution of the nervous system is closely paralleled by a respective evolution of behavior. Actually, it is the adaptive value of behavior which counts for survival.

The phylogenetic process has produced not only increasingly effective sense organs, faster action, more acute discrimination, and many specialities in many species but also a variety of more and more elaborate social systems, mediated by an increasing refinement of communication processes. It would lead too far to speculate about the most primitive forms of social behavior. Even for the vertebrates it would be extremely difficult to draw a line as to when during evolution one can speak of social behavior. There are four classes of behavior which, according to Lorenz (1965b) and Tinbergen (1953), might be called social. First, the interactions of the male and female for the purpose of reproduction; second, the actions and interactions of a male and a female for breeding and upbringing, as well as interactions of the young with parents and siblings; third, the interactions in herds, groups, troops, bands, and the like; and fourth, all kinds of agonistic interactions among members of the same species, such as attacking, defending, threatening, avoiding, withdrawing, and fleeing.

If we take an extreme reductionistic view in regard to behavior patterning, we might postulate that in the beginning the simplest modes of social behavior were nothing but approach and avoidance of members of the same species. The outcome of such an encounter was always unpredictable and depended upon the partner's move to action, which, as we know, depends not only upon external stimuli but also upon the internal state of the individual. In this connection we speak of the motivation of an animal. Social signals evolved, as the theory goes, because communication between partners was desirable, and signaling resulted as a more flexible way of an encounter and a greater degree of information about the outcome.

Whether we consider the vertebrates or other phyla, there seems to be a basic rule in the development of social signals which was first described by Julian Huxley (1923): "If it is of advantage to a sender that a recipient perceives the disposition or the state of the sender by a specific behavior, then this pattern is likely to be modified until it is conspicuous. The transformation of a behavior into a signal is called ritualization.

96

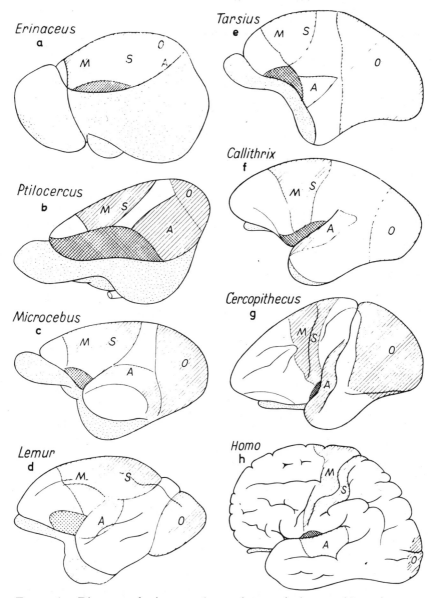

FIGURE 1.   Diagrams of primary and secondary cortical areas of Insectivores (*a, b*), Prosimians (*c, d, e*), Simians (*f, g*), and Man (*h*). Rhinencephalon (limbic cortex): stippled. Insular area: crosshatched. Secondary cortex: white. Other primary areas: hatched. M: Motor cortex; S: Somatosensory cortex; O: Optic (visual) cortex; A: Auditory cortex. (From D. Starck 1965).

97

Animal ritualization constitutes an adaptive canalization of expressive behavior produced by natural selection. It has a built-in genetic basis, although learning may also play a part." These transformed behavioral patterns are commonly derived from a basic repertoire not originally employed for communication purposes.

From a study of primitive forms surviving at the present time, for example, the tiny reptile Tuatara (*Sphenodon punctatus*) found on some of New Zealand's small southern islands, we are able to learn something about the fixed pattern of social signals which possibly in this case remained unchanged for 150 million years or so. This reptile shows head-nodding as one of the several social signals, just as it can also be seen in many more recent species of lizards. Figure 2 shows a South American lizard (*Iguana iguana*) studied in our laboratory, at the onset of his chief display. The signal is directed toward another male. Note the extended dewlap which makes the signal especially conspicuous. The signal consists of a sequence of head-noddings which are highly stereotyped in amplitude, frequency, and time course as shown in the curve above the head. Communication processes of this general kind, although more flexible, are obviously also present in mammals, including nonhuman primates (Ploog and MacLean 1963; Castell, Krohn, and Ploog 1969).

Besides movements of parts of the body with or without participation of autonomic responses, the vertebrates very early employed vocalizations as social signals, for instance in the mating croaks of frogs, the hissing of turtles, the vocalization of Tuatara, the songs of birds, and the vocal repertoire of monkeys of which I offer greater detail shortly.

These basic mechanisms of behavior—approach and avoidance with its extremes in attack and flight, and partner interaction for mediating within a species and for providing a means of reproductive isolation between the species—have their brain correlates which developed from very primitive to highly complex neuronal machinery, older parts being preserved though modified, while newer parts came into existence. The most comprehensive and ingenious view of this aspect of social behavior has been presented by MacLean (1958, 1968).

BRAIN STRUCTURES AND SOCIAL BEHAVIOR According to MacLean (1968), man has inherited the basic structure and organization of three brains, referred to on the basis of their prototypes as reptilian, old mammalian, and new mammalian (Figure 3). Man's brain of oldest heritage is basically reptilian. It forms the matrix of the brain stem and comprises much of the reticular system, midbrain and basal ganglia. The next intimately interconnected superstructure is the old mammalian brain which

FIGURE 2. Display behavior of *Iguana iguana,* a South American lizard. This social signal consists of a sequence of head noddings which are highly stereotyped in amplitude, frequency, and time course, as shown in the graph above the head.

is distinctive in its marked expansion of the primitive incipient cortex of reptilian origin. Finally, there mushrooms late in evolution a more complicated form of cortex called the neocortex, which culminates in man to become the brain of speaking, reading, writing, and arithmetic.

On the basis of the behavioral observations by ethologists, it may be inferred that the reptilian brain is bound to produce highly stereotyped behavior based on ancestral (phyletic) memories. It subserves basic functions of social behavior such as homing, mating, breeding, establishing territory, and forming group hierarchies. It seems to be a slave to

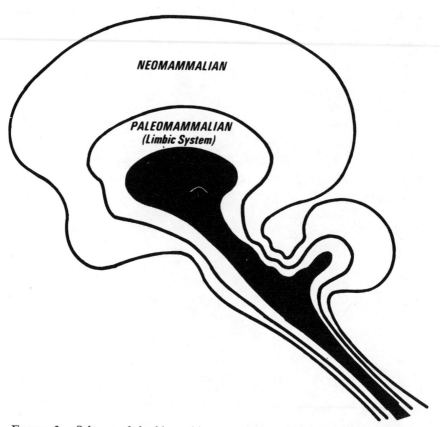

FIGURE 3. Schema of the hierarchic organization of the three basic brain types which, in the evolution of the mammalian brain, became part of man's inheritance. Man's counterpart of the old mammalian brain comprises the so-called limbic system, which has been found to play an important role in emotional behavior. (From P. D. MacLean 1949, 1968).

precedent, and therefore an inadequate machinery for learning to cope with new situations (MacLean 1968).

"The evolutionary development in lower mammals with a respectable cortex might be regarded as Nature's attempt to provide the reptilian brain with 'a thinking cap'" (MacLean 1968). This paleomammalian cortex "is found in a ringlike convolution that Paul Broca (1878) called the limbic lobe because it surrounds the brain stem." (Limbus is a border distinguished by its structure.) "This lobe, together with structures of the brain stem with which it has primary connections, is nowadays called the limbic system," according to MacLean's suggestion in 1952. "From the standpoint of behavioral implications, it should be emphasized that this lobe is found as a common denominator in the brain of all mammals." Research of the last twenty-five years followed the lines of Klüver and Bucy (1937, 1939), who demonstrated as early as 1937 that bilateral temporal lobectomy in rhesus monkeys resulted in complex behavioral deficiencies including emotional, sexual, and dietary alterations as well as changes in recognition and approach-avoidance behavior. Neuro-anatomically, it could be shown that not only the primarily severed portion of the limbic system, the hippocampus, was destroyed, but also that further interconnected parts of this system degenerated. Animal work and clinical experience led to the belief that the limbic system elaborates emotions and guides adaptive behavior in a changing environment. I believe that it is heavily involved in the elaboration of social behavior and in the refinement and differentiation of social communication systems.

Before going into this in greater detail, I wish to "refer briefly to a simplified anatomical diagram of the pathways linking three major subdivisions of the limbic system" (Figure 4). According to MacLean (1967), the figure focuses on three branchings of the medial forebrain bundle that connects the ring of limbic cortex with the reptilian counterparts of the brain stem. The two upper branches of this bundle meet with descending fibers from the olfactory apparatus and feed into the lower and upper halves of the ring through the amygdala and the septum at the points marked 1 and 2. Experimental findings suggest that the lower part of the ring, receiving connections from the amygdala (1), is primarily concerned with oral activity, feeding, attack, and defense behavior. On the other hand, the pathway diverging to the septum (2) and the structures in the upper part of the ring appear to be involved in expressive and emotional states that are conducive to sociability and sexual behavior. The third pathway (3) bypasses the olfactory apparatus and connects the hypothalamus with the anterior thalamic nuclei and the cingulate gyrus in the upper half of the ring. In evolution it is notable that structures comprising this third subdivision of the limbic system become progressively larger and reach a maximum size in man. According to MacLean (1968), this condition reflects a shifting of emphasis from olfactory to visual influences in socio-sexual behavior. Significant in this respect is the fact that in monkeys stimulation within parts of this third subdivision, as in the septal circuit, elicits genital responses (MacLean and Ploog 1962).

These findings are summarized in Figure 5. To quote from MacLean (1968): "Using the shield of Mars (O) as a symbol for responses involving the face and mouth, and his sword for genital responses ($\nearrow$), one obtains an interesting picture in plotting results of electrical stimulation of the brain on a diagram of the medical wall of the cerebrum. The symbols for mouth and face congregate in the region of amygdala, while those for genital responses cluster in the region of the septum. In proceeding caudally, one sees a reconstitution of the symbols (δ) in the anterior hypothalamus. Along the line of the junction of sword and shield is the

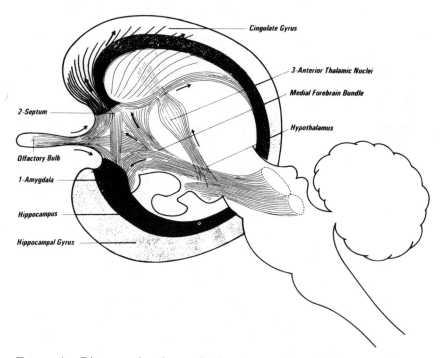

FIGURE 4. Diagram of pathways linking three main subdivisions of the limbic system. The ring of limbic cortex is shown in light and dark grays. See page 101. (From P. D. MacLean 1967, 1968).

region that is focal for congregating fibers involved in angry and defensive behavior. Since fighting is frequently a preliminary to mating as well as feeding, these findings suggest that Nature uses the same neural mechanisms for combat in both situations."

COMMUNICATION PROCESS AND BRAIN FUNCTIONS The neurological concept of the evolution of social behavior invites further consideration of the behavioral mechanisms involved. I have spoken of the increasing refinement and differentiation of communication processes and will give but one example. Electrical stimulation of subdivisions of the limbic system in squirrel monkeys resulted in penile erection, as already mentioned (MacLean and Ploog 1962; MacLean, Robinson, and Ploog 1959). In order to learn more about the sexual and social behavior of the squirrel monkey, I observed the first colony of these animals in Dr. Mac-

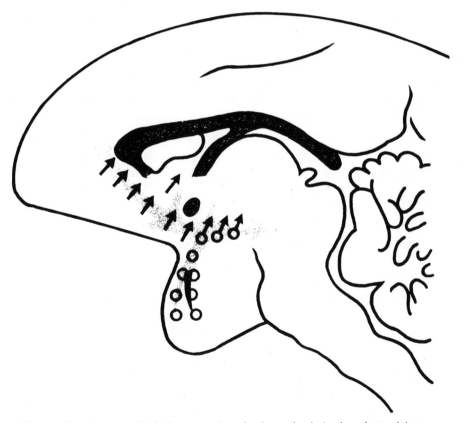

FIGURE 5. A parasagittal diagram of squirrel monkey's brain schematizing the localization of structures involved, respectively, in oral and genital functions. (From P. D. MacLean 1968, see page 102 for explanation).

103

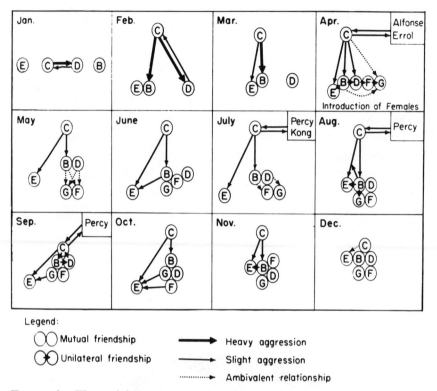

Legend:

◯◯ Mutual friendship   ➡ Heavy aggression

◯✳◯ Unilateral friendship   → Slight aggression

                                    ┄┄➤ Ambivalent relationship

FIGURE 6. The social development in a colony of squirrel monkeys. The circles and arrows indicate various cohesive and agonistic behavior patterns, including genital display as seen in Figure 7. The diagram is based on sociometric data. (From D. Ploog 1963).

Lean's laboratory and found among other social signals one which is now referred to as genital display (Ploog, Blitz, and Ploog 1963). This signal is used in various types of agonistic, dominance, and courtship behaviors. From sociometric data I have concluded that genital display is a social sign stimulus that contributes decisively to the formation of group structure (Ploog 1963, 1966, 1967). Figure 6 shows the overall results of a twelve-month observation period.

In a special study we could show that the frequency of occurrence and the distribution of genital display among group members are more indicative of the rank order in a colony than are ratings on food-getting (Ploog and MacLean 1963). Figure 7 shows two variations of genital display. This consists of several components: lateral positioning of the leg with the hip and knee bent and marked supination of the foot, abductions

FIGURE 7.   Genital display, a social signal of the squirrel monkey. For description of this behavior pattern see page 104. (From D. Ploog, Blitz, Ploog 1963; D. Ploog 1967).

of the big toe as well as erection of the penis. In females, the erection is replaced by an enlargement of the clitoris (Maurus, Mitra, and Ploog 1965). The display is frequently accompanied by specific vocalizations and occasionally by a few spurts of urine. It may last for a second or for many minutes.

Here again we may refer to the process of ritualization. Genital organs, when functioning as part of copulatory behavior, serve to maintain the species, whereas these same organs, when used in genital display, provide the individual with a means of intraspecific communication enabling him to assert himself in a communal situation. Genital display is a ritual derived from sexual behavior but employed as a social signal in agonistic behavior. We do not know precisely which brain structures are involved in mediating this signal, but we are sure that at least some of the areas which have yielded genital responses upon electrical stimulation contribute to the generation of the signal. In this connection we have been interested in the developmental aspects of brain functions and communication processes.

Various features of neonate behavior in nonhuman primates suggest the built-in nature of certain behaviors and their sequential order of occurrence, such as grasping the fur, rooting, and searching for and sucking the nipples as soon as the neonate has emerged from the birth canal (Bowden, Winter, and Ploog 1967). It was to our surprise that such a complex behavior as genital display can also be observed in the neonate. Motion picture analysis of a 1½-day-old infant revealed it displaying to a cagemate; its mouth was slightly opened for vocalization. The signal seems to be a highly integrated pattern including visual orientation and recognition, directed partner relation, and coordination of motor and autonomic functions. It indicates that brain structures involved in this response are already functionally mature at birth. The innate nature of genital display is also suggested by observations of a hand-reared squirrel monkey. He never had had an opportunity to observe genital display but nevertheless directed this signal against his substitute mother, a stuffed woolen sock. He was, by the way, the only squirrel monkey I have ever seen who sucked his thumb (Hopf 1970, Ploog 1969).

The age of first genital display varies greatly. Up to a certain age the signal, although used with increasing frequency, does not affect the adult partner's behavior. At the end of the first and the beginning of the second year, which is also the time of final weaning, the situation becomes different. I will take the example of the dominant male of a group and of the young (Figure 8c). Up to about nine months the "boss" of the group, the alpha male, only mildly and infrequently threatens when the young male displays toward him and makes use of this opportunity time and again. In fact, the boss and the mother (see Figure 8a) are the ones who are most frequently addressed by genital display. When the young animal grows older, however, relations with the alpha animal change radically. The latter threatens severely and may attack the young male when it displays toward him. There is an amusing transitional phase in which the young male does not want to give up his behavior and turns away while displaying but nevertheless glances over his shoulder at the boss. At the beginning of the second year the display behavior decreases markedly and the young male establishes a new relationship with the

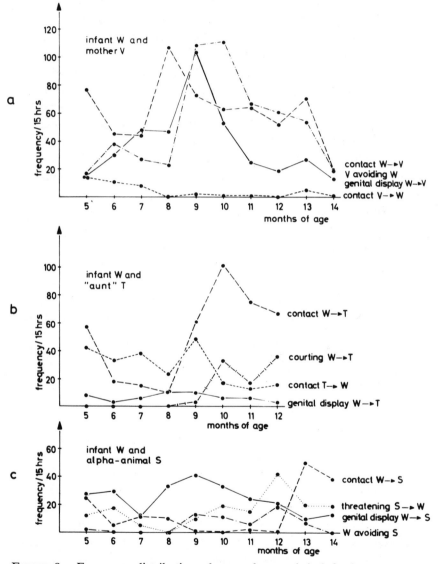

FIGURE 8. Frequency distribution of some characteristic behavior patterns of a male squirrel monkey infant in interaction with mother, "aunt," and alpha male. (From D. Ploog, S. Hopf, and P. Winter 1967).

dominant male. Before this time contact between them is rarely seen. Afterward contacts are more frequent, consisting mainly of huddling and playing. The play includes a characteristic form, which is no doubt schooling for fighting, a playful but well-controlled training by the alpha animal.

The example of genital display as a social signal shows some features which may be important for all primates including man. On the one hand this social signal is a built-in behavior pattern specific to the species; on the other hand—as we have found in long-term studies—infant and group change their interaction pattern with respect to a given signal during the process of growth and maturation. First, the signal is used by the infant over and over again with little or no consequence for sender or recipient. Despite this lack of reinforcement it persists up to a predetermined age. The signal is then followed by severe consequences and the young monkey learns within a short time the context in which he may or may not use this signal. This protracted maturation which coincides with other biological data such as second dentition and final weaning seems, in one form or another, to be dependent upon the species, and is characteristic of the social development of primates. This process of socialization is genetically determined by maturational processes in which innate and learning components are interlocked. This type of partner-related social learning seems to differ from learning which is related to objects.

So far we have considered communication processes which are guided by visual perception. From the other senses which can mediate social communication—such as olfaction and touch—I will choose audition since it eventually plays a fundamental role in human communication. The generation of sounds for auditory communication is, as I have already mentioned, an old capacity in vertebrates. Some classes, chiefly the birds, have developed a highly elaborated form of sound production which has never been achieved by mammals. Auditory communication, however, plays an important role among the nonhuman primates. Among them are some with only few, but variable calls—these are the Old World monkeys and the great apes. Others have a greater repertoire of rather discrete sounds which carry specific information—these are the New World monkeys. Among these, the adult squirrel monkey has a very elaborate repertoire of up to thirty calls, whose physical characteristics are distinguishable by means of sound spectrography. Figure 9 shows a schematic presentation of the vocal repertoire divided into five groups. The sixth group is comprised of calls formed by elements of the five

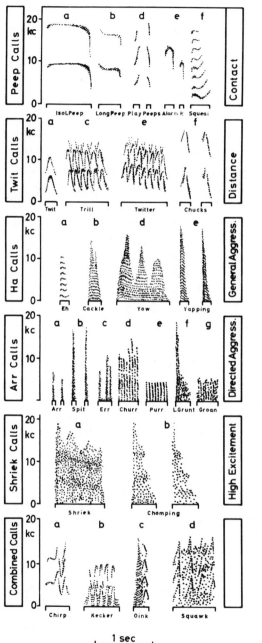

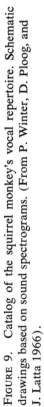

FIGURE 9. Catalog of the squirrel monkey's vocal repertoire. Schematic drawings based on sound spectrograms. (From P. Winter, D. Ploog, and J. Latta 1966).

1 sec

groups. Although the groups were formed primarily on the basis of physical characteristics, there was much evidence for a common denominator in each group with respect to the information content of the signals.

In order to investigate the meaning of the calls, four methods were employed: First, the calls were, whenever possible, elicited repeatedly by well-defined visual stimuli. Second, vocal and motor behavior patterns were elicited by playing back tape recordings of the animal's calls. Third, the animal's motivational state was varied, for instance by food deprivation, and the vocal behavior concurrently observed. Fourth, types of calls were correlated with the social role and status of the emitters and receivers of calls within the group (Winter, Ploog, and Latta 1966).

The discreteness of signals made this animal particularly suitable for electrical brain stimulation studies. A first attempt, which is shown in Figure 10, revealed the possibility of eliciting the majority of the naturally occurring calls reliably and repeatedly in specific brain sites by implanted electrodes. The brain diagrams of representative frontal planes show a concentration of vocalization points in the septal region as well as in sections of the lateral and dorsal hypothalamus with an emphasis on the periventricular region. A corresponding division was seen in the type of calls elicited from these regions. Peep and twit calls were representative of the septal region and adjacent structures of the caudate nucleus, whereas kecker and shriek calls were predominately elicited from the amygdala, hypothalamus, and the caudally adjoining periventricular gray (Jürgens, Maurus, Ploog, and Winter 1967). A much more elaborate study has been published recently (Jurgens and Ploog 1970).

It is not my intention here to go into anatomical details. But it is noteworthy that the brain structures which mediate these calls, especially the amygdala, the hypothalamus, the stria terminalis, and the midbrain periventricular gray are also associated with attack and defense behavior. Furthermore, almost all structures which are shown to mediate vocalizations are also known to yield other behavioral or autonomic responses, including genital responses. In connection with social signaling the latter is of special interest since erection during genital display is frequently accompanied by two types of vocalization, namely by calls of directed aggression in an aggressive context and by peep calls in a nonaggressive context. Both of these alternative types of vocalization could be elicited together with the genital response by brain stimulation.

The communication system we are dealing with in the squirrel monkey and, in fact, in all nonhuman primates, has reached a very high degree of complexity. The sender of signals can employ posture, motion, and

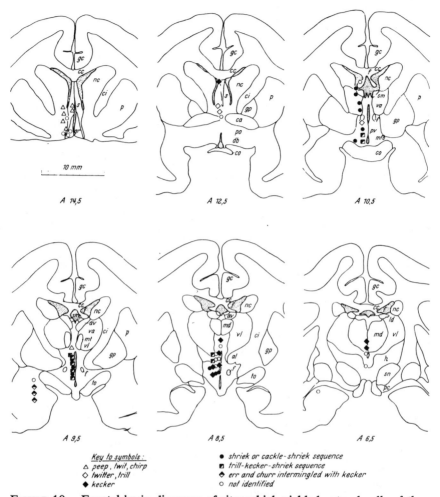

FIGURE 10.   Frontal brain diagrams of sites which yielded natural calls of the squirrel monkey upon electrical stimulation of implanted electrodes. (From U. Jurgens, M. Maurus, D. Ploog, and P. Winter 1967).

vocalization. He can address a whole group with certain vocal signals and a single individual either vocally, visually, or by combined signals without having the whole group respond. The recipient of these signals has to discriminate visual, auditory, and combined signals in a serial order and to respond appropriately. Furthermore, all of the partners communicate in an ever changing context of events, where the motive state and the social rank or role of each individual has to be taken into account at any given moment.

111

It takes a primate many years to attain not only physical maturity but also the social maturity typical of adult social behavior. The struggle for food and other goods seems, under normal conditions at least, less frequent than the struggle for partner relations and social status. Social interactions seem to be a basic need of all primates, including man.

Nonhuman primates handle their affairs, as we have seen, by means of vocal and other nonverbal communication. In man this older communication system with its highest representation in limbic and other subcortical structures still plays a role and is clearly seen in all vocal, facial, postural, and other motor expressions of emotions; in songs without words; and in the cooing and babbling of small infants. In fact, this older communication system is involved in every human conversation and in every direct partner interaction, but it is dominated by human language, the most effective and unique communication system which Nature has produced, constituting the chief trait of human social behavior and the basis for the cultural evolution of mankind.

SPEECH AND BRAIN MECHANISMS   Throughout the centuries of human history much thought has been devoted to the question of how language originated. In a chronicle about Emperor Friederich II, it is told that some 750 years ago he conducted an experiment to investigate the behavior, language, and speech of boys who had never talked with anyone. Accordingly, he instructed the nurses and attendants to provide the children with milk, to let them suckle on the breast, to wash and bathe them, but to neither talk with them nor show them affection. He hoped to determine whether their original language was Hebrew, Greek, Latin, Arabian or the language of their parents. But these efforts were in vain, since all of the children died. Without endearing words, friendly looks or caresses from those nursing and feeding them, they were unable to survive. So the chronicle goes. This idea can be traced back to Herodotus (fifth century B.C.), who relates a comparable experiment of the Egyptian king Psammetichos in the seventh century B.C. In the light of modern deprivation and isolation experiments, the interesting aspect in Frederick von Stauffen's experiment seems to me the idea of the narrator that human growth and development including speech depends upon the friendly social behavior and nonverbal communication ("friendly looks or caresses") of the person caring for the child. I shall come back to this notion when I speak of so-called autistic children who are unable to communicate by language. Before going into this clinical aspect I wish to deal briefly with the fact that man's language capacity is based on

112

specific, biologically determined propensities including species-specific ontogeny.

Quite clearly the most important differences between the prelinguistic and postlinguistic phases of development originate in the growing individual and not in the external world or in changes in the availability of stimuli. The onset of speech consists in a gradual unfolding of capacities; it is a series of generally well-circumscribed events which take place during the second and third years of life. Certain important speech milestones are reached in a fixed sequence and at a relatively constant chronological age.

At about five months of age the vowel-like cooing sounds produced up to then begin to be interspersed with more consonantal sounds. Acoustically, the vocalizations are very different from the sounds in the mature language of the environment. At six months, cooing changes into babbling which resembles one-syllable utterances. At eight months the intonation patterns become distinct; utterances can then signal emphasis and emotions. At twelve months of age identical sound sequences are replicated with higher frequency and words such as "mama" or "dada" begin to emerge. The child shows definite signs of understanding various words and simple commands. At eighteen months there is still much babbling but nevertheless a definite repertoire of words—more than three and usually less than fifty. At two years the child has a vocabulary of more than fifty items and begins to spontaneously join items of vocabulary into two-word phrases, such phrases appearing to be the child's own creations. At around thirty months the fastest increase in vocabulary takes place, many additions being made each day. Utterances now have a communicative intent. They consist of two, three, or even five words, although the sentences are rarely verbatim repetitions of adult utterances. With three years of age there is a vocabulary of some thousand words and the grammatical complexity of utterances is roughly that of colloquial adult language. At the completion of the fourth year, language is well established. Deviations from the adult norm tend to be more in style than in grammar (Lenneberg 1967).

A vast amount of observations on children with various abnormalities, such as the onset of deafness or the incidence of traumatic aphasia at one age or another, provides a convincing demonstration of the fact that the acquisition of language is regulated by maturational processes, much the way the acquisition of gait is dependent upon such a process. The many parameters of brain maturation obtained from neuroanatomy, neurochemistry, and neurophysiology show that the first year of life is characterized by a very rapid maturation rate. By the time language begins to make its appearance, about sixty percent of the adult maturational values, such as cell density, connectivity, and myelination have been attained. There is then a critical period in which primary language can be acquired. With the approach of puberty this capacity gradually declines. By then primary language acquisition has become inhibited, the brain has reached its mature state and dominance of one hemisphere is firmly established. Damage to it and specifically to certain areas of the dominant hemisphere may permanently incapacitate speech and language functions. The earlier in life a brain lesion is incurred, the brighter is the outlook for language recovery. On the other hand, *throughout* childhood sudden deafness has an immediate effect upon speech. Within a year or less a child up to the age of four will develop noises and habits seen in the congenitally deaf. Those who lose hearing after having been exposed to the experience of speech, however, even for as short a period as a year, can be trained much more easily in all language arts. It seems as if even a short exposure to language is sufficient to give a child a foundation on which later language can be based (Lenneberg 1967).

In the mature human brain the neocortex, referred to earlier in this lecture as the neomammalian brain, shows an enormously elaborated representation of those parts of the body which are involved in speech: lips, mouth, tongue, pharynx, and larynx (Figure 11). Early in this century, Grünbaum and Sherrington (1947) found that upon electrical stimulation a far greater number of different movements could be obtained from the cortex of chimpanzees, gorillas, and orangutans than from that of the dog or monkey. These movements may be called "fractional." Each is a unitary part of a more complex act. The authors observed that at a level as high in the nervous hierarchy as the cerebral cortex the movements are broken down into small local units. This discrete representation becomes increasingly evident in progressing up the mammalian scale. In man it clearly is elaborated most. Figure 12 shows results from electrical stimulation of the human neocortex. Patients under local anesthesia quite clearly can report what and where they sense when they are electrically stimulated.

Penfield and Rasmussen (1950) found two bilateral cortical areas of vocalization. One, where the sound-producing and speech-elaborating parts of the body are represented, is on the lateral surface of the hemispheres; it is indicated in Figure 12 by the vertical lines in the sensorimotor area. The other area is situated on the medial surface of the brain in the su-

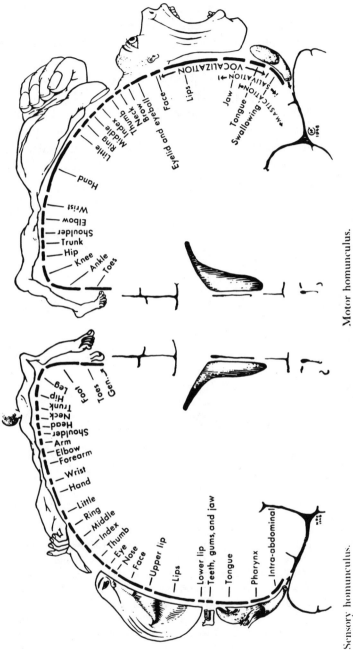

Sensory homunculus.

Motor homunculus.

FIGURE 11. Cerebral representation of the human body. Left side: sensory representation. Right side: motor representation. (From W. Penfield and Th. Rasmussen 1950).

perior frontal region and is indicated by broken arrows. Electrical stimulation of either of these areas, in either hemisphere, can produce either vocalization or arrest of speech, depending on conditions. The difficulty in speaking applies to all words alike. Interference with speech was also produced by stimulation outside of these two bilaterally represented zones in three cortical areas of the dominant hemisphere: frontal, parietal, and temporal as indicated by the horizontal lines. Penfield and Rasmussen (1950) designated these as areas of aphasic arrest since the stimulation effect was characterized by temporary confusion of words similar to that which confounds a patient suffering from aphasia. It would appear from

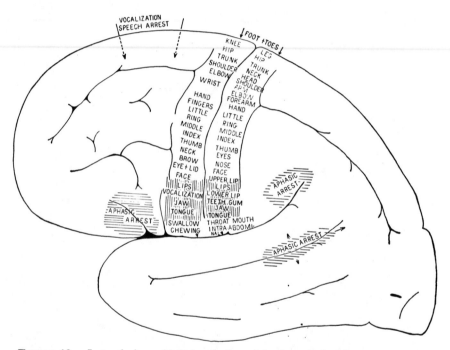

FIGURE 12. Lateral view of left hemisphere (dominant) showing sequence of motor-sensory representation and the areas concerned with speech, as determined by electric stimulation (modified from W. Penfield and Th. Rasmussen 1950). Vertical lines in somato-sensory areas indicate region responding with vocalization or speech arrest, depending on conditions. A similar area, indicated by dotted lines and arrows, occurs on medial surface. The motor area for foot and toes turns over the medial margin of the hemisphere (indicated by arrows on either side of foot and toes); the area for the alimentary tract sinks into the lateral fissure and extends onto the insula (as indicated by arrows under chewing and intra-abdominal). (From S. W. Ranson and S. L. Clark 1959).

116

these and other observations (Penfield and Roberts 1959) that faculties for vocalization are present in each hemisphere and that those for the production of speech are present in the dominant, that is the left hemisphere in right-handed individuals.

Returning to the subcortical vocalization system and its importance for social behavior and communication, it is true that language is not always dependent upon vocalization and that naming is also possible in communication without sound production as shown by the gesture language of the congenital deaf-mutes. It is not appropriate here to go into the problem of language and cognitive processes. It will simply be accepted as fact that no other creature but man has that constellation of capacities that makes naming possible and that in all natural languages this naming is brought about by vocal expressions. In this context it is of considerable interest to note that functioning of verbal language is dependent not only upon cortical but also upon subcortical structures such as certain thalamic nuclei which are connected with the cortical speech areas, and other subcortical structures such as the head of the caudate nucleus, parts of the diencephalon and the periaqueductal gray matter. Although there are not sufficient comparative data of man, apes, and monkeys, there is evidence for the homology of the subcortical vocal system between man and the rest of the primate community, although the behavioral product is species-specific. A squirrel monkey's vocal repertoire is different from that of the macaque, which is different from the chimpanzee's, and so forth (Robinson 1967).

Although the chimpanzee has a highly mobile face and, as already mentioned, a rather differentiated and extended cortical area for the representation of tongue and mouth, several scientists tried almost in vain to teach a chimpanzee elementary language. The young female chimpanzee Viki was eventually able to utter four poorly intelligible words, "mama," "papa," "cup," and "up," but she clearly had no idea of their meaning (Hayes and Hayes 1962). The teaching method employed here was based on imitation and contingent reinforcement, which is very similar to modern methods of speech therapy in language-incapacitated children. Gardner and Gardner's chimpanzee, Washoe, employed nineteen signs of American Sign Language appropriately in a two-way partner situation after sixteen months of conditional training. Whether this nonvocal form of communication meets the basic criteria for human language is a not-yet-settled question. (For a review on "speaking" chimpanzees, see Kellogg 1968.)

We are much interested in so-called infantile autism (Kanner 1951) because of the combined deficiency of social behavior and of speech. Autistic children relate to inanimate objects with fascination but fail to establish

117

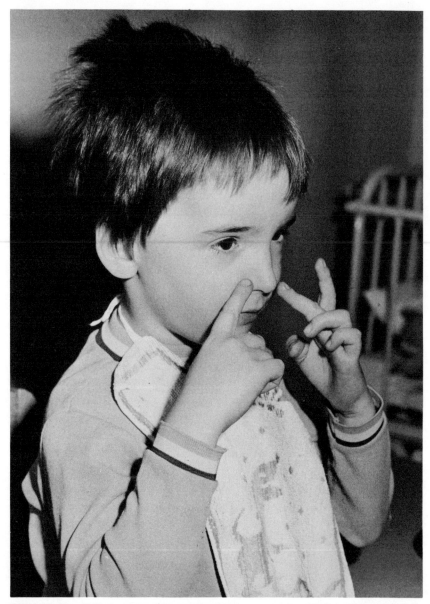

FIGURE 13. Autistic child in verbal imitation training. The boy imitates the therapist's supporting gesture and tries to generate the sound "n." Photo by P. Gottwald, Max Planck Institute for Psychiatry, Munich.

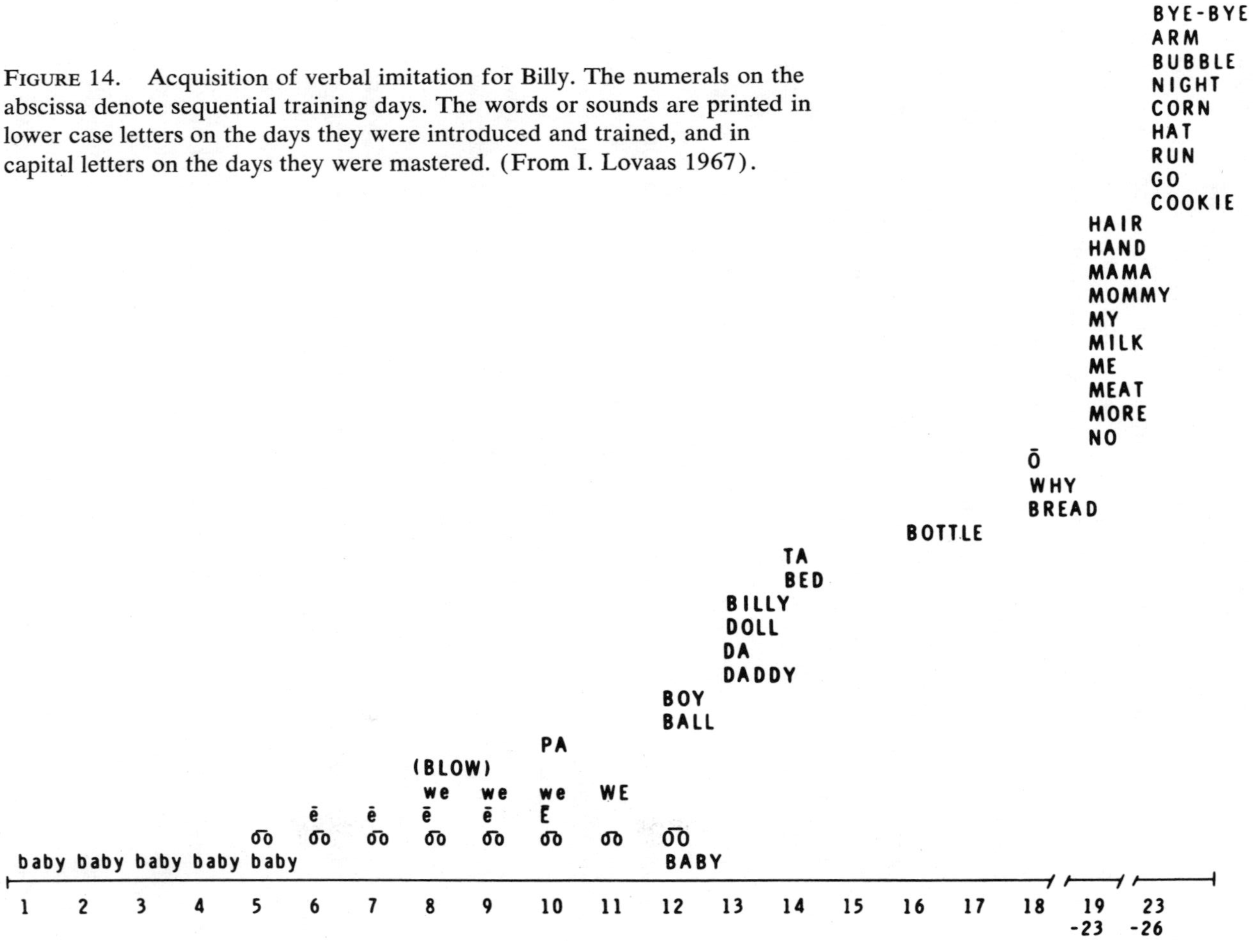

FIGURE 14. Acquisition of verbal imitation for Billy. The numerals on the abscissa denote sequential training days. The words or sounds are printed in lower case letters on the days they were introduced and trained, and in capital letters on the days they were mastered. (From I. Lovaas 1967).

1	2	3	4	5	6	7	8	9	10	11	12	13	14	15	16	17	18	19	23

baby baby baby baby baby
ē ē ē ē we we WE
ōō ōō ōō ōō ōō ōō ōō
(BLOW)
PA
BABY
ōō
BALL
BOY
DADDY
DA
DOLL
BILLY
BED
TA
BOTTLE
BREAD
WHY
ō
COOKIE
GO
RUN
HAT
CORN
NIGHT
BUBBLE
ARM
BYE-BYE
NO
MORE
MEAT
ME
MILK
MY
MOMMY
MAMA
HAND
HAIR

-23
-26

119

relations to persons or to use language for the purpose of communication. They are almost mute, although able to vocalize. It may be noted that these severe deviations of social behavior cannot be understood as the consequences of lack of language. Healthy deaf children get along famously despite the total inability to communicate verbally. They become very clever in their pantomime and have well-developed techniques for communicating their desires, needs, and even their opinions (Lenneberg 1967).

The verbal imitation training employed with an autistic child, as shown in Figure 13, has at least in some cases astounding success. Not only language acquisition, however slow it may be, but also a gradual adjustment to the environment and an improvement in partner-related behavior takes place.

The training starts with "shaping," in which the slightest vocalization is immediately reinforced with tiny candies or the like (Figure 14). Then the child may be shown how the lips are pursed and each imitation is reinforced. Sound production and the position of lips, tongue, etc., have to be brought into simultaneous connection. After many months and sometimes years the deficiency may be compensated. The children have by then improved their partner relationships and at the same time their speech habits. Some of them approximate normal behavior.

The etiology or the etiologies of early infantile autism are unknown. There obviously are conditions, however, which prevent the development of normal social behavior or cause a halt in this development, so that only rudiments of it remain. It appears that these children fail to respond to nonverbal social signals and therefore fail to establish regular partner relations during the pre-language period. Whether this inhibits language development or whether the total communication system, nonverbal and verbal, is defective, remains unknown. It has been suggested that many of the manifestations of autism are explicable in terms of cognitive and perceptual defects. Of all the hypotheses concerning the nature of autism, the one which views the primary defect in terms of language or coding problem appears most promising (Rutter 1968). In the present context we prefer to consider the social signal system, including language propensities, as being defective. In providing insight into the biological foundations of the nonverbal and verbal communication systems, this form of developmental deviation offers considerable promise for future work and has rightly become a worldwide subject for research.

FIGURE 15. A medieval warrior. (Private photo. School of Lucas Cranach, ca. 1545).

121

CONCLUDING REMARKS I have tried to depict the neurological aspects of comparative social behavior, with emphasis on communication processes and their brain correlates. The study of the natural history of social behavior can improve understanding of the present-day behavior of man. It would be erroneous to suppose that the most recent acquisitions of the primate family, such as logic, arithmetic, the language arts, and extension of the learning period, would completely suppress our earlier heritage and govern our lives exclusively. These newly acquired faculties are directed primarily at objects and their interdependencies. They are cognitive in nature. Our social communication, however, appears to contrast sharply with these, being more closely related to our primitive heritage and not necessarily being dominated by logic, reasoning, and cognition. Language, as a dominant part of our social communication, serves both sides; that is, it establishes interdependencies with objects and with partner relationships alike. To control the progress of the cultural evolution which has taken place so much more rapidly than our natural evolution, and to provide for the survival of mankind it seems of utmost importance that we study the nonlogical rules and principles of social communication in much greater detail and with less bias, and that we consider these in our plans for the forthcoming century. The trends in the cultural evolution may well change rapidly. The natural evolution of our social communication system will scarcely be so radical, however, as to change appreciably in the future. That is to say we will have to live with our heritage and to use it for our benefit in any way that may be made possible by advances in the sciences of brain functions and behavior. I am afraid that there is no easy answer as to how this can best be accomplished. This 16th century warrior (Figure 15) shows how prone to display behavior man has always been and probably will be for a long while.

REFERENCES

Bowden, D., P. Winter, and D. W. Ploog.
1967. "Pregnancy and Delivery Behavior of the Squirrel Monkey (*Saimiri sciureus*) and Other Primates." *Folia Primatologica,* 5:1–42.

Broca, P.
1878. "Le grand-lobe limbique et la scissure limbique dans la serie des mammiferes." *Revue d'anthropologie,* 7(1):385–498.

Castell, R., H. Krohn, and D. Ploog.
1969. "Rückenwälzen bei Totenkopfaffen (*Saimiri sciureus*) Körperpflege und soziale Funktion." *Zeitschrift für Tierpsychologie,* 26:488–497.

Friedrich II, F. von Stauffen.
  1968. In *Kaiser Friedrich II in Briefen und Berichten seiner Zeit*, K. J. Heinisch, editor. Darmstadt: Wissenschaftliche Buchgesellschaft.
Gardner, R. A., and B. T. Gardner.
  1969. "Teaching Sign Language to a Chimpanzee." *Science*, 165:664–672.
Grünbaum, A., and C. S. Sherrington.
  1947. In Sherrington, C. S. *The Integrative Action of the Nervous System*. Second Edition, pages 274–276. New Haven, Connecticut: Yale University Press.
Hayes, K. J., and C. Hayes.
  1952. "Imitation in a Home-raised Chimpanzee." *Journal of Comparative Physiology and Psychology*, 45:450–459.
Hopf, S.
  1970. "Report on a Hand-reared Squirrel Monkey (*Saimiri sciureus*). *Zeitschrift für Tierpsychologie*, 27:610–621.
Huxley, J. S.
  1923. "Courtship Activities in the Red-throated Diver (*Colymbus stellatus Pontopp*) Together with a Discussion of the Evolution of Courtship in Birds." *Journal of Linnean Society of London* (*Zoology*), 53:253–292.
Jürgens, U., M. Maurus, D. Ploog, and P. Winter.
  1967. "Vocalization in the Squirrel Monkey (*Saimiri sciureus*) Elicited by Brain Stimulation." *Experimental Brain Research*, 4:114–117.
Jürgens, U., and D. Ploog.
  1970. "Cerebral Representation of Vocalization in the Squirrel Monkey." *Experimental Brain Research*, 10:532–554.
Kanner, L.
  1943. "Autistic Disturbances of Affective Contact." *Nervous Child*, 2:217–250.
  1951. "Early Infantile Autism." *American Journal of Psychiatry*, 108:23–26.
Kellogg, W. N.
  1968. "Communication and Language in the Home-raised Chimpanzee." *Science*, 162:423–427.
Klüver, H., and P. Bucy.
  1937. " 'Psychic Blindness' and other Symptoms following Bilateral Temporal Lobectomy in Rhesus Monkeys." *American Journal of Physiology*, 119:352–353.
  1939. "Preliminary Analysis of Functions of the Temporal Lobes in Monkeys." *Archives of Neurology and Psychiatry*, 42:979–1000.
Lenneberg, E. H.
  1967. *Biological Foundations of Language*. New York, London, Sidney: John Wiley and Sons, Inc.
Lorenz, K.
  1965a. *Über tierisches und menschliches Verhalten*. Collected papers from 1931 to 1963, two volumes. Munich: Piper and Co.
  1965b. *Evolution and Modification of Behavior*. Chicago: University of Chicago Press.

123

Lovaas, I. O.
 1967. "A Behavior Therapy Approach to the Treatment of Childhood
 Schizophrenia." *Minnesota Symposium on Child Psychology.* Minnesota: University of Minneapolis Press.
MacLean, P. D.
 1949. "Psychosomatic Disease and the Visceral Brain." *Psychosomatic Medicine,* 11:338–353.
 1952. "Some Psychiatric Implications of Physiological Studies on Fronto-
 temporal Portion of Limbic System (Visceral Brain)." *Electro-
 encephalography and Clinical Neurophysiology,* 4:407–418.
 1958. "The Limbic System with respect to Self-preservation and the Preser-
 vation of the Species." *Journal of Nervous and Mental Disease,*
 127:1–11.
 1967. "The Brain in Relation to Empathy and Medical Education." *Journal
 of Nervous and Mental Disease,* 144:374–383.
 1968. "Alternative Neural Pathways to Violence." Pages 24–34 in *Alternatives to Violence, A Stimulus to Dialogue.* New York: Time-Life
 Books.
MacLean, P. D., and D. Ploog.
 1962. "Cerebral Representation of Penile Erection." *Journal of Neurophysiology,* 25:29–55.
MacLean, P. D., B. W. Robinson, and D. W. Ploog.
 1959. "Experiments on Localization of Genital Function in the Brain."
 Transactions of the American Neurological Association, 84:105–109.
Maurus, M., J. Mitra, and D. Ploog.
 1965. "Cerebral Representation of the Clitoris in Ovariectomized Squirrel
 Monkeys." *Experimental Neurology,* 13:283–288.
Penfield, W., and Th. Rasmussen.
 1950. *The Cerebral Cortex of Man.* New York: The Macmillan Company.
Penfield, W., and L. Roberts.
 1959. *Speech and Brain-Mechanisms.* New Jersey: Princeton University
 Press.
Ploog, D.
 1963. "Vergleichende quantitative Verhaltensstudien an zwei Totenkopfaf-
 fenkolonien." *Zeitschrift fur Morphologie und Anthropologie,* 53:92–
 108.
 1966. "Biological Bases for Instinct and Behavior: Studies on the Development of Social Behavior in Squirrel Monkeys." In *Recent Advances in
 Biological Psychiatry,* Joseph Wortis, editor, 8:199–223. New York:
 Plenum Press.
 1967. "The Behavior of Squirrel Monkeys (*Saimiri sciureus*) as Revealed
 by Sociometry, Bioacoustics, and Brain Stimulation." Pages 149–184,
 in *Social Communication Among Primates,* S. A. Altmann, editor.
 Chicago: The University of Chicago Press.
 1969. "Early Communication Processes in Squirrel Monkeys." In *Brain
 and Early Behaviour: Development in the Fetus and Infant,* R. J.
 Robinson, editor. London and New York: Academic Press.

124

Ploog, D., J. Blitz, and F. Ploog.
   1963. "Studies of Social and Sexual Behavior of the Squirrel Monkeys (*Saimiri sciureus*)." *Folia Primatologica*, 1:29–66.
Ploog, D., S. Hopf, and P. Winter.
   1967. "Ontogenese des Verhaltens von Totenkopf-Affen (*Saimiri sciureus*). *Psychologische Forschung*, 31:1–41.
Ploog, D., and P. MacLean.
   1963. "Display of Penile Erection in Squirrel Monkey (*Saimiri sciureus*)." *Animal Behaviour*, 11:32–39.
Ranson, S. W., and S. L. Clark.
   1959. *The Anatomy of the Nervous System*. 10th edition, page 378. Philadelphia and London: W. B. Saunders Company.
Robinson, B. W.
   1967. "Vocalization Evoked from Forebrain in *Macaca mulatta*." *Physiology and Behavior*, 2:345–354.
Rutter, M.
   1968. "Concepts of Autism: A Review of Research." *Journal of Child Psychology and Psychiatry*, 9:1–25.
Starck, D.
   1965. "Die Neencephalisation." Page 130 in *Menschliche Abstammungslehre. Fortschritte der Anthropogenie, 1863–1964*. G. Heberer, editor. Stuttgart: G. Fischer Verlag.
Stebbins, G. L.
   1966. *Processes of Organic Evolution*. Englewood Cliffs, New Jersey: Prentice-Hall, Inc.
Tinbergen, N.
   1953. *Social Behaviour in Animals, with Special Reference to Vertebrates*. London: Methuen.
Winter, P., D. Ploog, and J. Latta.
   1966. "Vocal Repertoire of the Squirrel Monkey (*Saimiri sciureus*), Its Analysis and Significance." *Experimental Brain Research*, 1:359–384.

PART II

WHAT ARE THE BASIC MECHANISMS OF SOCIAL BEHAVIOR IN ANIMALS AND MAN?

INTRODUCTION

J. F. EISENBERG

In this section we will turn away from a concentration on the physiological and genetical bases for expressed behavior patterns and instead take a close look at some of the fundamental behavior mechanisms involved in the maintenance of social bonds, the dispersal of animals in space, and the integration and coordination of group-living members' behaviors. Chapter 4 by Robert Zajonc considers the question of how permanent or long-term relationships are established among organisms. He draws his material from a wide range of living creatures and concentrates on the problem of how positive relationships are formed and maintained. Although a variety of mechanisms have been proposed to account for bonding among animals, this author proposes that such a simple process as repeated exposure to a stimulus object is in and of itself a sufficient condition for the enhancement of an individual's attraction and attachment to the given object. He deals specifically with the bases for an attraction relationship and does not concentrate on the formation of aversive reactions. The author proposes that imprinting, specific instincts, and associative learning do not explain the formation of attachment in all cases and, further, none of the preceding processes are a necessary condition for the formation of all types of affiliation. Rather, repeated exposure itself without any discrete reinforcement can be a sufficient condition for the establishment of a preference.

In this section the concept of imprinting or *Prägung,* as defined by Lorenz (1935), is reviewed. Lorenz defines imprinting as a type of rapid learning restricted to a specific critical period in development. He offered four criteria: (1) once a subject becomes imprinted on an object, it is almost impossible to reverse the imprinted tendencies; (2) the ability to imprint is restricted to a certain stage during the development of the animal; (3) once an imprinted response is fixed, certain general classes of behavior, such as sexual or parental care, tend to be directed toward the imprinted object; and (4) imprinting involves learning supra-individual characters so that the imprinted animal can generalize from a specific organism to a class of organisms that resemble the imprinted object. These criteria tended to define imprinting in the classic sense. Lorenz further speculated that there may be a succession of critical periods which would insure imprinting to correct "companions" at each stage of the animal's developing life cycle. Depending on the species in question, the critical periods may be discrete or show some broad overlap. In any event, his suggestions provided a fertile field of research on a comparative basis, especially with birds (Klinghammer 1967).

Zajonc in Chapter 4 uses the term imprinting in a broader context than was originally proposed by Lorenz (1935). Zajonc's suggestions are certainly thought provoking but he radically extends the concept of imprinting and further stretches the meaning of the term bonding. The formation of bonds may involve something more than just a preference for an object. Rather, in order for bonding to take place, it would appear that the organism must be able to perform some satisfying act of a self-reinforcing nature with the bonded object (Fischer 1965). Bonding is often used in the more restricted sense by ethologists.

With these qualifications in mind, Zajonc's chapter can be read with much profit, although the extended definitions employed by the author renders the overall conclusions not universally applicable to certain operationally defined experimental procedures. Nevertheless, the fact that repeated exposure can be involved in the establishment of preferences in a choice situation for animals as well as humans is indeed food for thought.

Wilson's essay opens with a reconsideration of the theories propounded by Lorenz with respect to aggressive behavior. He reemphasizes that the position of Lorenz involves the assumption that aggressive behavior has aspects of being under control of a drive center in the same sense that hunger, thirst, and sexual drives are manifested. Hence, aggressive behavior may have an appetitive phase where the organism actually seeks out an object to fight. There are counter arguments to this view which assume that the propensity for aggression is in part a function of early experience and further that there is not necessarily an aggressive drive to fight but rather that an organism can be conditioned to fight and positively reinforced by winning. Hence, there exists within the scientific community a disagreement with respect to the nature of aggression and its physiological basis.

The reader is referred to the recent critique by Robert Hinde (1969) for a balanced presentation of the issues wherein Hinde concludes that the evidence at hand would suggest that perhaps aggression does not have the same attributes as a classical drive and further that a unitary drive concept for explaining any functional class of behavior, such as parental care, sexual behavior, and feeding behavior is not necessarily the most realistic explanation. Furthermore, Hinde suggests that the thresholds to exhibit aggressive behavior and the readiness with which aggression can be reinforced may well vary from species to species and not enough evidence is at hand to make a conclusion with respect to how aggression is controlled physiologically in humans. Clearly then, the role of the student in comparative behavior is to continue with his comparisons, always striving to interrelate results but never attempting to be too rash in extending the results from the study of one species to another.

Wilson, utilizing insect studies, turns to the phenomenon of competition among organisms which is defined as a "density dependent" factor. That is to say, competition is a pattern of behavior which increases in the intensity of its manifestation as the population density increases. Classical competition in reality involves the activities of organisms attempting to gain access to resources which are limited, be they spatial resources, food resources, or sexual partners. Furthermore, competition is only one method of control exerted by species at high densities, and competition in and of itself is not the only method of regulating density and access to limited resources. Again, when one considers competition for resources in short supply, aggression is only one mechanism of competition. The animal kingdom is replete with examples of overt aggression, however, and in Chapter 5 the reader is asked to pay special attention to the descriptions of social insect "warfare."

A consideration of insect control mechanisms leads the author to delineate certain basic mechanisms by which competition is expressed. By establishing classes of activity, it is then possible to draw analogies with respect to the behavior of vertebrate populations. Wilson then moves on to consider territory as a method of dominance and control of members of the same species. He offers a re-definition of territory. He examines the fact that there are limits to which aggressive behavior can be expressed and, in some cases within natural populations, one may observe the phenomenon of "aggressive neglect" where offspring suffer reduced attention from parents, since the aggressive activities of parents lead to a total reduction in the time spent with the young. Under such cases of pathological behavior, the parents often cannot efficiently replace themselves in the forthcoming generation; hence, one would anticipate that to the extent that this behavior is genetically controlled there would be a decrease in the descendants of those animals exhibiting extreme forms of social pathology.

Wilson points out that aggression in and of itself is not necessarily maladaptive but may only become maladaptive under certain special

133

circumstances in the environment. Many populations of vertebrates and invertebrates have been subjected to experimental manipulations where a variety of social pathologies have appeared. Wilson reviews these studies in part, but whether these types of social pathology ever appear in nature is still open to some question; nevertheless, studies of responses to crowding using closely related species have amply demonstrated that there may well be different thresholds of responsiveness to crowding which reflect overall adaptations to a general population density which is characteristic of either the species in question or of the population from which the species is drawn. Hence, social pathologies under experimental conditions may indeed reflect different adaptive tendencies on the part of either species or populations (Eisenberg 1967).

Wilson returns to the consideration of the genetic contribution to behavioral traits and again poses the question "To what extent is man's behavior determined by heritable factors?" He demonstrates the possibilities that some human behavior traits may have a high heritability. In closing, Wilson suggests that one of the major goals for the anthropology of the future may well be the development of genetic studies related to uncovering the extent to which culturally different behavior patterns are in part under the regulation of heritable factors.

Following on Wilson's consideration of the role of competition in nature by vertebrates and invertebrates, Kummer considers spacing mechanisms as a method of adapting to various environmental conditions. As he points out, many factors influence spacing, most of which are related to the ecology of the species in question or the manner in which the species exploits its environment. Kummer draws his examples from primate studies and shows that within the primates aggression is very often used as a mechanism to insure spacing among individuals or between different troops of the same species. It is used as a control mechanism for the orderly distribution of individuals or troops within the habitat. He points out that individual spacing differs when one considers age classes, sex classes, and species. Ultimately these differences may well be related to the mode of habitat utilization.

The defense of a territory is one method of spacing out troops. It is characteristic of species which habitually do not migrate. Within the troop itself the maintenance of certain distances among the members prevents overstimulation by individuals within the troop but there must be a limit on the distance among members or the troop cannot maintain its integrity through a reduction in the ability to communicate among themselves. Hence (within a troop at the individual level) there is always a balance between mechanisms insuring some form of spacing and mechanisms which tend to keep troop members in a somewhat cohesive grouping.

One of the mechanisms aiding in the reduction of interindividual distances within a troop are behavior patterns referred to as "submissive" which are display patterns that indicate that the sender is not predisposed to attack or to direct adverse behaviors on the receiver. A further mechanism for insuring control within a troop is the regulation of access to resources by means of an established dominance order. Kummer then goes on to demonstrate how submission, dominance orders, and territories vary in their manifestations when different species of primates are compared. He convincingly shows that there are infinite variations on the interplay of mechanisms for spacing and attraction.

He turns then to a consideration of the use of space by human beings and points out that modern humans must interact with virtual strangers in contradistinction to the interacting individuals within a primate troop or the members of a preurbanized human community. Modern urbanized man is forced to associate the better part of his day with other humans who are unknown to him; hence, modern man has invented spacing patterns such as compartmentalizing his housing and locks on his doors which are based on the biological foundations reflected in the spacing patterns of his primate relatives.

Crook's essay reviews mechanisms of cooperation within animal societies. He proposes to examine the processes of animal cooperation and to relate, if possible, to the basic sources of human cooperation. He prefers not to consider behavior primarily determined by heredity but rather to enter a middle ground between considerations of environmental influences and heritable tendencies. For Crook, cooperation is equivalent to the collaborative effort of two individuals to bring about a desired end, and it is a group characteristic.

He sees the formation of bonds between adult females as an emergent property within primate societies. In this example one female without an infant acts to aid and assist a second female in the rearing of her infant. He points out that this may indeed be the beginnings of a form of cooperation. Indeed, such cooperative behavior with respect to infant care need not be confined to another female, even subordinate males may "use" infant primates to improve their status with high-ranking males. Furthermore, in some primate societies, male child care patterns are involved and indeed the harem formation of the hamadryas baboon very often begins with the adoption of an infant female by an adult male which then grows up to form the nucleus of this adult male's new harem. Hence, harem formation in the hamadryas baboon often begins with a parental care behavior pattern.

Crook adopts a new viewpoint by demonstrating that the analysis of social structure based solely on a dominance hierarchy method of description is totally inadequate to explain group behavior. In short, he advocates that a modified use of role theory derived from sociology may be the most useful way of describing group behavior in nonhuman primates. Roles may be expressed quantitatively by calculating the percentage of time spent by each individual in performing various sequences of behavior. Only by such an analysis is it possible to show that in those primate societies which characteristically have more than one adult male associated with the group, mutual cooperation among beta males is necessary to maintain the status of an alpha male within a troop. Contrastingly, in such species as the hamadryas baboon where habitually the social unit contains only one adult male, a single young adult male may remain submissive to an older male and maintain his presence in a troop until he becomes sexually mature. By cooperation he may eventually take over the alpha position as the alpha male himself ages.

Crook points out that the parent-young relationship is the basic unit for the derivation of most cooperative behavior which one may discern in primate troops; hence, affiliation tendencies within primate troops are based upon kin groups. Compare this conclusion with the theories concerning the evolution of altruistic behavior as propounded by Hamilton in Chapter 2.

Crook is careful to point out that cooperative behavior in macaque and baboon troops has arisen within the context of competition. If we reconsider the examples, males which are to an extent in competition with each other will nevertheless cooperate to support an alpha male, an action which is apparently of some adaptive advantage by conferring an overall stability on the troop. Furthermore, a single male may be submissive to an older male, in the one-male troop baboon organization as displayed by the hamadryas, and, although in competition with him, may act cooperatively for many years before taking over the alpha position as the older male ages. Furthermore, when two female monkeys show a mutual care relationship with respect to an infant, to an extent the female without an infant who participates in parental care is competing with the true mother for the infant as a course of satisfaction. Hence, mild forms of competition are necessary as precursers to the emergent phenomenon of cooperation. In short, mildly competitive mechanisms and the regulation of the degree of competition give rise to a complex system of reinforced behavior patterns which we refer to as cooperative. Such forms of cooperation are related to the achievement of individualistic goals on a deferred basis.

In this section, Wilson draws in the main on social insects for some of his examples whereas Kummer and Crook lean heavily upon the primates for their source material. All of these men are well aware that similar behavior mechanisms are operative in the social systems of other vertebrates; indeed, Crook reviews some of the pertinent literature to underscore this theme. The emphasis is undeniably on primates and the rationale is that since man arose from a primate stock, homologies may be better established by turning to the primates than by considering more distantly related mammals. Nevertheless, it is prudent to bear in mind that many of the emergent mechanisms one can discern in the primates have developed in a parallel fashion if not in a homologous fashion within other related mammalian taxa.

The formation of unisexual subgroupings in mammalian societies is well known in the ungulates. The formation of an extended mother family deriving from surviving generations of a given female's progeny is the fundamental mechanism whereby cohesive social groupings are structured in other mammalian groups. An extended mother family which persists over several generations may not move cohesively in space but rather assemble at given times in given places as demonstrated by the semi-solitary roe deer, *Capreolus capreolus,* in the publication by Kurt (1968).

Even in such relatively solitary species of carnivores as the tiger, *Panthera tigris,* and the puma, *Felis concolor,* one can discern extended mother families which persist for several years (Schaller 1967, Hornocker 1969). In contrast within the Carnivora, one may note the cohesive social groupings formed by certain species of the family Canidae, e.g., the wolf *Canis lupus,* where a persistent family unit stays together for several generations with reproduction generally being performed by one male and one or two dominant females; where cooperative care of the young is demonstrated on the part of both adult sexes; and where provisioning of the bitch and her litter is part of the normal rearing process (see Kleiman 1967, Mech 1966).

It is instructive not to lose sight of common basic trends in the evolution of social structure exhibited within the class Mammalia and which are not unique to the primates alone (Eisenberg and Kuehn 1966). I may mention that within the two major radiations of the class Mammalia [e.g., the marsupial radiation in Australia and the placental radiation in the northern hemisphere] we can discern parallel trends in the formation

137

of extended social groupings as the result of adaptation for the utilization of grassland on the part of herbivorous mammals (Eisenberg 1966).
With the emergence of more extended social units, there has been a
parallel evolution in mechanisms for maintaining cohesion yet retaining
spacing and all of this has been accomplished in part by selection
operating upon a female-young unit and an extended mother family as the
core grouping.

When larger mammals are compared with smaller ones, it often appears
that the larger forms have more complicated organizations and more complex communication mechanisms. This may be more apparent than real,
in that extremely complicated mechanisms for spacing and social integration may be discerned within the extended kin groups of very small and
so-called primitive mammals (Eisenberg and Gould 1970). Further, the
differences between primate social systems and the social systems of other
mammals have been overemphasized to the point of being nonrealistic,
and in fact very similar mechanisms and trends may be observed if the
appropriate taxa are compared (see Eisenberg and Kuehn 1966).

Such a comparative perspective does not deny the existence of the
mechanisms already described within primate societies but rather de-
emphasizes these mechanisms as being necessarily unique to primates and
restores our understanding of how these mechanisms function in nature
and how they may be called forth under the appropriate selective pressures into functional patterns as social life is favored in the ongoing
process of adaptation to the exploitation of specific habitats. Knowledge
of the existence of functionally similar behavioral mechanisms within
mammalian societies other than these primates is fundamental to an
understanding of social evolution. Only when mechanisms for spacing,
promoting cohesion, bonding, and cooperation have been defined for
many species can we meaningfully examine the questions of homology
with respect to physiological substrates. Much confusion concerning the
biological bases for so-called "drives" can be dispelled only if we continue
to study and infer within a broadly based series of comparisons.

REFERENCES

Eisenberg, J. F.
  1966. "The Social Organizations of Mammals." *Handbuch der Zoologie,*
    volume VIII (10/7), lieferung 39:1–92.
  1967. "A Comparative Study in Rodent Ethology with Emphasis on Evolu-
    tion of Social Behavior." *Proceedings U.S. National Museum,*
    122(3597):1–51.

Eisenberg, J. F., and E. Gould.
1970. "The Tenrecs: A Study in Mammalian Behavior and Evolution." *Smithsonian Contributions to Zoology*, number 27:1–135.

Eisenberg, J. F., and R. E. Kuehn.
1966. "The Behavior of *Ateles geoffroyi* and Related Species." *Smithsonian Miscellaneous Collection*, 151(8):1–63.

Fischer, H.
1965. "Des Triumpschrei der Graugans (*Anser anser*)." *Zeitschrift fur Tierpsychologie*, 22:247–304.

Hinde, R. A.
1969. "The Bases of Aggression in Animals." *Journal of Psychosomatic Research*, 13:213–219.

Hornocker, M. G.
1969. "Winter Territoriality in Mountain Lions." *Journal of Wildlife Management*, 33:457–464.

Kleiman, D. G.
1967. "Some Aspects of Social Behavior in the Canidae." *American Zoologist*, 7:365–372.

Klinghammer, E.
1967. "Factors Influencing the Choice of a Mate in Altricial Birds." Pages 5–42 in *Early Behavior*, Stevenson, H. W., et al. New York: Wiley & Sons.

Kurt, F.
1967. "Das Sozial Verhalten Des Rehes (*Capreolus capreolus*)." *Mammalia Depicta*. Frankfurt a.m.: Paul Parey.

Lorenz, K.
1935. "Der Kumpan in der Umwelt des Vogels." *Journal fur Ornithologie*, 80(heft 1). Translation in K. Lorenz, *Studies in Animal and Human Behavior*. Volume I. Cambridge: Harvard University Press, 1970.

Mech, L. D.
1966. "The Wolves of Isle Royale." *Fauna of National Parks of the U.S.*, number 7. Washington, D.C.: United States Government Printing Office.

Schaller, G.
1967. *The Deer and the Tiger*. Chicago: University of Chicago Press.

CHAPTER 4

ATTRACTION, AFFILIATION, AND ATTACHMENT

ROBERT B. ZAJONC

UNIVERSITY OF MICHIGAN

The inhabited regions of the earth extend over an area of some 52 million square miles. Dispersed today over this area are, according to recent estimates, approximately 3.3 billion people. According to this the population density is 63 persons per square mile.

If the dispersion of people over all the inhabitable areas were random, the average distance between a given person and the *nearest* other person would be approximately 590 feet. This is certainly not the case. The probability that at any given time a given square foot of habitable ground on earth is occupied by an individual is certainly quite low, in fact, one in 500,000. But once we have located one individual, we will almost certainly find another within a few yards. It is a rather safe assumption that the average distance between a given individual and the nearest other person is today less than ten yards.

Three hundred years ago the world population did not exceed 545 million. Hence the population density during the seventeenth century was somewhat over ten persons per square mile. Again, if they were distributed over the habitable area at random, like the molecules of oxygen in a room, the average distance between one person and the nearest other one would have been roughly 1320 feet. But again, this certainly was not the case, and probably, *there never was a period on earth* when the average nearest distance between people exceeded ten yards. It is, of course, no news to us that we are not randomly distributed, and it is certainly obvious that all species at all times manifest a dispersion which markedly departs from chance, as is revealed by successive samples of the same habitat. Unfortunately, there are no precise figures at the present time for most species. Nevertheless, common observations lead us to believe that each species displays a characteristic average minimal distance. It should be stressed that we are not speaking here of population density and not even of local population density, that is, size of the population averaged

Research of the author reported in this paper was supported by the National Institute of Mental Health, Grant MH 12174.

over the area of a particular habitat. Both overall density and local density do vary depending on a variety of ecological factors, and may be taken as basic indications of the species' adaptation to its environment. The average distance between an individual and the nearest conspecific, however, is as distinct a characteristic of a given species as is its coloring, diet, bone structure, or breeding pattern; unlike average dispersion, it represents a form of adaptation which each individual of an aggregation has achieved with respect to the others. For the vast majority of species this distance is no more than a few body lengths. It is curious, therefore, that there are only meager, descriptive data on the problem.[1]

Not only is the average nearest distance between two individuals of the same species peculiar to each given species, but individuals that are found near to each other on one observation remain so for extended periods of time. This is not saying more than that people and other animals live in aggregations of groups and crowds, that their dispersion over an area resembles more the disperison of molecules in heterogeneous matter, such as organic tissues, than in liquids or gases, and that the social organization of these groups has some stability over a period of time. But saying that species live in aggregations tends to conceal a rather basic problem because it implies in an Aristotelian manner that such is the nature of beasts and that we might as well take it, *a priori*. Research in this area has tended to take as its main objective the *description* of the social organization of aggregations of the various species, while the *mechanisms* maintaining social organization are only rarely the subject of systematic inquiry. The observation that animals live in organized groups has in fact prevented us from asking some rather basic and significant questions, questions which only recently have been recognized as significant, as Professor Kummer has pointed out in Chapter 6.

In science all constancies are precious, precious because they are the terms by which some of our stubborn equations become solvable. If the average distance between the individual and his nearest neighbor is indeed constant over different groups and communities of the same species, then other characteristics of the distribution of these nearest distances, such as their standard deviations, skewness, and kurtosis, *might* also be important benchmarks of the given social organization and *must* then directly

---

[1] *Editor's note:* Rather than think in terms of each species as displaying a characteristic average minimal distance, which may well be true for some species, it is more prudent to think in terms of a characteristic average minimal distance as an attribute of a given population. (J.F.E.)

relate to the social behavior of the individuals. Each of them raises interesting research questions about the underlying social and psychological processes.

Why then is there for all species a characteristic average distance between individuals? Not a great deal is known today about the dispersion of animal populations. It is known, however, that animal populations are self-limiting (Wynne-Edwards 1962). Once a certain level of crowding is reached, behavioral changes may occur: a drastic decrease in the number of breeders or the number of eggs which are laid, an increase in newborn fatalities, retardation in growth and maturity, ejection of group members, rejection of newcomers, migration of the colony, an increase in frequency of agonistic behavior, and cannibalism are not out of the question. Wynne-Edwards' keen analysis points out that most of these adaptations occur *before* the population begins *to suffer drastically from density,* that is, before signs of starvation. "On the contrary, the ceiling is normally imposed, and the level indefinitely maintained, while the members of the population are in good health—sometimes actually fat—and leading normal lives" (Wynne-Edwards 1962, page 10).

When guppies reach a certain density they begin eating their young a few minutes after birth. Breder and Coates (1932) reared guppies in two aquaria, one having a single pregnant female and the other containing fifty mixed fish. In a few months *both* colonies reached a stable level of population—nine individuals. But it is interesting that in the first aquarium all the young in the first brood survived, while succeeding broods fared less well. In fact, the entire fourth brood was eaten by the mother, although food in excess was provided at all times. These behavioral adaptations to crowding are only beginning to be understood today. It appears, for instance, that aggression within a species reduced mating, and other forms of behavior that appear with crowding might be related to demonstrable changes in endocrine functions.

Thiessen and his colleagues (1962), for instance, have shown that in mice the secretion of adrenocorticosteroids increases with crowding, and Christian (1955) found under similar conditions an increase in adrenal weights. Endocrine changes, which are typical responses to stimuli which elicit emotional strain, might initiate certain behaviors, the collective consequence of which would be to maintain the population density below a certain level. Christian (1956) reports that androgen production, and hence the onset of puberty, is delayed in male mice that live in crowded conditions. He also found lower gonadal weights and suppression of spermatogenesis in mature males living in such quarters. Hence reproductive functions, too, may be directly affected by overcrowding.[2]

Conditions that make crowding persist are no doubt closely tied to social organization (Zajonc, ed. 1969). Also, such mechanisms explain that within a given distance from a given individual the *number* of other individuals never (or extremely rarely) exceeds certain magnitudes. But they do not explain why, even during periods of abundance and affluence, the distance between one individual and the *nearest* other individual of the same species remains fairly constant. From the point of view of exploitation of the habitat's resources, it would be most efficient for the individuals to disperse as far apart as possible. If the average nearest distance between individuals is indeed a constant across communities of the given species, it would be absurd to speak of a *relationship* between this distance and crowding. We must also account for the temporal stability of these distances between *particular* individuals. There is nothing in the behavioral mechanisms that control density which suggests an explanation of *particular* social bonds.

What then are the behavioral mechanisms that maintain distances? It is useful to assume, as did Professor Kummer in the case of spacing in Chapter 6, that the stability of these distances represents an equilibrium maintained by two opposing forces: the forces of attraction or cohesion and the forces of dispersion and repulsion. As the title of this paper implies, however, I shall be exclusively concerned with the forces of attraction.

Since the three terms of my title—attraction, affiliation, and attachment—have been used interchangeably in the literature, they will also be used interchangeably in this paper. All three refer to the emotional bond between the individual and a given stimulus object. There are some differences in emphasis which are not critical for our purposes but which may be pointed out in passing. *Attraction* emphasizes the individual's tendency to approach the given stimulus object, animate or inanimate. *Attachment* places stress on the temporal and more permanent aspects of

---

[2] It is interesting in this respect that in humans the age of puberty has been decreasing in spite of increases in population densities. But one should not overlook the fact that along with rapidly growing densities, human populations have been able to improve their exploitation of the environment at an even faster rate. *Editor's note:* Evidence from the field for the cited captive pathologies is still equivocal. It would appear that other mechanisms for population control may manifest themselves before the pathologies referred to in this text appear (see D. Lack, *Appendix in Population Studies of Birds,* Oxford, 1968, for a critique). (J.F.E.)

emotional bonds. *Affiliation* is merely attachment or attraction of the individual to animate objects.

What is the source of attraction and attachment between individuals of the same species and what leads to the formation of social bonds of animal and human groups?

Explanations in terms of specific gregarious or herd instincts are no longer satisfactory. And if we are prevented from relying on such traditional answers, we immediately turn to experiential factors, such as learning and reinforcement. Filial attachment seems to be developed by rewards the mother provides for her offspring, and some theories of attachment make this claim. But some experiments show that attachment can develop without rewards. Harlow (1958) and Igel and Calving (1960) report the development of filial attachments of mammals in the absence of lactation. Brodbeck (1954) has shown that puppies fed by mechanical means attach themselves to humans as readily as hand fed subjects. Puppies can even form attachments when punished. Fisher (1955) punished puppies whenever they approached their human handler. But as soon as punishment was stopped, the puppies went back to their handler. In an experiment on imprinting (the early acquisition of strong attachment), Hess (1964) found that shock administered to chicks facilitated rather than inhibited imprinting. Moreover, attachment and attraction of one individual to the other is not sufficient to explain the stability of the social bond *between* them. Such a social bond requires reciprocity and mutuality. Why should the mother become attached to her offspring? Perhaps because of the pleasurable aspects of lactation in mammals? But what earthly joys might a goose derive from having a number of goslings trail behind her for weeks on end?

In 1963 Scott reviewed the literature on attraction and within species and concluded that while reinforcement might enhance attachment, it is not a *necessary* condition for its occurrence. If neither specific instincts nor associative learning explain the formation and maintenance of attractions and attachments between individuals of the same species, what are the underlying psychological processes?

We shall examine in this paper a rather simple process—namely, repeated exposure—and attempt to show that the mere repeated exposure of one individual to another is enough to produce attraction. An attempt will be made to show that this phenomenon is a special case of a more general hypothesis, namely, that *the mere repeated exposure of an individual to a given stimulus object is a sufficient condition for the en-*

hancement of his attraction toward it, be this stimulus object a member of the same species, a member of different species, or an inanimate object. By "mere" exposure is meant a situation which makes the stimulus object just accessible to the individual's perception and which is unencumbered by other processes or contingencies, such as positive or negative reinforcement, requirement on the individual that he make particular responses (instrumental or consummatory), or other stimulation systematically associated with the exposure of the critical stimulus object.

IMPRINTING AND EXPOSURE EFFECTS IN ANIMALS Modern ethology represents a compromise between instinctual and experiential bases of animal behavior. Imprinting represents such a compromise with respect to the development of attachment and attraction. The early concepts of imprinting treated it as a "process by which certain stimuli become capable of eliciting certain 'innate' behavior patterns (during) a critical period of the animal's behavioral development" (Jaynes 1956, p. 201). While imprinting was believed restricted to certain specific conditions and behaviors, it is now clearly apparent that it can occur in a variety of species, in a large variety of situations, for a variety of behaviors, at various ages of the animal, to almost any stimulus object (Bateson 1966), and that it is not irreversible (Sluckin 1965).

While the concept was initially restricted exclusively to birds, imprinting was successfully accomplished with a variety of mammalian species (Altmann 1958; Cairns 1966a, 1966b; Collias 1962; Cross, Holcomb, and Matter 1967; Gray 1958; Hediger 1950; Scott 1958; Shipley 1963; Thorpe 1956), fishes (Candland and Milne 1966; Greenberg 1963), and reptiles (Burghardt and Hess 1966).

Evidence indicates that attachments within species are deeply influenced by early social experience. Mainardi (1967) reported that normal orange fruitflies (*Drosophila melanogaster*) court orange females when given a choice between orange and yellow females. Individuals reared in isolation, however, do not discriminate between orange and yellow females, and court the one as often as the other. Pinckney and Anderson (1967) reared guppies (*Lebistes reticulatus*) in groups and in isolation. They found that isolated subjects tended to avoid other fish during the early stages of testing, but eventually they increased the amount of time spent near display guppies and behaved like normal fish. The rat, which has been regarded as having a minimal social life (Tolman 1951), is also not free from the social effects of experience. Latané, observing pairs of rats in an open field test, found that the average distance between the rats of each pair decreased with time. This study confirms others (Eckman and Meltzer 1969, Latané 1969, Latané and Glass 1968), in which it is consistently found that attraction between rats increases over successive experiences.

While imprinting is more likely to occur as the result of attachment between individuals of the same species, exposures to members of a different species are no less powerful. Cairns (1966b) used lambs which prior to the experiment, lived under normal conditions for several weeks with their mothers and other lambs. At the beginning of the experiment the lambs were separated from their small flock and for a period of seventy-one days confined to live either with a dog in the same cage, with a dog in an adjacent cage, with a nonmaternal ewe, or with a continuously operating television set. At various points of the cohabitation, tests were made in which the lamb was placed in a U-shaped maze and allowed to choose between an empty compartment or one containing the cohabitant. Figure 1 shows the results of Cairns' experiment from which it is clear that when lambs have the choice between solitude and their cohabitant they always prefer the cohabitant, and this preference increases over the period of cohabitation. But it also shows that dogs, ewes, and television sets are equally effective in gaining the lambs' affection as a function of exposure.

After nine weeks Cairns allowed his lambs to choose between their cohabitants and a tethered ewe. Having lived with a dog for a period of nine weeks, the lambs chose their canine companions in preference to a ewe. Having to choose between a tethered ewe and the television, lambs reared with a continuously playing television set preferred the ewe, but this preference was not overwhelming, and reliably lower than that exhibited by the control animals.

In similar experiments Candland and Milne (1966) reared chickens, kittens, guppies, and rats in the company of their respective species or in isolation, and either with or without manipulable objects such as balls on strings, marbles, mirrors, or moving toys. Regardless of their previous experience, when given a choice, rats showed a preference for other rats. But in all the remaining animals exposure to objects had a profound effect on their subsequent social choices. Cats did prefer other cats but not absolutely; in several instances they preferred the toy, especially during the early series of testing. Chickens, too, preferred other chickens. Those reared with objects and in isolation, however, showed least preference for other chickens. Guppies, however, preferred objects to other guppies in all conditions.

Denenberg, Hudgens, and Zarrow (1964) reared four groups of mice

149

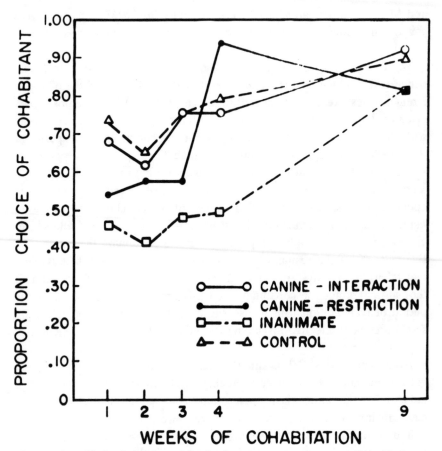

FIGURE 1. Choice behavior of lambs in noncontrast maze series, with ten trials at each test week (from Cairns 1966a).

under different conditions. One group lived with other mice, another group was exposed to male and female rats after weaning, a third group was fostered to a rat mother when three days old, and the fourth group was kept in isolation after weaning. When given a choice to enter a chamber adjacent to a mouse or one adjacent to a rat, the subjects reared with rats or by a rat mother preferred to stay near chambers with rats. Mice living with other mice or in isolation chose chambers adjacent to mice.

Attachment and imprinting are also possible between prey and predator. Using a circular runway and a sparrow hawk, Melvin, Cloar, and Massingill (1967) achieved strong imprinting in seven out of eighteen quail chicks. Imprinting was especially strong in one chick which the experimenters were not able to protect from being picked up by the hawk and nearly devoured. Kuo (1930) was able to show that kittens reared in the same cage with a rat will not kill their cage mate upon reaching adulthood. Three of the eighteen kittens reared in such a manner, however, did kill other rats. Of twenty kittens reared in isolation nine killed rats when adults, and of twenty-one kittens reared in a rat-killing environment eighteen killed rats before reaching four months of age.

As the results of some of the previous experiments suggest, imprinting is not limited to animate targets. In fact, almost any object or repeated occurrence of an event can become such a target. Food preferences are rather readily and easily established by means of repeated exposure. For instance, Rabinowitch (1968) fed herring gulls (*Larus argentatus*) and ring-billed gulls (*Larus delewarensis*) a diet of either fresh earthworms, pink catfood, or catfood dyed green. The animals were placed on this diet shortly after hatching and were fed the given food exclusively for a period of five days. The results showed a clear preference for the diet with which the chick had experience. Out of a total of 132 tests the familiar food was chosen 122 times. These preferences were of the order of 90 to 100 percent. They applied equally to choices between catfood and worms, even though worms are closest to the natural diet of these birds. Burghardt and Hess (1966) report that snapping turtles (*Chelydra serpentina*) fed either meat, fish, or worms preferred the familiar diet in sixteen out of twenty cases.

Experiments with food preferences, however, are not a convincing evidence that *mere* exposure or experience with a particular stimulus object results in attraction to that object. Food has reinforcing properties. Hence, in these studies the presentation and ingestion of the given food during imprinting is always associated with reducing hunger, and is therefore likely to acquire reinforcing effects.

But reinforcement is not required and imprinting also can occur to a variety of objects in the absence of rewards. Thus, for instance Pitz and Ross (1961) were able to produce imprinting in chicks to a small red cardboard box. Gottlieb (1963) imprinted ducklings to a male mallard decoy either emitting the exodus call of the wood duck (*Aix sponsa*) or silent. Both the silent and the vocalizing models induced the same response—that is, the ducklings reacted to the decoys as if they were mothers—although the vocal model seemed to be more effective. Salzen and Meyer (1968) used green or dark blue cloth-covered paper balls and a rectangular sponge dyed either green or yellow. Their chicks imprinted on all of these objects. Hoffman and Kozma (1967) imprinted Peking ducklings on a white plastic milk bottle mounted on an electric train, and Peterson (1960) had equal success with an illuminated yellow cylinder. While many researchers used a moving object to produce imprinting, Salzen and Meyer (1968) used stationary objects with considerable success. Taylor, et al. (1967) reared chicks in boxes that were just large enough to accommodate the birds and were lined with either a smooth or rough material. Preference tests revealed that the chick preferred to enter the box which had the familiar texture.

Not only tactile but auditory stimuli that have no intrinsic reinforcing qualities and have never been associated with other reinforcing events, can easily become objects of preference and attraction just by virtue of their exposure to the animal. Grier, Counter, and Shearer (1967) exposed chicken eggs during the third week of incubation to a series of one-second tones. Another group of eggs was incubated and hatched in a quiet and sound-attenuated incubator. Six hours after hatching each chick was presented with two sound sources—one producing the familiar tone and the other of a different frequency. The control chicks which spent their incubation in silence showed no preference for one tone over the other, although they did show movement toward both sound sources. But there was preferential movement toward the familiar tone for chicks which had prenatal experience with the auditory stimulus.

A remarkable attachment to a complex auditory stimulus was produced by Cross, Holcomb, and Matter (1967). These experimenters reared three groups of rats under three different conditions. One group of animals lived in a chamber equipped with a speaker which, for fifty-two successive days and twelve hours each day, regaled the rats with selections from Mozart, such as Symphonies No. 40 and 41, Violin Concerto No. 5, and *The Magic Flute.* Another group of rats lived for the same period of time in a similar chamber but their program consisted exclusively of music by Schoenberg. This group heard pieces such as *Pierrot Lunaire,* Chamber Symphonies No. 1 and 2, and *Verklaerte Nacht.* A third, less fortunate group, was placed in similar compartments for the same period of time, but alas, it was totally deprived of music. After fifty-two days all animals were given a fifteen-day rest, and were then tested for their musical preferences during a period of sixty days. These tests were performed by placing the rats in a chamber equipped with a floor hinged in the center and suspended over two microswitches, one on each side of the hinge. The rat's weight was sufficient to lower either one side or the other side of the floor and thus to activate the given microswitch. Thus, one microswitch controlled access to Mozart, the other to Schoenberg. I must hasten to add, however, that Cross and his co-workers provided the animals not with the same musical selections which they had heard earlier, but with new and distinct pieces by the same composers. Figure 2 shows the results of these tests. Without prior training, the rats preferred Mozart to Schoenberg. It is clear from the data that experience with Mozart made the animals true Mozart lovers and experience with Schoenberg led to preference for his form of music. But we must stress, not without some feelings of sympathy, that the preference for Mozart of animals reared with Mozart was stronger than the preference for Schoenberg of animals that lived with Schoenberg. These results are entirely consistent with those of the control group. In the absence of prior training, the rats prefer Mozart to Schoenberg. Perhaps some higher mammals will find it rather disturbing that some lower animals share their musical tastes.

These latter studies show not only that the rat may have a more tender soul than we have come to believe, but also, that very little is required beyond mere exposure to produce differential preference and attraction. Of course, one could argue that such experiments are unconvincing because they do not deal with the formation of strong social bonds but with the formation of trivial preferences. Usually, it cannot be determined whether the animal's choice in these experimental situations is indicative of social attachment having some enduring qualites, or whether it is simply a passing fancy. There are, however, two experiments which bear on this question and which do suggest that exposure effects leave more than trivial consequences on the social choice of the individual. In the first experiment, Peterson (1960) was able to utilize the imprinted stimulus as a reinforcer in establishing the acquisition of new responses. First, shortly after hatching, ducks were presented with a moving stimulus for six 45-minute periods. Following this initial exposure series, the bird was separated from the stimulus and an attempt was made to train the duck to peck at a key which would present the previously imprinted stimulus. The duck was eventually trained to peck at the key in such a way that every eighth peck would present the stimulus for a period of forty seconds. A stable response output was obtained by Peterson, and no appreciable decline in response rate was observed, even after twelve hours of testing. The ducks reached rates that exceeded thirty responses per minute.

Using a similar procedure Hoffman and Kozma (1967) have demonstrated that such instrumental behavior, acquired by rewarding responses with the exposure of the imprinted stimulus, is maintained for as long as

153

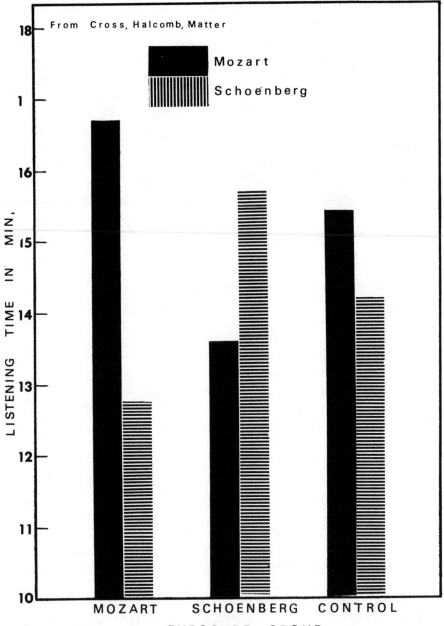

FIGURE 2.   Musical preferences of rats reared with music by Mozart, of rats reared with music by Schoenberg, and of rats without musical background (from Cross, Halcomb, and Matter 1967).

sixty days. While it is dangerous to make anthropormorphic conjectures about animal behavior, it is tempting to regard these results as showing that the ducks really "wanted" to see the stimulus on which they were imprinted.

Perhaps the most consistent finding in the area of imprinting is that it occurs with a greater vigor and greater probability in young animals. This, of course, is true of other learning as well. Imprinting, however, is considerably more sensitive to age than other forms of acquired behavior patterns. The Peking duck, for instance, has a remarkably stable period of sensitivity to imprinting (Gottlieb 1961). In fact, Scott (1962, 1967) and Lorenz (1937) believe that if attachments are not formed at a given period they will not be formed at all. Scott (1967) considers the period between the third and seventh week as the only time during which puppies can become attached to people. But, depending on the behavior to be imprinted and on the criterion test of imprinting, the critical period may be restricted or extended. Salzen and Sluckin (1959) observed imprinting in five-day old chicks, and Fabricius and Boyd (1952–1953) even in ten-day-old ducklings.

The most effective means of extending the period of imprinting consists of restricting the early experience of the animal. Social and visual isolation prolong the period of imprinting by a considerable amount (Guiton 1958, 1959; Moltz and Stettner 1961; Sluckin 1965; Sluckin and Salzen 1961). But even with a restricted early social and sensory experience the period when it is possible to achieve imprinting by conventional techniques terminates. While several explanations were offered for this phenomenon (Kaufman and Hinde 1961), the most important is the observation that, like marriage, imprinting exercises a priority right such that once the animal has become attached to one object, his attachment to other objects is less likely. One explanation of this priority may be that the attraction to these new objects must now compete with the attraction that has developed to the primary target. We shall return to these points later.

EXPOSURE EFFECTS IN HUMANS Beside critical periods, the literature on imprinting reveals one, and perhaps the only one, other solid generalization: repeated exposure of a given object is sufficient to produce an attachment of the individual to a given stimulus object, be that object stationary or mobile, animate or inanimate. This generalization applies to human subjects equally well and, as we shall see, it is not limited to a particular age of the individual.

A few years ago when the new hair styles for men began to appear among the younger age groups, many of us on the other side of the generation gap were aghast. Some of us treated the phenomenon as a passing fad, some as a protest against the war, and others as a symptom of the utter perversity which besets the entire offspring reared according to the permissive philosophy of Dr. Spock. Regardless of what antecedents we attributed to the new hair fashions, we did not think of our "new" youth in kindly terms. Many of us reserve judgment still today. It simply does not seem proper to combine the hair styles of Louis XIV and the garb of a Davy Crockett on the same male body. But now more and more of our children look that way and fewer and fewer of the older generation are appalled by these looks. Many of our high schools have rescinded restrictive rulings about the boys' hair length.

We have gotten used to it, you say. But what does that mean? We have accepted it. Have we here the effects of repeated exposure?

I have recently published a monograph (Zajonc 1968) in which I reviewed some evidence showing that the mere repeated exposure of an individual to a stimulus object enhances his attraction to it. This evidence covers primarily the attitudes of persons toward inanimate or symbolic objects; but I believe that attraction between members of the same species, though more complex, is a special case of this more general phenomenon.

Such a special case of the exposure effect can be found in the meanings of words. Let me give you a few illustrations. For many languages there exist counts of the frequencies with which certain words occur. In English we have such a count for 30,000 words collected by Thorndike and Lorge (1944). A careful reading of the Thorndike-Lorge tables will reveal a remarkable relationship between the frequency of words and their meaning, especially the evaluative aspect of their meaning. This remarkable relationship can be summarized by simply saying that words that occur often in language mean good things, and that infrequent words mean bad things.[3] We will all agree that "love" is better than "hate."

---

[3] *Editor's note:* It is interesting to speculate that infrequent words also contain more consonants, furthermore, such words are often harder to pronounce (see G. Zipf, *Human Behavior,* 1949). According to Zipf's law then, words that take more effort are more infrequently used; furthermore, I might point out that words containing a great number of consonants are harsher and such harsh sounds to the ear may predispose them to be more negatively associated. This relates to an early idea developed in part by Sir R. Paget (*Human Speech,* 1930, pages 148–153) wherein it is suggested that the roots for many words are developed from movements of the tongue and mouth bearing a mimetic or symbolic equivalent to the idea or action to which the word refers. (J.F.E.)

According to the Thorndike-Lorge count "love" is more frequent than "hate"—it is more frequent by a factor of seven. We will all agree that "good" is better than "bad." It is more frequent than "bad" by a factor of five.

In an attempt to examine this relationship more extensively we have employed a list of 154 antonym pairs. A large number of subjects, all college students, judged which member of each antonym pair had "the more favorable meaning, represented the more desirable object, event, state of affairs, characteristic, etc." Words from all parts of language were included. Table 1 presents the results of this inquiry showing preference ratings together with frequency values taken from the Thorndike-Lorge count. It is clear, above all, that our subjects agreed in their preferences on most of the antonym pairs. It is also clear that the vast majority of the pairs reflect the general phenomenon, that is, if the member of the pair is more frequent, it is also the preferred member of the pair. Moreover, the majority of the reversals occur toward the bottom of the list where agreement about preference is less pronounced. We note that words of which we do not ordinarily think in evaluative terms, but which nevertheless show stable evaluative preference, also conform to the general relationship between goodness of meaning and the frequency of occurrence. Thus for instance "on" is much better than "off," "in" is much better than "out," and "add " is clearly superior to "subtract."

There are pairs of antonyms about which there should be no surprise in this culture. "White" occurs twice as often as "black," and it is preferred. "Success" occurs twice as often as "failure," and it is preferred. We should take heed, however, from the data on "peace" and "war." While our own subjects expressed overwhelming preference for the former, the frequency data which presumably represent the feelings of the entire population, show that "war" is favored. I might also add that the relative frequencies of the German equivalents of these words are the same. But in French and Spanish, the words "paix" and "paz" occur more frequently than "guerre" and "guerra." I shall refrain from making any conjectures about these comparisons.

It turns out that this relationship between frequency is not limited to the meanings of words, but that it also applies to the people's attitudes toward the things for which these words stand. We asked for attitudes toward countries and American cities, and we found that the relationship between our subjects' attitudes toward the cities and countries related quite highly to the frequencies with which the names of these countries and cities occurred in the written language. We have also asked a number

TABLE 1.—Preference and frequency of 154 antonym pairs.
(From Zajonc 1968.)

Percentage Agreement	Preferred Alternative (a)	Non-Preferred Alternative (b)	Frequency of (a)	Frequency of (b)
100	able	unable	930	239
100	attentive	inattentive	49	4
100	better	worse	2354	450
100	encourage	discourage	205	147
100	friendly	unfriendly	357	19
100	honest	dishonest	393	41
100	possible	impossible	1289	459
99	advance	retreat	452	105
99	best	worst	1850	292
99	clean	dirty	781	221
99	comfortable	uncomfortable	348	112
99	favorable	unfavorable	93	25
99	good	bad	5122	1001
99	grateful	ungrateful	194	13
99	peace	war	472	1118
99	present	absent	1075	65
99	pure	impure	197	4
99	responsible	irresponsible	267	30
99	reward	punishment	154	80
99	right	wrong	3874	890
99	smile	frown	2143	216
99	tolerant	intolerant	42	13
99	victory	defeat	118	166
98	add	subtract	2018	6
98	advantage	disadvantage	404	41
98	agreeable	disagreeable	58	43
98	capable	incapable	176	30
98	desirable	undesirable	160	42
98	find	lose	2698	593
98	fortunate	unfortunate	136	108
98	forward	backward	736	139
98	friend	enemy	2553	883
98	high	low	1674	1224
98	honorable	dishonorable	58	8
98	kind	unkind	1521	34
98	legal	illegal	180	34
98	life	death	4804	815
98	love	hate	5129	756
98	mature	immature	91	17
98	moral	immoral	272	19

TABLE 1.—Preference and frequency of 154 antonym pairs.—Continued

Percentage Agreement	Preferred Alternative (a)	Non-Preferred Alternative (b)	Frequency of (a)	Frequency of (b)
98	pleasant	unpleasant	457	114
98	polite	impolite	115	3
98	reliable	unreliable	78	9
98	success	failure	573	262
98	valid	invalid	22	56
98	voluntary	involuntary	28	26
97	adequate	inadequate	95	59
97	competent	incompetent	69	23
97	found	lost	2892	1074
97	important	unimportant	1130	40
97	likely	unlikely	364	25
97	on	off	30224	3644
97	patience	impatience	139	39
97	patient	impatient	392	79
97	patiently	impatiently	85	82
97	popular	unpopular	418	12
97	positive	negative	92	28
97	profitable	unprofitable	57	12
97	promote	demote	90	2
97	remember	forget	1682	882
97	satisfactory	unsatisfactory	154	32
97	willingly	unwillingly	66	13
96	above	below	941	529
96	active	passive	186	29
96	early	late	1022	2859
96	front	back	1094	6587
96	full	empty	1129	395
96	live	die	4307	1079
96	presence	absence	277	163
96	probable	improbable	64	14
96	rational	irrational	33	9
96	reasonable	unreasonable	155	56
96	resolutely	irresolutely	30	4
96	strong	weak	770	276
96	succeed	fail	264	620
96	superior	inferior	166	40
96	timely	untimely	27	6
95	accept	reject	667	51
95	direct	indirect	416	23
95	include	exclude	533	38
95	increase	decrease	781	86

TABLE 1.—Preference and frequency of 154 antonym pairs.—Continued

Percentage Agreement	Preferred Alternative (a)	Non-Preferred Alternative (b)	Frequency of (a)	Frequency of (b)
95	most	least	3443	1259
95	practical	impractical	340	12
95	regularly	irregularly	122	5
95	rich	poor	656	857
95	wealth	poverty	243	146
94	approve	disapprove	171	45
94	conscious	unconscious	299	116
94	leader	follower	373	45
94	obedient	disobedient	70	4
94	together	apart	1835	276
93	agreement	disagreement	143	21
93	certain	uncertain	800	107
93	first	last	5154	3517
93	major	minor	366	83
93	normal	abnormal	335	43
93	regular	irregular	340	44
93	unselfish	selfish	32	137
93	upwards	downwards	9	40
93	wide	narrow	593	391
92	more	less	8015	1357
92	now	then	7665	10208
92	up	down	11718	5534
92	upward	downward	111	27
92	visible	invisible	110	74
92	yes	no	2202	11742
91	always	never	3285	5715
91	familiar	unfamiliar	345	39
91	maximum	minimum	43	86
91	optimism	pessimism	28	11
90	agree	disagree	729	38
90	necessary	unnecessary	715	107
90	over	under	7520	2961
90	sweet	sour	679	102
90	whole	part	1663	1585
89	light	dark	2387	1005
88	deep	shallow	881	104
88	smooth	rough	346	294

TABLE 1.—Preference and frequency of 154 antonym pairs.—Continued

Percentage Agreement	Preferred Alternative (a)	Non-Preferred Alternative (b)	Frequency of (a)	Frequency of (b)
86	white	black	2663	1083
85	in	out	75253	13649
85	independent	dependent	134	18
84	fast	slow	514	434
83	comedy	tragedy	126	189
83	fasten	unfasten	142	16
79	day	night	4549	3385
78	dry	wet	592	319
78	long	short	5362	887
78	unshaken	shaken	6	83
77	usually	unusually	718	91
74	upstairs	downstairs	314	226
72	inner	outer	143	97
72	interior	exterior	185	48
70	near	far	1338	1835
70	unlimited	limited	43	67
68	inside	outside	656	921
68	wrap	unwrap	293	17
67	infinite	finite	71	2
67	internal	external	36	26
65	coming	going	1486	4623
64	informal	formal	64	166
63	answer	question	2132	1302
63	men	women	3614	2552
61	different	same	1194	1747
59	inward	outward	43	54
59	man	woman	7355	2431
58	husband	wife	1788	1668
58	usual	unusual	516	273
57	offense	defense	86	223
55	hot	cold	1006	1092
55	import	export	86	88
55	inwardly	outwardly	32	33
54	inconspicuous	conspicuous	33	59
52	play	work	2606	2720
51	mortal	immortal	54	26

ROBERT B. ZAJONC

TABLE 2.—Preference ratings of trees, fruits, vegetables, and flowers and their corresponding frequencies. (From Zajonc 1968.)

Trees	f*	A.P.R.**	Fruits	f	A.P.R.
Pine	172	4.79	Apple	220	5.13
Walnut	75	4.42	Cherry	167	5.00
Oak	125	4.00	Strawberry	121	4.83
Rosewood	8	3.96	Pear	62	4.83
Birch	34	3.83	Grapefruit	33	4.00
Fir	14	3.75	Cantaloupe	1.5	3.75
Sassafras	2	3.00	Avocado	16	2.71
Aloes	1	2.92	Pomegranate	8	2.63
Yew	3	2.83	Gooseberry	5	2.63
Acacia	4	2.75	Mango	2	2.38

Vegetables	f	A.P.R.	Flowers	f	A.P.R.
Corn	227	4.17	Rose	801	5.55
Potato	384	4.13	Lily	164	4.79
Lettuce	142	4.00	Violet	109	4.58
Carrot	96	3.57	Geranium	27	3.83
Radish	43	3.13	Daisy	62	3.79
Asparagus	5	2.33	Hyacinth	16	3.08
Cauliflower	27	1.96	Yucca	1	2.88
Broccoli	18	1.96	Woodbine	4	2.87
Leek	3	1.96	Anemone	8	2.54
Parsnip	8	1.92	Cowslip	2	2.54

* Frequency of usage (L-Count).   ** Average preference rating.

of subjects to rate a large variety of other items such as trees, fruits, vegetables, and flowers. Table 2 shows these ratings (made on seven-point scales from zero to six), together with their frequencies according to Thorndike and Lorge. Again, we note that the relationship between frequency and the attractiveness of the various trees, fruits, vegetables, and flowers is rather pronounced.

Ordinarily we do not think of letters of the alphabet as being pleasant or unpleasant. Alluisi and Adams (1962), however, found that some letters are consistently better liked than others. Checking on the relationship between preference for letters and the likelihood of their occurrence in English, these authors found a correlation of .84. We found a similar effect with numbers (Figure 3). Contrary to the cultural truisms (the "bigger the better" and "the more the merrier") calling for larger quantities to be more valued than small quantities, our subjects rated these numbers in inverse relation to their magnitudes. But the relationship between their love for these numbers and the frequency of their occurrence in English was clearly supported.

Since the above findings are correlational it is, of course, entirely

FIGURE 3.   Scatter plot of the relationship between the frequency of occurrence and the affective ratings of numbers of 1 to 20.

162

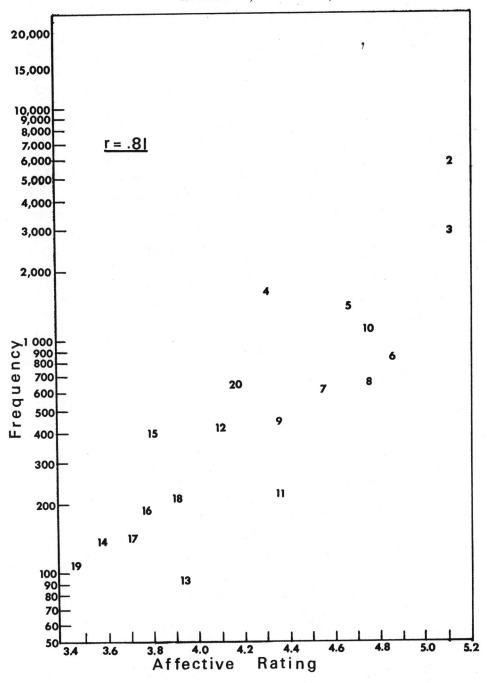

presumptuous to make conjectures about causal directions. Thus, we do not know whether we rate the word "sweet" more favorably than the word "bitter," because "sweet" is used more frequently, or we use it more frequently because it means something more pleasant than "bitter." We do not know whether apples are liked because there are many apples, or many apples are produced because they are an attractive fruit. While these questions remain virtually unanswerable, we cannot say the same about the letters of the alphabet and about numbers. It would be difficult to defend the proposition that the letter B occurs often in our language because it is a well-liked letter, or that the number 2 occurs so frequently because for some outside reason it is a well-liked number. For these two types of material we must assume that it is the frequency which determines their attractiveness.

In concluding the correlational evidence on frequency and exposure I should like to cite two poems. The frequencies of the critical words in these poems were averaged. The first is by Robert Browning, and it is a light thing, full of life, joy, and looking to the future with naive but fervent hope:

> *Song from "Pippa Passes"*
> The year's at the spring
> And day's at the morn;
> Morning's at seven;
> The hill-side's dew-pearled;
> The lark's on the wing;
> The snail's on the thorn;
> God's in his heaven—
> All's right with the world!

The average word frequency[4] in this poem is 1,380. But, here is another poem, this time by Percy Bysshe Shelley, in which he reaches a conclusion which stands in stark contrast to Browning's optimism:

> *A Dirge*
> Rough wind, that moanest loud
> Grief too sad for song;
> Wild wind, when sullen cloud
> Knells all the night long;
> Sad storm, whose tears are vain,
> Bare woods, whose branches strain,
> Deep caves and dreary main,—
> Wail, for the world's wrong!

---

[4] Only nouns, verbs, adjectives, and adverbs were counted. Connectives, articles, and auxiliary verbs were ignored.

The average word frequency of Shelley's woeful piece is 728. I do not mean to suggest that word frequency be taken as the cornerstone of a new literary criticism. I am using these poems merely as a further illustration of the effects of frequency of exposure. Nevertheless, we have examined several samples of literature, and the relationship between average word frequency and the mood of a given piece is rather compelling.

Supporting these correlational studies on exposure and attraction is also some good experimental evidence indicating that the attractiveness of a given stimulus object may be enhanced by virtue of its repeated exposure. Johnson, et al. (1960) have found that the semantic ratings of nonsense words can be enhanced when they are presented repeatedly. We have similar evidence. A number of Turkish words were shown to our experimental subjects different numbers of times. Some words were seen by them frequently, others infrequently. These presentations were randomized such that each of the words appeared in different frequency for different subjects, and what word appeared on any one presentation was determined by chance. After viewing these words, the subjects were told that what they just saw were Turkish adjectives, and we unashamedly asked them to guess what the words they just saw meant. We proceeded to explain that we appreciated how nearly impossible this task was, given their lack of familiarity with Turkish. Nevertheless, we insisted that they try. To help our subjects guess these meanings we told them that each of these adjectives meant either something good or something bad, and that it was their task merely to guess for each Turkish word if it meant something good or something bad. Figure 4 shows the results of this experiment.

The same experiment was replicated using different stimuli. Thus, for another instance, Chinese ideographs were substituted for Turkish words and used in the same manner. The subject first observed these ideographs in different frequencies and subsequently he was asked to rate their meanings. In the same way photographs of men's faces were exposed different numbers of times and the subjects were subsequently asked how much they liked them. Figures 5 and 6 show these results. While the comparisons for the ideographs and for the photographs are somewhat weaker than those found with the Turkish words, there are no reversals, and the overall effect still stands up. Out of a total of thirty-six comparisons, thirty-two favor a positive relation between frequency and liking, while four show no differences in liking as a function of previous

165

ROBERT B. ZAJONC

experience. There is other evidence showing similar trends, but I will not describe it here.

Currently we are studying some psychological processes which might explain why repeated exposure increases the attractiveness of the stimulus object. These processes are more fully outlined in my monograph on the effects of exposure (Zajonc 1968) and in a recent article by Harrison (1968). It suffices for present purposes to make a few observations. First, the effect of exposure is most pronounced when we expose the subject to novel stimuli. Secondly, the effects of exposure on attraction are logarithmic. That is, early exposures produce the strongest effects, while each successive exposure adds less and less to the total attractiveness of the object. Thirdly, the effect of exposure is easiest to demonstrate when the stimulus is emotionally neutral, and when exposures are not accompanied by other psychological events—such as stimuli that are noxious, positive, or negative reinforcers—or demands on subjects that they respond to the stimuli in some systematic way.

The psychological processes underlying a change of attraction which results from repeated exposure are perhaps fairly simple. Consider a stimulus encountered for the first time. By definition, the subject has no ready response to this novel stimulus, because if the stimulus has never occurred, the stimulus could not have been conditioned to any of his responses. But in many ways the novel stimulus is similar to stimuli that the subject has encountered in the past. By virtue of generalization from these familiar stimuli several response tendencies may be elicited. Many of these response tendencies might be mutually incompatible, leading the individual to experience a state of mild stress. Since the stress occurs in direct association with the novel stimulus, the stimulus receives a low attractiveness rating. Over successive exposures many of these incompatible responses drop out, and eventually a stable response pattern to the given stimulus is established. This progression is accompanied by reduction of the mild stress and discomfort which the organism experienced when it encountered the novel stimulus for the first time, and the stimulus object becomes more attractive. Harrison (1968) has performed a series of experiments to show that this indeed may be the type of process that occurs with successive exposures, and Margaret Matlin (1967) has collected further evidence. Thus, for instance, Harrison (1968) has demonstrated that in word association tests, the lag between

FIGURE 4.   Average rated affective connotation of nonsense words exposed with low and high frequencies (from Zajonc 1968).

166

ATTRACTION, AFFILIATION, AND ATTACHMENT

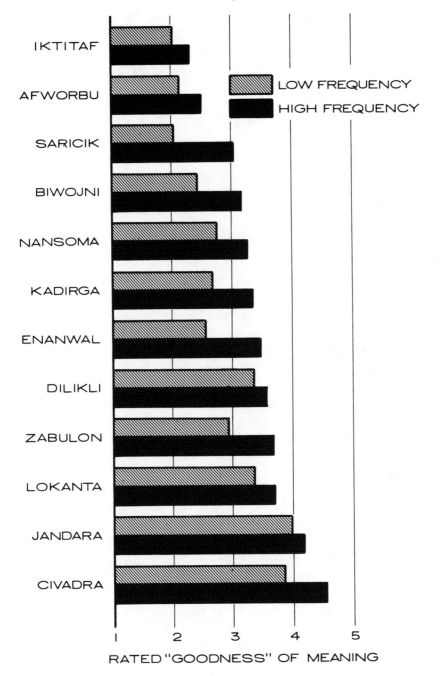

RATED "GOODNESS" OF MEANING

the presentation of a stimulus to a subject and his response (a good indication of tension or response competition) is longer when made to novel stimuli than when made to familiar stimuli; and Matlin (1967) confirmed his results. In independent experiments both Harrison and Matlin have shown that stimuli which produce mild response competition, that is which tend to elicit a number of incompatible weak response tendencies, are less well liked than stimuli to which a single response has been attached.

Whatever the nature of the psychological processes which lead the organism to increase its attachment or attraction to a repeatedly encountered stimulus object, it is still necessary to explain why animals become attracted and attached to members of their own species, and why certain periods are especially favorable for the formation of these attachments. The answer which immediately suggests itself is that these attachments arise because members of the same species (conspecifics) are the most frequent stimuli for each other. While this solution has some merits, it ignores the problem of critical periods. Moreover, the assertion that conspecifies are the most frequent stimuli for each other is not entirely tenable. Why should a newly hatched chick not become strongly attached to a twig or a rock which happens to be nearby? And some species are rather widely dispersed during certain periods of their lives. Oyster larvae and larvae of the barnacle, *Elminius modestus,* drift freely in the plankton and settle only in the communities of other oysters or barnacles. They are apparently able to postpone their metamorphosis for long periods of time until they have located the appropriate settlement (Wilson 1952, Cole and Knight-Jones 1949, Knight-Jones and Stevenson 1951).

The fact that there exist periods particularly suitable for the formation of attachments is in part due to the process of sensory maturation of the animal (Sluckin and Salzen 1961). To the extent that the animal is unable to make fine discriminations, as is the case with a few-day-old puppy, objects of attachment cannot be clearly distinguished, and the animal's behavior toward his environment is marked by a great deal of generalization. Thus Scott (1967) could not establish attachments in puppies before they were three weeks old, and Gottlieb (1961) found no imprinting in seven-hour-old Peking ducklings.

Imprinting and attachment have a form of exclusiveness such that

FIGURE 5. Average rated affective connotation of Chinese-like characters exposed with low and high frequencies (from Zajonc 1968).

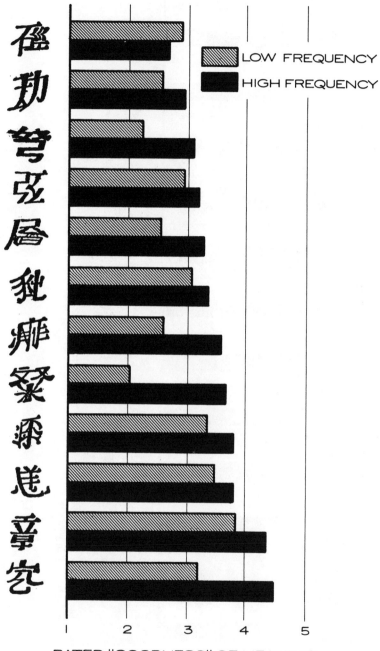

RATED "GOODNESS" OF MEANING

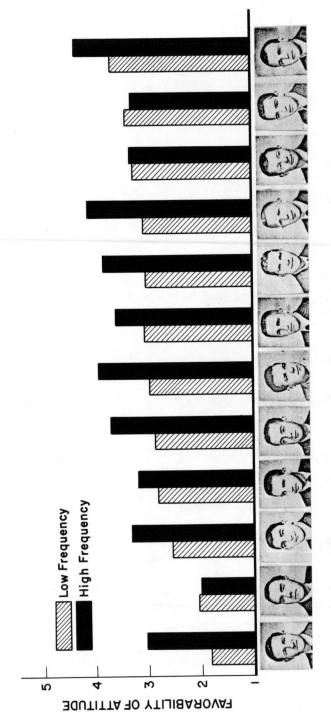

FIGURE 6. Average attitude toward photographs exposed with low and high frequencies (from Zajonc 1968).

once a commitment has been made, new attachments are less likely to form. The attraction which the organism has acquired first is in conflict with later attractions that the animal may develop toward another object. The exclusiveness of imprinting is demonstrated by a study carried out by Guiton (1961) in which he found that chicks imprinted to an inanimate object less effectively in groups than when trained alone. Of course, in groups, they were imprinting on each other. The greylag gosling cannot follow Konrad Lorenz and its dam at the same time, unless Konrad Lorenz and the gosling's dam become inseparable companions (a condition which is not altogether out of the range of possibilities).

The priority rights exercised by first attachments, however, cannot in themselves explain the end of the critical period because of two facts. First, animals kept in isolation during periods most favorable to attachment still show over a period of time, a marked drop in their ability to form attachments (Bateson 1966, Sluckin 1965, Sluckin and Salzen 1961, Scott 1967, Moltz and Stettner 1961). Second, inexperienced and isolated animals show preference for members of their own species even on their first encounter (Cairns 1966b, Lorenz 1937, Sluckin 1965). When ducklings and chicks are reared in mixed groups and given social choice tests between a chick and a duckling, they prefer their own kind, although many choose individuals of the other species (Schooland 1942).

But consider an animal reared in isolation. While experiments using the isolation technique prevent it from exposure to social objects and restrict its physical environment, they do not delay its sensory maturation, and hence they do not prevent its exposure to one very important stimulus object—*itself*. After all, the animal emits sounds which it can learn to discriminate, it sees various parts of its own body (legs, wings, feet, or its coloring), it can feel its texture, it can smell its own odor, and there must be thousands of other cues associated with the animal's own body and own behavior that are very much like those associated with the bodies and behavior of other members of his particular species. It is, therefore, false to assume that an animal that has been isolated from birth has had no exposure to social stimuli, and that a member of the same species presented to an animal kept in isolation since its birth is as novel to it as is a football, an electric train, or a member of another species. By virtue of the same process whereby exposure leads to the formation of attachment to other objects, the isolated animals develop some form of attachment to the only objects and events to which it is exposed: its own body and its own behavior. Perhaps what is known by psychoanalysts as primary narcissism has an experiential basis after all.

171

ROBERT B. ZAJONC

The hypothesis that familiarity with the patterns of one's own behavior is an important determinant of attraction to other conspecifics was first proposed by Salzen and Cornell (1968). Their experimental results, however, did not provide a clear support for it. But the results of Pratt and Sackett (1967), although not interpreted in this way by the authors, do show some form of self-imprinting rather dramatically. Three groups of rhesus monkeys were reared in the laboratory in the absence of their mothers. Eight monkeys lived in nearly complete isolation for a period of nine months except for the first five to seven days when they saw a human. Between the ninth and eighteenth month these monkeys lived in wire cages from which they could see and hear humans and each other. The second set of eight monkeys was housed from birth to eighteen months in wire cages kept in a large room. A third set of eight monkeys was reared in peer groups of various sizes during the entire first eighteen months of their lives. Following this initial experience the animals were tested for their social choices. Figure 7 shows the amount of time each group spent by associating with animals which had either the same or different early experience as the test subject. In no case did the test animal and the stimulus animal have previous contact. It is clear from the data that totally deprived monkeys are, on the whole, less sociable than animals partially deprived or animals raised in full contact with their peers. They are less attracted to other animals. But more striking is the fact that animals *prefer others which had the same rearing experience.* Totally deprived monkeys prefer others that were totally deprived. Partially deprived monkeys prefer partially deprived monkeys, and monkeys reared in full contact with others prefer peers that also had full contact. This occurred, it must be stressed again, when the animals were given social choices between test monkeys with which they were previously not acquainted. Apparently the rearing condition produces a discriminable overall behavior pattern and discriminable emotional responses that are distinct for the various conditions. A normally reared monkey becomes a desirable social object only for other normally reared monkeys. But the same monkey is rejected by one that was totally deprived of contact with monkeys.

If exposure is a sufficient condition for the development of attraction and attachment in animals and in humans, what then is the factor which maintains a characteristic average distance between the individual and his nearest neighbor of the same species? This question is considerably more complex than the one with which we were dealing. If there were only forces of attraction, affiliation, and attachment, all species would live like barnacles, in communities where there is "standing room" only. But of course, only few species would survive under these conditions.

172

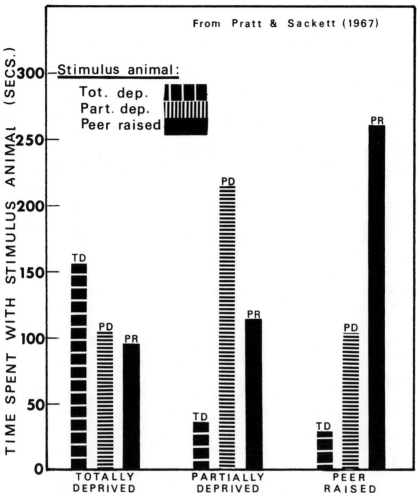

FIGURE 7. Association responses of Rhesus monkeys reared under three deprivation conditions to three differentially reared stimulus animals. Although monkeys reared with peers are more sociable, in all cases associations are made more readily with a stimulus animal having the same quality of rearing experience.

Various mechanisms exist, different for different species, which counteract the forces of attraction. First is the factor of primacy of attachments discussed above. By virtue of these attachments one animal maintains physical proximity with another. Once a given attachment has been formed, this reduces the development of attachments to other social objects. If the animal remains close to its first attachment, it is less respon-

173

sive to other stimuli. Second, while imprinting and attachment claim primacy and exclusiveness they do not claim *total* primacy (Salzen and Meyer 1968) nor *total* exclusiveness. The individual that has become attached to one member of his community is, by virtue of exposure to other members and by virtue of their similarity to the primary object of his attachment, also attracted to them. Third, all these other individuals have attachments of their own. The total configuration of all primary attachments in a community can, then, in itself act as a force of dispersion. These networks of diverse attractions may lead to a homeostatically maintained social distance that is characteristic of given animal grouping.

The relation of the species to its habitat, and in particular territorial mechanisms which regulate this relation, are also important factors in preventing complete agglomerations of individuals. In the same way priority rights over mating privileges, dominance structures, and other forms of social organization which determine the individuals' access to scarce resources and which are associated with agonistic behavior, are clearly very significant factors in counteracting attachment and attraction. Each species and each grouping probably has its own particular equilibrium whereby the tendencies to approach and become attached are restrained by their opposites. Each species has probably developed particular homeostatic behavioral mechanisms which maintain such an equilibrium, and there are probably some differences between different groupings of the same species as well. What these mechanisms are is far from known today, and their discovery and description will require an enormous research effort.

But we may now conclude that man and other animals are endowed with a similar capacity for attachment to others. It consists simply of one's capacity to gain love from exposure. Familiarity does not breed contempt. Familiarity breeds!

REFERENCES

Alluisi, E. A., and O. S. Adams.
    1962. "Predicting Letter Preferences: Aesthetics and Filtering in Man." *Perceptual and Motor Skills,* 14:123–131.
Altmann, M.
    1958. "Social Integration in the Moose Calf." *Animal Behaviour,* 6:155–159.
Bateson, P. P. G.
    1966. "The Characteristics and Context of Imprinting." *Biological Review,* 41:177–220.

Breder, C. M., Jr., and C. W. Coates.
  1932. "A Preliminary Study of Population Stability and Sex Ratio of *Lebistes.*" *Copeia,* 147–155.
Brodbeck, D. J.
  1954. "An Exploratory Study of the Acquisition of Dependency Behavior in Puppies." *Bulletin of the Ecological Society of America,* 35:73.
Burghardt, G. M., and E. E. Hess.
  1966. "Food Imprinting in the Snapping Turtle, *Chelydra serpentina.*" *Science,* 151:108–109.
Cairns, R. B.
  1966a. "Development, Maintenance, and Extinction of Social Attachment Behavior in Sheep." *Journal of Comparative and Physiological Psychology,* 62:298–306.
  1966b. "Attachment Behavior of Mammals." *Psychological Review,* 73:409–426.
Candland, D. K., and D. Milne.
  1966. "Species Differences in Approach Behavior as a Function of Development and Environment." *Animal Behaviour,* 14:539–545.
Christian, J. J.
  1955. "Effect of Population Size on the Adrenal Glands and Reproductive Organs of Male White Mice." *American Journal of Physiology,* 181:477–480.
  1956. "Adrenal and Reproductive Response to Population Size in Mice from Freely Growing Populations." *Ecology,* 37:258–273.
Cole, H. A., and E. W. Knight-Jones.
  1949. "The Settling Behavior of Larvae of the European Flat Oyster, *Ostrea edulis* (L.) and Its Influence on Methods of Cultivation and Spat Collection." *Fishery Investigations, London,* series 2, 17(3).
Collias, N. E.
  1962. "Social Development in Birds and Mammals." In *Roots of Behavior,* E. L. Bliss, editor. New York: Harper and Bros.
Cross, H., A. Holcomb, and C. G. Matter.
  1967. "Imprinting or Exposure Learning in Rats Given Early Auditory Stimulation." *Psychonomic Science,* 7:233–234.
Dennenberg, V. H., G. A. Hudgens, and M. X. Zarrow.
  1964. "Mice Reared with Rats: Modification of Behavior by Early Experience with Another Species." *Science,* 143:380–381.
Eckman, J., and J. D. Meltzer.
  1969. "Gregariousness in Rats as a Function of Familiarity of Environment." *Journal of Personality and Social Psychology,* 11:107–114.
Fabricius, E., and H. Boyd.
  1952–1953. "Experiments on the Following Reactions of Ducklings." *Wildfowl Trust Annual Report,* 6:84–89.
Fisher, A. E.
  1955. "The Effects of Early Differential Treatment on the Social and Exploratory Behavior in Puppies." Unpublished PhD thesis, Pennsylvania State University.

175

Gottlieb, G.
  1961. "Developmental Age as a Baseline for Determinations of the Critical Period in Imprinting." *Journal of Comparative Physiology and Psychology*, 54:422–427.
  1963. "A Naturalistic Study of Imprinting in Wood Ducklings (*Aix sponsa*)." *Journal of Comparative and Physiological Psychology*, 58:86–91.
Gray, P. H.
  1958. "Theory and Evidence of Imprinting in Human Infants." *Journal of Psychology*, 46:155–166.
Greenberg, B.
  1963. "Parental Behavior and Imprinting in Cichlid Fishes." *Behaviour*, 21:127–144.
Grier, J. B., S. A. Counter, and W. M. Shearer.
  1967. "Prenatal Auditory Imprinting in Chickens." *Science*, 155:1692–1693.
Guiton, P.
  1958. "The Effect of Isolation on the Following Response of Brown Leghorn Chicks." *Proceedings of the Royal Physiological Society* (Edinburgh), 27:9–14.
  1959. "Socialization and Imprinting in Brown Leghorn Chicks." *Animal Behaviour*, 7:26–34.
  1961. "The Influence of Imprinting on the Agonistic and Courtship Responses of the Brown Leghorn Cock." *Animal Behaviour*, 9:167–177.
Harlow, H. F.
  1958. "The Nature of Love." *American Psychologist*, 13:673–685.
Harrison, A. A.
  1968. "Response Competition, Frequency, Exploratory Behavior, and Liking." *Journal of Personality and Social Psychology*, 9:363–368.
Hediger, H.
  1950. *Wild Animals in Captivity*. London: Butterworth.
Hess, E. E.
  1964. "Imprinting in Birds." *Science*, 146:1128–1139.
Hoffman, H. S., and F. Kozma, Jr.
  1967. "Behavioral Control by an Imprinted Stimulus: Long-term Effects." *Journal of the Experimental Analysis of Behavior*, 10:495–501.
Igel, G. J., and A. D. Calving.
  1960. "The Development of Affectional Responses in Infant Dogs." *Journal of Comparative Physiological Psychology*, 53:302–305.
Jaynes, J.
  1956. "Imprinting: The Interaction of Learned and Innate Behavior, I: Development and Generalization." *Journal of Comparative Physiological Psychology*, 49:201–206.
Johnson, R. C., C. W. Thomson, and G. Frincke.
  1960. "Word Values, Word Frequency, and Visual Duration Thresholds." *Psychological Review*, 67:332–342.

Kaufman, I. C., and R. A. Hinde.
1961. "Factors Influencing Distress Calling in Chicks, with Special Reference to Temperature Changes in Social Isolation." *Animal Behaviour,* 9:197–204.
Knight-Jones, E. W., and J. P. Stevenson.
1951. "Gregariousness During Settlement in the Barnacle, *Elminus modestus* Darwin." *Journal of the Marine Biological Association, United Kingdom,* 29:281–297.
Kuo, Z. Y.
1930. "The Genesis of Cat's Responses to Rats." *Journal of Comparative Psychology,* 11:1–35.
Latané, B.
1969. "Gregariousness and Fear in Laboratory Rats." *Journal of Experimental Social Psychology,* 5:61–69.
Latané, B., and D. C. Glass.
1968. "Social and Nonsocial Attraction in Rats." *Journal of Personality and Social Psychology,* 9:142–146.
Lorenz, K.
1937. "The Companion in the Bird's World." *Auk,* 54:245–273.
Mainardi, M.
1967. "Scomparsa delle preferenze sessuali intraspecifiche nel maschio di *Drosophila melanogaster* allevato in isolamento." *Atti dell' Accademia Nazionale dei Lincei,* 43:107–108.
Matlin, M. A. W.
1967. "Response Competition as a Mediating Factor in the Frequency-affect Relationship." PhD dissertation, University of Michigan.
Melvin, K. B., J. F. Cloar, and L. S. Massingill.
1967. "Imprinting of Bobwhite Quail to a Hawk." *Psychological Record,* 17:235–238.
Moltz, H., and L. J. Stettner.
1961. "The Influence of Patterned-light Deprivation on the Critical Period for Imprinting." *Journal of Comparative Physiology and Psychology,* 54:279–283.
Peterson, N.
1960. "Control of Behavior by Presentation of an Imprinted Stimulus." *Science,* 132:1395–1396.
Pinckney, G. A., and L. E. Anderson.
1967. "Rearing Conditions and Sociability in *Lebistes reticulatus.*" *Psychonomic Science,* 9:591–592.
Pitz, G. F., and R. B. Ross.
1961. "Imprinting as a Function of Arousal." *Journal of Comparative Physiology and Psychology,* 54:602–604.
Pratt, C. L., and G. P. Sackett.
1967. "Selection of Social Partners as a Function of Peer Contact during Rearing." *Science,* 155:1133–1135.

Rabinowitch, V. E.
1968. "The Role of Experience in the Development of Food Preferences in Gull Chicks." *Animal Behaviour,* 16:425–428.

Salzen, E. A., and J. M. Cornell.
1968. "Self-perception and Species Recognition in Birds." *Behaviour,* 30:44–65.

Salzen, E. A., and C. C. Meyer.
1968. "Reversibility of Imprinting." *Journal of Comparative Physiology and Psychology,* 66:269–275.

Salzen, E. A., and W. Sluckin.
1959. "The Incidence of the Following Response and the Duration of Responsiveness in Domestic Fowl." *Animal Behaviour,* 7:172–179.

Schooland, J. B.
1942. "Are There Any Innate Behavior Tendencies?" *Genetic Psychology Monographs,* pages 219–287.

Scott, J. P.
1958. *Animal Behavior.* Chicago: University of Chicago Press.
1962. "Critical Periods in Behavioral Development." *Science,* 138:949–958.
1963. "The Process of Primary Socialization in Canine and Human Infants." *Monographs of the Society for Research in Child Development,* 28(85).
1967. "The Development of Social Motivation." Pages 111–132 in *Nebraska Symposium on Motivation,* D. Levine, editor. Lincoln: University of Nebraska Press.

Shipley, W. U.
1963. "The Demonstration in the Domestic Guinea Pig of a Process Resembling Classical Imprinting." *Animal Behaviour,* 11:470–474.

Sluckin, W.
1965. *Imprinting and Early Learning.* Chicago: Aldine.

Sluckin, W., and E. A. Salzen.
1961. "Imprinting and Perceptual Learning." *Quarterly Journal of Experimental Psychology,* 13:65–77.

Taylor, A., W. Sluckin, R. Hewitt, and P. Guiton.
1967. "The Formation of Attachments by Domestic Chicks to Two Textures." *Animal Behaviour,* 15:514–519.

Thiessen, D. D., J. F. Zolman, and D. A. Rodgers.
1962. "Relation between Adrenal Weight, Brain Cholinesterase Activity, and Hole-in-wall Behavior of Mice under Different Living Conditions." *Journal of Comparative Physiology and Psychology,* 55:186–190.

Thorndike, E. L., and I. Lorge.
1944. *The Teacher's Wordbook of 30,000 Words.* New York: Teachers College, Columbia University.

Thorpe, W. H.
1956. *Learning and Instinct in Animals.* London: Methuen.

Tolman, E. C.
　1951. *Behavior and Psychological Man.* Berkeley: University of California Press.
Wilson, D. P.
　1952. "The Influence of the Nature of the Substratum on the Metamorphosis of the Larvae of Marine Animals, Especially Larvae of *Ophelia bicornis* Savigny." *Annales del' institut oceanographique,* 27:49–156.
Wynne-Edwards, V. C.
　1962. *Animal Dispersion in Relation to Social Behavior.* New York: Hafner.
Zajonc, R. B.
　1968. "Attitudinal Effects of Mere Exposure." *Journal of Personality and Social Psychology, Monograph Supplement,* 9(2):1–27.
Zajonc, R. B., editor.
　1969. *Animal Social Psychology.* New York: Wiley and Sons.

CHAPTER 5

COMPETITIVE AND AGGRESSIVE BEHAVIOR

EDWARD O. WILSON

HARVARD UNIVERSITY

The current popularity of animal behaviorists comes in good part from the comfort and assurance their discoveries offer to humanity. It is, after all, comforting to think that our sins are only animal sins (original sin if you wish) and that we are no more than naked apes momentarily disoriented by our jerry-built civilization. We want to believe that the beastliness in human nature is beastliness in the primordial sense and not some dark angelic flaw, to trust that we have not escaped so far from our ancestral genes as to be due for an early extinction. Perhaps all that is needed, the popular exponents of ethology seem to be saying, is to understand the adaptedness of our behavior and to learn to operate within its constraints. These writers—Robert Ardrey (1961), Konrad Lorenz (1966), Desmond Morris (1967), Anthony Storr (1968), and others—speak of territorial and aggressive instincts which long ago originated as stereotyped, strictly inherited behavioral repertories in our primate ancestors. The instincts are said to survive today in man in slightly abated and more diffuse form, hedged in by social conventions that tend to minimize their overt effects.

Of course nothing so starkly Darwinian could go unchallenged for very long. The contrary view has been argued by those of liberal humanist persuasion, such as that of Edmund Leach (1968) and Ashley Montagu (1965), and also by animal behaviorists with experience in the raw source material, including S. A. Barnett (1967) and Peter Klopfer (1968). These critics declare that there are no such things as unitary instincts, or drives, that persist through phylogenetic lineages as do vertebrae and eardrums. They point out that territorial behavior and aggression are not universal in lower animals, and that when such traits do occur they are expressed in myriad ways, performing functions that shift subtly from species to species. They condemn as facile and un-scientific the analogies between animal and human behavior.

In the midst of these contradictions, what are we to believe?

When I was invited to deal with the subject of competitive behavior, I welcomed it as an opportunity to attempt an objective comparative approach to this most contemporary of subjects. A comparative behaviorist is above all an evolutionist, and he can thus contribute to the discussion of the given problematic species—in this case, man—in at least two ways. First, he can try dispassionately to catalog the phenomenology of the subject. Each species of animal displays a pattern of behavioral phenomena with a texture of emphasis and clarity uniquely its own. What is rudimentary or hidden in one species might be exaggerated and obvious in the next. By considering many species, it is possible to catalog and perceive the significance of a much larger set of phenomena than would be possible from a study of a single example. Each of the behavioral acts in the repertory of the problematic species, however weakly or deceptively expressed, thus stands a better chance of being recognized and understood. This in essence is the approach to man already taken by ethologists of the Lorenz school.

The second contribution to be desired from the comparative behaviorists is less obvious in nature. It consists of extrapolating trends beyond species already analyzed to encompass the problematic species. The method is not limited simply to fixing the species as a point on a subjective curve. It also evaluates the variability of behavioral characters among species in order to judge the lability of the characters during evolution. For example, if characteristics evolve so quickly as to shift markedly in the course of evolution at the species level, then extrapolation to the genus level or higher in the taxonomic scale is risky and probably worthless. The second approach seems to be the key in evaluating competitive and aggressive behavior in man, yet it has been largely neglected in prior discussions of the subject. I would like to make it the theme of the exposition to follow.

THE OCCURRENCE OF COMPETITION AND AGGRESSION IN ANIMAL SPECIES
Competition, as Miller (1967) modified the original Clements and Shelford (1939) definition, is "the active demand by two or more individuals of the same species (intraspecies competition) or members of two or more species at the same trophic level (interspecies competition) for a common resource or requirement that is actually or potentially limiting." This definition is consistent with the assumptions of the Lotka-Volterra equations, which still form the basis of the mathematical theory of competition (Levins 1968). It also matches the intuitive conception held by most modern ecologists concerning the underlying behavioral processes (Miller 1967). Competition arises only when populations become crowded enough for a shortage to develop in one or more resources. When it does come into play, it reduces population growth; and if permitted to increase

unimpeded it will eventually reduce the growth rate to zero. When the growth rate is zero, competition can no longer increase in intensity. In short, competition is a self-limiting process. It follows that population growth is also a self-limiting process; and we speak of competition as being a *density-dependent factor*—a factor, in other words, whose depressing influence grows as population density increases. But note that competition is not the only density-dependent factor, and furthermore that other *density-independent factors* can play a role in the population regulation of any given species. Figure 1 presents a very simplified classification of both density-dependent and density-independent factors. According to the particular species involved, these can operate singly or in combination to bring the average, long-term growth of a population to zero. The point to bear in mind in looking at this scheme—one which will be documented shortly—is that population growth can be halted before competition occurs. Therefore competition is by no means a necessary consequence of population growth.

Aggression within animal species is almost always associated with competition. Insofar as aggressive behavior is adaptive, it can usually be regarded as a competitive technique and placed within our scheme as one of the devices of the "contest" form of competition. Since other forms of competition exist, aggressive behavior can be expected to be less common in nature than competitive behavior.

There are probably more than three million species of animals living on the earth today. Our knowledge of the occurrence of competitive and aggressive behavior among them is extremely meager. In Table 1 are tabulated the highly varied forms of population control encountered in eight species of insects. These species were chosen by Clark et al. (1967) solely on the basis of their being among the best-studied cases to date. Aside from the fact that most are also pest species capable of mounting very large populations, there is no reason to suspect that they are atypical in ecology and behavior. It can be seen that although density-dependent controls affect all eight, in only five are the controls known to involve competition; and of the five with competitive controls only two (the codling moth and sheep blowfly) are under the primary influence of competition.

The following generalizations can be made about competition in animals as a whole:

1. The mechanisms of competition between individuals of the same species are qualitatively similar to those between individuals of different species.

2. There is nevertheless a difference in intensity. Where competition

185

THE FACTORS THAT REDUCE POPULATION GROWTH RATES

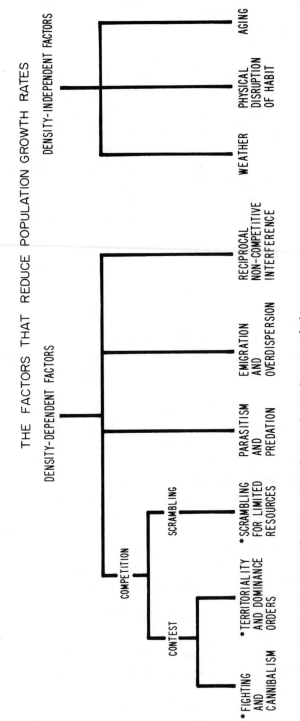

FIGURE 1. A simplified classification of the factors that reduce population-growth rates. Those factors grouped under competition are starred to stress that competition comprises but one set of such phenomena and is not a necessary outcome of population growth for all animal species.

186

TABLE 1.—The frequency and nature of density-dependent controls in the population growth of eight insect species. (Based on Clark et al. 1967.)

Species	Occurrence of density-dependent controls	Nature of the controls
Codling moth (*Cydia pomonella*) introduced populations in Australia	Very frequent	Competition for feeding-space among larvae and for cocooning sites among grown larvae.
Grasshopper (*Phaulacridium vittatum*)	Very frequent	Primarily emigration; also (under extreme conditions) competition for food.
Sawfly (*Perga affinus*)	Very frequent; weather also an occasional influence	In some regions, emigration coupled with competition; in other regions, parasitism by other insects.
Cabbage aphid (*Brevicoryne brassicae*)	Very frequent	Primarily emigration (by special alate forms); also reduced fecundity.
Sheep blowfly (*Lucilia cuprina*) in laboratory populations	Very frequent	Competition for food among adults, resulting in reduced fecundity.
Larch budmoth (*Zeiraphera griseana*)	Very frequent	Hymenopterous parasites and granulosis virus, which alternate in prevalence.
European spruce sawfly (*Diprion hercyniae*), introduced populations in Canada	Erratic; weather plays a major role in these unstable populations	Disease and insect parasitism.
Psyllid (*Cardiaspina albitextura*)	Very frequent	At low densities, predation by birds and insect parasites; at high densities, competition for food.

occurs at all, it is generally more intense within species than between species.

3. Several theoretical circumstances can be conceived under which competition is perpetually sidestepped (Hutchinson 1948, 1961). Most involve the intervention of other density-dependent factors of the kind

just outlined or fluctuations in the environment that regularly halt population growth just prior to saturation.

4. Field studies, although still very fragmentary in nature, have tended to verify the theoretical predictions just mentioned. Competition has been found to be widespread but not universal in animal species. It is more common in vertebrates than in invertebrates, in predators than in herbivores and omnivores, and in species belonging to stable ecosystems than in those belonging to unstable ecosystems. It is often forestalled by the prior operation of other density-dependent controls, the most common of which are emigration, predation, and parasitism.

5. Even where competition occurs, it is frequently suspended for long periods of time by the intervention of density-independent factors, especially unfavorable weather and the frequent availability of newly created empty habitats.

6. Whatever the competitive technique used—whether direct aggression, territoriality, nonaggressive "scrambling," or something else—the ultimate limiting resource is usually food. Although the documentation for this statement (Lack 1966, Schoener 1968) is still thin enough to be authoritatively disputed (Chitty 1967a), there still seem to be enough well-established cases to justify its provisional acceptance as a statistical inference. It is also true, however, that a minority of examples involve other limiting resources: growing space in barnacles and other sessile marine invertebrates (Connell 1961, Paine 1966); nesting sites in the pied flycatcher (Von Haartman 1956) and Scottish ants (Brian 1952a,b); resting places of high moisture in salamanders (Dumas 1956) and of shade in the mourning chat in African deserts (Hartley 1949); nest materials in rooks (C. J. F. Coombs in Crook 1965) and herons (A. J. Meyerriecks, University of South Florida, Tampa, personal communication).

THE MECHANISMS OF COMPETITION   As aggressive behavior is only one form of competitive technique, consider now a series of cases that illustrate the wide variation in this technique actually recorded among animal species. We will start with aggression in its direst and most explicit form and then, by passing from species to species, examine the increasingly more subtle and indirect forms.

Direct aggression.—When the barnacles of the species *Balanus balanoides* invade rock surfaces occupied by the second barnacle species *Chthamalus stellatus,* they eliminate these competitors by direct physical seizure of the attachment sites. In one case studied by Connell (1961) in Scotland, ten percent of the individuals in a colony of *Chthamalus* were overgrown by *Balanus* within a month, and another three percent were undercut and lifted off in the same period. A few others were crushed laterally by the expanding shells of the dominant species. By the end of the second month twenty percent of the *Chthamalus* had been eliminated, and eventually all disappeared. Individuals of *Balanus* also destroy each other but at a slower rate than they do members of the competitor species.

Ant colonies are notoriously aggressive toward each other, and colony "warfare" both within and between species have been witnessed by many entomologists. Pontin (1961, 1963) found that the majority of the queens of *Lasius flavus* and *L. niger* attempting to start new colonies in solitude are destroyed by workers of their own species. Colonies of the common pavement ant *Tetramorium caespitum* defend their territories with pitched battles conducted by large masses of workers (McCook 1909). The adaptive significance of the fighting has been made clear by the recent discovery that the average size of the worker and the production of winged sexual forms at the end of the season, both of which are good indicators of the nutritional status of the colony, increase with an increase in territory size (Brian, Elmes, and Kelley 1967). The following description by Brian (1955) of fighting among workers belonging to different colonies of *Myrmica ruginodis* is typical of a great many territorial ant species. The dispute in this particular case was brought about when workers from one colony approached those of another colony at a sugar bait.

If its approach is incautious, the feeder turns round . . . and grapples, and the pair fall to the ground and break. On the other hand, the incomer may approach slowly, and examine the abdomen of the feeder carefully without disturbing it; then it grips it by the pedicel (with the mandibles) and lifts it up. In this grip the lifted ant invariably remains quiescent, and is carried right back to the nest of the incomer. Sometimes under circumstances when a perfect grip is not obtained, other ants may become involved, and a group of three or four workers, composed of individuals from both nests, may struggle backwards and forwards along a line between the nest and the source (no perceptible track is formed). Mortality does not occur in the field, but those ants that are successfully dragged into the opposing nest will probably be dismembered. Hence the outcome of these struggles should favor the colony that brings the most workers to the site; that is, it will be related to colony size, proximity and recruitment ability.

Direct aggression among colonies of both the same and different ant species is a common occurrence (Talbot 1943, Haskins and Haskins 1965, Yasuno 1965). One of the more dramatic spectacles of insect biology is provided by the large-headed soldiers of certain species belonging to the genus *Pheidole*. These individuals have mandibles shaped approximately like the blades of wire clippers, and their heads are largely filled by massive adductor muscles. When clashes occur between colonies the soldiers rush in, attack blindly, and leave the field littered with the severed antennae, legs, and abdomens of their defeated enemies. Brian (1956) has provided evidence that interference among colonies leads to replacement and "dominance hierarchies" among Scottish ant species that places the winners in the warmest nest sites. He identified the three following competitive techniques: (1) gradual encroachment of the nest; (2) occupation of nest sites abandoned by competitor colonies following adverse microclimatic change (e.g., the nest chambers becoming temporarily too wet or cold), the occupation being accomplished when conditions improve but before the competitor can return; (3) siege, involving continuous harassment and fighting, until the competitor evacuates the nest site. Interference at the colony level sometimes leads to the total extirpation of one species by another from a local area. This extreme result occurs most frequently in unstable environments, such as agricultural land, or when newly introduced species invade native habitats. An example is given in Figure 2.

There can be no question that fighting and even cannibalism are normal among the members of some insect species. In the life cycle of certain species of parasitic Hymenoptera belonging to the families Ichneumonidae, Trigonalidae, Platygasteridae, Diapriidae, and Serphidae the larvae undergo a temporary transformation into a bizarre fighting form that kills and eats its brothers and sisters occupying the same host insect. This reduces the number of parasites to a number that more easily grow to the adult stage on the limited host tissue available. Two of the cannibalistic species are illustrated in Figure 3.

These facts from the biology of the ants and other Hymenoptera should dispel the impression created by some popular writers that the killing of members of the same species is never a normal event in nature. Lorenz (1966), for example, has stated, "Though occasionally, in territorial or rival fights, by some mishap a horn may penetrate an eye or a tooth an artery, we have never found that the aim of aggression was the extermination of fellow members of the species concerned." This is a purely empirical generalization about vertebrates, one which cannot be extended to the rest of the animal kingdom. I make the point primarily to establish that there are no universal "rules of conduct" in competitive behavior. Species are entirely opportunistic. Their behavior patterns do not conform to any general innate restrictions but are guided, like all other biological traits, solely by what happens to be advantageous over a period of time sufficient for evolution to occur. Thus, if it is of even temporary

190

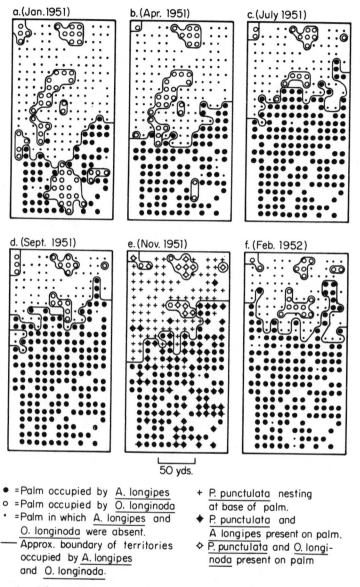

a.(Jan.1951)   b.(Apr. 1951)   c.(July 1951)

d. (Sept. 1951)   e.(Nov. 1951)   f. (Feb. 1952)

50 yds.

● =Palm occupied by A. longipes   + P. punctulata nesting
○ =Palm occupied by O. longinoda   at base of palm.
· =Palm in which A. longipes and   ◆ P. punctulata and
   O. longinoda were absent.   A longipes present on palm.
— Approx. boundary of territories   ◇ P. punctulata and O. longi-
   occupied by A. longipes   noda present on palm
   and O. longinoda.

FIGURE 2.   The exclusion of the ant *Oecophylla longinoda* by its competitor *Anoplolepis longipes* in a coconut plantation in Tanzania. The exclusion occurs through fighting at the colony level. In areas of sandy soil with sparse vegetation, *Anoplolepis* replaces *Oecophylla,* but where the vegetation is thicker and the soil less open and sandy, the reverse often occurs. A third species, *Pheidole punctulata,* is occasionally abundant but plays a minor role. (From Way 1953.)

191

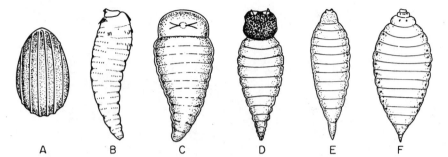

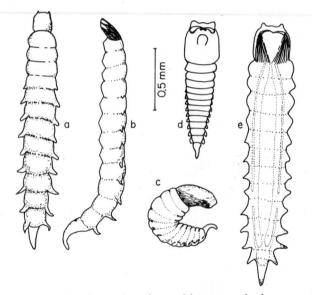

FIGURE 3. In certain species of parasitic wasps, the larvae undergo a temporary transformation into a bizarre fighting form, equipped with a sclerotized head and large mandibles. While in this instar the larvae inhabiting a single host insect fight together until only one is left alive. In the upper row are shown the egg and successive larval instars of the trigonalid *Poecilogonalos thwaitesii,* the fighting stage is the fourth instar (D). In the lower row are the first (a,b) and second (c-e) larval instars of the ichneumonid *Collyria calcitrator,* the fighting stage in this case is the second instar. (From Clausen 1940.)

selective advantage for individuals of a given species to be cannibals, one can expect that the entire species will evolve toward cannibalism.

Mutual repulsion.—When workers of the ants *Pheidole megacephala* and *Solenopsis globularia* meet at a feeding site, some fighting occurs, but the issue is not settled in this way. Instead, dominance is based on organizational ability. Workers of both species are excitable and run off the odor trails and away from the food site when they encounter an alien. The *Pheidole* calm down, relocate the odor trails, and assemble again at the feeding site more quickly than the *Solenopsis.* Consequently they build up their forces more quickly during the clashes and are usually able to control the feeding sites. *Solenopsis globularia* colonies are nevertheless able to survive by occupying nest sites and foraging areas in more open, sandy habitats not penetrated by *Pheidole megacephala* (E. O. Wilson and R. Levins, unpublished).

Other examples are known in which competition for resources is conducted by indirect forms of repulsion. Females of the tiny wasp *Trichogramma evanescens* parasitize the eggs of a wide variety of insect host species by penetrating the chorion with their ovipositors and inserting their own eggs inside. Other females of the same species are able to distinguish eggs that have already been parasitized, evidently through the detection of some scent left behind in trace amounts by the first female; thus alerted, they invariably move on to search for other eggs of their own (Salt 1936). At high population densities adults of the flour beetle *Tribolium confusum* remain neatly spaced-out because they repel one another by means of two specific quinonic substances secreted by glands in the abdomen and thorax (Loconti and Roth 1953, Naylor 1959).

Chemical aggression and interference can be both insidious and unpredictable in their effects. If a female mouse recently inseminated by one male is placed with a second male belonging to a different genetic strain, she will usually abort and quickly become available for a new insemination. The aborting stimulus is an as yet unidentified pheromone produced in male urine which is smelled by the female and activates the pituitary gland and corpora lutea (Bruce 1966, Bronson 1969). An equally significant effect has recently been demonstrated by Ropartz (1966, 1968). Investigating the causes of reduced fertility in crowded populations, he found that the odor of other mice alone causes the adrenal glands of individual mice to grow heavier and to increase their production of corticosteroids, resulting eventually in a decrease in reproductive capacity and even death of the animal. Here we have part but surely not all of the explanation of the well-known stress syndrome of mammals. Some ecologists have invoked the syndrome as the explanation of population fluctuation, including the occasional "crashes" of overly dense populations.

Territory, dominance, and social distance.—Territory was defined by G. K. Noble (1939) and other early students of the subject as any defended area. By this definition the territorial response was understood to consist of an overt action on the part of the territorial animal against intruders of the same species and, in a few cases, intruders belonging to other species as well. In recent years there has been a tendency to employ a broader definition, of the kind suggested by Pitelka (1959) in the following statement: "The fundamental importance of territory lies not in the mechanism (overt defense or any other action) by which the territory becomes identified with its occupant, but the degree to which it in fact is used exclusively by its occupant." We now know that territoriality varies gradually among species from immediate aggressive exclusion of intruders to the subtler use of chemical signposts unaccompanied by threats or attacks.

Maintenance of territories by aggressive behavior has been well documented in a great many different kinds of animals. Dragonflies of the species *Anax imperator,* for example, patrol the ponds in which their eggs are laid and drive out other dragonflies of their species as well as those of the similar appearing *Aeschna juncea* by darting attacks on the wing (Moore 1964). Miller (1967) has described how overt territorial aggression in the red-winged blackbird *Agelaius phoeniceus* and yellow-headed blackbird *Xanthocephalus xanthocephalus* results in the partial exclusion of the former species. The males of both species space themselves by frequent exchanges of vocal and visual displays delivered from perches in the marshy land where they nest. At one study area near Saskatoon, Canada, *Agelaius* males arrived an average of thirteen days earlier than the *Xanthocephalus* and set up their territories throughout the marsh. When the *Xanthocephalus* males appeared they displaced the *Agelaius* from the emergent vegetation in deep water at the center of the marsh. Orians (1961) has found that where the tricolored blackbird *Agelaius tricolor* occurs with *A. phoeniceus* in the western United States, a different kind of interaction occurs. Colonies of the former species do not defend territories and are consequently interspersed in the seemingly less favorable nesting sites not preempted by the aggressive *A. tricolor* males.

Horn (1968) has considered the implications of the variation in social organization among such bird species. He points out that if the food supply is evenly distributed in a stable pattern, it is of advantage for pairs to establish territories over which they have more or less exclusive control.

194

But if the food supply is both concentrated and shifting in location, it is of advantage for pairs to cluster together in a central location—and perhaps go so far as to forage in flocks. Thus it is theoretically possible for a change in a single parameter in the environment of a species to transform its optimal strategy from one employing open aggression and a tendency toward solitary existence to one of cooperative coexistence. Other aspects that may have equally profound influence on the evolution of aggression include the intensity of predation, the need for cooperative action in flushing and securing prey, the selection of nest sites that may be in short supply, competition for mates, and the degree of danger of a total population crash that results from overpopulating a given habitat (Hinde 1956, Crook 1965).

A somewhat less direct device of territorial maintenance consists of repetitious vocal signaling. Familiar examples include some of the more monotonous songs of crickets and other orthopteran insects (Alexander 1968), frogs (Blair 1968), and birds (Hooker 1968). Such vocalizing is not directed at individual intruders but is broadcast as a territorial advertisement. An even more circumspect form of advertisement is seen in the odor "signposts" laid down at strategic spots within the home range of mammals. Leyhausen (1965) has pointed out that the hunting ranges of individual house cats overlap considerably, and that more than one individual often contributes to the same signpost at different times. By smelling the deposits of previous passersby and judging the duration of the fading odor signals, the foraging cat is able to make a rough estimate of the whereabouts of its rivals. From this information it judges whether to leave the vicinity, to proceed cautiously, or to pass on freely.

We do not have the information needed to decide whether occupied land is generally denied at certain times to other members of the species by means of chemical advertisement. Animal behaviorists have naturally focused their attention on the more spectacular forms of aggressive behavior that arise during confrontations. When such behavior is lacking, one is tempted to postulate that exclusion is achieved by advertisement of one form or other. But such indirect effects have seldom been documented. I suggest that it would be useful to refine our definition of territory in the following way: *Territory is an area occupied more or less exclusively by animals or groups of animals by means of repulsion through overt defense or advertisement.* It remains to be pointed out that the exclusive use of terrain must be owing to: (1) overt defense, (2) repulsion by advertisement, (3) the selection of different kinds of living quarters by different life forms or genetic morphs, (4) the sufficiently diffuse

195

scattering of individuals through random effects of dispersal, or (5) some combination of these effects. Where interaction among animals occurs, specifically in the first two listed conditions, we can say that the occupied area is a territory.

Most of the same considerations apply to those closely related social mechanisms, the social space and the dominance hierarchy. Social space is a kind of floating territory in which the exclusive area is generated simply by the existence of a distance below which an individual animal will not permit another animal to approach it. It produces the sometimes astonishingly regular spacing patterns of roosting birds and swimming schools of fish. Social distance is sometimes maintained by an overt threat. For example, a brooding hen begins to show agitation when another hen comes within twenty feet; if the approach is less than ten feet, she lowers her wings and prepares for attack. In other cases, such as the *Tribolium* flour beetles, it is maintained by chemical repulsion or some other form of indirect exclusion.

Dominance behavior can be conveniently viewed as the analog of territorial behavior in which a group of animals coexist within one territory. The result is that one of them, the equivalent of the territory holder, comes to dominate the others. Below this alpha individual there may be a second, "beta" animal that similarly controls the rest of the underlings, and beneath it a third-ranking individual, and so on. Dominance hierarchies based on direct interaction are very widespread but not universal among social animals. They have been recorded, for example, in social wasps, bumblebees, hermit crabs, lizards, birds, and mammals. In a few cases they are interchangeable with territories. When territorial iguanid lizards are forced to live together in cages smaller than their natural territories, a single male despot comes to dominate the rest of the group, utilizing the same threat displays employed in natural territorial defense.

The expression of hierarchies may shift with the spatial position of the animals. A group of domestic cats forced to feed together from the same dish form, what Leyhausen has called, an "absolute hierarchy," the rigid ordinal relationship of the classic hen-pecking kind. But when it comes to resting places, the group displays a "relative hierarchy," that is, each individual is dominant in its own chosen spot.

Hierarchies are formed in the course of the initial encounters by means of threats and fighting, but after the issue has been settled, each individual gives way to its superiors with a minimum of hostile exchange. The life of the group may eventually become so peaceable as to hide the existence

196

of such ranking from the observer—until some minor crisis or other happens to force a confrontation. Troops of the baboon *Papio cynocephalus,* for example, often go for hours without enough hostile exchange occurring to reveal the form of the hierarchy; then in a moment of tension—a quarrel over an item of food is sufficient—the ranking is suddenly displayed, like the image on a negative dipped in developer fluid. In its pacific state the hierarchy is often supported by "status" signs. The identity of the leading male in a wolf pack is unmistakable from the way he holds his head, ears, and tail, and the confident, face-forward manner in which he approaches other members of his group. He controls his subordinates in the great majority of encounters without any display of overt hostility (Schenkel 1947). Similarly, the dominant rhesus male maintains an elaborate posture signifying his rank: head and tail up, testicles lowered, body movements slow and deliberate and accompanied by unhesitating but measured scrutiny of other monkeys that cross his field of view (Altmann 1962).

Finally, dominance behavior is mediated not only by visual signals but also by acoustic and chemical signals. Mykytowycz (1962) has found that in male European rabbits (*Oryctolagus cuniculus*) the degree of development of the submandibular gland increases with the rank of the individual. By means of "chinning," in which the lower surface of the head is rubbed against objects on the ground, dominant males mark the territory occupied by the group with their own submandibular gland secretions. Recent studies of similar behavior in flying phalangers and black-tailed deer (reviewed by Wilson 1969) indicate that territorial and other agonistic pheromones (chemical signals) of these species are complex mixtures that vary greatly among members of the same population. As a result individuals are able to distinguish their own scent from that of others.

Scramble competition.—Let us now consider the less direct forms of competitive behavior. So far the account has been deliberately simplified by the adoption of Nicholson's (1955) dichotomy of competitive forms into "contest" versus "scramble" forms, even though more sophisticated (and complicated) classifications can be devised. The following point I wish to make, however, is not compromised by the simplification. It is generally true that the population growth rate of family groups and other genetically allied groups within species, as well as the population growth rate of other species, can be diminished by mere appropriation of resources in short supply, without any aggression or other kinds of behavior leading to repulsion. Thus scramble competition can be correctly described by the same basic mathematical models used to analyze contest

197

competition. This rather formal way of putting the matter is meant to take care of the celebrated objection by Andrewartha and Birch (1954) to the effect that a mere shortage of resources does not ipso facto provide a density-dependent control of the population.

The curtailment of population growth and even reduction in total population size due to periodic starvation has been well documented in birds (Ashmole 1963, Lack 1966) and mammals (Chitty 1967b). In times of severe food shortage the local effects can be ameliorated by territoriality and emigration, but they cannot be avoided altogether. The effects of capricious climatic change together with a relentless pressure from predators keeps most insect species from ever reaching levels that create shortages (Miller 1967). When competition for food does occur— and there are a few species such as the codling moth in which it is a frequent event—its effects are less likely to be buffered by intervening contest competition of the kinds prevailing in the vertebrates. Under uniform conditions the outcomes of scramble competition among differing genetic strains and species can be predicted with reasonable accuracy. The issue is by no means settled simply by who is able to eat or seek shelter the fastest. In his studies of *Drosophila melanogaster,* which like most species of flies exhibits the purest form of scramble competition, K. Bakker (in Miller 1967) detected at least five factors which act together to determine the outcome: (1) rate of feeding, (2) duration of the molting periods, (3) special food requirements, (4) initial larval weight, and (5) resistance to the mechanical and chemical effect of crowding.

THE LIMITS OF AGGRESSION   Why is pacifism the rule among animal species? Even if we discount the very large number of species in which density-dependent controls are sufficiently intense to prevent the populations from reaching competitive levels, it still remains to be explained why overt aggression is lacking among most species that do compete. The answer is almost certainly that for each species, depending on the details of its life cycle, its food preferences, and its courtship rituals, there exists some optimal level of aggressiveness above which individual fitness is lowered. For some species this level must be zero, in other words the animals should be wholly nonaggressive. There are in fact at least two kinds of constraints on the evolutionary increase of aggressiveness. First, as Tinbergen (1956) and others have pointed out, an aggressor spends time that could be invested in courtship, nest building, and the feeding and rearing of young. The adverse effects of such "aggressive neglect" on reproduction have been documented in the gannet (*Sula bassana*) by Nelson (1964, 1965) and in sunbirds and honeyeaters by Ripley (1959,

1961). Its theoretical implications have been explored by Hutchinson and MacArthur (1959).

For the aggressor there also exists a danger that its hostility will be directed against unrecognized relatives. If the rates of survival and reproduction among relatives are thereby lowered, then the replacement rate of the genes held in common descent between the aggressor and its relatives will also be lowered. Since these genes will include the ones responsible for aggressive behavior, such a reduction in the "inclusive fitness" (the summed fitness of the aggressor and genes held in common descent) will work against aggressive behavior as well. This process will continue until the difference between the advantage and disadvantage, measured in units of inclusive fitness, is maximized. The theory of the subject has recently been developed mathematically by Hamilton (1964).

The constraints on aggression are such that even when aggression occurs as a genetically determined trait it can be expected to be programed in such a way as to be brought into play only when it gives a momentary advantage. Such episodes in the life of an animal may be few and far between, yet their rarity in a particular case must not mislead us into assuming that the behavior is not "natural," i.e., adaptive and genetically programed. Let me illustrate this point with several examples. Well-fed honeybee colonies are very tolerant of intruding workers from nearby hives, letting them penetrate the nest and even take supplies without opposition. But when the same colonies are allowed to go without food for several days, they attack every intruder at the nest entrance. When snowy owls (*Nyctea scandica*) live at normal population densities, each bird maintains a territory, about 12,000 acres in extent, and it does not engage in territorial defense. But when the owls are crowded together, particularly during the time of lemming highs in the Arctic, they are forced to occupy territories covering as few as 300 acres. Under these conditions, they defend the territories overtly, with characteristic sounds and postures (Pitelka in Schoener 1968). Aggressive encounters among adult hippopotami are rare where population densities are low to moderate. However, when populations in the Upper Semliki near Lake Edward became so dense that there was an average of one animal to every five meters of river bank, males began to fight viciously, sometimes even to the death (Verheyen 1954).

Aggression in primate societies is also strikingly limited in time and space. Hall (1965) describes its occurrence in *Papio cynocephalus* as follows: "Even in baboon groups in the wild, many hours may pass without any signs of aggression, but its readiness to occur is clearly seen when there is competition for an oestrus female, or when tension is experimentally created in a group by presenting it with a disturbing or frustrating situation to which a male may react by directing his aggression onto subordinate males."

This brings us to the subject of the crowding syndrome and social pathology. Leyhausen (1965) has graphically described what happens to the behavior of cats when they are subjected to unnatural crowding: "The more crowded the cage is, the less relative hierarchy there is. Eventually a despot emerges, 'pariahs' appear, driven to frenzy and all kinds of neurotic behaviour by continuous and pitiless attack by all others; the community turns into a spiteful mob. They all seldom relax, they never look at ease, and there is a continuous hissing, growling, and even fighting. Play stops altogether and locomotion and exercise are reduced to a minimum." Still more bizarre effects were observed by Calhoun (1962) in his experimentally overcrowded laboratory populations of white rats. In addition to the hypertensive behavior seen in Leyhausen's cats, some of the rats displayed hypersexuality and homosexuality and engaged in cannibalism. Nest construction was commonly atypical and nonfunctional, and infant mortality among the more disturbed mothers ran as high as 96 percent.

Such behavior is obviously abnormal. It has its close parallels in certain of the more dreadful aspects of human behavior. There are some clear similarities, for example, between the social life of Calhoun's rats and that of people in concentration and prisoner-of-war camps, dramatized so remorselessly, for example, in the novels *Andersonville* and *King Rat*. We must not be misled, however, into thinking that because aggression is twisted into bizarre forms in conditions of abnormally high density, it is therefore nonadaptive. A much more likely circumstance for any given aggressive species, and one which I suspect is true for man, is that the aggressive responses vary in what can properly be called a genetically programed manner. At low population densities, to take one conceivable example, all aggressive behavior may be suspended. At moderate densities it may take a mild form such as intermittent territorial defense. At high densities territorial defense may be sharp, while joint occupancy of land is also permitted under the regime of dominance hierarchies. Finally, at extremely high densities, the system may break down almost completely, transforming the pattern of aggressive encounters into "social pathology." Whatever the specific program that slides individual responses up and down the aggression scale, however, each of the various degrees of aggressiveness is adaptive at an appropriate level of population density— short of the rarely recurring pathological levels. In sum, it is the total *pattern* of responses that is adaptive and has been selected for in the course of evolution.

The lesson for man is that personal happiness has very little to do with all this. It is possible to be unhappy and very adaptive. If we wish to reduce our own aggressive behavior to levels that make us all happier, we should consider altering our population densities and social systems in such a way as to make aggression nonadaptive.

Is aggression in man *really* adaptive? From the biologist's point of view it certainly seems to be. It is hard to believe that any characteristic so widespread and easily invoked in a species, as aggressive behavior is in man, could be neutral or negative in its effects on individual survival and reproduction. To be sure, overt aggressiveness is not a trait in all or even a majority of human cultures. But in order to be adaptive it is enough that aggressive patterns be evoked only under certain conditions of stress such as those that might arise during food shortages and periodic high population densities. It also does not matter whether the aggression is wholly innate or is acquired part or wholly by learning. We are now sophisticated enough to know that the capacity to learn certain behaviors is itself a genetically controlled and therefore evolved trait.

Such an interpretation, which follows from our information on patterned aggression in other animal species, is at the same time very far removed from the sanguinary view of innate aggressiveness which was expressed by Raymond Dart (1953) and had so much influence on subsequent authors:

The blood-bespattered, slaughter-gutted archives of human history from the earliest Egyptian and Sumerian records to the most recent atrocities of the Second World War accord with early universal cannibalism, with animal and human sacrificial practices or their substitutes in formalized religions and with the worldwide scalping, head-hunting, body-mutilating and necrophiliac practices of mankind in proclaiming this common blood lust differentiator, this mark of Cain that separates man dietetically from his anthropoidal relatives and allies him rather with the deadliest of Carnivora.

This is obviously bad anthropology, bad ethology, and as I shall show shortly even bad genetics. It is equally wrong, however, to accept cheerfully the extreme opposite view, espoused by many psychologists, that aggressiveness is only a neurosis brought out by abnormal circumstances and hence, by implication, nonadaptive for the species. When T. W. Adorno, for example, demonstrated (in *The Authoritarian Personality*) that bullies tend to come from families in which the father was a tyrant and the mother a submerged personality, he identified only one of the

201

environmental factors affecting expression of certain human genes. It says nothing, as Barnett (1967) seems to believe it does, about the adaptiveness of the trait. Bullying behavior, together with other forms of aggressive response to stress and unusual social environments, may well be adaptive —that is, programed to increase the survival and reproductive performance of individuals thrown into stressful situations. A revealing parallel can be seen in the behavior of rhesus monkeys. Individuals reared in isolation display uncontrolled aggressiveness leading frequently to injury. Surely this is neurosis and nonadaptive for the individuals whose behavioral development has been thus misdirected. But it does not lessen the importance of the well-known fact that aggression is a way of life and an important stabilizing device in free-ranging rhesus societies.

DOES MAN GENETICALLY TRACK HIS CULTURE? It is true that we do not inherit a particular language or a set of customs and attitudes. In the same sense a mammal does not inherit knowledge of its parent's home range. But it does not automatically follow that dominant traits of cultures are never genetically fixed through selection of genotypes conforming to the prevailing culture. The process whereby a trait ("phenotype") is induced first by environmental influences and later fixed by selection of the genes most prone to exhibit the trait is called genetic assimilation. The process has been well demonstrated in laboratory experiments with *Drosophila* (Wallace 1968).

The key to the genetic assimilation of given culture traits, if such is possible, lies in their heritability. In simplest terms, heritability is a precise measure that includes the total amount of variability of a trait in a given population and how much of this variation is due to variation in genes.

Heritability can be defined and measured as follows: The total *phenotypic variance* (V_P) of a trait is the total variation in the population in the outward manifestation of the trait where variation is given precise form as the statistic variance. It is the sum of the *genetic variance* (V_G) and *environmental variance* (V_E). The genetic variance in turn is the variance due to differences among genes affecting the trait, and the environmental variance is the variance due to differing environments as they affect individual development. *Heritability in the broad sense* (h_B^2) is the proportion that genetic variance contributes to the total variance:

$$h_B^2 = \frac{V_G}{V_G + V_E} \ .$$

In the case of additive inheritance, $V_G = V_A + V_D + V_I$, where $V_A =$ variance due to additive genes, $V_D =$ variance due to dominance deviations, $V_I =$ variance due to epistatic interactions. Ignoring V_D and V_I for the moment as interaction effects chiefly of interest to geneticists, it is possible to separate out a measure of heritability that permits a direct estimate of the rate at which evolution can occur. This *heritability in the narrow sense* (h_N^2) is defined as follows:

$$h_N^2 = \frac{V_A}{V_P} \cdot$$

Further explanations of these measures and the genetic techniques for obtaining them are given in the textbooks by Falconer (1960) and Parsons (1967).

The speed with which a trait is evolving in a population increases as the product of its heritability and the intensity of the selection process. (To be exact, $R = h_N^2 S$, where R is the response to selection, h_N^2 is heritability in the narrow sense as defined in the preceding paragraph, and S is a parameter determined by the proportion of the population included in the selection process and the standard deviation, i.e., amount of variation, of the trait.) In other words the susceptibility of human behavioral characteristics to evolution depends on the amount of genetic material there is to work on in a given population and the intensity with which certain genetic types are favored in the process of differential reproduction. These components can be exactly defined, and the genetic tools exist with which to estimate them.

Hirsch (1967), however, has called attention to a major unsolved problem in the study of human behavioral evolution—how to classify behavioral traits in a way that will permit them to be genetically analyzed as separate entities. Even though this and other technical difficulties stand in the way of any thoroughgoing investigations in the immediate future, there exists abundant evidence that many of the most important measurable behavioral characteristics do possess a moderately high heritability. These include introversion-extroversion measures, personal tempo, psychomotor and sports activities, neuroticism, dominance, depression, and the tendency toward certain forms of mental illness such as schizophrenia (Parsons 1967, Lerner 1968).

It is therefore safe to assume that many important behavioral traits in man can evolve. This leads to the question of the speed with which such evolution occurs. Does it ever move fast enough, say, for human populations to adapt to some of the cultural norms of particular societies? In other words, does behavioral evolution occur faster than some forms of cultural change? At the risk of being dismissed by anthropologists as an ignorant heretic, I would like to present the case for such a possibility in the form of two arguments. First, I will show that strong evolution at the level of single genes can occur under moderate selection pressure in ten generations or less. Such evolution is not only well accommodated by genetic theory but is a commonplace in experimental animal populations. Second, the great variation in social organization among related animal species, especially primates, will be taken as evidence that moderate behavioral evolution can occur at rates at least comparable to the process of ordinary species formation.

Few persons, including even biologists, appreciate the speed with which evolution can proceed at the level of the gene. Consider first the theoretical possibilities. Let the frequency of a given gene in a population be represented by q (so that when $q = 0$ the gene is absent and when $q = 1$ it is the only gene of its kind at its chromosome locus); and let selection pressure against homozygotes of the gene be represented by s. When $s = 0$, individuals possessing nothing but the gene survive and reproduce as well as individuals with other kinds of genes. When $s = 1$, no such individuals contribute offspring to the next generation. In nature most values of s fall somewhere between 0 and 1. The rate of change in each generation in a large population will be $\dfrac{-sq^2(1 - q)}{1 - sq^2}$, for which the simpler expression $-sq^2(1 - q)$ is a good approximation, since sq^2 is usually a negligible quantity. The rate of change is greatest when $q = 0.67$ but falls off steeply as the gene becomes either rare or very abundant.

Figure 4 illustrates an actual case of microevolution of a character involving behavior in *Drosophila*. Here $s = 0.5$, because the homozygote males (possessing two raspberry genes) are about half as successful in mating as those males which possess one raspberry gene or none at all. The experimental curve of evolutionary change can be seen to be nicely consistent with the theoretical curve. In only ten generations the frequency of the gene declines from 50 percent to approximately 10 percent. Other eye mutants of *Drosophila* often show this degree of reduction in reproductive performance. The exact behavioral basis in the *yellow* mutant of *D. melanogaster* was elucidated by Bastock and Manning (1955) and Bastock (1956). They found that successful courtship by males of the species entails the following rigid sequence of maneuvers: (1) "orientation," in which the male stands close to or follows the female; (2) "vibration," in which he rapidly vibrates his wings close to her head; (3) "licking," wherein the male extends his proboscis and licks the female's ovipositor; and (4) attempted copulation. The *yellow* homozygote males are wholly normal in the movements and sequence of these maneuvers, but they are less active at vibrating (movement number 2) and licking (movement number 3). Hence they are less effective in achieving copulation. Such behavioral components are commonplace in

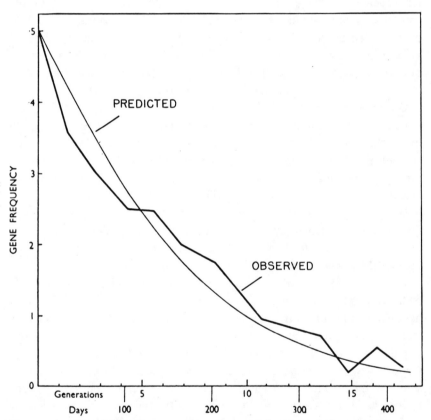

FIGURE 4. The decline in percentage of a gene in a population when the homozygotes (individuals bearing only that gene at the chromosome locus) reproduce at 50 percent the rate of other kinds of individuals in the population. The smooth curve is the one predicted by theory. The irregular one, which fits the theoretical curve closely, shows the actual decline of the "raspberry" gene, which affects both eye color and behavior, in a laboratory population of the fruit fly *Drosophila melanogaster*. The frequency of the gene declines from 50 to about 10 percent in only ten generations. (From Falconer 1960; the experimental curve was based on data from Merrell 1953).

the phenotypes of rapidly evolving *Drosophila* populations (Spiess and Langer, 1964a, b).

There exist numerous other examples in which significant evolution in major behavioral characters has been obtained in laboratory populations in ten generations or less—in accordance with the generous limits predicted by theory. Starting with behaviorally neutral stocks, Dobzhansky and Spassky (1962) and Hirsch (1963) have created lines of *Drosophila* whose adult flies orient toward or away from gravity and light. In only ten generations Ayala (1968) was able to achieve a doubling of the equilibrial adult population size within *Drosophila serrata* confined to overcrowded bottles. He then discovered that the result had come about at least in part because of a quick shift to strains in which the adults are quieter in disposition and thus less easily knocked over and trapped in the sticky culture medium (Ayala, personal communication).

Gibson and Thoday (1962), while practicing disruptive selection on a population of *D. melanogaster* in order to create coexisting strains with high and low numbers of thoracic bristles, found that their two lines stopped crossbreeding in only about ten generations. In this brief span of time they had created what were, in effect, two species. The explanation, elucidated in later experiments by Thoday (1964), appears to be that linked genes favoring "homogamy"—the tendency for like to mate with like—were simultaneously and accidentally selected along with bristle number. Evolution leading to rapid species formation can occur even without the application of such intense selection pressure.

In the late 1950s, M. Vetukhiv set up six populations from a single highly heterozygous stock of *Drosophila pseudoobscura* derived from hybrids of populations from widely separate localities. Fifty-three months later the males were observed to prefer females from their own laboratory populations over those originating from the other five (Ehrman 1964). Quite a few cases of rapid microevolution of natural insect populations, some of them entailing behavioral traits, have been reported by Ford (1964) and his colleagues in England. In these examples selection coefficients (*s* in our earlier formula) typically exceeded 0.1.

Equally rapid behavioral evolution has been achieved in rodents through artificial selection, although the genetic basis is still unknown due to the greater technical difficulties involved in mammalian genetics. Examples of the traits affected include running behavior in mazes, defecation and urination rates under stress, fighting ability, tendency of rats to kill mice, and tameness toward human observers (Parsons 1967). Behavior can also evolve in laboratory rodent populations in the absence of artificial selection. When Harris (1952) provided laboratory-raised prairie deer mice (*Peromyscus maniculatus bairdii*), a form whose natural habitat is grassland, with both simulated grassland and forested habitats in the laboratory, the mice chose the grassland. This response indicated the presence of a genetic component of habitat choice inherited from their immediate ancestors. Ten years and 12–20 generations later, however, the laboratory descendants of Harris' mice had lost the tendency to choose the habitat (Wecker 1963).[1]

To summarize, there is every justification from both genetic theory and experiments on animal species to suppose that rapid behavioral evolution is at least a possibility in man. By rapid I mean significant alteration in, say, emotional and intellectual traits within no more than ten generations —or about three hundred years. The changes could affect genes shared by a large proportion of the population. Moreover, the necessary conditions are present for such swift microevolution. I have already mentioned that many measurable behavioral characteristics in man have been demonstrated to have moderate degrees of heritability. There is also overwhelming evidence for the existence of the second prerequisite for continuing evolution, namely varying reproductive performance among different families and family groups within the same society. This is especially characteristic of primitive and impoverished societies (Spuhler 1959, Stern 1960, Dunn 1962, Mayr 1963). Finally, some cultures evolve slowly enough so that their dominant features remain essentially unchanged for hundreds of years, long enough it would seem to permit the occurrence of some amount of genetic assimilation.

Man therefore has the genetic *capacity* to track some of the dominant features of particular cultures. Whether he does so—and to what degree —remains an open question. In order to provide the answer, human geneticists would have to accomplish the following difficult feats: (1) classify behavioral traits in a form amenable to genetic analysis, (2) estimate the heritability of the traits, (3) measure the cross-cultural

---

[1] *Editor's note:* Although in Wecker's experiments, the prairie deer mouse, *P. maniculatus bairdii* did not retain a preference for the grassland habitat which is its normal habitat type, the captive individuals could, after a brief exposure to grassland habitat, select this habitat preferentially after not being exposed to it again for various periods exceeding a month. The reverse experiment was not true, in that, the same subspecies could not be induced to prefer a woodland habitat based on equivalent early experience. Hence, even though the predisposition to select the appropriate habitat type was no longer present without experience, Wecker's experiments amply demonstrated that this subspecies was still susceptible to a form of early experience predisposing it to choose its ancestral habitat type. (J.F.E.)

genetic differences, and (4) estimate intensities of within-culture selection pressures on the heritable traits. I believe it is much too early to attempt to make a judgment on the matter, as Dobzhansky (1963a) has done with the following statement: "Culture is not inherited through genes, it is acquired by learning from other human beings. . . . In a sense, human genes have surrendered their primacy in human evolution to an entirely new, nonbiological or superorganic agent, culture. However, it should not be forgotten that this agent is entirely dependent on the human genotype." Obviously human genes have surrendered a great deal, but perhaps they have kept a little of their old heritability and responsiveness to selection. This amount should be measured, because it is crucial to the planning of future society. Above all, it is not enough to point to the absence of a behavioral trait in one or a few societies as conclusive evidence that the trait is environmentally induced and has no genetic disposition in man. The difference could still be genetic and, in fact, only recently evolved. Meanwhile, the primitiveness of the science of human genetics and its inadequacy to the task at hand cannot be overstressed.

Having completed this excursion into population genetics, let us now return to competition, aggression, and the image of man as the killer primate. Suppose it were true that fifteen million or more years ago our australopithecine ancestors evolved into carnivores who hunted in packs, that these creatures were highly aggressive and territorial, and that their habits persisted to the dawn of agricultural societies around five thousand years B.P. Even if Raymond Dart's most sanguinary imaginings were thus momentarily accepted for the sake of argument, would it follow that australopithecine traits persisted as a genetic legacy into civilized times? The answer is no. If there were selective pressures in other directions, time enough has elapsed since the appearance of the first agricultural and urban societies, and even since the fall of Rome, for evolution of some behavioral traits to have reversed itself many times over. Given even small amounts of heritability and selection pressure, both of which are indicated by our rudimentary understanding of behavioral genetics in man, it seems inevitable that man makes himself genetically as he goes along. If aggressive behavior under stress has a genetic basis, it is likely to be due less to Pleistocene genetic inertia than to the fact that such behavior has continued to be adaptive into modern times.

The conception of great evolutionary plasticity in behavioral and social traits is additionally supported by recent studies of free-ranging primate societies. To the surprise of almost everyone who was ever swayed by the early writings of Sir Solly Zuckerman, the higher primate species have been found to vary enormously in the most basic properties of individual behavior and social organization. Furthermore, as Hall (1965) has pointed out, the correlations between social behavior and the grosser aspects of ecology are quite weak. The most aggressively organized species, particularly the baboons and rhesus macaques, utilize varied habitats, from trees in gallery forests to clumps of bushes and open ground in savannas. Their versatility fits our intuitive conception of dominant species. But it is also true that the common langur, a monkey with a relatively placid form of social behavior, utilizes an equally wide range of habitats. Even more interesting is the case of the chimpanzee, the most manlike of the great apes. Chimpanzee troops patrol their forest habitats in much the same way as the compact baboon and rhesus groups. Yet they have a remarkably loose and pacific social organization, and they display no trace of the fierce territorial hostility that marks baboon and rhesus behavior. In view of these facts it would be clearly an error to infer anything about the social behavior of man's Pleistocene ancestors from our meager knowledge of their ecology. The science of comparative primate sociology will have to become far more sophisticated before that can be tried again.

This review should make it clear that we are in grave need of a truly scientific and powerful anthropology. Dobzhansky (1963b) put the matter exactly right in the following statement: "The ultimate function of anthropology is no less than to provide the knowledge requisite for the guidance of human evolution. . . . But to fulfill its function, anthropology cannot belong entirely either to biology or to social sciences or to humanities. It must, in the fullness of time, become a synthesis of all three."

From my own point of view as a biologist, the task now before anthropology seems almost overwhelming. Anthropology must encompass human genetics, extending that science to generate a new discipline, anthropological genetics, the study of the heredity of the behavioral traits that affect culture. Only by this means can a measure be taken of heritability and evolutionary potential of the basic personality and cultural traits. Anthropology must continue to promote primate sociology, but in such a way as to translate it into the most advanced theory of population genetics and ecology. Only by this means can an understanding be gained of the adaptive radiation that has occurred in primate social systems. When both of these great tasks are achieved, some of the guesswork can at last go out of comparisons between man and beast.

CONCLUSIONS Competition is widespread but not universal in animal species. Current ecological theory predicts that there are several easily obtained conditions under which competition could be permanently avoided. It is not surprising, therefore, that in numerous instances empirical studies have either failed to uncover evidence of competition or else have revealed it to be of secondary importance.

Aggressive behavior among members of the same species without competition is improbable. Aggression is only one of several competitive techniques that have been documented in animal species. Among the species that engage in competition, the more overt forms of aggression are less common in the vertebrate species than in the invertebrates. A small minority of invertebrate species employ killing and even cannibalism as normal competitive techniques, but the occurrence of such behavior seems to be extremely rare in vertebrates.

Within the species that engage in competition and aggression, these phenomena nevertheless tend to be suspended in periods of low population density and accentuated as population density increases. Aggressiveness is viewed as a pattern of adaptive response—most commonly increasing along the ascending scale of population density—rather than as a "neurotic" response to "abnormal" stresses.

The idea that man's immediate ancestors, the primitive Hominidae, were territorial and very aggressive may be true. But the evidence from comparative studies of primate sociology is wholly inconclusive on this point, and ecological correlation can no longer be invoked with any degree of confidence to argue the matter either way.

Some degree of aggressiveness in man is nevertheless probably adaptive —that is, genetically programed by means of natural selection to contribute to fitness in the narrow reproductive sense. This complex trait cannot be assumed to be due to a useless or harmful genetic residue left over from prehistoric times. It is more plausibly viewed as a trait that has been adaptive within the past few hundreds or, at most, thousands of years. Some of its components might even have *originated* during historical times, since both theoretical considerations and empirical studies on animal populations show that some behavioral traits can evolve significantly within ten generations or less.

ADDENDUM

Robert Ardrey, working from a preprint of this article, has taken issue on several points in his recent book *The Social Contract*.[1] I now have the

---

[1] Robert Ardrey, *The Social Contract: A Personal Inquiry into the Evolutionary Sources of Order and Disorder*. 405 pages. New York: Atheneum, 1970.

rare luxury of responding in the very article criticized. Ardrey believes that "competition" occurs everywhere in nature. He asks, "Can one speak of natural selection without it?" The answer is yes, one can. Ardrey, whose grasp of ecology is somewhat less firm than his grasp of sociobiology, confuses competition between alleles (natural selection itself) with ecological competition. Ecological competition, as biologists define it, is only one of the processes which contribute to the differential reproduction of genotypes and hence the substitution of alleles. Ardrey assails the definition of competition presented as "Triassic" in obsolescence because it was first proposed in 1939. That is irrelevant. What is important is the fact that it is the working definition of most contemporary ecologists. To call it obsolete is equivalent to calling the concept of natural selection obsolete just because it was proposed back in 1858. I can only repeat my generalization: theory predicts that competition is not an essential property of species, and data from empirical studies (for example, see Table 1) show that competition is in fact very far from being universal.

REFERENCES

Alexander, R. D.
    1968. "Arthropods." Pages 167–216 in *Animal Communication, Techniques of Study and Results of Research,* T. A. Sebeok, editor. Bloomington: University of Indiana Press.

Altmann, S. A.
    1962. "A Field Study of the Sociobiology of Rhesus Monkeys, *Macaca mulatta." Annals of the New York Academy of Sciences,* 102:338–435.

Andrewartha, H. G., and L. C. Birch.
    1954. *The Distribution and Abundance of Animals.* Chicago: University of Chicago Press.

Ardrey, R.
    1961. *African Genesis: A Personal Investigation into the Animal Origins and Nature of Man.* New York: Atheneum.

Ashmole, N. P.
    1963. "The Regulation of Numbers of Tropical Oceanic Birds." *Ibis,* 103b:458–473.

Ayala, F. J.
    1968. "Evolution of Fitness, II: Correlated Effects of Natural Selection on the Productivity and Size of Experimental Populations of *Drosophila serrata." Evolution,* 22:55–65.

Barnett, S. A.
    1967. Review of "On Aggression," by K. Lorenz. *Scientific American,* 216:135–138.

Bastock, M.
  1956. "A Gene Mutation which Changes a Behavior Pattern." *Evolution,*
     10:421–439.
Bastock, M., and A. Manning.
  1955. "The Courtship of *Drosophila melanogaster.*" *Behaviour,* 8:85–111.
Blair, W. F.
  1968. "Amphibians and Reptiles." Pages 289–310 in *Animal Communica-
     tion, Techniques of Study and Results of Research,* T. A. Sebeok,
     editor. Bloomington: University of Indiana Press.
Brian, M. V.
  1952a. "Interaction Between Ant Colonies at an Artificial Nest-site." *En-
     tomologist's Monthly Magazine,* 88:84–88.
  1952b. "The Structure of a Natural Dense Ant Population." *Journal of
     Animal Ecology,* 21:12–24.
  1955. "Food Collection by a Scottish Ant Community." *Journal of Animal
     Ecology,* 24:336–351.
  1956. "The Natural Density of *Myrmica rubra* and Associated Ants in
     West Scotland." *Insectes Sociaux,* 3:473–487.
Brian, M. V., G. Elmes, and A. F. Kelley.
  1967. "Populations of the Ant *Tetramorium caespitum* Latreille." *Journal
     of Animal Ecology,* 36:337–342.
Bronson, F. H.
  1969. "Pheromonal Influences on Mammalian Reproduction." In *Perspec-
     tives in Reproduction and Sexual Behavior,* M. Diamond, editor.
     Bloomington: University of Indiana Press.
Bruce, H. M.
  1966. "Smell as an Exteroceptive Factor." *Journal of Animal Science,* 25
     (Supplement): 83–89.
Calhoun, J. B.
  1962. "Population Density and Social Pathology." *Scientific American,*
     206 (February): 139–148.
Chitty, D.
  1967a. "What Regulates Bird Populations?" *Ecology,* 48:698–701.
  1967b. "The Natural Selection of Self-regulatory Behavior in Animal
     Populations." *Proceedings of the Ecological Society of Australia,*
     2:51–78.
Clark, L. R., P. W. Geier, R. D. Hughes, and R. F. Morris.
  1967. *The Ecology of Insect Populations in Theory and Practice.* London:
     Methuen; New York: Barnes and Noble.
Clausen, C. P.
  1940. *Entomophagous Insects.* New York: McGraw-Hill.
Clements, F. E., and V. E. Shelford.
  1939. *Bio-ecology.* New York: John Wiley and Sons.
Connell, J. H.
  1961. "The Influence of Interspecific Competition and Other Factors on
     the Distribution of the Barnacle *Chthamalus stellatus.*" *Ecology,*
     42:710–723.

Crook, J. H.
1965. "The Adaptive Significance of Avian Social Organizations." *Symposia of the Zoological Society of London,* 14:181–218.

Dart, R. A.
1953. "The Predatory Transition from Ape to Man." *International Anthropological and Linguistic Review,* 1:201–208.

Dobzhansky, T.
1963a. "Genetics of Race Equality." *Eugenics Quarterly,* 10:151–160.
1963b. "Anthropology and the Natural Sciences—The Problem of Human Evolution." *Current Anthropology,* 4:138–148.

Dobzhansky, T., and B. Spassky.
1962. "Selection for Geotaxis in Monomorphic and Polymorphic Populations of *Drosophila pseudoobscura.*" *Proceedings of the National Academy of Sciences,* 48:1704–1712.

Dumas, P. C.
1956. "The Ecological Relations of Sympatry in *Plethodon dunni* and *Plethodon vehiculum.*" *Ecology,* 37:484–495.

Dunn, L. C.
1962. *Heredity and Evolution in Human Populations.* Cambridge: Harvard University Press.

Ehrman, L.
1964. "Genetic Divergence in M. Vetukhiv's Experimental Populations of *Drosophila pseudoobscura,* I: Rudiments of Sexual Isolation." *Genetical Research* (Cambridge), 5:150–157.

Falconer, D. S.
1960. *Quantitative Genetics.* New York: The Ronald Press Company.

Ford, E. B.
1964. *Ecological Genetics.* London: Methuen.

Gibson, J. B., and J. M. Thoday.
1962. "Effects of Disruptive Selection, VI: A Second Chromosome Polymorphism." *Heredity,* 17:1–26.

Hall, K. R. L.
1965. "Social Organization of the Old World Monkeys and Apes." *Symposia of the Zoological Society of London,* 14:265–289.

Hamilton, W. D.
1964. "The Genetical Evolution of Social Behaviour." *Journal of Theoretical Biology,* 7:1–52.

Harris, V. T.
1952. "An Experimental Study of Habitat Selection by Prairie and Forest Races of the Deer Mouse, *Peromyscus maniculatus.*" *Contributions of the University of Michigan Laboratory of Vertebrate Biology,* number 56.

Hartley, P. H. T.
1949. "The Biology of the Mourning Chat in Winter Quarters." *Ibis,* 9:393–413.

213

Haskins, C. P., and E. F. Haskins.
  1965. *"Pheidole megacephala* and *Iridomyrmex humilis* in Bermuda—Equilibrium or Slow Replacement?" *Ecology,* 46:735–740.
Hinde, R. A.
  1956. "The Biological Significance of the Territories of Birds." *Ibis,* 98: 340–369.
Hirsch, J.
  1963. "Behavior Genetics and Individuality Understood." *Science,* 142: 1436–1442.
  1967. "Intellectual Functioning and the Dimensions of Human Variation." In *Genetic Diversity and Human Behavior,* J. N. Spuhler, editor. Chicago: Aldine.
Hooker, B. I.
  1968. "Birds." Pages 311–337, in *Animal Communication, Techniques of Study and Results of Research,* T. A. Sebeok, editor. Bloomington: University of Indiana Press.
Horn, H. S.
  1968. "The Adaptive Significance of Colonial Nesting in the Brewer's Blackbird *(Euphagus cyanocephalus).*" *Ecology,* 49:682–694.
Hutchinson, G. E.
  1948. "Circular Causal Systems in Ecology." *Annals of the New York Academy of Sciences,* 50:221–246.
  1961. "The Paradox of the Plankton." *American Naturalist,* 95:137–146.
Hutchinson, G. E., and R. H. MacArthur.
  1959. "On the Theoretical Significance of Aggressive Neglect in Interspecific Competition." *American Naturalist,* 93:133–134.
Klopfer, P. H.
  1968. "From Ardrey to Altruism: A Discourse on the Biological Basis of Human Behavior." *Behavioral Science,* 13:399–401.
Lack, D.
  1966. *Population Studies of Birds.* Oxford: Clarendon Press.
Leach, E.
  1968. "Ignoble Savages." *The New York Review,* 11:24–29.
Lerner, I. M.
  1968. *Heredity, Evolution, and Society.* San Francisco: W. H. Freeman and Company.
Levins, R.
  1968. *Evolution in Changing Environments.* Princeton, New Jersey: Princeton University Press.
Leyhausen, P.
  1965. "The Communal Organization of Solitary Mammals." *Symposia of the Zoological Society of London,* 14:249–263.
Loconti, J. D., and L. M. Roth.
  1953. "Composition of the Odorous Secretion of *Tribolium castaneum.*" *Annals of the Entomological Society of America,* 46:281–289.
Lorenz, K.
  1966. *On Aggression.* New York: Harcourt, Brace, and World.

Mayr, E.
  1963. *Animal Species and Evolution.* Cambridge: Harvard University Press.
McCook, H. C.
  1909. *Ant Communities and How They Are Governed: A Study in Natural Civics.* New York and London: Harper and Brothers.
Merrell, D. J.
  1953. "Selective Mating as a Cause of Gene Frequency Changes in Laboratory Populations of *Drosophila melanogaster.*" *Evolution,* 7:287–296.
Miller, R. S.
  1967. "Pattern and Process in Competition." *Advances in Ecological Research,* 4:1–74.
Montagu, A.
  1965. *The Human Revolution.* Cleveland: The World Publishing Company.
Moore, N. W.
  1964. "Intra- and Interspecific Competition among Dragonflies (*Odonata*)." *Journal of Animal Ecology,* 33:49–71.
Morris, D.
  1967. *The Naked Ape: A Zoologist's Study of the Human Animal.* New York: McGraw-Hill.
Mykytowycz, R.
  1962. "Territorial Function of Chin Gland Secretion in the Rabbit, *Oryctolagus cuniculus* (L.)." *Nature,* 193:797.
Naylor, A. F.
  1959. "An Experimental Analysis of Dispersal in the Flour Beetle *Tribolium confusum.*" *Ecology,* 40:453–465.
Nelson, J. B.
  1964. "Factors Influencing Clutch-size and Chick Growth in the North Atlantic Gannet, *Sula bassana.*" *Ibis,* 106:63–77.
  1965. "The Behaviour of the Gannet." *British Birds,* 58:233–288.
Nicholson, A. J.
  1955. "An Outline of the Dynamics of Animal Populations." *Australian Journal of Zoology,* 2:9–65.
Noble, G. K.
  1939. "The Role of Dominance in the Life of Birds." *Auk,* 56:263–273.
Orians, G. H.
  1961. "The Ecology of Blackbird (*Agelaius*) Social Systems." *Ecological Monographs,* 31:285–312.
Paine, R. T.
  1966. "Food Web Complexity and Species Diversity." *American Naturalist,* 100:65–75.
Parsons, P. A.
  1967. *The Genetic Analysis of Behaviour.* London: Methuen.
Pitelka, F. A.
  1959. "Numbers, Breeding Schedule, and Territory in Pectoral Sandpipers of Northern Alaska." *Condor,* 61:233–264.

215

Pontin, A. J.
    1961. "Population Stabilization and Competition Between the Ants *Lasius flavus* (F.) and *L. niger* (L.)" *Journal of Animal Ecology*, 30:47–54.
    1963. "Further Considerations of Competition and Ecology of the Ants *Lasius flavus* (F.) and *L. niger* (L.)" *Journal of Animal Ecology*, 32:565–574.

Ripley, S. D.
    1959. "Competition Between Sunbird and Honeyeater Species in the Moluccan Islands." *American Naturalist*, 93:127–132.
    1961. "Aggressive Neglect as a Factor in Interspecific Competition in Birds." *Auk,* 78:366–371.

Ropartz, P.
    1966. "Contribution à l'étude du déterminisme d'un effet de groupe chez les souris." *Comptes Rendu Academie Science* (Paris) 263:2070–2072.
    1968. "Role des communications olfactives dans le comportement des souris males." In *L'effet de groupe chez les animaux,* R. Chauvin and C. Noirot, editors. *Colloques Internationaux du Centre National de la Recherche Scientifique,* 173:323–339.

Salt, G.
    1936. "Experimental Studies in Insect Parasitism, IV: The Effect of Superparasitism on Populations of *Trichogramma evanescens.*" *Journal of Experimental Biology,* 13:363–375.

Schenkel, R.
    1937. "Ausdrucksstudien an Wölfen." *Behaviour,* 1:81–130.

Schoener, T. W.
    1968. "Sizes of Feeding Territories Among Birds." *Ecology,* 49:123–141.

Spiess, E. B., and B. Langer.
    1964a. "Mating Speed Control by Gene Arrangements in *Drosophila pseudoobscura* Homokaryotypes." *Proceedings of the National Academy of Sciences of the United States of America,* 51:1015–1019.
    1964b. "Mating Speed Control by Gene Arrangement Carriers in *Drosophila persimilis.*" *Evolution,* 18:430–444.

Spuhler, J. N.
    1959. "Physical Anthropology and Demography." In *The Study of Population,* P. M. Hauser and O. D. Duncan, editors. Chicago: University of Chicago Press.

Stern, C.
    1960. *Principles of Human Genetics.* Second edition. San Francisco: W. H. Freeman & Company.

Storr, A.
    1968. *Human Aggression.* New York: Atheneum.

Talbot, M.
    1943. "Population Studies of the Ant, *Prenolepis imparis* Say." *Ecology,* 24:31–44.

Thoday, J. M.
    1964. "Genetics and the Integration of Reproductive Systems." *Symposia of the Royal Entomological Society of London,* 2:108–119.

Tinbergen, N.
  1956. "On the Functions of Territory in Gulls." *Ibis,* 98:401–411.
Verheyen, R.
  1954. *Monographie éthologique de l'hippopotame* (Hippopotamus amphibius *Linne*). Institut des Parcs Nationaux du Congo Belge. Exploration du Parc National Albert. Bruxelles.
Von Haartman, L.
  1956. "Territory in the Pied Flycatcher *Muscicapa hypoleuca.*" *Ibis,* 98: 460–475.
Wallace, B.
  1968. *Topics in Population Genetics.* New York: Norton.
Way, M. J.
  1953. "The Relationship between Certain Ant Species with Particular Reference to Biological Control of the Coreid, *Theraptus* sp." *Bulletin of Entomological Research,* 44:669–691.
Wecker, S. C.
  1963. "The Role of Early Experience in Habitat Selection by the Prairie Deer Mouse, *Peromyscus maniculatus bairdii.*" *Ecological Monographs,* 33:307–325.
Wilson, E. O.
  1969. "Chemical Communication within Animal Species." In *Chemical Ecology,* E. Sondheimer and J. B. Simeone, editors. New York: Academic Press.
Yasuno, M.
  1965. "Territory of Ants in the Kayano Grassland at Mt. Hakkôda." Scientific Reports of Tôhoku University (Sendai, Japan). Fourth Series. *Biology,* 31:195–206.

CHAPTER 6

SPACING MECHANISMS IN SOCIAL BEHAVIOR

HANS KUMMER

UNIVERSITY OF ZURICH

Social relations and spatial arrangement of animals are connected in many ways. Societies, for example, use space as the safest technique of regulating social interactions. Incompatible individuals can live tolerably at a great distance from each other. On the other hand, evolution makes individuals incompatible when a great distance between them is desirable for other than social reasons. Ecological pressures thus can realize certain advantageous spatial arrangements in a population by means of social affinities and antagonisms (Wynne-Edwards 1962). In general, social affinity and spatial proximity are so highly correlated that the distribution of animals in space can be used as a first reading of their social structure. An ideal aerial photograph of a population would show whether its members adhere to a solitary life, whether they live in pairs, or in large groups. Even within the group, affinities are revealed by spatial arrangements (Carpenter 1964; McBride, James, and Shoffner 1963; Kummer 1968).

Social life uses space for its own purposes, but it has not the only claim on determining spatial arrangements. Where complex selective pressures favor life in groups, individuals must live together even if they are not ideally compatible. Society may then have to find new means of regulating interactions. In this review I shall attempt to show how group life in primates gradually replaced purely spatial regulations by substitute techniques that permit the shaping of social relationships without altering spatial arrangements which are vital in other contexts. These developments take place on two fronts, within groups and between groups. *Within* the group, the main problem is how to stay together, how to prevent group members from physically escaping each other. The existing solutions were, in their basic forms, evolved by many nonhuman primates. Refining relationships *between* groups, however, is a task left to man. We shall see that the primate ways of emancipation from social space are never totally efficient. Spacing behavior remains the ultimate refuge when social relationships become unmanageable.

Social life in space can be reduced to two opposing tendencies, attraction and repulsion. Both have ecological origins. The resources of animal life are in general evenly distributed over the habitat. They are best exploited if the individuals scatter themselves, each one keeping as far as possible from its neighbors. The most general dispersing mechanism in vertebrates is intraspecific aggression and its counterpart, escape. Aggression is also one of the most problematic inventions in behavioral evolution. It required a host of refinements, checks, and counterdesigns.

Aggression necessarily conflicts, for example, with an even older design, that of sexual reproduction. In land animals, the male and the female must periodically come into physical contact to procreate. Such intimate contact arouses aggression which a strong sexual attraction must overcome. Hormones periodically produce this shift in favor of attraction, and the behavior of courtship is a device to synchronize the female's and the male's readiness to mate. Parental care for the young solves similar difficulties with similar means—by hormonal predisposition and by signals directing the partner's behavior and inhibiting his aggression. The attractions evolved for mating and for the care of the young are the evolutionary raw materials for the development of more complex societies (Wickler 1967).

THE BASIC PARAMETER: DISTANCE BETWEEN INDIVIDUALS   The metric distance between two animals emerges as a compromise between the forces of repulsion and attraction. By altering the ratio of these forces distance can be directly manipulated, as an example may show. Patas monkeys spend the day foraging in closed groups at a few meters from each other. At night they reduce the risk of massive predation by spacing out, each monkey sleeping alone on one of the scattered little trees of the savanna. As I observed in captive patas, this daily rhythm is caused by a fluctuation of intragroup aggression. Two monkeys that foraged five meters apart in the evening become intolerant of each other as dusk approaches. They begin to threaten each other; weaker animals withdraw from trees occupied by more dominant ones, and the group finally rests widely scattered when night falls.

The particular social structure of a species in part depends on different degrees of attraction between various types of members. Gelada baboons and patas monkeys are naturally organized in family groups containing only one male but several females. From this structure we may expect that the attraction between males is weaker (or counteracted by a stronger repulsion) than the attraction between females or between males and females. A study on the spatial behavior of the two species shows just that (Kummer, unpublished material). In addition, all patas distances are about ten times longer than the corresponding distances in geladas. Wild gelada groups actually live together in compact troops, whereas patas groups live far apart from each other. Our study indicated that the repulsion between patas males often outweighs attraction, whereas gelada males definitely prefer to stay close together. Preferred distances thus vary among species, and they are further differentiated according to sex. The typical spatial layout of a population or group appears as an expression of these differential affinities.

DISTANCE AND COMMUNICATION   Distance is manipulated by communication, but in turn, distance affects communication. At close range, social stimuli become so powerful that communicating becomes a compulsion. Crowding carries in it a constant provocation to react, to make one's activities dependent on others. The individual in a crowd tends to act and feel like its neighbors, due to a mechanism called social facilitation. This tendency, often deplored in humans, has its function. An animal approaching a water hole with its group must be induced to drink by seeing others drink even if it is not very thirsty. The group may not seek out water for the next twenty-four hours. Sufficient distance, on the other hand, gives freedom of movement, renders some social stimuli such as odors inefficient, and permits individual activity. By spacing out, an animal can remove itself from the compulsion to respond to its neighbors. In studying wild baboons I became convinced that the tendency to protect oneself against overstimulation is a second factor, besides aggression, that keeps individuals at a distance. Too great a distance, finally, will break communication completely, and this means losing the group.

Because distance and communication are interdependent, any change in the means of communication must thoroughly alter the spacing behavior of a species.

HANDLING INTERGROUP SPACE: THE TERRITORY   A freely mobile population constantly communicating about its spatial arrangements appears as a workable solution of attributing space to its members. But reality often goes a step further. Societies tend to formalize relationships between members, and between members and space, thus replacing the need for constant communication by fixed and recognized relationships which make the behavior of members mutually predictable. A first important formalization is a fixed relationship between animal and space known as the territory. A territory is a field of repulsion (and sometimes attraction) fixed in space. It includes all resources which its inhabitant or inhabitants require either for a specific activity like rearing young, or for permanent life. Instead of wandering about in search of these resources and clashing at intervals with other wanderers the animal settles

223

down. Territorial behavior is the rule where the animals *create* resources in many days' work. The great apes build nests every evening, which takes them only a few minutes; they are not territorial. Houses and stores for the winter months encourage territorial behavior in man.

Aggression may initially decide on who occupies the better sites and where the borders will be. Once this is settled, the movements of the owners become formalized and predictable; conflict is minimized. Everybody learns where the borders are and respects them at least for some time. An essential characteristic of the territory is that its boundaries are defended, but even this activity tends to settle in routine. Neighboring groups of Callicebus monkeys, for example, converge daily on fixed areas at their common boundary. A fight may follow, but usually the encounter is a harmless demonstration of power and presence by chases, visual displays, and calls (Mason 1968).

The territorial design, in general, works against change. It does so by a peculiar relationship between the owner and his space. Being on his own ground enhances the aggressive and assertive motivation of the owner and thereby his success in encounters with competitors (Leyhausen 1965). This effect is most marked in the center of the territory, and it fades out as the border is approached. Why this is so has never been fully explained, although Zajonc, in Chapter 4, contributes part of the answer. The fact is that an intruder fighting an owner must be very strong or very highly motivated to win. (In this light it seems deplorable that governments direct their wars from their own and not from the enemy's capital.)

Nonterritorial species, which live in undefended and overlapping home ranges, show a similar increase of escape motivation near the borders of their range. The center of a home range of hamadryas baboons is the cliff on which they sleep at night. Sometimes a troop will attempt to pass a night in a cliff of a neighboring troop, far away from its regular cliff. But even a large intruding troop hastily withdraws when it finds the cliff—unexpectedly perhaps—occupied by even a few of the regular residents. The increasing wariness of an animal leaving the center of its range must reduce its tendency to migrate. As a stabilizing factor, it helps to keep even nonterritorial groups where they are and to prevent the fusion of groups.

REDUCING INTRAGROUP DISTANCE: SUBMISSION   The territorial design eases the spacing problem by fixing "properties" in space, but it cannot do so for animals that must live together on the same grounds, in the same group. A male and a female living together as a breeding pair are faced with the original problem of attraction and repulsion in a mobile situation requiring constant equilibration and communication. No matter how aggressive the male is, the female must not escape him and the breeding site. A widely used solution is a complex of behavior called submission. The weaker animal, usually the female, no longer responds to aggression by the primitive means of escape in space. Instead, it communicates its inferior strength by submissive gestures that convey its helplessness. It turns its teeth away, exposes its more vulnerable parts to the aggressor, makes itself small. This reduces the challenge to the aggressor, his aggression is inhibited, and the weak may remain near the strong. Communication is not severed, and the pair or group is prevented from breaking up. Like the territory, submission reduces permanent conflict to a settled and recognized relationship.

The elegance of the submission design appears when we compare the behavior of patas monkeys and gelada baboons in a large enclosure (Kummer, unpublished material). Two patas males newly introduced to each other will fight. It soon becomes clear who is the stronger of the two. The loser will flee, but being prevented by the fence he cannot remove himself from the winner's sight. The winner continues to chase him at intervals, day after day, until the loser ceases to feed properly and has to be removed. The situation cannot be resolved except by spacing out beyond sight and hearing. The observation explains why natural patas groups contain only one male.

Two gelada males will also fight when they meet for the first time in the enclosure, and a winner will emerge within minutes. But once the loser has given up and withdraws, the stronger male completely changes his behavior. Instead of chasing, he slowly approaches the loser with the friendly gesture of lip-smacking. The weaker male will again withdraw or even attack when cornered, but the winner does not give in. He continues his friendly approaches until, after an hour perhaps, the loser's tension wears off. Finally, still nervously, the loser will present his rear to the winner as a gesture of submission. The winner continues in his efforts until the loser eventually dares to groom the winner's hair. From that point onward, friendly gestures and mutual grooming prevail; the two males wander side by side and feed at a few meters distance, and no other fight occurs. The essence of this bond is dominance and submission. Whereas a patas fight leads to total separation, the gelada fight must merely determine the fighters' relative status and, after an initial increase of distance, ends in bringing the males together. This explains why gelada males live together in large troops.

The dominance-submission design does not abolish the forces of attraction and repulsion, but it so much alters their ratio that communication need never be interrupted. It makes group life possible even for the aggressive.

SOCIAL CONTROLS OF GROUP SIZE   It would now be possible to add more and more males to such a gelada group, and the process of bond formation would be repeated. At a certain point, however, the group would split up; spacing out would take over again, now to separate the groups. What are the mechanisms that limit group size and prevent the accumulation of a whole population in one enormous group which no longer could survive on the resources within its reach?

First, a dominance order requires that all members are acquainted with the individual dominance positions. Such knowledge must be acquired and kept up to date by experience, which is obviously impossible when the group grows beyond a certain limit. Second, the scale of dominance has a limited extent. A very large group would include too many individuals of nearly equal status. The fighting of such equals would not readily be resolved and might, after some time, result in spatial separation.

At this point another and rather striking mechanism may come into play. Aggression, like other behavior, may be directed at another object than the one that arouses it, as we can observe in ourselves. The stranger and outsider may become the routine object of aggression originally generated within the group. Our geladas offer examples of this mechanism. In a pause between fights, two male geladas discovered their mirror images in the window of the observation cabin. The dim reflections must have appeared to them as strangers. Both started to threaten the reflections, and of course the strangers threatened back. Engaged in this common action against the outsiders, the two males gradually shifted closer to each other than ever before and even exchanged friendly lip-smacks between the threats against the mirror. In another instance, two gelada females fought intermittently for three days, unable to determine their dominance positions. We then released a number of juveniles into the enclosure. Immediately the two females threatened the newcomers. After a while, the females joined forces; within fifteen minutes they groomed each other for the first time, and they did not fight again as long as the youngsters were present. Thus the visible presence of outsiders may ease the aggressive pressure within the group. The mechanism has two distinct effects: It strengthens cohesion within the group and increases aggression and separation between the groups. The result is the

226

strikingly different treatment given by some animals to group members and outsiders. This, of course, is the very phenomenon which Halle (in Chapter 12) calls "the fallacy of the two species" in man. In monkeys, the mechanism is adaptive both in social and in ecological terms, since *their* groups must not cooperate, but separate.

Distinct and organized groups thus result from two sets of spacing mechanisms. Within the group, normal spacing-out is reduced by the spatial effect of submission and familiarity. Between the groups, the undiluted effect of spacing-out remains in force. It is probably increased by redirected intragroup aggression and by the wariness experienced by the group when it leaves its home range. These factors can vary in degree and they may selectively affect one sex or a certain age class. Their combination, together with nonsocial factors, determines the size of a group, the number of tolerated males, and whether it is open or closed to strangers.

HANDLING SPACE IN THE GROUP: PRIVACY, INHIBITIONS, AND TACTICS
Within the organized group the further evolutionary tendencies are to refine the handling of space, to overcome the effects of repulsion, and to reduce the compulsion to respond when distance is short. Emancipation from purely spatial equilibration is a necessity in large groups because no more than three animals can respect all preferred distances among them; with more individuals this is geometrically impossible. By being at the right distance from A and B a group member is automatically too close to C or too far from D. Being too far usually does no harm, but being too close may be disturbing or even dangerous. A simple solution in this case is to interrupt visual communication by hiding. A male hamadryas baboon attacks his female when he sees her mating with a subadult male. A female who has such intentions selects a place behind a rock, where her mate cannot see her. Man has extended the scheme by providing his houses not only with roofs but also with walls. The wall is a substitute for distance. Hiding is most often practiced by animals of inferior rank. Dominant ones, in contrast, may impose their visual effects by choosing a conspicuous place.

The addressee, too, has ways of avoiding communication. An animal can protect itself from visual stimuli by looking away. By sitting quietly and looking to the ground a monkey can virtually remove himself from the social field, thus substituting behavior for distance. By such "cut-off" behavior (Chance 1962) a monkey not only controls his own escape response, he is also less likely to be attacked.

Finally, the social stimulus can be made ineffective *within* the animal, by an inhibition to respond. Hamadryas baboons live in troops of a hundred or more animals. About 80 percent of the adult males own an exclusive harem of females to which no other male has access (Kummer 1968). The females are sexually receptive for only a few days each month. During these days they display a conspicuous swelling which is visible throughout the troop and which induces the males to mate. At any time, most of the males of a troop have no receptive females; those who have no females at all may have no chance to mate for months or years. For them, the constant presence of receptive females in the same troop is no little provocation. Nevertheless no adult male was ever seen to mate with a female of another male, regardless of an occasional opportunity. This is not because a male has no interest in another female; as soon as the owner of a harem is trapped and removed, the remaining males eagerly take over his females. Our recent field study has demonstrated that males are inhibited to touch a female of an established pair. The inhibition enables hamadryas family groups to live together in a troop. It depends, however, on one condition: In tense situations the harems must not mix in space. The mobile "social territory" of the male and his females, only a few meters in diameter, must be respected. This condition can be artificially destroyed by pouring out a pile of corn. The hamadryas groups then crowd at the corn, mix again and again, and finally the males' inhibitions break down. They begin to fight over their females. At this point the function of the now lost inhibition becomes clear. Many of the males lead their females away from the troop onto surrounding hills; the troop falls apart. With the inhibition lost, the baboons have to revert to the safe old mechanism of spacing out, just like the families of Bushmen mentioned by DeVore in Chapter 9.

An interesting though rare technique of keeping groups together is a reversal of the spacing effect of aggression. The hamadryas male must attempt to keep his female close to him within the troop. He trains her to remain near him by attacking her whenever she is too far away. Every hamadryas female has learned this lesson and, paradoxically, responds to a threat by coming closer.

Apart from the described suppressions of spacing-out the group, especially the primate group, there develops a refined use of space. When two animals compete for access to a third, a triangle situation arises. Among three animals distance is no longer the only spatial parameter; relative position in space becomes just as important. Primates are quite able to use elementary tactics. Captive gelada females competing for a male actually fight for the position between him and the rival female. The female who gains this central position has practically won. She is now able to prevent her rival from approaching the male but she has free access to him herself. The distant rival will attempt to bypass and outmaneuver the winner, while the winner carefully follows on a circle of smaller radius. The same tactics are used in larger gelada groups. When two males and several females had newly organized themselves in two harems, each female held a place in a straight spatial line between the two males. The two most dominant females kept closest to the males whereas the two least dominant ones were neighbors in the center of the line. Once dominance and group membership were stabilized and acknowledged the line of defense positions disappeared. Spacing behavior again was used as the safest social technique in a time of crisis.

CROWDING Submission, cutoff, and inhibition permit life in groups, but group life nevertheless means life in a crowd. The average primate group allows no privacy day or night.

A high rate of social stimuli may eventually produce the detrimental symptoms of stress (Christian and Davis 1964). Little research has been done on crowding in our closest animal relatives, but it seems that the mere density of individuals is not the most important cause of stress as long as the crowded group is stable and well organized. It is the social unrest following, for example, the introduction of strangers to a group, which most increases stressful encounters. Southwick (1967) found that reducing the size of a rhesus macaque cage by fifty percent raised aggression among the inhabitants by only twenty percent. A fifty-percent reduction in food diminished the frequency of aggression. But the introduction of strangers to the group upset the social balance and the frequency of aggression multiplied by five. In wild hamadryas baboons crowding provokes fighting indirectly, by creating uncertainty about group membership. The tiny almost-primate tupaia exhibits stress as a consequence of both crowding and aggression (Autrum and von Holst 1968). In the case of aggression, only the subordinate tupaia shows signs of stress, and these signs return whenever the dominant animal walks past, even long after the decisive fight. As in other mammals, stress in tupaia leads to sterility. Stressed females exhibit male copulatory behavior; hamadryas females do so in captivity, but not in the wild. Calhoun's work (1962, 1967) has demonstrated similar and more serious disturbances of social behavior in crowded rats.

The study of the more tense and complex societies of primates suggests at first that their members are more resistant to social stress than modern man. The primate tolerates a lifetime within six feet of his fellows; western man needs privacy. It is obvious that certain primate species have developed an extraordinary tolerance of social stimulation, but their lot is easier than ours in an important respect. Nonhuman primates, although crowded, live among familiar group members whose behavior they learned to predict. Since the primate group is acted out and separated in space, contacts with strangers are rare. Modern human groups, in contrast, are no longer spatially distinct; their members mix for most of the day. Many people spend much more time with virtual strangers than with truly familiar group members. An encounter with a stranger is not only less predictable but—in the context of work—it is often of great importance to the outcome of our own endeavors. Social encounters with unpredictable but critical outcome are comparable to the rare rank-establishing encounters between two unfamiliar monkeys; both involve an element of stress. Certain rules of human politeness (very obvious in past Chinese societies) offer a partial check. Two strangers may both insist on assuming the inferior status, thus avoiding an out-and-open exploration of their relative social positions. We quite generally refuse to establish relationships based on personal qualities with most people whom we meet for the first time.

In certain mammals population growth appears to be limited by the very stress induced by crowding. Crowded and stressed tupaia mothers fail to rub their young with the protective scent of their sternal glands. In consequence, the unscented young are killed and eaten by other group members. It is possible that the killing of infants by males helps to regulate population density in langur monkeys (Yoshiba 1968) and hamadryas baboons. In both species infant-killing is observed after drastic changes in social structure. In hamadryas baboons this very change of structure can be induced by artificial crowding. In man, approved practices of killing or abandoning infants as a means of population control were abandoned in historic times, and the rate of stress-induced death is unable to restrict the growth of populations. We have, of course, every reason to precede the action of such mechanisms with other measures, since few cultures might survive it. An ancillary measure to reduce stress from crowding is the appropriate structuring of available space. Experience with animals and humans demonstrates that adaptive architectural design eases or prevents the effects of high density (Hall 1966). Research into architecture must establish the relevant relationships (Sommer 1969). The results of such research must become at least as important in practical building as esthetic or financial considerations.

THE HERITAGE AND ITS LIMITS   This symposium has been stimulated by the theory that human social behavior has a biological basis inherited from nonhuman ancestors. The theory implies that cultural developments of social behavior are possible only within the limits set by our behavioral heritage. If this is true, research on these limits of our behavioral adaptability is of first-rate importance. In my view these limits exist beyond any reasonable doubt; but where exactly are they?

Some human ways of handling social space resemble common animal techniques. We may experience attraction and, at short distance, repulsion. It has been shown for at least one sample (Sommer 1959) that the prefered distances among women may be smaller than those among men. We feel an urge to interpret very close distances by communicating our intentions. In a crowd we tend to act and feel like the crowd. We may seek privacy behind visual screens; in addition, we reduce social stimulation by clothing and deodorants (Hall congratulates man for being a microsmat). Nations defend "territories." Individuals may give an angry look to intruders on their premises. Approaching the center of another person's private area reduces our self-confidence. An executive therefore meets an esteemed visitor at the door of his office, but he awaits at his desk a subordinate whom he wishes to reduce in status. Armies and business organizations seem to operate by a formalized dominance. Since these groups are too large to allow personal experience of all individual ranks, status is marked by brass on shoulders and by titles on office doors. Enemies may be as necessary to the cohesion of some human groups as they are to some animal groups. The human inhibitions that secure the integrity of territorial property and social ties resemble those found in primates, although for some reason human inhibitions must often be reinforced by ancestral spirits or courts. Relative position in space is used on the battlefield and to separate incompatible dinner guests. The human male, like other primate males, is more apt to leave the group, to wander, and to explore than the human female.

Examples of such similarities between man and animals (*some* animals, that is) could be amplified almost *ad libitum*. Many of them will not withstand scrutiny, but in their totality they make it more probable that we inherited much of our spatial behavior from prehuman ancestors than that we invented the same patterns all over again on the cultural level. Assuming for the moment that this is so, we shall be most interested, in relation to present human problems, in the flexibility of such behavior, that is, in the limits within which it may safely be altered *beyond* the range of known cultural variation.

The study of primate behavior offers some hopes that spacing behavior may be relatively open to environmental influence. Aggressive spacing, territoriality, and closed groups are not engrained, pervading attributes of the primate order. They appear here and there in varying intensity, often with little relationship to taxonomic positions. They seem to be common primate potentials which, however, appear and disappear relatively fast in evolution. Man's closest relatives for instance, the great apes, are relatively unaggressive; they do not defend territories, and their groups are open to strangers. We do not know whether this resembles our own ancestral condition. If it does, we have, in a relatively short period, swung toward the opposite (Reynolds 1966), approaching the style of macaques and baboons.

More relevant to man's problems is the flexibility observed within the same species. The vervet monkey is territorial in some areas but not in others (Gartlan and Brain 1968). Gibbons, naturally organized in territorial pairs, are not territorial in small cages but breed there nevertheless. One of our recent field experiments has demonstrated a high flexibility of spacing behavior in baboons. Transferred into a group of anubis baboons, a hamadryas female reverts her spacing behavior. After half an hour she no longer approaches an attacking male but flees like an anubis female. The reverse experiment is yet more instructive; an anubis female in a hamadryas troop learns, within one hour, to approach the male who attacks her although it is almost certain that none of her ancestors behaved this way. But the really interesting lesson of this experiment is that most anubis females, after learning the new behavior to perfection, suddenly escaped the herding male and left the troop for good. Learning was not enough; these females had gone beyond some limit of their behavioral adaptability. They provide a model case of what I meant by the "limits within which behavior can be *safely* altered."

CONCLUSIONS Let me conclude by characterizing the evolutionary stage of spacing mechanisms at which primates leave off and man, perhaps, takes over. The use of ecological resources requires animals to space-out, and aggression provides the principal means to do so. In primates, selective pressures introduced the life in permanent groups. The spacing problem thus took two different forms: Groups still had to keep apart for ecological reasons, but group members had to remain together. Nearly all subsequent refinements in the handling of social space were designed for intragroup use, as checks on the factors that tend to disperse. In comparison, intergroup relations could safely be left at an archaic state, with territorial behavior as the only major elaboration. Intergroup relations in man still show archaic traits. Social behavior in foreign politics certainly falls short of the standards of the average citizen.

In considering spatial behavior in modern man we must keep in mind that space and distance in themselves are socially meaningless. What matters is the behavioral potential of a spatial arrangement. Being far apart means having time to respond, being close means having to respond at short notice. Being between two other animals prevents their interaction. These implications of a spatial situation entirely depend on two factors: the participants' speed of movement and the range of their means of communication. Both factors remain constant in animal societies and their importance is easily overlooked. But both speed and the range of communication undergo drastic changes in our own species. A total application of electrical technology would make our arrangement in space socially irrelevant, except at the one-to-ten-meter level of a cocktail party. This development would by itself close the chapter of spacing behavior in technical man, were it not for another behavioral heritage. Behavior is easily redirected and transferred to new objects and contexts. Territorial tendencies, for example, can reemerge in the handling of information. Crowding and privacy are now possible without any connection to meters and miles, but our responses to them remain. Our attention should follow the old mechanisms into the new media.

REFERENCES

Autrum, H., and D. von Holst.
1968. "Sozialer 'Stress' bei Tupajas (*Tupaia glis*) und seine Wirkung auf Wachstum, Körpergewicht und Fortpflanzung." *Zeitschrift für vergleichende Physiologie,* 58:347–355.
Calhoun, J. B.
1962. "Population Density and Social Pathology." *Scientific American,* 206 (February):139–148.
1967. "Ecological Factors in the Development of Behavioral Anomalies, Part I: Sociocultural Environmental Factors." In *Comparative Psychopathology,* Grune and Stratton, editors.
Carpenter, C. R.
1964. *Naturalistic Behavior of Nonhuman Primates.* University Park, Pennsylvania: Pennsylvania State University Press.
Chance, M. R. A.
1962. "An Interpretation of Some Agonistic Postures: the Role of 'Cut-off' Acts and Postures." *Symposium of the London Zoological Society,* 8:71–89.

Christian, J. J., and D. E. Davis.
  1964. "Endocrines, Behavior, and Population." *Science,* 146:1550–1560.
Gartlan, J. S., and C. K. Brain.
  1968. "Ecology and Social Variability in *Cercopithecus aethiops* and *C. mitis.*" In *Primates: Studies in Adaptation and Variability,* Phyllis Jay, editor. New York: Holt, Rinehart & Winston.
Hall, E. T.
  1966. *The Hidden Dimension.* New York: Doubleday.
Kummer, H.
  1968. *Social Organization of Hamadryas Baboons.* Chicago: Chicago University Press.
Leyhausen, P.
  1965. "The Sane Community—A Density Problem?" *Discovery,* 26:27–33.
Mason, W. A.
  1967. "Use of Space by *Callicebus* Groups." In *Primates: Studies in Adaptation and Variability,* Phyllis Jay, editor. New York: Holt, Rinehart & Winston.
McBride, G., J. W. James, and R. N. Shoffner.
  1963. "Social Forces Determining Spacing and Head Orientation in a Flock of Domestic Hens." *Nature,* 197:1272–1273.
Reynolds, V.
  1966. "Open Groups in Hominid Evolution." *Man,* 1:441–452.
Sommer, R.
  1959. "Studies in Personal Space." *Sociometry,* 22:247–260.
  1969. *Personal Space.* New Jersey: Prentice Hall.
Southwick, C. H.
  1967. "An Experimental Study of Intragroup Agonistic Behavior in Rhesus Monkeys (*Macaca mulatta*)." *Behaviour,* 28:182–209.
Wickler, W.
  1967. "Vergleichende Verhaltensforschung und Phylogenetik." In *Die Evolution der Organismen,* G. Heberer, editor. Stuttgart: Gustav Fischer.
Wynne-Edwards, V. C.
  1962. *Animal Dispersion in Relation to Social Behavior.* Edinburgh: Oliver and Boyd.
Yoshiba, Y.
  1968. "Local and Intertroop Variability in Ecology and Social Behavior of Common Indian Langurs." In *Primates: Studies in Adaptation and Variability,* Phyllis Jay, editor. New York: Holt, Rinehart & Winston.

CHAPTER 7

SOURCES OF COOPERATION IN ANIMALS AND MAN

JOHN H. CROOK

UNIVERSITY OF BRISTOL

The current public and academic fascination with the implications of animal behavior research for an understanding of human society is in part a consequence of an extraordinary neglect of man's biological roots by social scientists. After vigorously establishing the autonomy of social anthropology, sociology, and other related disciplines the practitioners of these subjects are at last considering the impact of Darwin's thought on humanity as a whole. So far, however, the interest in ethology has focused upon a Darwinism largely dressed in a fashionable Lorenzian form.

Unfortunately, this particular formulation of the subject, based largely on the ethology of the late 1930s, is for the most part inadequate as a tool in the analysis of the complex social processes of higher vertebrates —especially community-living mammals. Many questions posed by ungulate, carnivore, or primate societies simply cannot be answered meaningfully using the limited propositions of an earlier ethology developed in studies of fish, reptiles, and birds. The subject today needs additional or new approaches for an adequate examination of these problems. Thus, while social anthropologists show an increasing interest in ethology, modern ethologists, in their turn, are inspecting social psychology and sociology for possible analytical tools.

The phenomenon of cooperation between individuals in producing a behavioral effect poses questions of exactly the kind of complexity that current ethology finds difficult to treat. Indeed, biologists generally have found themselves at a loss in formulating an analytical approach to such cases. In the context of natural selection, of micro-evolution, and of behavioral genetics, the cooperative behavior often shown by higher animals remains an undigested lump that many have evidently preferred to ignore. Yet, for man, perhaps the most fundamental problem of our time is an adjustment between competition and cooperation at every level of human function: the international, the institutional, the township, the familial, and the personal. Possibly an understanding of those processes of cooperation occurring in higher mammals may provide us with an

237

account of the sources from which human cooperative behavior springs and of some of the forces that prevent its expression.

Our initial problem is to identify those animal analogs of human cooperation that may be useful to such an inquiry. Although of manifest academic interest, the proto-cooperative behavior and contingent environmental conditioning shown by the lower phyla of the animal kingdom (Allee 1938) will not concern us here; nor will we be interested in behavior that appears to be programed purely genetically. The cooperative behavior that concerns us consists rather in the high-order consequences of multifactorial behavioral determination during the ontogeny of advanced mammals and birds. While genetics, child-rearing processes, and social and proto-cultural influences are all involved, it is not in our interest here to attempt a disentangling of such factors. The identification of cases of sufficient complexity and a look at the processes operating at the social level at the time of their occurrence must, for the moment, suffice.

To begin with we need some definition of human cooperation to use as our model in choosing relevant animal examples for study. Cooperation, we may say, is the collaborative behavior of two or more persons in the production of some common behavioral effect. Such behavior is commonly directed toward some goal or to the completion of some preconceived task in which there is common interest, emotional satisfaction or reward. The collaborative behavior may entail work in common or varying degrees of division of labor to produce the required effect. The motivational sources of the behavior are not likely to be simple and their analysis may require an understanding of the person's history—possibly in psychodynamic terms. Cooperation normally occurs within the context of shared social norms and a common code of conduct. The proximate causal determinants of the behavior lie at several levels including the innate and learned bases of reciprocal action, traditional habits, and contractual obligations.

Human cooperation occurs at its most complex in the integrated work schedules of complex institutions—governments, universities, business firms, banks, ships—but even in such cases it comprises elements also found in the football match, in assistance given after a road accident, or in domestic washing-up. The term cooperation refers to a characteristic type of intragroup behavior rather than to the specific behavior of an individual participating in it. Cooperation, moreover, occurs within a social structure based in part upon caste and class distinction, status hierarchy and other products of group and individual competition. Both cooperation and competition exist together in any human organization; they are not simply the opposites of one another. Both belong to the process.

In observing animals we have no means of asking the subject for its "reasons" for doing something, although the past history of an organism and the environmental context may allow us to infer something regarding its motivation. Nevertheless, an intensive study allows us to determine the size of an animal's behavioral repertoire and the probability of a cooperative response occurring in relation to a given set of stimuli. There is, in fact, a gradient or range of cases in which the autonomy of the individual in relation to its milieu steadily increases and in which the flexibility of response becomes increasingly pronounced.

At this point it is worthwhile emphasizing an important distinction. We have said that cooperation comprises a type of intragroup or inter-individual behavior rather than denoting simply the behavior of individuals. Cooperation thus refers to a group process—it is a group characteristic. Now in discussing behavioral evolution it is usual for ethologists to argue from a neo-Darwinian viewpoint—that is to say they commonly attribute change solely to the natural selection of the genetic basis of individual behavior. Few ethologists have ever considered whether such an approach is adequate to an analysis of group processes although this is clearly the basis of what social anthropologists would call culture. It seems that in asking what factors act to program the patterns of group behavior, close attention must be paid to the direct intervention of both the physical and the social milieus. The programing of what goes on in a herd, for example, depends not only on the genetics of the individuals in it but also on the social composition of the herd membership and the frequency of water holes.[1] So also with cooperation. This means that in tracing the emergence of the phenomenon we are not concerned solely with adaptation from the genetic selectionist viewpoint but also with the direct reactivity of a system in relation to its circumstances. Such a system is open rather than closed, adaptive rather than merely homeostatic and responsive rather than autonomic, Lamarckian as well as Darwinian. It has history—let us say—rather than evolution in the strictist biological sense of that term.

---

[1] *Editor's note:* The author here is referring to the fact that within the home range of a species, the water-hole distribution can profoundly affect the distances that have to be traversed and the dependent concentration effect of the herd on a daily basis at restricted watering places. This is used as just one example of the influence of environment upon social behavior. (J.F.E.)

JOHN H. CROOK

The evolution of group processes cannot be reduced simply to a study of the nature of the separate members. Reductionism is not enough. And this seems to be as true of the higher animals as it is obviously true with regard to man.

ADVANCED COOPERATIVE BEHAVIOR IN ANIMALS   Cooperative behavior in nonhuman mammals and in birds crops up quite frequently in many contexts and in a diversity of species. A prime requirement for its occurrence appears to be some structural complexity in the social relations of a population. Mammals that live solitarily in burrow-centered territories for the greater part of the year and whose most complex social unit is the mother-litter family usually have a limited repertoire of patterns of social interaction. The same applies to the more solitary birds usually living in large territories. By contrast, birds and mammals living in densely congregated colonies, in mobile troops, or in groups in which long-term monogamous or polygamous pair-bonding has developed commonly show some emergence of group coordination. It is among these species that instances of cooperation are most readily found.

The adaptive significance of living in complex social organizations is receiving increasing attention at the present time (Crook 1965, 1970; Wynne-Edwards 1962; Lack 1968; Orians 1968). Briefly we may say that the emergence of animal societies with complex structures reflects an adaptation of the species in relation to aspects of its ecological niche. Gregarious birds breed in colonies where nesting habitats are relatively inaccessible to predators, large enough to contain nests, and with an adequate food supply near at hand for the rearing of young. In some colonies the reduction of territory size contingent upon crowding has led to the formation of vast fused nests or "lodges," the structure of which may be maintained cooperatively. Communal behavior in birds probably occurs in "clans" arising through the continued association of young with parents. The participation of the young in brood care rather than attempting to reproduce themselves appears, in certain limiting environments, to be the most likely way to ensure the participants' contribution to the next generation. Such species may show communal nest construction, brooding, care of young, and in one case food storage. Among mammals, herd and troop formation appear related to particular conditions of predation and food-resource dispersion in time and space (Eisenberg 1966).

Cooperative behavior in birds and mammals occurs in a number of contexts but particularly in relation to food storage, territorial defense, mutual protection against predators, in group hunting, in parental care

240

and also in infant care by individuals other than the actual parents, and, finally, at its most complex in the cooperative control of social interaction in certain primate groups.

In food storage certain group-living species work together to establish stores which are utilized by the communal group as a whole (Ritter 1938, Morris 1962). Individuals here work separately, however, and the behavior does not involve either a close interlinking of the behavior of two or more individuals or the reciprocally related response delays of individuals alternating in performance of complex task-oriented cooperation (Crook 1966a). In several mammals, members of a group territory will act together in its defense against a neighboring group and complex battles sometimes occur (Mykytowicz 1960; King 1955; Southwick, Beg, and Siddiqi 1965). Sometimes certain individuals give vocal and visual signal support to displaying primate males on territorial boundaries (Carpenter 1965, Gartlan 1966, Jolly 1966). Mutual protection against predators is well known in certain group-living mammals including musk oxen, the water vole, baboons, and the rhesus monkey (Ryder 1962, Wilson 1968, etc.). Cooperative hunting in group fishing activities is known from both cormorants and pelicans (Bartholomew 1942). Many cases of cooperative hunting by wolves and hunting dogs are reported in which some animals trail the prey while others cut corners to shorten the chase.

Assistance at the nests in the care of young by birds other than the parents is known in a number of species (Skutch 1935, Davis 1942), and can be shown to be functional in relation to the ecological niche of the species (Lack 1968). Instances of assistance in parental care are found among several species of mammals and are the focus of rapidly developing research. Probably the number of species in which it occurs is much larger than is at present known. It happens for instance in mice, also among dolphins where the newborn has to be taken rapidly to the surface if it is to commence breathing. The group hunting of hunting dogs (Kühme 1965) includes a complex cooperation between hunters and den-dwelling mothers in the feeding of young. Further cases occur among primates and, because of their complexity and their significance to man, we will examine them in detail.

PARENTAL "AUNT" AND "UNCLE" BEHAVIOR IN PRIMATES   An interest in newborn babies by female companions of a mother has been reported in several species—certain lemurs, howlers, langurs, rhesus, Japanese and barbary macaques, baboons, and gorillas (DeVore 1965). Studies of such behavior using captive groups has clarified many of the problems

241

involved. In particular R. A. Hinde and his collaborators at Madingley, Cambridge, have analyzed so-called aunt[2] behavior within a rhesus group, the members of which had been studied in detail for several years.

Aunt behavior arises from the responses of a (usually) childless female to the presence of a mother-baby pair (Spencer-Booth 1968) and at first may be resented by the mother. It gradually becomes a highly cooperative activity with survival value for the young. Rowell, Hinde, and Spencer-Booth (1964) report that most of the rhesus mothers eventually accepted the attentions of at least one aunt with whom they were willing to leave the babies. The aunt was usually a female that had been a chief sitting and grooming companion. One mother which had allowed her "best friend" to hold the baby when it was only six days old subsequently died when the baby was aged eight months. The aunt adopted the baby with minimum disturbance.

In the wild, aunt behavior probably has great survival value, aiding in the protection of the child during the mother's lifetime and leading to its adoption on her death. Macaque troops are apparently structured into castes (Imanishi 1960) and contain many affiliative subgroups. It is highly likely that a mother's "best friends" are usually those who, if themselves childless at the time, play the role of aunt. Probably, too, the aunts are close kin to the mother. If so, their behavior may well help perpetuate their own genes in the forthcoming generations (Hamilton 1963, also chapter 2 in this volume).

Mother-aunt interaction is complex. Mothers of newborn babies at first resist the approach of aunts and keep the babies to themselves. Aunts are persistent animals, however, and during the first few weeks of a baby's life they use various cunning devices that enable them to approach the baby without upsetting the mother: sidling up while pretending to forage, or grooming the mother until her attention is elsewhere and then surreptitiously grooming the baby until she looks again.

As babies become mobile they inevitably interact frequently with the ever-hovering aunts. Aunts carry and cuddle babies, play with them and look after them both in relation to swinging cage doors and to the occasional antagonisms of other companions. Babies sometimes anger the aunt and then, if the mother is not too near, the baby gets a cuffing.

---

[2] *Editors' notes:* The "aunt" phenomenon is not necessarily confined to primates but an emergent form of cooperation in long-lived group-living mammals, e.g., *Elephas, Loxodonta,* and *Tursiops* (Eisenberg 1966) (J.F.E.). The term "aunt" as used here does not imply any particular geneological relationship although kinship studies in monkeys suggest that some females showing aunt behavior in nature may be quite close kin to the mothers of the young involved. (W.D.)

Aunt-infant interactions change in type and relative frequency as the infant gets older and they gradually develop into "friendly relations" characterized by adult patterns of mutual grooming. The relations between aunt and mother are affected by the relative dominance of the two animals. The aunts which showed most carrying and cuddling toward infants were all subordinate to the mother. Mothers appeared to prefer attention from subordinate aunts rather than from those dominant to them. High-ranking mothers could control the interactions of others with their babies by low-intensity threat, but low-ranking mothers had to "grin" or "present" to potential aunts more dominant than they. The pattern of interactions is thus intimately related to the social position of the participants within the group defined in terms of age status, relative dominance, degree of mutual affiliation, age of the baby, and the resultant frequencies of behavioral interactions of specified types.

The long-term effects of the activities of aunts on the behavior of infants remain to be assessed, but Hinde and Spencer-Booth (1967) have shown that their presence affects the frequencies of a number of interaction patterns of infant and mother rhesus. In the absence of aunts and other adult companions mothers are less restrictive and infants wander more. Because these babies lack play and aunt companions, however, they also return more frequently to the mother. This leads to a higher proportion of infant rejections in the behavior of the isolate mother when compared with those living in normal groups.

In the Madingley study, male rhesus macaques were found to show very little behavioral interaction with babies, although males about two years older than the infant tended to show more of such behavior than did others (Spencer-Booth 1968). Likewise, in the wild, rhesus males do not evidently show much interest in infants (Southwick, Beg, and Siddiqi 1965), although in some five *Macaca* species a degree of male interest in young animals is known (Gifford 1967). Particularly notable is the generalized "paternal" behavior of wild male Japanese macaques investigated by Itani (1959). Males behaving in this way may perhaps be called "uncles."[3] Adult male Japanese macaques become interested in juvenile animals when the latter are one year old. At this time females are in the birth season and cease protecting the young of the previous year. The males appear to restrict their interest in young animals primarily to this period. Their behavior consists in hugging and sitting

---

[3] *Editor's note:* Again there is no implication regarding geneological relationship, although some degree of kinship is likely in nature. (W.D.)

with the infant, accompanying it on the move, protecting it from other monkeys and dangerous situations, and grooming it.

Although Itani found no relationship between dominance, as such, and the frequency of child care, he did find the behavior to be especially developed in middle-class animals of the caste-structured troops. The behavior indeed seemed pronounced in animals that were sociable, not aggressive and oriented toward high-caste animals. Itani suggests that certain monkeys by showing care to high-caste infants succeed in being tolerated by leaders and their affiliated females and may therefore rise in rank. Protectors usually behave in a mild manner which may facilitate both their association with infants and their rise in rank. It is not clear, however, whether the effect on rank lasts for more than the birth season. Itani gives no details on permanent changes in social structure so produced. The adult males appear to protect one-year-old males and females equally, but more second-year females than males are protected owing to the peripheral social ranking of young males. Any protected two-year-olds are moreover often poorly grown individuals that were protected by the same male in the previous year. Protection has a further interesting effect in that adults more readily learn to investigate the new foods a progressive infant has discovered than would otherwise be the case.

Itani found cases of paternal care to be common only in three of eighteen troops investigated. It occurred very rarely in seven others and was not observed in the remaining eight. The behavior thus appears to be a local cultural phenomena. It undoubtedly provides additional chances of survival for young animals likely to be relatives, may improve their social status in the group, increases the rate of spread of new patterns of behavior in the group, and—since its frequency differs between troops—may increase the reproductive success of some monkey groups over others.

Recent observations on the Barbary macaque (*Macaca sylvana*) both in captivity (Lahiri and Southwick 1966, Gifford 1967) and in wild groups in the Moyen Atlas of Morocco (Deag and Crook 1971) show that adult males exhibit an extraordinary amount of interest in young babies of the year. An interest in babies this young was relatively uncommon in Itani's study. Furthermore, the wild male Barbary macaque does not seem, on present evidence, to limit his interest to a particular infant. He appears to appropriate babies from females in the group and to groom and care for them for short periods, usually under fifteen minutes in length. Babies may, moreover, move away from their mothers to accompany males, commonly riding off on their backs. Babies also move from one male to another. Males carrying babies frequently approach

244

males without them in such a way as to encourage the approached animal to engage in a mutual grooming session with the baby as target. In some of these sequences babies are presented to the second male while on the back of the approacher, the first male turning its rear toward the other male (as it would do in sexual presenting), as it does so. In some cases the approached male was seen to mount and thrust an animal that had done this. It appears, too, that most males approaching with babies are relatively juvenile animals that are relatively subordinate. They may be using the babies in some way to improve their relations with higher ranking males.

Thus, far too little is known about the social structure of the Barbary macaque to show whether there is a caste system comparable to that described from Japan. Whether males are using the babies as a means to increase their social standing and, hence, their freedom to behave without the constraints imposed by low rank, remains unknown. It does seem, however, that in both species not only does the male's behavior increase the chances of survival for young animals but it appears to be closely related to the structure of the monkey group and the pattern of constraints regulating social mobility of individuals within it. We do not know yet whether the behavior of the Barbary macaque male is restricted, as it is with the Japanese macaques, to certain troops and localities or whether it is a general phenomenon found throughout the species.

In the hamadryas baboon, behavior by subadult males toward juvenile females has effects of the utmost consequence for the social organization of the species. Kummer (1968) describes how such animals steal young females from their mothers and attend them with every semblance of solicitous maternal care. The young female is trained under punishment not to run away. At this stage there is no sexual behavior for the female is as yet too young. Nevertheless this acquisition of females is one of the ways by which the maturing male gradually acquires a harem. Apparent cooperation in child care is thus again seen to have a profound relationship to group structure and social dynamics.

SOCIAL CONTROL OF INDIVIDUAL BEHAVIOR IN PRIMATE GROUPS For many years the structure of primate groups was analyzed primarily in terms of dominance. The existence of a status hierarchy was generally thought to stabilize relationships through the reduction of social tension— each animal knowing its place. Often animals were found to cooperate either in the enforcement of existing rank relations or, by contrast, in upsetting them. Cooperation in social control emerges as an important problem area in primate social research. Recently it has become apparent, however, that the simple dominance concept was not only inadequately defined and carrying many unwarranted motivational overtones but that the description of group structure in dominance terminology was in many species not only a difficult task but also an inappropriate procedure (Gartlan 1968).

In an important discussion of dominance in a captive baboon group, Rowell (1966) implies that relative rank depends upon a continuous learning process in relation to rewards in inter-individual competition for environmental or social goals. This occurs, moreover, against a background of differential kinship status and the observational learning of the behavioral styles of companions. Relative rank is much affected by health. Dominance ranking is based upon the approach-retreat ratio in encounters between two individuals in a group. Measures of rank by differing criteria do not, however, necessarily correlate and Rowell found no single criterion for high rank. Using simpler organisms (weaver birds) Crook and Butterfield (1968) also showed that ranking according to the maintenance of spatial position on perches, ranking according to competitive access to nest-building materials, and ranking by the amount of building done did not necessarily correlate. The rank hierarchies in these birds depend upon different hormonal factors or combinations of such factors in the three cases. The same is probably true of primate behavior.

Rowell (1966) also shows that apparent rank is a function of the behavior of the relatively subordinate. High-rankers evidently feel free to initiate interactions. These initiations commonly lead to some suppression in a continuing activity by a subordinate or to an outright conflict. Subordinates learn to avoid such situations. Avoidance learning leads to behavioral restraint that leaves high-rankers even greater freedom of movement, easy access to commodities and freedom to initiate behavior with others. In competition for commodities in short supply, low-rankers are likely to suffer deprivation (see discussion in Crook and Butterfield 1970) and, in social relations, repeated constraint may involve physiological "stress" and concomitant behavioral abnormality.

Hall and DeVore (1965) describe the "dynamics of threat behavior" in wild baboon troops. A male's dominance status relative to others is a function not only of his fighting ability but also of his ability to enlist the support of other males. In one group studied, two adult males formed a central hierarchy—the pivot around which the social behavior of the group was organized. When one of these two died, the remaining one was unable to prevent the third-ranking male in cooperation with a newcomer (a subordinate male that had left another troop) from establishing themselves as central. The third male and the newcomer had evidently become affiliated when both had been relatively peripheral in the group structure. Common mutually supporting behavior seems to have been the pre-condition for their "success" in later assuming high rank. By so doing they gained the freedom to express behavior in the absence of previous constraints and to initiate behavior as and when they wished.

Wilson (1968) provides further information on mutual support in a study of the feral rhesus troops on Cayo Santiago Island. Young males tend to leave the smaller groups and move into the all-male peripheral areas of larger ones. When they do this they are commonly attacked unless they gain the protection of another male already established there. It so happens that males that give support are usually relatives, even brothers, who originated from the same natal group as the "protegé."

The inadequacies of the dominance terminology have led Bernstein and Sharpe (1966), Rowell (1966), and Gartlan (1968) to describe the social positions of individuals in a group in terms of roles. Roles are defined in terms of the relative frequencies (percent of group occurrence, for example) with which individuals perform certain behavioral sequences. When the behavior set of an individual or class of individuals is distinct the animal is said to show a "role."

Bernstein (1966) emphasizes the importance of the role of "control animal" in primate groups and shows that such a role may occur in a group of capuchins in which no clear status hierarchies can be established. The prime responses of a control animal are assuming a position between the group and a source of external disturbance or danger, attacking and thereby stopping the behavior of a group member that is distressing another, and generally approaching and terminating cases of intragroup disturbance. Whether a control animal is also recognizably "dominant" or a "leader" (in the sense of determining direction of march) depends upon the social structure in which he or she is situated.

Control animals in baboon and macaque troops are commonly also either the dominant (at least by certain criteria) or at least a prominent member of a central class. In addition to the properties listed above, the control animal shows a capacity for enlisting aid from affiliated animals in carrying out his activities of social control, in being a recipient for the "presenting" responses of subordinates and in being the focal point of "protected threat" (Kummer 1957) whereby lower-ranking animals regulate their agonistic encounters by reference to his spatial position. In baboons and macaques it seems that a male maintains his role primarily by gaining the cooperative support of other males, but his often superior

247

physical strength cannot always resist a combination of assertive animals should such a subgroup develop in his troop. In addition, Japanese workers have established that mutual support and affiliation often comes from close kin so that a central hierachy may, in some troops of Japanese macaques at least, virtually represent a caste or "establishment." This is, however, by no means always the case. Baboons and macaques moving into a troop or group from outside, either directly from another group or after a period of relatively solitary existence, can attain high rank and even control by virtue of establishing affiliations with others. Clearly the social skills involved must relate to the individual personalities of the animals concerned. The process of attaining high rank is unlikely to depend on accidental social conditioning.

In species whose reproductive unit is a one-male group (harem), rather than a multi-male troop, the nature of the hierarchical structure differs. There are usually many males peripheral to the reproductive units or living in separate all-male groups. Kummer (1968) has shown that young male hamadryas baboons, in addition to establishing the nucleus of a harem by appropriating juvenile females from the mothers, also manage to enter existing harems and become established there. In this most important field study, Kummer shows that a young male enters by adopting a submissive behavior style that makes him acceptable to the harem male. The two gradually develop a working partnership. As the older male ages the younger animal acquires sexual access to the females but the older animal retains control of group movement and daily routine. A complex system of mutual "notification" is set up between them whereby the possibility of mutual misunderstanding is greatly reduced. As Chance (1967) has emphasized, primates living in groups are constantly watching one another and their mutual attention underlies the control of behavior in a group.

So far we do not know how far the hamadryas "two-male team" is paralleled in other harem living primates. Geladas certainly live in harems that often contain a large subadult male in addition to the adult (Crook 1966b). How this association is established is not yet known. Among patas monkeys, females appear to play important roles in controlling group behavior, for the male spends much time partially withdrawn from the group and behaving as a watchdog in relation to predators (Hall 1965).

In all these cases cooperative behavior between males ensures the relative stabilization of group behavior, thereby providing optimum social circumstances for the rearing of young. Vandenbergh (1967) records how the absence of a kinship structure and clear male control in macaque groups newly established on a small island apparently accounted for their social instability. Similar effects have been noted in other mammals. Calhoun (1962) has demonstrated that female rats living in groups controlled by the activities of a powerful male were reproductively more successful and such groups were more socially stable than others.

It may be that cooperative behavior in social control is biologically advantageous for the practitioners. Cooperation with powerful kin—for instance, a brother—may enhance the chances of the passage of some of one's own genes to a later generation. The kinship structure of macaques makes this seem likely even though relatively few males (the dominants) appear to fertilize females in estrus. Furthermore, for the fathers, it is essential that the social stability of the group is such as to optimize the chances for successful rearing of young by the mothers.

Peripheral males in coordination may, as we have seen, upset a given hierarchy and then play the usurped roles. Peripheral males also have the option of leaving the group with affiliated females and setting up a freshly structured unit. In Kummer's hamadryas harems the old male gains the assistance of a physically strong youngster in defense and in social control, while the youngster gradually acquires sexual control of the females and can utilize the wisdom of the elder with regard to food foraging in various seasons.

All these cases of cooperation occur, nevertheless, in a highly competitive situation giving rise to the various types of hierarchy, classes, and castes. The motivational sources of cooperation thus appear to be exceptionally complex. Do the animals practice cooperation as a subterfuge for gaining or maintaining rank? Do they perhaps mitigate the disastrous effects of direct competition through aggression by an indirect competition mediated through cooperation? How is the genuine "altruism" of both males and females in relation to young animals in danger related to the complex competitive environment of the group? If we could answer these questions, we would be a long way toward stating in what way nonhuman primate studies are relevant to man.

COMPETITION AND CONTINGENT COOPERATION: A WORKING HYPOTHESIS We may try to pull together the existing shreds of evidence into an open-end working hypothesis that may prove useful in future research direction. Child-care behavior and mutual affiliation are considered the basic behavior systems from which cooperative behavior in higher mammals, particularly in nonhuman primates, emerges.

Parental care of young animals in distress or danger is well known and is also commonly shown by individuals of the same (occasionally of other) species that are not the actual father or mother of the juvenile concerned. Probably the basis for these responses is genetically programed. In populations with relatively limited dispersal from natal areas, and also in those societies partly or largely composed of blood relatives, the behavior would appear biologically advantageous to an individual in that it increases the chances of passing on some elements of its own gene compliment to the next generation. Selection may thus favor the evolution of child-oriented behavior by some such process as kin selection (Hamilton 1963).

Animals brought up in groups of more or less common descent are likely to affiliate more strongly with those nearest to them in the same matrilineal family or reproductive group. Such affiliation is likely to be compounded from the experience of mutual play, supporting behavior in juvenile "protected threat" situations, and a common aversion to a novel animal. The affiliative process also ensures a preference for in-group company. In addition the common experience of males, for example, in the periphery of the same social unit, may lead to an affiliation between animals even though they may not be descended from the same natal group. This seems, however, likely to be a less frequent basis for affiliation than familial relationship and kinship.

Child-care behavior and mutual affiliation occur in social contexts commonly marked by high competitiveness in relation to both environmental (food, drink, sleeping ledges) and social commodities (access to estrous females, opportunities for motivational expression without social constraints). Since some animals are "more equal than others," the stronger will tend to gain access to commodities of both categories more easily. They will also have greater freedom for the expression of behavior advantageous to them in numerous contexts (such as in foraging and copulating). Open aggressive conflict in competitive situations is likely to be both painful and harmful particularly to weaker animals, and hence increasingly avoided by them. In every generation an individual discovers its relative social position in relation to its peers both through real competition and through mock competition particularly during play. Many behavior mechanisms, such as mutual grooming, are apparently used to lessen the impact of antagonism, to reduce the tension between individuals, and in some cases to maintain sexual bonds outside a mating period. The effect of these interactions will be the emergence of an individual style of behavior for each animal. The style adopted by an individual in encounters with each other member of the group defines the animal's social position.

250

Within this perspective the relative dominance of an individual is seen as an aspect of the individual's social position and not a cause of it.

Social position in primate groups may perhaps be best described in terms of roles but little attention has been given as yet to an appropriate set of descriptive terms. An effective analysis of cooperative behavior requires a means of designating social position precisely and this the following categorization may supply. The occurrences of cooperation can then be analyzed in terms of which roles and social contexts are involved in cooperative behavior. We may be able to describe cooperation not so much as interactions between known individual organisms but as the necessary relations obtaining between any set of individuals occupying particular role categories in a group.

Using concepts derived from writers such as Sarbin (1954) and Nadel (1957), we can describe a primate's social behavior in terms of the individual's age and sex status, social position, role, and group-type affiliation. In any given group each individual shows characteristic patterns of response in relation to others in the group—to older animals, dominant animals, subordinates, peers. The variety of an animal's behaviors in relation to others in the group comprises its *social behavior repertoire;* and comprises the complete *set of behavior styles* adopted in relation to every possible companion. An observer may prepare a social position network or matrix by allocating the relative frequency of interaction patterns shown by each member to a particular point or cell. In a more general statement each individual may be defined by its proportion of the total of the various interacting patterns shown within the group (Bernstein and Sharpe 1966, Gartlan 1968) and allocated a *social position.*

It so happens that macaque social positions may be categorized into consistent types that recur repeatedly in new groups formed from the division of the old or in separately analyzed independent groups. Such categories may be termed *roles.* There is, for example, the *control-animal role,* the central subgroup *secondary male role* (competitive with another in the subgroup, dominant to peripheral males but subordinate to the central animal and commonly supportive of him) and the roles of the *peripheral male,* the *isolate male,* the *central female* and the *peripheral female.* We may also bracket together certain types of behavior to describe roles of animals of high-status kinship and low-status kinship, respectively. Now, these styles of behavior are called roles because they are not fixed and immutable aspects of given individuals. On the disappearance of a control animal another male typically adopts the same behavior. A male falling

251

in a dominance hierarchy may, however, march out of the group with affiliated females and establish a new group in which he may adopt the behavioral style of a central animal. Isolated males have been known to enter a group and form a central subgroup—one of them perhaps being the control.

While not every conceivable role is necessarily present in any given group, there is an overall consistency that makes this approach meaningful. Furthermore, the basic data consists of quantified reports of individual behavior in relation to companions. Certain roles are usually characteristic of some kinds of groups and not of others—the harem "overlord" occurs in hamadryas, patas, and gelada groups but not in other baboons nor among macaques.

Different sorts of roles occur in groups differentially composed in terms of age and sex categories. Species populations are commonly dispersed in a pattern of groups that is consistent for a given habitat. In some cases the whole species population is dispersed in groups of the same type while in other species there are contrasts across the geographical range. All such contrasts in group composition are intimately related to the ecological adaptations of a species and its social adaptability. These relations have recently been reviewed elsewhere and we need not develop the point further here (Crook 1970).

The behavior characteristic of a particular role is not the "property" of the individual playing it. Such behavior is not fixed by conditioning so that the individual remains continuously in the same role. Physiological and social changes impel behavioral shifts so that in a lifetime individuals may play many roles in their social structure. Social mobility in the sense of role changing is an important attribute of primate groups. It seems more characteristic of males than of females. Young and subadult males may become solitary, live peripherally or in all-male groups, or shift from one reproductive unit to another. Females are more loyal to their natal group and provide the more fixed social positions around which males revolve. This mobility is an expression of a set of tensions or forces characteristic of group life.

At least three types of factors interact in the social sorting process that underlies the dynamics of primate social groups and determines the place of individuals in their respective social positions at any one time. First, periodic shortages of environmental (food and water shortage in the dry season) and social commodities (mates) provide conditions in which aggressive competition may occur. As in birds, severe damage, particularly to subordinates, is avoided by withdrawal upon threat and the gradual establishment of a social hierarchy giving prior access to commodities to more dominant individuals. The ranking system is maintained primarily by the avoidance behavior of those relatively subordinate and becomes habitual even when actual competition is not involved in an encounter. The behavior of the relatively low-ranking individuals is inhibited whereas high-rankers show a free-style confidence that their cringing companions lack. This constraint is liable to place an individual in physiological stress; a behavioral depression that affects comportment, health, chances of survival, and chances of reproduction. The escape from constraint would appear highly rewarding and means of escape are sought and found.

A second factor concerns the aging of individuals. A sexually maturing male will seek a social position wherein he may mate females. If this behavior is denied expression he is likely to enforce a social change or to withdraw. The means whereby young males enter reproduction units may be quite elaborate, particularly in the case of harem species. Likewise, old macaque males may change role. Although their social positions may no longer be defined by threat and mating behavior, they may retain the respect of their companions and remain as control animals almost into senility. The experience of age is valuable in a leader. Dominant animals lacking in local wisdom may perhaps fall rapidly into peripheral status.

The third factor in the sorting process concerns the growth in size of the reproductive unit. In well fed and enlarging groups splits must eventually occur with the re-creation of old roles in new groups. Some Japanese workers have talked in terms of a fission threshold. In relatively small, cohesive groups of Japanese macaques, high behavioral constraint may force some young males into isolation. Larger groups, comprising mutually affiliated subsections, are liable to split up into branch units— again each with its set of roles. The process of change naturally varies with the species population and the social structure concerned.

If this picture is substantially correct, then there appear to be two opposed social forces operating at any one time within a baboon or macaque troop. One consists of the assertive, freely expressed utilization of available physical and social commodities by high-status animals, which has the effect of constraining the behavior of juveniles and subordinates. The other consists of the adoption of behavioral subterfuge by certain subordinates whereby such behavioral constraint can be avoided (e.g., by temporary solitary living or by splitting up the group into branch groups permitting a greater freedom of expression to the new leaders).

It is not suggested that the subterfuge is conscious or deliberate. It appears to arise from the need of certain subordinates to free themselves from the behavioral constraints to which they have been exposed. There are in fact relatively few social routes along which an aspirant may move. In our review of the evidence we have noted three: (a) temporary solitude, followed sometimes by take-over of a small branch group; (b) the use of an affiliated companion to ensure the rise of a dominant animal into a higher or even a centrally located position; and (c) the use of infants and babies as a means of entering high-status subgroups and so to affiliate with them.

In each of these cases individuals closely affiliated with others can combine cooperatively to bring about the liberating effect, an effect which, furthermore, in times of shortage (food, females) would ensure an increased probability of survival and reproductive success in addition to the psychological freedom from the effects of "stress" that undoubtedly accompany in some degree a continuing social restraint on individual behavioral expression. Similarly, by enlisting the cooperation of affiliated animals, often relatives, in their "control" behavior, animals that are already established in social positions of high rank will be able to maintain such positions, and the access to commodities they provide. We have already quoted examples of such behavior.

It seems, then, that cooperative behavior of the high order found in macaque and baboon groups has arisen within the context of competition for access to both physical and social commodities. Both direct affiliative behavior and indirect affiliation through a common interest in child care may provide the basis for common action. As we have seen, such cooperation provides numerous advantages for the participants—and not only for the most dominant animals among them. It also provides the behavioral basis for the complex class-structured society of these animals with its tolerance of individual mobility between roles.

Finally, the stable social structure maintained by a powerful clique around a control animal seems to provide the optimum circumstances for maternal security and child rearing. Females appear to form the more cohesive elements of primate groups and, as a consequence, their affiliative relations and kinship links may play a much greater role in determining who emerges as "control" than is at present known. Males by contrast, subject to the full force of social competition, are more mobile than females, and can transfer themselves, as recent research shows, quite frequently from one group to another.

This outline model of primate group dynamics has some consistency and has been based carefully upon existing field data. Nevertheless, detailed accounts of cooperative behavior are few and still largely anecdotal. Only further field research can clarify its extent and nature. Until we have more data we must also be suspicious of a natural tendency to anthropomorphize. It remains unknown to me how far my explanatory model reflects unconsciously the social tensions clearly present within both Western and Japanese societies during the period of research under review and to which the human observers themselves are exposed. In discussing primate behavior, reflective caution may be vital in preventing the promulgation of misleading interpretations of field reports.

FROM MONKEYS TO MAN   Although perennially outsung by the trumpeters of orthodox Darwinism, the idea that a biology of cooperative behavior may be essential for the understanding of man has surfaced periodically ever since Darwin (1871) himself made the point. Kropotkin (1902) provided the significant impetus and he has been followed by Geddes and Thompson (1911), Allee (1938), and Ashley Montagu (1957). The concept of cooperation in all these works was, however, never clearly defined; sometimes meaning little more than reflexive mutuality or a general sociability and occasionally identified with love. In almost all cases cooperation was raised to a "principle" and opposed to "competition." Some passages in these works had a certain missionary intent, and in any case the crucial data from the field studies of wild primates was not yet available. These idealistic ventures may now give place to critical analyses.

The picture of the relationship between cooperation and competition between members of macaque and baboon troops does perhaps suggest an analogy to modern human relations that looks too close for comfort. For example, the relationships within the New York law firms described so beautifully by Louis Auchincloss in his *Tales of Manhattan* seem structured in a markedly simian fashion. Were early hominid structures also similar?

Reynolds and Reynolds (1965), Reynolds (1966), and Goodall (1965) have described the relatively unstructured "open" groups of chimpanzees, and Reynolds (1968) has further argued the case for such a social organization as primordial in man. Both these studies were made, however, in forest or woodland. The available information suggests that baboons, chimpanzees, and men may have all acquired increasingly structured societies in relation to ecological conditions in the savannah (Crook and Gartlan 1966, Itani and Suzuki 1967, Crook 1970).[4] This struc-

---

[4] *Editor's note:* Not only did primates acquire increasingly structured societies in relation to the ecological conditions in the savannah but the adaptation of marsupials, ungulates, and carnivores to the savannah habitat has exhibited the same trends in social organization (Eisenberg 1966, and Pfeiffer 1969, *The Emergence of Man*). (J.F.E.)

tural differentiation may be based upon the seasonal shortage of crucial commodities and the resulting competition for them. Learning in relation to competition is a prime factor in the formation of status hierarchies in these animals.

We may infer that far from being a remote analogy to human life, the social sorting process in baboon and macaque troops, the emergence of kinship, role, and cooperation as vital to the social organization, and the social mobility of the male players may be a very close homolog of the early social systems of protohominids. Upon such a basis the accultura-tive and communication processes were added as human society emerged into its primitive forms. Competition-contingent cooperation may thus lie at the root of our behavioral heritage—but it lies there in no simple instinctual sense. It was already the complex, multifactorially governed process such as we have described.

The moral of our story lies in a close focus on socially induced com-petition in man. Human cooperation, as the studies of Sherif and Sherif (1953) show, is linked closely to the identification of a person with the needs of the group to which he belongs and of which he considers himself a member. Cooperation within such an "in group" may be high espe-cially if the group is in competition with another. Men, like monkeys, ap-pear to cooperate best when at their most competitive. Nevertheless, hu-man beings, again like monkeys, are socially mobile and may change the frame of reference of their activities from a narrow sectarian concern to broader issues of wider significance. An understanding of the forces con-trolling the maintenance of social position in relation to human needs in terms of identity, ingroup membership, self-esteem, and compassionate empathy would much improve our chances of social control.[5] Ultimately the problem moves to an economic and educational level with a focus on the needs of humanity as a whole (Tajfel 1966). From this viewpoint local issues may be seen in a more balanced perspective.

---

[5] For example, certain group processes such as those involved in sensitivity train-iny, can promote high levels of cooperation contingent upon the mutual sense of trust and affiliation that such treatment may induce (T. R. Gibb and L. M. Gibb, "Humanistic Elements in Group Growth," in *Challenges of Humanistic Psychology*, J. F. T. Bugental, editor, New York: McGraw-Hill, 1967).

REFERENCES

Allee, W. C.
1938. *Cooperation among Animals.* New York: H. Schuman.

Bartholomew, G. A.
1942. "The Fishing Activities of Double-crested Cormorants on San Francisco Bay." *Condor,* 44:13–21.
Bernstein, I. L.
1966. "Analysis of a Key Role in a Capuchin (*Cebus albifrons*) Group." *Tulane Studies in Zoology,* 13(2):49–54.
Bernstein, I. S., and L. F. Sharpe.
1966. "Social Roles in a Rhesus Monkey Group." *Behaviour,* 26:91–104.
Calhoun, J. B.
1962. *The Ecology and Sociology of the Norway Rat.* United States Department of Health, Education, and Welfare.
Carpenter, C. R.
1965. "The Howlers of Barro Colorado Island." In *Primate Behavior,* I. DeVore, editor. New York: Holt, Rinehart & Winston.
Chance, M. R. A.
1967. "Attention Structure as the Basis of Primate Rank Orders." *Man,* 2(4):503–518.
Crook, J. H.
1965. "The Adaptive Significance of Avian Social Organizations." *Symposia of the Zoological Society of London,* 14:181–218.
1966a. "Cooperation in Primates." *Eugenics Review,* 58:63–70.
1966b. "Gelada Baboon Herd Structure and Movement—A Comparative Report." *Symposia of the Zoological Society of London,* 18:237–258.
1970. "The Socio-ecology of Primates." In *Social Life in Birds and Mammals,* J. H. Crook, editor. London: Academic Press.
Crook, J. H., and P. A. Butterfield.
1968. "Effects of Testosterone Propionate and Luteinising Hormone on Agonistic and Nest-building Behavior of *Quelea quelea.*" *Animal Behaviour,* 16:370–384.
1970. "Gender Role in the Social System of *Quelea.*" In *Social Behavior in Birds and Mammals,* J. H. Crook, editor. London: Academic Press.
Crook, J. H., and J. S. Gartlan.
1966. "Evolution of Primate Societies." *Nature* (London), 210:1200–1203.
Darwin, C. R.
1871. *Descent of Man and Selection in Relation to Sex.* London: Murray.
Davis, D. E.
1942. "The Phylogeny of Social Nesting Habits in Crotophaginae." *Quarterly Review of Biology,* 17:115–134.
Deag, J., and J. H. Crook.
1971. "Social Behaviour and 'Agonistic Buffering' in the Wild Barbary Macaque, *Macaca sylvana.*" *Folia Primatologica* (in press).
DeVore, I., editor.
1965. *Primate Behavior.* New York: Holt, Rinehart & Winston.
Eisenberg, J. F.
1966. "The Social Organizations of Mammals." *Handbuch der Zoologie,* Band 8, Leiferung 39. 10(7):1–92.

257

Gartlan, J. S.
1966. "Ecology and Behavior of the Vervet Monkey, Lolui Island, Lake Victoria, Uganda." PhD thesis. Bristol University Library, Bristol, England.
1968. "Structure and Function in Primate Society." *Folia Primatologica* (Switzerland), 8:89–120.

Geddes, P., and J. A. Thompson.
1911. *Evolution.* New York: Holt, Rinehart & Winston.

Gifford, D. P.
1967. "The Expression of Male Interest in the Infant in Five Species of Macaque." *Kroeber Anthropological Society Papers,* 36:32–40.

Goodall, J. van L.
1965. "Chimpanzees of the Gombe Stream Reserve." In *Primate Behavior,* I. DeVore, editor. New York: Holt, Rinehart & Winston.

Hall, K. R. L.
1965. "Behavior and Ecology of the Wild Patas Monkey, *Erythrocebus patas,* in Uganda." *Journal of Zoology,* 148:15–87.

Hall, K. R. L., and I. DeVore.
1965. "Baboon Social Behavior." In *Primate Behavior,* I. DeVore, editor. New York: Holt, Rinehart & Winston.

Hamilton, W. D.
1963. "The Evolution of Altruistic Behavior." *American Naturalist,* 97:354–356.

Hinde, R. A., and Y. Spencer-Booth.
1967. "The Behavior of Socially Living Rhesus Monkeys in Their First Two and a Half Years." *Animal Behaviour,* 15:169–196.

Imanishi, K.
1960. "Social Organization of Subhuman Primates in Their Natural Habitats." *Current Anthropology,* 1:5–6, 393–407.

Itani, J.
1959. "Paternal Care in the Wild Japanese Monkey, *Macaca mulatta.*" Pages 91–97 in *Primate Social Behavior,* C. H. Southwick, editor. Princeton, New Jersey: Van Nostrand.

Itani, J., and A. Suzuki.
1967. "The Social Unit of Chimpanzees." *Primates,* 8:355–381.

Jolly, A.
1966. *Lemur Behavior: A Madagascar Field Study.* Chicago: University of Chicago Press.

King, J. A.
1955. "Social Behavior, Social Organization, and Population Dynamics in a Black-tailed Prairie Dog Town in the Black Hills of South Dakota." *Contributions from the Laboratory of Vertebrate Biology,* number 67. Ann Arbor: University of Michigan Press.

Kropotkin, P.
1902. *Mutual Aid: A Factor of Evolution.* London: Heinemann.

Kühme, W. von
1965. "Freilandstudien zur Soziologie des Hyanenhundes (*Lycaon pictus lupinus* Thomas 1902)." *Zeitschrift fur Tierpsychologie,* 22:495–541.

Kummer, H.
1957. *Soziales Verhalten einer Mantelpavian-Gruppe*. Bern and Stuttgart: Huber.
1968. "Social Organization of Hamadryas Baboons." *Bibliotheca Primatologia*, number 6. Basel: S. Karger.

Lack, D.
1968. *Ecological Adaptations to Breeding in Birds*. London: Methuen.

Lahiri, R. K., and C. H. Southwick.
1966. "Parental Care in *Macaca sylvana*." *Folia Primatologica*, 4:257–269.

Montagu, M. F. A.
1957. *On Being Human*. New York: Schuman.

Morris, D.
1962. "The Behavior of the Green Acouchi (*Myoprocta pratti*) with Special Reference to Scatter Hoarding." *Proceedings of the Zoological Society of London*, 139:701–732.

Mykytowycz, R.
1960. "Social Behavior of an Experimental Colony of Wild Rabbits, *Oryctolagus cuniculus* (L), III: Second Breeding Season." *CSIRO* (Commonwealth Scientific and Industrial Research Organization, Australia), *Wildlife Research*, 5:120.

Nadel, S. F.
1957. *The Theory of Social Structure*. Glencoe, Illinois: Free Press.

Orians, G.
1968. *The Study of Life*. New York: Allyn and Bacon.

Reynolds, V.
1966. "Open Groups in Hominid Evolution." *Man*, 1:441–452.
1968. "Kinship and the Family in Monkeys, Apes, and Man." *Man*, 3:209–223.

Reynolds, V., and F. Reynolds.
1965. "Chimpanzees of the Budongo Forest." In *Primate Behavior*, I. DeVore, editor. New York: Holt, Rinehart & Winston.

Ritter, W. E.
1938. *The California Woodpecker and I*. Berkeley: University of California Press.

Rowell, T. E.
1966. "Hierarchy in the Organization of a Captive Baboon Group." *Animal Behaviour*, 14:430–443.

Rowell, T. E., R. A. Hinde, and Y. Spencer-Booth.
1964. " 'Aunt'-Infant Interaction in Captive Rhesus Monkeys." *Journal of Animal Behaviour*, 12:219–226.

Ryder, S. R.
1962. "The Water Vole." *Animals of Britain No. 4*. London: Sunday Times.

Sarbin, T. R.
1954. "Role Theory." In *Handbook of Social Psychology*, G. Lindzey, editor. Cambridge, Massachusetts: Addison-Wesley.

Sherif, M., and C. W. Sherif.
1953. *Groups in Harmony and Tension*. New York: Harper.

Skutch, A.

    1935. "Helpers at the Nest." *Auk,* 52:257–273.

Southwick, C. H., M. A. Beg, and M. R. Siddiqi.

    1965. "Rhesus Monkeys in North India." In *Primate Behavior,* I. DeVore, editor. New York: Holt, Rinehart & Winston.

Spencer-Booth, Y.

    1968. "The Behavior of Group Companions Towards Rhesus Monkey Infants." *Animal Behaviour,* 16:541–557.

Tajfel, H.

    1966. "Cooperation between Human Groups." *Eugenics Review,* 58(2): 77–84.

Vandenbergh, J. G.

    1967. "The Development of Social Structure in Free-ranging Rhesus Monkeys." *Behavior,* 29:179–194.

Wilson, A. P.

    n.d. "Intergroup Relations and Individual Association in Free-ranging Rhesus Monkeys." (In press.)

Wynne-Edwards, V. C.

    1962. *Animal Dispersion in Relation to Social Behavior.* Edinburgh: Oliver and Boyd.

PART III

IS MAN UNIQUE?

INTRODUCTION

J. F. EISENBERG

In this the third section of our symposium, the emphasis shifts to a consideration of those behavioral attributes of man which tend to set him apart from the rest of the animal kingdom. The question proposed as a subtitle for this section indicates a basic consideration, "Are the behavioral attributes which characterize man unique to him?" If not unique, do all of man's behavioral attributes have a continuity in the past and, in an evolutionary sense, are the wellsprings for man's behavior tied to physiological mechanisms which are indeed homologous to those mechanisms that can be discerned in other animals?

The contribution by Fox considers the unique attribute of man's behavior as his culture. He attempts to demonstrate that cultural manifestations of behavior are in part rooted in biological drives which are expressed by physiological mechanisms which in turn are broadly homologous for many of man's infrahuman relatives. There are historical reasons for the fact that "culture" has been studied separately from the biologically based elements of human behavior. Culture is seen as an aggregate of learned activities and constraints passed from generation to generation by the uniquely interconnected cultural processes of abstract thought and language.

Obviously some aspects of human behavior have biological roots and certain aspects of cultural differences in behavior may be approached from the standpoint of biological origins. As two examples, Fox points out that (1) men in almost all cultures form into groups from which they exclude women, and (2) courtship preceding marriage is an almost universal process in all cultures. He poses the question: What are the biological roots for such universals in human behavior? Further, he points out that there are limits on the forms of human behavioral expression and, although man's imagination "is almost boundless," his overt behavior is structured into units many of which are certainly universal to all cultures. He uses the analogy of language to show that, although language is varied in its phonemic structure, all languages obey certain basic laws which are reflections of the common biological heritage of man. Thus, by analogy, it must certainly be so with other classes of human behaviors.

Fox re-echoes the theme discussed in the introduction to Part I, namely, that man's biological predisposition to learn is in part an inherited trait and, further, he is predisposed to learn in certain ways at certain critical times. Hence, in the course of a man's development, his neurophysiology "anticipates" certain restricted behavior patterns and, in a sense, man is patterned to learn in a certain way and this patterning has a heritable basis. Thus, to correctly prescribe for man's behavioral ills, one must know the limits of his biological system; in short, one must know what essential sensory inputs are anticipated at certain life phases and what limits for assimilation and modification man may possess with respect to his learning capacity and with respect to the overt expression of his biological drives.

For Fox, man's animal heritage is quite large and sets the stage for types of learning which result in the expression of such culturally transmitted patterns as exogamy and incest taboos. He explores the question as to why large brains and culture evolved at all. Obviously there was a stage where man's ancestors became more and more dependent on their brains—the cultural way preceded in time the very marked morphological divergence from other primates. In short, dependency on symbolic forms of communication surely must have preceded the evolution of larger and larger brains, so the culture became, by a feed-back process, the major selective pressure operating on humans to shape their forms of behavior and indeed their ultimate brain size.

Although Fox points out that man's forms of symbolic communication and highly developed culture set him apart from other primates, at the same time man's biological heritage predisposes him to form culture in a certain way, to speak in a certain way, and to think in a certain way; furthermore, his developmental patterns in time are controlled so that he is preprogramed, as it were, to accept certain key stimuli at certain critical phases in his life. Fox attempts in his chapter to form a synthesis between man, the cultural animal, and man, the biological animal, and to an extent he certainly succeeds.

The contribution from DeVore, although not a complete paper, is nevertheless very instructive, especially when one considers the conceptual framework upon which DeVore bases his efforts. He is attempting to define the probable behavior mechanisms in hominid-like primates, the Australopithecines (which are totally extinct) from both a consideration of the behavior of present-day primates and the culture and behavior

266

patterns of the remaining hunter-gatherer societies of man. To paraphrase DeVore's own words, one is attempting to project forward from primate studies to discern what might have been the Australopithecine way of life and then to project backward from studies of contemporary hunter-gatherer societies to what may have been the emergent pattern of behavior displayed by man as he evolved from Australopithecine ancestors.

In considering primate patterns of behavior, DeVore points out that there is great variability in the form of social organization within this order. In fact, the same grades of sociability have been achieved within the order Primates in at least three lines having had separate evolutionary histories since the Eocene (Pfeiffer 1969). Because of the range in the form of social organization exhibited by primates, it is most instructive to look at those primate species which are probably exhibiting the same trends in habitat-utilization as those primates which gave rise to the Australopithecines. As a result, DeVore confines his remarks to the behavior of macaques and baboons which have, within recent geological times, begun the exploitation of the open country savanna terrain and have become much more terrestrial than other primate species.

He reviews the roles of the baboon male, female, and subadult male, pointing out that the inclusion of male primates within the troop as active participants in troop behavior is the result of the advantage derived from the fact that the males serve to protect the females and young against the potential attacks of predators. The adult females, on the other hand, provide a cohesive core and are, in a sense, the true promoters of cohesiveness within the baboon troop. Offspring of given females form a closely affiliated matrilineal descent subgroup and, when baboon troops split, they generally do so along matrilineal lines.

If then the primate ancestors of the Australopithecines lived somewhat like baboons or macaques, DeVore raises the interesting hypothesis that the formation of the human family probably did not result from the coalescing of separate family bands each with their own males into a troop but rather the family, as we know it in man today, differentiated out of a troop already composed of adults of both sexes. In his consideration of the role of the subadult males in a baboon troop, he draws some astonishing functional parallels between the activities of young male baboons [their exposure to danger, their super-abundant energy, and their highly developed aggressive instincts] and those attributes within human society which characterize adolescent males.

Turning to the hunter-gatherer society, DeVore draws from the results of the studies initiated by himself and Lee. Within the Bushman society, we find tribes composed of individual families in the conventional human sense, with a strict division of labor whereby the men hunt and the women gather staple foods, such as wild beans or nuts. Incredible as it seems, the Bushmen live on an adequate diet and have in all respects a healthy balanced society. Some of the unique attributes of Bushmen society upon which DeVore focuses include the fact that the women through their efforts provide up to eighty percent of the tribe's sustenance; and, although the hunting of the men is important, it contributes less than twenty percent to the support of the group. Stability in food supply is thus a function of the activity of the women.

One of the major differences that DeVore sees between hunter-gatherer societies and baboon-macaque societies, aside from the family-type organization, is the fact that men and women can separate for a day's work and return to the same place to share food. Food sharing, planning strategies for food collection, and the sharing of resources in an equitable fashion within the tribe is something that is not accomplished by any primate species and appears to be a culturally emergent phenomenon in man.

With respect to our considerations of man's aggressive behavior, DeVore points out that the Bushman's solution to internal conflicts within the tribe is simple. Since the ownership of property extends to only a few basic implements, each family upon arriving at an impasse in social relationships with another may opt to leave rather than to fight and, packing their belongings on their backs, are at liberty to shift to a neighboring tribe and settle in complete freedom. Generalizations about territorial defense simply do not hold up within the context of present-day Bushman's social organization.

In Professor Langer's chapter, we begin to consider for the first time a realistic case for maintaining a clear-cut distinction between aspects of human behavior and the behavior of infrahuman animals. In her contribution she sounds a warning that conceptual barriers prevent the development of an adequate theory of behavior and, although throughout her article she refers to instinct, she makes a definite distinction between her belief in the use of instinct as an adjective but not in the use of instinct as a noun. That is, there are instinctive acts but no instincts.

In the departure from the animal level of organization to the human level, she points out, from her viewpoint, that a definite shift has occurred: a shift from instinctive responses to intuition. Man has the capacity to deliberately exclude certain stimuli from his perceptual world, and one can defer responding to stimuli or even choose to ignore them. In so doing very often mental images of consummation or mental images corresponding to discrete perceptions are reflected upon in the mind of a human but are not necessarily carried out as a real activity.

This ability to abstract to the stage of forming mental images or executing activities in a mental sphere, she believes, is directly related to the increase in human brain size. Furthermore, the ability to substitute a mental image for action and to associate discrete sounds or behavior patterns with the "image" that they conjure up is the beginning of communication and the basis for language formation. Indeed, communal rites in which human groups participate involve the ability to form mental images corresponding to the symbolic actions being carried out during such rites.

For Professor Langer, an intuition is a mental construct resulting from an organization of perception, coupled with a corresponding mental imagery; indeed, while her concept of perception and the corresponding mental imagery is not in accord with a strict "stimulus-response" psychology, this formulation is beautifully discussed from a psychological standpoint in the works of D. O. Hebb (1949). Speech was primarily developed to express mental images or symbols. Speech involves symbols and permits the symbolic exchange of ideas. Values, then, for humans are an emergent symbolic property attributed to classes of things and acts. The whole fabric of society and its organization is upheld by values. Ethnological institutions such as the church, the army, and the legislature are maintained by symbols of their power.

Granted, however, that values are a symbolic property of classes, nevertheless they are derived from human wants which are related ultimately to human needs. Needs arise from deficits which set in motion the physiological mechanisms responsible for drive states. Values are not divorced from biologically determined mechanisms and the reader is urged to turn to a reading of Pepper (1958) for a further development of this idea.

For Langer, it is important to study differences and distinctiveness between the behavior of animals and man. One must avoid blurring the differences by subsuming apparently similar acts under the same term, since one inadvertently blurs real differences and creates a false sense of similarity. She does not believe that there is any direct application of animal sociology to human social problems; furthermore, she feels that the control of human society needs the application of rational principles formulated by "vigorous conception and consistent thinking."

In the contribution by Jaynes and Bressler, a psychologist and a sociologist, the case is made for interdisciplinary cooperation between biologists and social scientists. Once more the uniqueness of man is re-considered and the question is posed: What meaning have animal studies for the students of human behavior? They pose two alternative ways of looking at the data from multidisciplinary research: (1) One can con-sider studies from an evolutionary standpoint seeking to find in the behavior of man reflections of physiologically similar behavior patterns in animals. They reiterate the position presented by Fox that man has, as part of his heritable equipment, not only the potentiality to learn but the constrained potentiality to learn best at certain times in only certain ways. (2) They contrast this view of partial limits with the position that man obviously has freedom from physiological constraints, and he possesses a syntactic language system. Perhaps with these freedoms and modes of communication, animal behavior has little relevance for human studies. These two points of view may be taken as polar opposites. How is one to decide which argument is correct?

If we compare a given behavior pattern from an animal subject with a behavior pattern from a human subject, then it is possible to establish an identity between the two behavior patterns. By identity, one means that the underlying physiological mechanisms leading to the overt expression of the behavior are similar for the two forms. Given that a similar phys-iological basis is discovered for two functionally equivalent behavior pat-terns between an animal subject and a human subject, then the next question to be asked is what binding contingencies then limit the mode of expression of such a physiologically based behavior for man?

In order to clarify the problem, the authors suggest that the first steps would involve the determination of various kinds of "universals." Two of their five types of universals are of particular interest. These are functional universals—behavioral configurations which serve the same function but may have had differing phylogenetic origins and variform universals—those having a common basis in terms of physiological mechanism. Be-havioral universals are patterns and mechanisms found in all species. Given the establishment of different classes of universals, one can then ask the question: What continuities are exhibited between universals in human behavior and universals in animal behavior? For the purposes of the authors' discussion, they restrict animal considerations to primate be-havioral universals. In establishing continuities, it is important to avoid making the mistake of attributing a human universal to be equivalent to an animal universal because of a similarity in function. The authors caution that in order to establish evolutionary continuities we must establish homologous continuities or continuities between variform universals rather than analogous continuities, or continuities between functional universals.

A brief digression may be necessary here, since the authors are using the word homology in the sense of the comparative anatomist. A homology—be it between two organs or between two behavioral functions—is established only when we are reasonably certain that the expressed form—be it behavioral or morphological—has a common physiological basis which reflects a common embryological basis which reflects a common genetic basis, thus indicating a relationship by descent between the compared forms. Only after a certain required series of cross-checks have been applied to the data can a homology be established (see Wickler 1961). A *homology* must be kept conceptually separate from an *analogy* because a behavioral or morphological analogy may be expressed by an entirely different set of physiological, developmental, and genetic mechanisms and, thus, although it is functionally equivalent, it is not phylogenetically equivalent.

The authors suggest a first-order conceptual framework for the intercorrelation of universals between primates and man and conclude that there are indeed some correlations and some noncorrelations. Given that there exist continuities between primates and man with respect to universally displayed behavioral mechanisms, the question then becomes: Given a continuity, does this necessarily imply that there is one method of expression for the behavioral act or are there alternatives? Given that the same neural mechanisms may underlie the overt expression of the behavior in question, need it necessarily be expressed in a single way? The answer, of course, is that even if similar physiological mechanisms mediate behavior in men and in primates that reflect an evolutionary continuity and reflect a basic homology, it does not necessarily follow that man can express a given activated drive only in a single way. There are indeed many alternative outlets for the expression of a given physiological drive state. In this conclusion, the authors re-echo the warning by Langer in the sense that it is perhaps the function of man's reason to choose between outlets and to weigh the consequences of alternative outlets even when under the influence of strong physiological drives.

The authors, however, indicate the desirability of a synthesis between animal and human-oriented studies and suggest the distinct possibility of establishing a cross-species catalog of behavior universals.

Such a possible cataloging of responses and response mechanisms could well begin with a consideration of aggressive behavior. Often in the literature aggressive behavior is treated as if it were under the control of a single physiological response mechanism. Yet there are several different kinds of behavior called aggressive which on the basis of animal studies appear to have different underlying physiological control systems (Moyer 1968). A cross-cataloging of animal-human aggressive systems could go a long way toward clarifying the methods of control which could be employed to reduce or redirect human behavior.

REFERENCES

Hebb, D. O.
   1949. *The Organization of Behavior.* New York: Wiley.
Moyer, K. E.
   1968. "Kinds of Aggression and Their Physiological Basis." In *Communications in Behavioral Biology,* Part A, 2:65–87.
Pepper, S.
   1958. *The Sources of Value.* Berkeley: University of California Press.
Pfeiffer, J.
   1969. *The Emergence of Man.* New York: Harper Row.
Wickler, W.
   1961. "Okologie und Stammesgeschichte von Verhaltensweisen." *Fortschrifte der Zoologie,* 13:303–365.

CHAPTER 8

THE CULTURAL ANIMAL

ROBIN FOX

RUTGERS UNIVERSITY

Primitive mythologies testify to the enduring fascination of man with the problem of his own relationship to the natural world. For *Homo* is burdened with being *sapiens,* and one thing this *sapientia* drives him to is a ceaseless and almost passionate inquiry about his status—what T. H. Huxley aptly called *An Enquiry into Man's Place in Nature.* And like Darwin and Huxley, the primitive seeks an answer to the eternal paradox: We are obviously part of nature, and in particular we are part of the animal world, and yet we are set apart from nature by the very fact of knowing that we are part of it. Not only does no other animal know it is going to die, but no other animal knows it is alive—in any sense in which we would normally use the word "know." And no other animal concerns itself with the problem of its own uniqueness. But man is obsessed with it. He is forever seeking to define himself—a task as yet uncompleted—and to do so he has to establish the boundaries between himself and the animal world.

In their mythologies the primitives solve the problem in various ways, most usually by having man descend from an animal ancestor, or rather, various groups of men descend from various animal ancestors. We might like to think that this represents an anticipation of Darwin, but unfortunately most primitives believe in acts of special creation, so we have to disqualify them. One of these acts of creation, however, is usually the clue to the essential difference: be it language, fire, the art of cooking, rules about incest, and so on, that are the diacritics of humanity. We do not communicate, convert energy, eat, or breed quite like the animals, and hence we make that crucial breakthrough from nature to culture, and become the cultural animal.

Not only do we become cultural, we become divine. In many of our

---

This paper is a very slightly revised version of Part One of the original paper written for the symposium, and is substantially the same as the actual address delivered there. The second part, which will be published elsewhere, consisted of an examination of some areas of human behavior such as politics, territory and population, social bonds, aggression, and thought and language.

ego-boosting mythologies we do not differ simply in degree from the animals, we differ in kind. It is not some simple attribute—like the ability to make fire—but the possession of a divine spark that renders us *in essence* different, that carves out a gulf between us and "brute creation." Here again we cannot seem to settle the matter, and much argument, as we know, ensues about where brute creation stops and the divine human starts. Any human group is ever ready to consign another recognizably different human group to the other side of the boundary. It is not enough to possess culture to be fully human, one must possess *our* culture. Even universalistic religions, which were happy to define man as an animal with a soul, were often not too sure by what criterion one recognized the possession of the *anima,* and categories of *Homo sylvestris* and *Homo feralis* were invented to take care of marginal cases. But at least in the western world this definition sufficed (and for many still suffices) until the eighteenth century savants began to look down on such arguments as perhaps too emotional, and substituted reason as the defining characteristic of man. Linnaeus, to whom we owe our pretentious zoological title, was very much a child of the eighteenth century. Souls were not to be trusted, it seems, since one never knew quite what they were up to, and animals may very well have them. But brute creation did not have reason and that was obvious enough. Soulful our furry friends may be, but rational they are not. They could probably adore God, but they could not understand Pythagoras.

Darwin undermined this stance as much as the position of the religiously orthodox. He noted what in fact many predecessors, including Linnaeus himself, and even Immanuel Kant, had noted—the striking anatomical similarity between ourselves and the rest of the order *Primates* and ultimately between ourselves and the rest of the vertebrates. What Darwin added was theory that could explain how this striking relationship came about, other than by some whim of the Almighty or by Lamarckian effort of will. Now this caused many people other than Bishop Wilberforce to feel that human dignity and uniqueness were in danger. That great anticleric Samuel Butler castigated Darwin for "banishing mind from the universe." He had blurred the distinctions that we had assumed were inviolable. We had emerged gradually from the animal world by a natural process, not suddenly by a supernatural one. The moral was plain to the soul merchants and the reason merchants alike: We in fact differed only in degree and not in kind from our cousins. The reaction was interesting. The anatomical argument was quickly adopted and became its own kind of orthodoxy. Despite a few skirmishes the battle was over before it was fought.

The anatomist W. E. LeGros Clark (1957) said recently that it is astonishing to think people ever doubted the anatomical continuity between ourselves and the other primates. And indeed it does seem absurd today, to the extent that when I am faced with an unrepentant fundamentalist I confess I am unable to cope with him. I have no ready-made arguments for defending the self-evident, and so fare badly, thus confirming his worst fears about the conspiracy of the ungodly.

In the hundred years between the appearance of *The Origin of Species* and today, a large (although still too limited) amount of fossil evidence has come to light documenting the gradual transition that what Darwin saw *must* have happened, even in the absence of direct evidence. As far as anatomy was concerned then, the case rested. But human behavior was somehow exempted from the same rubric.

Darwin published in 1873 his most remarkable work, *The Expression of the Emotions in Man and Animals.* Whatever we may think of his specific conclusions, his message was clear enough: In many areas of behavior we show great similarities to our cousins; their behavior, like their anatomy, has evolved through the process of natural selection, ergo, so has ours. Anatomy and behavior, structure and function, were of course intimately linked, and what was true for one was true for the other.

Even in the biological sciences, the impact of this line of thinking was not immediate, and it is only comparatively recently that biologists have been investigating in a serious way the evolution of animal-behavior systems. The reasons for this are not our concern here, although the historians of science should be working on them. But one reason we should note: Investigations of animal behavior really got going under the aegis of Pavlovian-style behaviorism, which is not evolutionary in orientation and has scant respect for anything that is claimed to be innate. A similar reaction (or was it even a reaction?) happened in the social sciences. Darwin had blurred the distinctions all right, and even reason did not appear to be so firmly enthroned now, so anthropology took on the role of "Defender of the Faith" in human uniqueness and weighed in with culture as the defining characteristic. Of course, as with their predecessors, they were never able to define very clearly what this was.

So, as in the older myths of those other primitives, the nature of our uniqueness remains something of a mystery. Very roughly, "culture," in anthropological parlance, refers to traditional modes of behaving and

277

thinking that are passed on from one generation to another by social learning of one kind or another. We get a little uneasy when told that animal communities also have "traditions" that get passed on, so we retreat into symbols. Culture is couched in symbols and it is by means of these that it is passed on. Preeminent among the symbol systems is language, and when all else fails we can cling to language. "By their speech ye shall know them"—and to this we will return later.

The social and behavioral sciences thus side-stepped Darwin's challenge. This maneuver was aided by a number of developments. Behaviorism dominated psychology, and "instinct theory" fell into disrepute. Behaviorism was rigorous and "scientific" while instinct theory—primarily under McDougal—seemed nothing more than a kind of thesaurus of human attributes. The eugenics movement which put such store in biological aspects of behavior became more and more entangled with racism, and any attempt to show that there were important biological components in behavior was regarded as incipient racism, and still is in many quarters. In sociology, the "social Darwinists" also fell into disrepute. They were not really Darwinians in the sense in which I am using the term; they simply used analogies from Darwinian biological theory and applied them, usually wrongly, to social processes. Their wrongheaded use of evolutionary doctrines to support the excesses of laissez-faire capitalism eventually sent them into oblivion. With them, the proverbial baby went out with the proverbial bath water. Henceforth, any explanation of a social phenomenon that was "Darwinian" or "biological" was ipso facto erroneous in the social sciences, and that was that. Marx and Durkheim dominated sociology, and while the latter had problems with the autonomy of the subject, his doctrine that the social must be explained in terms of the social and not reduced to any lower level (like the biological, of course) held almost complete sway.

Anthropologists continued to pronounce. Sir Arthur Keith (1948) even set a limit below which culture was impossible. The brain, he said, had to reach a size of 750 cubic centimeters before any fossil primate could be considered a "man." This gave substance to the anthropological belief that culture was, in the words of Malinowski, "all of a piece." One never found people with religion but no language, or law but no religion, and so on. If they had one they had all, and it must have happened at that point when the brain reached the size necessary for culture to "occur."

One can immediately see the similarities between this and the Catholic doctrine as ennunciated in the encyclical *Humani generis* where it is al-

278

lowed that man may have evolved in body à la Darwin, but insisted that at some point an immortal soul was injected into the painfully evolving body. God would have had to wait, it seems, until his chosen primate had crossed Keith's "cerebral rubicon" before doing anything so presumptuous. Anthropologists, also, were almost maniacally preoccupied with explaining cultural differences. They were really not very interested in what made men man, but in what made one lot of men different from another lot.

As a student I had the litany chanted at me: Biological universals cannot explain cultural differentials. And of course at one level they cannot. Muslims, I was told, take off their shoes to go into church while Christians take off their hats. Now find me a biological explanation for that! I was never sure I wanted to find any kind of explanation for it. It seemed to me a pretty arbitrary thing. And anyway, what explanation was I offered? I will not bore you with the answer since I do not want to shake your faith in anthropology too much. But I will confess that even in those salad days I was plaguing my teachers with the question: If we do not really know what biological universals there are, then how can we study the cultural differentials in the first place? How to study the variables without the constants? In response, I was told that biological universals were simply primitive drives like hunger and sex. The fact that sex was universal did not explain why some cultures were polygynous and others monogamous. Maybe not, I thought, but it might explain why they were all adulterous. After all, sex is a very complex business, and might it not be that behavior resulting from it was more than just these rather gray and amorphous urges that I was presented with. Look at the courtship of birds and animals, for example. Ah, came back the answer, but that is *genetic,* whereas human courtship is *cultural.*

When all this was going on—some fifteen years ago in London— I had no ready answer. Anyway, I wanted to pass my exams. It all depends, I thought to myself and in secret, upon what you want to explain. All human cultures have some kind of courtship ceremonies, and when you look at them they look very much alike despite the different cultural trappings. If all you want to explain is why in America girls wear their date's fraternity pins while in Fiji they put hibiscus flowers behind their ears, that is fine. But (a) it does not seem worth explaining, and (b) there probably is no explanation in any scientific sense—it is just what they do. These are simply ways of getting the same courtship job done, and the interesting thing to me is the universality of various similar symbolic devices. Has each culture independently invented the idea that the girl

279

should declare her allegiance in this kind of way, or is there perhaps something more subtle about courtship than we imagined, something uncultural, something unlearned?

To be fair to anthropology, it was fighting on several fronts and often shot at the wrong targets. The "no links between biology and culture" argument was partly an attack on the racists who wanted to explain seeming inequalities between cultures as a result of biological differences. Again the baby went out with the soapsuds when anthropology strenuously set its face against *any* connection between culture and biology, even at the universal level. At best—as for example in the work of Malinowski—culture could be seen as a response to a rather drab set of "biological imperatives," but then this kind of Malinowskian functionalism soon fell into disrepute as well, since it did nothing to explain cultural differences. While I am on with my catalog of complaints, let me add that as far as I could see, for all its obsession with cultural differences, anthropology in fact did nothing to explain them. What it did was to take cultural differences as given and use them to explain other things—largely other cultural differences. All the things that might have explained cultural differences, such as racial variation, environment, history, and diffusion, were at one time or another ruled out of court.

All in all, for a variety of ideological reasons, the anthropological profession, along with psychology and sociology, kept the world safe for humanity by refusing to allow that anything about culture could be "reduced" to biology, and hence kept the gap between us and the brutes nicely wide. We were the "cultural animal" all right, but stress was entirely on the cultural while the animal was relegated to a few odd things like blinking, sucking, feeling hungry, and copulating. Ninety-nine percent of our behavior, it was held, was "learned" and hence cultural. And what was more there was no limit to what could be learned. The human infant was a *tabula rasa* on which culture imprinted itself, and the subsequent behavior of the infant was therefore wholly a matter of which particular culture had been imprinted on it. The differences between cultures in their beliefs, behaviors, and institutions was so great that any considerations of common biological traits were totally irrelevant.

We get to the crux of what I want to say by raising the question: Were not anthropologists suffering from ethnographic dazzle? I borrow the term from linguistics where "orthographic dazzle" refers to the difficulty some people have of sorting out pronunciation from spelling. In some respects and at some levels—the levels of beliefs, of formal institutions—cultures are dazzlingly different. Why are the Japanese the way they are, as opposed to the Americans, the Russians, the Hottentots, and so on? This is a fascinating question. But as I have said, the anthropological answer is rather lame "they are different because they do things differently." Mostly anthropology tells us about the *consequences* of doing things differently, and tells it very well indeed. But are societies and cultures really very different at the level of forms and processes? Or are they not in some ways depressingly the same? Do we not time after time in society after society come up with the same processes carried out under a variety of symbolic disguises? I think we do, and if we can get past the cultural or ethnographic dazzle we can see that this is so. Thus, if you look at the behavior of what my colleague Lionel Tiger (1969) has called *Men in Groups,* you find that whatever the overt cultural differences in male-group behavior at the level of symbolism, actual practices and beliefs, and even emotional and other expressive features, in society after society one thing stands out: Men form themselves into associations from which they exclude women. These associations vary in their expressed purposes but in many of their processes they are remarkably uniform. A seemingly bewildering variety of male behavior can be reduced in effect to a few principles once this is grasped.

Similarly I have tried to show that the seemingly endless variety of kinship and marriage arrangements known to man are in fact variations on a few simple themes. The same can be said of political arrangements, which, despite their cultural variety, are reducible to a few structural forms. Once one gets behind the surface manifestations, the uniformity of human behavior and of human social arrangements is remarkable. None of this should surprise a behavioral zoologist; we are, after all, dealing with a uniform species divided into a number of populations. This being a species of rather highly developed mammals one would expect a lot of local differences in traditions between the various populations, but one would expect these differences to reflect species-specific units of behavior. Thus, every species has a complex of social behavior made up of recognizable units—a complex which distinguishes it from other species—but these units may well be put together in different ways by different populations adapting to different environments. But one does not find a baboon troop, for all its ingenuity, adapting like a herd of horses and vice versa. The baboons can only adapt with the material at hand in their stock of behavior units, and the same is true of man.

The degree of flexibility in human populations is obviously greater, but a great deal of it is at the symbolic level. We can tell the story in many different ways, but it is the same old story we are telling. And if we depart too far from the plot—which we have the capacity to do—the result may well be a truly dramatic chaos. For this is man's hang-up. Unlike the baboon or the horse, we can imagine things that are different from the plot laid down for us, and we can put our dreams into practice. The question then is, will the dream work? If you accept that all behavior is culturally learned and that man can learn anything, then the answer is yes. The only limit is human ingenuity. We can invent any kind of society and culture for ourselves. If you believe, as by now it should be obvious I do, that we have a species-specific repertoire of behavior that can be combined successfully only in certain ways, then the answer is no. There are definite limits to what this animal can do, to the kinds of societies it can operate, to the kinds of culture it can live with. But there is no end to its dreams and its fantasies. While its social behavior may have strict limits, its imagination has none.

I have jumped here to my conclusion without detailing the whole route. Let me postpone the latter for a little longer to press home this point. We mentioned earlier that language was the chief characteristic of our species, the crucial distinguishing feature. This is true and can be used to illustrate the point. It is now well established that the capacity for language acquisition and use lies in the brain on the one hand and in the speech organs on the other, and overall in the complex relations between the two. Linguists like Chomsky (1957, 1964, 1965) and psychologists like Lenneberg (1967) argue that the capacity for grammatical speech is somehow "in" the brain, and matures as the child matures. Thus every human child has the capacity for grammatical speech, and is ready, as it were, to be programed with whatever actual grammar its culture provides. Now we know that the latter are many and astonishing in their variety, and that their variation is arbitrary.

There is no "explanation" why the English say "horse," the French "cheval," and the Germans "pferd." There is no explanation why any particular pattern of sounds signifies an object or action (with the possible exception of onomatopoeia). This is quite arbitrary. Nevertheless, the speech patterns of all languages are known to operate on a few basic principles which linguists have worked out, and the semantic patterns may well also be reducible in this way, once what Chomsky calls the "deep structures" of all languages are known. Once these are discovered, we can write the "universal grammar" which will tell us the few principles upon which all actual grammars rest. We can do this because despite the enormous variety of "surface grammars" they all are doing the same job and are constrained to do it in a limited number of ways. Thus no language exists that a linguist cannot record with the universal phonetic alphabet in the first place, and analyze with universally applicable techniques of semantic analysis in the second. We can invent artificial languages based on binary signals, or other codes, which require different "grammars," but "natural languages" all can be broken down, first into phones, then phonemes, then morphemes, then lexemes, and so on up to the higher levels of grammaticality.

The rest of culture is probably like this. The potential for it lies in the biology of the species. We have the kinds of cultures and societies we have because we are the kind of species we are. They are built out of our behavioral repertoire and are analyzable into its elements and their combinations. Like language, the capacity for specific kinds of behavior is in us, but exactly how this will be manifested will depend on the information fed into the system. The system here is the behavior potential of the individual; the information is the culture he is socialized in. But in the same way as he can only learn a language that follows the normal rules of grammaticality for human languages, so he can only learn a grammar of behavior that follows the parallel rules in the behavioral sphere. Of course in either case he can try departing from normal grammaticality, but in either case he will then get gibberish, linguistic or behavioral.

We generally do not try to manipulate language because the matter is out of our hands, but with behavior we are continually producing gibbering illiterates, and until we understand the deep structure of the behavioral grammar within which we weave our cultural variations, we will continue to do so. No one wants to produce linguistic gibberish since verbal communication breaks down; but we constantly produce behavioral gibberish and then wonder why social communication breaks down. The answer of those who believe that anything is possible since everything is cultural is: Try to invent yet more and more different languages with any kind of grammaticality you can think of. My answer is: Find out how the universal grammar works and then bring changes within that framework; invent new behavioral languages that do not violate the principles of basic grammaticality.

At least two monarchs in history are said to have tried the experiment of isolating children at birth and keeping them isolated through childhood, to see if they would spontaneously produce a language when they matured. The Egyptian Psammetichos, in the seventh century B.C., and later James IV of Scotland, in the fifteenth century A.D. Both, it seemed did not doubt that untutored children would speak, although King James' hope that they would speak Hebrew was perhaps a little optimistic.

I do not doubt that they *could* speak and that, theoretically, given time, they or their offspring would invent and develop a language despite their never having been taught one. Furthermore, this language, although totally different from any known to us, would be analyzable by linguists on the same basis as other languages and translatable into all known languages. But I would push this further. If our new Adam and Eve could survive and breed—still in total isolation from any cultural influences—then eventually they would produce a society which would have laws about property, rules about incest and marriage, customs of taboo and avoidance, methods of settling disputes with a minimum of bloodshed, beliefs about the supernatural and practices relating to it, a system of social status and methods of indicating it, initiation ceremonies for young men, courtship practices including the adornment of females, systems of symbolic body adornment generally, certain activities and associations set aside for men from which women were excluded, gambling of some kind, a tool- and weapon-making industry, myths and legends, dancing, adultery, and various doses of homicide, suicide, homosexuality, schizophrenia, psychosis and neuroses, and various practitioners to take advantage of or cure these, depending on how they are viewed. I could extend the list but this will suffice.

In short, the new Adam and Eve would not only produce, as our monarchs suspected, a recognizable human language, but a recognizable human culture and society. It might not be in content quite like any we have come across: Its religious beliefs might be different, but it would have some; its marriage rules might be unique (I doubt it), but it would have them and their type would be recognized; its status structure might be based on an odd criterion, but there would be one; its initiation ceremonies might be unbelievably grotesque but they would exist; its use or treatment of schizophrenia might be bizarre, but there it would be. All these things would be there because we are the kind of animal that does these kinds of things.

In the same way, in a zoo one can rear infant baboons who know nothing of the state in which their ancestors and wild cousins lived, and yet when they reach maturity they produce a social structure with all the elements found in the wilds and of which they have no experience. Their capacity to produce a unique "language" is of course much more limited than that of our hypothetical naive group of humans, but in both cases the basic grammaticality of behavior will be operative. In the same way that a linguist could take our Garden of Eden tribe and analyze its totally unique language, so an anthropologist would be able to analyze its totally unique kinship system or mythology or whatever, because the basic rules of the universal grammar would be operating.

(Actually in the interests of accuracy I should add a rider here to the effect that the experiment might be impossible to perform. It is one of the ground rules of the universal behavioral grammar of all primates— not just humans—that if you take young infants away from maternal care at a critical period they will grow up to be very disturbed indeed and may well perpetuate this error by maltreating their own children in turn. Thus our experiment may well produce a group of very malad-justed adults and the whole thing founder rather quickly. But at least this gives us one element of the universal system: Some method has to be found of associating mother and child closely and safely during certain critical periods. If isolated during critical periods, not only can the animal not learn *anything* at all, it loses the potential to learn at any other time. It has to learn certain things at certain times—true of language and of many other areas of behavior.)

To return to our human tribe developed *de novo* in our experimental Eden: What I am saying may not seem very remarkable but it goes against the grain of the anthropological orthodoxy. Without any exposure to cultural traditions our tribe would develop *very specific* and highly complex patterns of behavior, and probably very quickly—within a matter of a few generations, once they had developed a language. They would do so for the same reason that the baboons produce a baboon social system in captivity—because it is in the beast. And it is not just a very general capacity that is in the beast—not just the capacity to learn, and to learn easily—which is all the culturalists need to assume, it is the capacity to learn some things rather than others, and to learn some things easily rather than others, and to learn some rather specific things into the bargain.[1]

This is a very important point. I am not positing that initiation cere-monies or male rituals are instinctive, in any old sense of that term. I am positing that they are an outcome of the biology of the animal because it is programed to behave in certain ways that will produce these phenomena, given a certain input of information. If this input does not occur then the behavior will not occur or will occur only in a modified or

---

[1] *Editor's note:* For experimental evidence on this point, see W. Thorpe, *Bird Song,* pages 80–86, Cambridge University Press, 1961; where he discusses the case of isolated chaffinches. Without previously hearing its own song, the bird is pre-disposed to select the "correct" song to be learned from a mixture of bird songs which are played to it. (J.F.E.)

distorted form. (This is, in fact, more like the modern theory of instinct, but to go into the ramifications of this would take too long.) The human organism is like a computer which is set up or "wired" in a particular way. It is thus in a state of readiness—at various points in the life cycle —to process certain kinds of information. The information has to be of a certain type, but the actual "message" can vary considerably. If the information is received, then the computer stores it and uses it to go on to the next task. If you confuse the system, the machine very easily breaks down and might even blow the fuses if you really mix up the program. Of course to push this analogy to its logical conclusion we would have to have computers feeding each other information to simulate the human situation. Only when they were synchronized would the total system run properly.

This is—although very crude—a different model from that of the old "instinctivists" or of the "behaviorists." To the instinctivists, behavior resulted simply from the manifestation of innate tendencies which in interaction produced such things as territorialism, maternal behavior, or acquisitiveness. To the behaviorists the infant was, as we have seen, a *tabula rasa* and behavior ultimately was the result of learning via conditioning. (Psychoanalysis leans to the instinctivist end, but is a special case in some ways.) Culturalists in anthropology and the social sciences share the *tabula rasa* view and see all behavior above the primitive-drive level as a result of the learning of a particular culture. My view sees the human organism as wired in a certain way so that it can process information about certain things like language and rules about sex, and not other things, and that it can only process this information at certain times and in certain ways. This wiring is geared to the life cycle so that at any one moment in a population of *Homo sapiens* there will be individuals with a certain "store" of behavior at one stage of the cycle giving out information to others at another stage, the latter being wired to treat the information in a certain way. As an outcome of the interaction of these individuals at various stages, certain "typical" relationships will emerge. This may seem either tortuous or obvious, but I can assure you it *is* a different way of viewing human behavior and social structure than the orthodox one. The orthodox view says: When in trouble, change the program because we can write any program we want to. What we should say is: When in trouble, find out what is in the wiring, because only then will we know what programs we can safely write.

The culturalists only acknowledge a very general "capacity for culture," if they acknowledge anything at all about the general characteristics of the species. To them, all culture is pure human invention and is passed on from generation to generation by symbolic learning. Thus, logically, it follows that if ever this store of culture should be lost, it is improbable that it would be invented again in the same forms. Thus something as specific as totemism and exogamy—that old anthropological chestnut— has to be seen in this view as a pure intellectual invention, and it would be unlikely that it would be invented again. I do not think so. I think my tribe with no experience of any other human culture and no knowledge of totemism and exogamy would produce both very quickly, and what is more these phenomena would be immediately recognizable and analyzable by anthropologists. In fact those anthropologists like Tylor who argued for the "psychic unity of mankind" were acknowledging a similar position.[2] They argued that such customs had not been invented in one area and diffused throughout the world, but were stock responses of the human psyche to external pressures. They were somehow reflections of "human nature," a phrase that we have been discouraged from using. The argument for psychic unity also had to face the "constants can explain variables" charge, but we have dealt with that one already.

The phychic unity argument, however, was never pushed as far as I am pushing it. The universal psyche for these anthropologists had no specific content; it was a capacity to do human things, but most of its proponents would have maintained it was a general learning capacity and that culture was invented. As I have said, at one level this is true—at the level of specific content—but we must not be dazzled by this into ignoring those basic processes and forms that crop up with regular monotony. (Here we must not slip into the error of thinking that *universal processes* necessarily produce *uniform results*. Far from it. This is not true even in the plant kingdom and is even less true in the animal.)

I can now return to the problem of the route by which I reached this conclusion. The question that had been plaguing me throughout my undergraduate career was really, "How do we know what's in the wiring and how did it get there?" For we can find out really what it is all about only if we know how it was constructed and to what end it was produced. It is no good trying to use an analog computer as if it were a digital computer since they were designed for different uses. The answer to this should have been obvious, and soon became so. What is in the wiring of

---

[2] *Editor's note:* Fox may well have noted that not only such cultural constructs as exogamy and incest taboo have the potential to be invented again but the steps toward urban growth may be just as determinate. This thesis is developed by R. McC. Adams in *The Evolution of Urban Society,* Chicago; Aldine, 1966. (J.F.E.)

the human animal got there by the same route as it got into any other animal—by mutation and natural selection. These "great constructors" as Konrad Lorenz calls them, had produced remarkable end products in the social behavior of all kinds of animals, reptiles, birds, fishes, and insects. And it is here that the message of Lorenz and his associates becomes important: Behavior evolves just as structure evolves and the evolution of the two is intimately linked.

Now we are back to Darwin's principle from which this paper started and from which anthropology so disastrously departed at the turn of the century. What the behavioral zoologists (in Europe usually known as ethologists) showed us was that units of behavior evolve on the same principle as units of anatomy and physiology—that a head movement that was part of a bird's innate repertoire of actions has an adaptive significance as great as the evolution of the wing itself. The head movement may be precisely the thing that inhibits the attack of another bird, for example, and over the millennia has become "fixed" as a signal recognized by the species as an inhibitor. Even if one does not accept that humans have "instincts" of this kind (I think they have a few but not many), the point is well taken that one should look at behavior as the end product of evolution and analyze it in terms of the selection pressures that produced it. If we have this marvelous flexibility in our learning patterns then this is a feature of the biology of our species and we should ask *why* we have this flexibility. What selection pressures operated to bring about this particular biological feature? Our enormous dependence on culture as a mode of adaptation itself stands in need of explanation, for this too is a species-specific characteristic, and it gets us into trouble as much as it raises us to glory. It is a two-edged weapon in the fight for survival, and the simple brutes with their instinctive headwagging may well live to have the last laugh.

But the brutes, it has transpired, are not so simple. When one looks at our cousins, the other primates, the complexity of their social behavior is amazing. One thing the ethologists taught us to do was to compare the behavior of closely related species in order to get at the "proto-behavior" of the group of animals concerned. The continuing flow of excellent material on nonhuman primates in the wild shows us how many and subtle are the resemblances between ourselves and our simian relatives. Wider afield, the growing science of animal behavior shows that many mammals, and vertebrates generally, have social systems which duplicate features of our own society, and in which similar processes occur, and even similar social pathologies. Lorenz (1966) showed how aggression was the basis of social bonding; Wynne-Edwards (1962) postulated that the "conventionalized competition" which controlled aggression was itself rooted in the control of numbers; Chance (1962) demonstrated that among primates the elementary social bond was that between males rather than that between males and females, and so on. The politics of macaque monkeys suggests that Aristotle was right: Insofar as he is a primate, man is by nature a political animal. (It is significant that quoting this, the phrase *by nature* is often omitted.) Ants can have societies, but ants cannot have politics. Politics only occurs when members can change places in a hierarchy as a result of competition. So man is more than social; he is political, and he is political because he is that kind of primate —terrestrial and gregarious.

As a consequence it becomes more and more obvious that we have a considerable animal heritage and hence a great store of comparative data to draw on in making generalizations about our own species. It forces upon us this observation: If we find our own species displaying certain patterns of social behavior that duplicate those of other similar species— depending, of course, on the level of similarity—we will often need to say only that these patterns are what we would expect from a terrestrial primate, a land-dwelling mammal, a gregarious vertebrate, or whatever. Of course some aspects of these patterns and a great deal of their content will be unique, but this is only to say that they will be species-specific. Every species is unique since it is the end product of a particular path of evolution.

The real question—What is the nature of the uniqueness?—brings us back to where we started. And we cannot answer that question until we know what we have in common with all other species, and with some other species, and with only closely related species. Thus the argument that we differ from all other species as a result of the triumph of culture over biology I find false, because culture is an aspect of our biological difference from other species. It is the name for a kind of behavior found in our species which ultimately depends on an organ, the brain, in which we happen to have specialized. Thus differences between ourselves and other primates for example do not stem from the fact that we have in some way *overcome* our primate natures, but stem from the fact that we are a different kind of primate with a different kind of nature. At the level of forms and processes we behave culturally because it is in our nature to behave culturally, because mutation and natural selection have produced this animal which must behave culturally, must invent rules, make myths, speak languages, and form men's clubs in the same way as

289

the hamadryas baboon has to form harems, adopt infants, and bite his wives on the neck.

But why culture? Why did our simian ancestors not content themselves with a much less flexible, and perhaps at the time less vulnerable, way of coping with nature's exigencies? This is where another strand of evidence comes in—the material on human evolution. In Darwin's day this was practically nonexistent and even now it is relatively meager. But we now can trace with some confidence the general picture of man's evolution over at least four million years, and we have evidence that the hominoid line may well go back over thirty million. This is not the place for a detailed exposition of what we know, and all I can do is to point out some of the implications of our new knowledge.

You will remember that Sir Arthur Keith set the limit of brain size below which was mere animal at 750 cc. The modern human brain averages about 1400 cc, roughly twice that of Keith's minimum. The brain of the chimpanzee is roughly 400 cc, that of the gorilla 500 cc. Now to cut a long story short, the modern discoveries have shown that hominids have existed for at least two million years and probably longer, and that at that early date in their evolution they were indulging in activities that imply the existence of cultural traditions, even if of a rudimentary form. The most striking evidence of this is the existence of tool-making industries first in bone and horn and then in stone (wood does not survive but was undoubtedly used) in small-brained hominids in East and South Africa. Two million years ago, our ancestors with brain sizes ranging from 435 cc to 680 cc—little better, you see, than the gorilla—were doing very human things, cultural things, before having reached the Rubicon. They were hunting, building shelters, making tools, treating skins, living in base camps and possibly many other things (speaking languages perhaps?) that we cannot know directly, while their morphology was still predominantly ape-like and their brains in some cases smaller than the modern apes. What was not ape-like about them was their dentition and their bipedal stance. In these features they were well launched on the road to humanity since both reflect the adaptation to a hunting way of life which differentiates these animals from their primate cousins.

You will note that I say these "animals"—I might just as easily have said these "men"—and this is the moral of the story. What the record of evolution shows is no sharp break between man and animal that can be pinpointed at a certain brain size or anything else. What it shows is a very gradual transition in which changes in locomotion led the way and

290

in which the brain was something of a sluggard. The pelvis of the Australopithecinae—those man-apes of South and East Africa—is strikingly human and totally unlike anything in an ape, because these were bipedal creatures; but the brain was, if anything, smaller than that of a gorilla—an animal not noted for its cultural achievements.

The moral goes deeper. Once launched on the way to humanity through bipedalism, hunting, and the use of tools, our ancestors became more dependent on their brains than their predecessors had been. If they were going to survive largely by skill and cunning and rapid adaptation to the changing circumstances of the Pleistocene epoch, then a premium was put on the capacity for cultural behavior about which we have been speaking. Man took the cultural way before he was clearly distinguishable from the animals, and in consequence found himself stuck with this mode of adaptation. It turned out to be very successful, although for a while it must have been touch and go. But because he became dependent on culture, mutation and natural selection operated to improve on the organ most necessary to cultural behavior, namely the brain and in particular the neocortex with its important functions of association and control. Those animals, therefore, that were best able to be cultural were favored in the struggle for existence. Man's anatomy, physiology, and behavior therefore are in large part the *result* of culture. His large and efficient brain is a consequence of culture as much as its cause. He does not have a culture because he has a large brain; he has a large brain because several million years ago his little-brained ancestors tried the cultural way to survival. Of course, the correct way to view this is as a "feedback" process. As cultural pressures grew, so did selection pressures for better brains, and as better brains emerged, culture could take new leaps forward thus in turn exerting more pressures, and so on.

Again this is an over-simplified account, and the actual picture of the evolution of the brain is much more complex. But in essence it is true, and for our immediate purposes enough to make the point that our uniqueness is a biological uniquenesses and that culture does not in some mysterious sense represent a break with biology. Our present biological makeup is a consequence among other things of cultural selection pressures. We are, therefore, biologically constituted to produce culture, not simply because by some accident we got a brain that could do cultural things, but because the cultural things themselves propelled us into getting a larger brain. We are not simply the *producers* of institutions like the family, science, language, religion, warfare, kinship systems, and exogamy; we are the *product* of them. Hence, it is scarcely surprising

291

that we continually reproduce that which produced us. We were selected to do precisely this, and in the absence of tuition our mythical tribe would do it all over again in the same way. It is not only the *capacity* for culture then that lies in the brain, it is the *forms* of culture, the universal grammar of language and behavior.

This then is how it all got into the wiring of the human computer. Once we know these facts about human evolution there is no great mystery in principle about the production of culture by human beings and the relative uniformity of its processes. There are many mysteries of fact which will never be solved since we can only infer the behavior of fossil man and never observe it. But in principle, once we accept that culture is the major selection pressure operating on the evolution of human form and behavior, and that it has produced an animal wired for the processing of various cultural programs, then the problem of the uniqueness of man becomes a problem on the same level as the problem of the uniqueness of any other animal species.

Putting together the insights of the ethologists and the students of human evolution, we can scan the behavior of related species for aspects of behavior that are common to all primates, and beyond that we can look to mammals and vertebrates for clues. For in the process of evolution we did not cease to be primates or mammals. In fact, as Weston LaBarre (1955) has said, part of our success lies in exaggerating certain mammalian tendencies rather than in losing them—length of suckling, for example. Much of our behavior and in particular our social arrangements can be seen as a variation on common primate and gregarious mammalian themes. Certain "unique" aspects—such as the use of true language—can be investigated for what they are, biological specializations produced by the unique evolutionary history of the species.

This perspective enables us to look at human society and behavior comparatively without any necessity to propound theories of the total and essential difference between ourselves and other animals. It puts the obvious uniqueness into perspective and does not allow us to lose sight of our commonality with the animal kingdom. We are the cultural animal all right, but both terms should be given equal weight, and one does not contradict the other. For the last time then, let me say that culture does not represent a triumph over nature, for such a thing is impossible; it represents an end product of a natural process. It is both the producer and the product of our human nature, and in behaving culturally we are behaving naturally.

To bury this issue once and for all, at least to my own satisfaction, let

292

me add a word about the nature of culture as opposed to the nature of instinct. It is often said that man has "lost" all his instincts. I think this is a bit too extreme. If we might paraphrase Oscar Wilde: To lose some of one's instincts is unfortunate, to lose all of them smacks of carelessness. No species could afford to be that careless. But it is true that in terms of innate mechanisms which produce items of behavior complete at their first performance and relatively unmodifiable by experience, man has very few. Instead, it is often claimed, he has intelligence, foresight, wisdom and the like, and the enormous capacity to learn. Now in ditching instinct and opting for intelligence man took something of a risk, since instinct does provide a surety of response that has been evolved from trial and error over millions of years. Ant societies are much better organized and more efficient than any human societies and are driven wholly on instinctive mechanisms. But again instinct has its costs. It is too rigid. Changed circumstances cannot be met by a rapid adjustment in behavior, and insects and animals heavily dependent on instinct have to wait for processes of genetic change to effect changes in the instincts themselves before they can adjust. The higher we go up the phyletic scale the less true this is of course and with man least true of all. Thus there is a cost-benefit analysis involved in the shedding of innate instincts in favor of more complex modes of behaving.

The crux of the matter is this: Even if a species sheds its dependence on instincts, it still has to do the same things that instincts were designed to do. To put it into our earlier language, culture has to do the same job that instinct had been doing. This is another paradox, I suppose, but an intriguing one, because to get culture to do the same jobs as instinct had been doing, one had to make cultural behavior in many ways like instinctive behavior. It had to be unconscious so that it did not require thought for its operation, it had to be "automatic" so that certain stimuli would automatically produce it, and it had to be common to all members of the population.

If we look at our cultural behavior, how much of it is in fact intelligent and conscious, and how much is at that unthinking automatic response level? The answer, of course, is that the vast majority of our behavior is the latter, absorbed during our socialization and built into our patterns of habitual thought, belief, and response. Habit indeed is, as William James said, the great flywheel of society. Anthropologists speak of covert or unconscious culture to refer to this iceberg of assumptions, values, and habitual responses. And sitting over all of them, of course, is the great evolutionary invention of conscience, superego, moral sense, or whatever you want to call it. The sense of guilt, of having broken the taboos, the rules, the laws of the tribe, keeps most of us in line most of the time. Conscience is an empty cannister that culture fills, but once filled, it becomes a dynamic controller of behavior. Most of our behavior, however, never even rises to the point where conscience and the sense of guilt need to step in. We do what we do from habit, even down to tiny little details of gestures and twitches of the facial muscles. Most of this we never think about, but we rapidly recognize when other people are not behaving "normally" and we lock them up in asylums as lunatics. Think only of the example of the man walking down the road in the rain without a raincoat, smiling, shoulders back, head facing the sky. Clearly a madman. He should be hunched, hurrying, and looking miserable, with his jacket collar up at least.

The genius of nature here stands revealed and the paradox is resolved. Of course most of our learned cultural behavior in fact operates almost exactly like instinct and, as we have seen, this has to be the case. The customs and usages of the tribe, although not instinctive themselves, had to do the same jobs as instincts and hence had to be built into the automatic habit patterns of the tribal members, with guilt as a safeguard. (This was not foolproof, but neither is instinct itself.) So the same effect is achieved, and those habits which have proved useful in survival become part of the behavioral repertoire of the people. But—and here is the genius bit—these habits can be changed within a generation. One does not have to wait for the long process of natural selection to operate before these quasi-instinctual behaviors can be modified. They can be modified very rapidly to meet changing circumstances. Thus one has all the benefits of instinctive behavior without waiting for instincts to evolve. At any one time the rigidity of cultural habits will be just as invulnerable to change as any instinct—as we well know if we reflect on the persistence of traditions—and habits are very conservative. Since most of them are passed on by means other than direct tuition, they tend to persist over generations despite changes in overt education. But they can be changed relatively rapidly compared with the time span needed for changes in genetic material. Thus man can make rapid adjustments without anarchy (which does not mean that he always does so).

Here again we see learned, cultural behavior as yet another kind of biological adaptation. At this level, other species also display behavior of the same kind, and the higher in the scale they are, the more dependent they become on habits transferred over the generations by learning rather than instincts transferred in the genetic code. But always we must keep in mind that this is not a sharp distinction. The code is not silent about learning and habits. If the position taken here is anywhere near correct, then instructions about habitual behavior are as much in the code as instructions about instinctive behavior.

The model of behavior sees the human actor as a bundle of potentialities rather than a *tabula rasa:* potentialities for action, for instinct, for learning, for the development of unconscious habits. These potentials or predispositions or biases are the end product of a process of natural selection peculiar to our species. One consequence of this view is that much of the quasi-instinctive cultural behavior of man can be studied in much the same way and by much the same methods as ethologists study the truly instinctive behavior of other animals. Many strands of investigation seem to be leading in this direction at the moment.[3]

The kind of overall investigation that emerges from this theoretical position would utilize primarily three kinds of data: Data from human behavior both contemporary and known in history; data on animal behavior, particularly that on wild primates; data on hominid evolution with special attention to the evolution of the brain. Eventually data from genetics—molecular genetics, behavior genetics, and population genetics —will have to be included. But this is perhaps jumping ahead too far. At the moment the best we can say is that we should be prepared to use genetic data when we become sophisticated enough to incorporate it.

We began with the theme of human uniqueness and should end with my point that our uniqueness has to be interpreted in the same way as the uniqueness of any other species. We have to ask "How come?" How did culture get into the wiring? How did the great constructors operate to produce this feature, which, like everything else about us is not anti-nature, or superorganic, or extrabiological, or any of the other demagogic fantasy-states that science and religion imagine for us? Darwin did not banish mind from the universe as Butler feared; indeed, he gave us a basis for explaining how mind got into the universe in the first place. And it got there—as did every other natural and biological feature—by natural selection. The tool-making animal needed mind to survive; that is, he needed language and culture and the reorganization of experience that goes with these. And having got the rudiments and become dependent on them, there was no turning back. There was no retreat to the perilous

---

[3] *Editor's note:* Such work is already in progress as exemplified by studies conducted by N. G. Blurton Jones, "An Ethological Study of Some Aspects of Social Behavior of Children in a Nursery School," pages 337–368, in *Primate Ethology,* D. Morris, editor, Chicago: Aldine, 1967. (J.F.E.)

certainty of instinct. It was mind or nothing. It was classification and verbalization, rules and laws, mnemonics and knowledge, ritual and art, that piled up their pressures on the precarious species, demanding better and better brains to cope with this new organ—culture—now essential to survival. Two related processes, thought and self control, evolved hand in hand, and their end product is the cultural animal, which speaks and rules itself because that is the kind of animal it is; because speaking and self-discipline have made it what it is; because it is what it produces and was produced by what it is.

REFERENCES

Chance, M. R. A.
  1962. "The Nature and Special Features of the Instinctive Social Bond of Primates." In *Social Life of Early Man,* S. L. Washburn, editor. London: Methuen.
Chomsky, N.
  1957. *Syntactic Structures.* The Hague: Mouton & Co.
  1964. *Current Issues in Linguistic Theory.* The Hague: Mouton & Co.
  1965. *Aspects of the Theory of Syntax.* Cambridge: MIT Press.
Keith, Sir A.
  1948. *A New Theory of Human Evolution.* London: Watts & Co.
LaBarre, W.
  1955. *The Human Animal.* Chicago: University of Chicago Press.
Le Gros Clark, W. E.
  1957. *History of the Primates.* Chicago: University of Chicago Press.
Lenneberg, E. H.
  1967. *Biological Foundations of Language.* New York: John Wiley and Sons.
Lorenz, K.
  1966. *On Aggression.* London: Methuen.
Tiger, L.
  1969. *Men in Groups.* New York: Random House.
Wynne-Edwards, V. C.
  1962. *Animal Dispersion in Relation to Social Behavior.* London: Oliver and Boyd.

CHAPTER 9

THE EVOLUTION OF
HUMAN SOCIETY

IRVEN DEVORE

HARVARD UNIVERSITY

There is so much in the behavior of our nearest primate relatives that reminds us sometimes rather uncomfortably of ourselves. It is no accident that the majority of papers in this symposium are concerned to some degree with the burgeoning field of primate studies. The recorded debate over man-beast relationships is at least as old as Aesop's fables and the Egyptian tomb paintings that venerated Thoth, the sacred baboon. In this country the uncomfortable assumptions made by Darwin and Huxley a century ago became a national *cause celebre* during the Bryant-Darrow debates. The Scopes trial clearly revealed the polarization between what W. W. Howells has called "little lower than the angels" school and the "nothing-but" school. The late Earnest Hooton of Harvard stated the point of view of the latter school most succinctly when he said, "Man is a made-over ape with no fundamental distinctions at all."

These earlier comparisons between man and the great apes were based entirely on anatomical features, but recent evidence of genetics, seriology, and immunology suggest that we are yet closer to these primate relatives than even Huxley had realized when he reported his detailed comparisons in *Man's Place in Nature*. At least one immunologist has had the temerity to suggest that on the basis of biochemical evidence there is no reason even to separate man into the distinct genus *Homo;* man should by this argument swallow his pride and admit that he belongs in a common genus with the gorilla and chimpanzee. Nevertheless it is not the possibility of close physical and biochemical similarity with the great apes that has recently caught the public eye and ear but the possibility that there are important behavioral continuities between ourselves and other animals—a thesis most ably presented by such writers as Konrad Lorenz, Robert Ardrey, and Desmond Morris. Thus, more than a century after Darwin, we again find our noses being rubbed in the pungent juices of our putative animal ancestors.

Editor's note: Dr. DeVore was unable to complete his manuscript for publication. As a result we have included a modified transcript of the talk which he presented at the Man and Beast Symposium in May of 1969. (J.F.E.)

By contrast to the situation a century ago, however, today one senses an almost too willing eagerness to accept the notion that there are important continuities in the behavior from beast to man, perhaps even a masochistic pleasure in that acceptance. And what better excuse for our frustrating inability to solve the persistent domestic crises and international problems than to embrace the idea that mankind is driven by an ancient and inexorable heritage from the beasts? Unable to alleviate our condition, we turn once again to biological explanations, even as the last generation thought to rationalize the status quo through social Darwinism. That some social anthropologists are now willing to look to the primates for clues to understanding human behavior is a quite recent and, to me, very interesting phenomenon.

When I was a graduate student in the mid-50s, the whole subject of human behavioral evolution was surrounded with a sort of taint and suspicion otherwise reserved for research on human sexual behavior. Social anthropology had only too recently purged itself of the excesses of the nineteenth century evolutionists to be comfortable with the same devil in a new guise. The suggestion that one might study living peoples or living creatures for clues to human prehistory was considered a special heresy. In those days we looked somewhat smugly across the chasm which seemed to separate us from our benighted primate relatives, secure in the knowledge that man was, in almost all respects, unique—in his social life, his family, his social groups, his tool-use, his language. In the intervening years, the increasing prominence of ethology and the burgeoning number of primate field studies has steadily eroded this notion of human uniqueness. The "nothing-but" school is clearly in the ascendance and the studies of primates by several of us at this symposium has clearly contributed to this changing view.

In the past decade, so many clear homologies between human and nonhuman primate behavior have come to light that we can now assert with confidence that there are no basic patterns of human social behavior that are not found in one or another Old World monkey or ape; none, that is, except language and language-dependent behavior. But this simple example, apparently a guileless assertion, is at once a succinct statement of what is truly, uniquely human as well as a warning that language has permeated every aspect of human life. A monkey that will not mate with his mother strikes a responsive oedipal chord in the monkey watcher but there can be little comparison between an incest *aversion* and a rationalized incest *taboo*. In the same way, only language can convert a cluster of uterine kin into a matrilineal descent group. My own interest in primate behavior, in other words, is not to give comfort to the "nothing-but" school but to better understand and sharpen our definition of the uniquely human.

BEHAVIORAL BASELINES   I interpret my topic to be the same as understanding human behavioral evolution. For this task the only primary evidence is the tools and the bones of the toolmaker uncovered by the archeologist, and any attempt to reconstruct behavior from this is necessarily speculative, but this speculation need not be entirely unfettered; the mere bones of our remote ancestors, as S. L. Washburn has remarked, can reveal much about the behavior of these ancestors. Still, when speculative reconstruction proceeds even cautiously, there are many problems of interpretation over which men of good will can, and do, differ. And there are many problems that we can recognize better than we can explain. To mention only one: The processes of evolution are continuous but the nature of our evidence requires that we treat the processes as "stages." Here I will be speaking of only two such stages.

What we wish to reconstruct is the behavior of the Australopithecines, their kin, and their descendants during the Pleistocene—from about 3 million to 100,000 years ago. The difficulty is obvious. No living creature is comparable to these hominid ancestors. So, if we are interested in reconstructing behavior, we are left with two baselines that bracket this period. One on the order of five to fifteen million years ago (depending on how one interprets the evidence of our split with our pongid relatives), when we are concerned with creatures that were more ape-like than hominid. In the present state of knowledge, this ten-million-year disparity is not necessarily crucial; whenever the division took place, it marked the emergence of the hominid line from a primate stock. The second baseline concerns the behavior of hunter-gatherers who were morphologically identical to ourselves, *Homo sapiens,* in a period that began about 75,000 years ago and continues, in isolated pockets of the world, to the present time.

For reconstructing the first baseline, we have available the accumulating evidence of the behavior and ecology of nonhuman primates; for the second, we have the studies of living hunter-gatherers. At present the only strategy for reconstructing the evolution of human behavior is to take the data from living hunter-gatherers and extrapolate backward as best we can into the Pleistocene while trying to project the primate data forward. Obviously the first task is to understand these two baselines as

301

clearly as possible and what particularly interests me is that neither of these bodies of data has turned out to be very much like what we thought it would be only five years ago.

In the following discussion, I have dodged some important theoretical and semantic difficulties, such as, the proper use of analogy and homology and the consideration of genetic and behavioral continuities over long periods of time. Instead I have assayed the simpler task of trying to clarify and reinterpret what I feel are some current misunderstandings about the nature of the primate and hunter-gatherer baselines. This reinterpretation seems to me to take precedence. Once we understand the baselines better, the task of describing the probable behavior of early man can proceed with greater confidence.

EVIDENCE FROM THE NONHUMAN PRIMATES The primates are one of the most successful orders of mammals, numbering about 50 genera, 200 species, and 600 varieties. Probably no interesting statement about social behavior is true of every variety. In the following discussion, I am concerned with selected aspects of behavior and some of the best studied of our nearest relatives, the Old World monkeys and apes. In particular I want to focus on the roles of males and females and the nature of monkey and ape social organization.

Despite the considerable variation in social organization found in the Old World primates, there are ways in which most of them contrast rather sharply with many other mammals. The typical primate group is a persistent heterosexual, organized social group, to a large extent unaffected by the pronounced seasonal changes found among other mammals, birds, and reptiles. Nonprimate social groups are typically subjected to periodic seasonal disruption during which, under strong hormonal influences, the members of a group disperse and coalesce according to different stages in the reproductive cycle. The cohesion of the Old World primate group is intimately associated with other prominent features of primate life such as prolonged infant dependency and the crucial role of learning. But, however one views cause and effect, one generally finds in the Old World primates, a persisting stable social group. From the point of view of an individual primate, most are born, grow up, mate, and die in the same small face-to-face group.[1]

---

[1] *Editor's note:* The formation of persistent groups is a phenomenon not confined to primates within the class Mammalia. Large, long-lived mammals, with a considerable generation overlap resulting from an extended maturation period have a tendency to form social groupings of related individuals which persist through time. In many cases such social groupings may be matriarchally organized as, for

THE ROLE OF THE PRIMATE MALE Again it is useful to contrast the role of the primate male to the role of the male vertebrate generally. With notable exceptions, for example among many birds, the vertebrate male usually has only one important function: to contribute his share of the genes to the next generation. Having completed this brief and important duty, the male becomes a potential ecological embarrassment to the species. If he continues to stay near the female after copulation, he is in the position of competing with her for food.[2]

After impregnation, the females of many vertebrate species quite sensibly drive the males away. In other species, the female withdraws into seclusion, returning to the group only when her offspring are capable of keeping up. Whenever we find a species in which the male continues to live with the female after mating, it suggests that there are strong selective pressures in the opposite direction; that is, the males must be important in other ways if they are to compensate for their feeding competition with the female. Among most primates where the males are present at all times, the male contribution is to defend the group against predators and, in some species, to defend against territorial encroachment by neighboring groups. The role of the male as a defender is most obvious in some of the ground-adapted monkeys such as the baboons and macaques, where protection from predators is crucial for group survival. But even in many arboreal primates, the male may serve this important function. When a monkey-eating eagle swooped suddenly over a group of Colobus monkeys, feeding in the forest canopy, the females and young plummetted to the lower branches but an adult male scampered even higher in the tree to bark at the predator. Such incidents may be rare and are certainly seldom seen by ground-based human observers but must be significant in the survival of slow-breeding organisms like primates.

It is surely no accident that we find the largest cohesive social group-

---

example, in the African and Asiatic elephant (R. M. Laws and I. C. Parker, "Recent Studies on Elephant Populations in East Africa," pages 319–366, in *Comparative Nutrition of Wild Animals,* M. Crawford, editor; New York: Academic Press, 1968); but males may form persistent members of the social group throughout the annual cycle in such species as the wolf (D. G. Kleiman, "Some Aspects of Social Behavior in the Canidae," *American Zoologist* (1967), 7:365–372). (J.F.E.)

[2] *Editor's note:* Although this seems at first sight to be the case in many vertebrates, very often the male has an additional role in maintaining an area for exclusive occupancy for the female(s) and her (their) progeny. One or two dominant males may not travel consistently with a female group but may by their activities insure the dispersion of excess males into other areas. This would appear to be the rule in many mammalian forms (J. F. Eisenberg, *Handbuch der Zoologie* (1966), VIII (10/7), Leiferung 39). (J.F.E.)

ings including many adult males acting as group defenders among the baboons and macaques. This very successful radiation of Old World monkeys is the most terrestrially adapted of all the primates except man himself,[3] and like early man, they are thereby exposed to the greatest number and variety of predators. In thinking about the baseline of primate behavior from which our ancestors evolved, it was this ability to move freely from forest to open savannah, secure in the protection of a group defended by many males, that seems far more fundamental to me than the emergence of, say, the family organization.

It is useful, in fact, to compare this "troop organization" to that of the gibbon, a species with a so-called family organization (Carpenter 1940). The resemblance of a gibbon group (a mated pair of adults plus one or two immature offspring) to the elementary human family is entirely fortuitous except that the gibbon group is stable throughout the year; it might better be compared to a nesting pair of birds. Like the mated pair of birds, once gibbons have formed a pair bond, they vigorously repel all other gibbons except their own immature offspring and, again, like the birds, one result is that gibbon groups are isolated from each other. Their tiny territories divide the jungle in a checkerboard pattern. All human families are based on an entirely different set of principles but in the present context I merely want to emphasize that human families always occur as subunits within a larger social organization. Since there is no single kind of primate social organization and one must make a choice in reconstructing the primate baseline, my predeliction is to look at the larger types of primate groupings, and speculate how human families might have come to differentiate within the group (rather than trying to imagine how isolated pairs were able to overcome mutual antagonisms and join in a larger social cluster).

It was almost as if patterns of the human family were already waiting in at least some of those organized Old World primate groups—waiting for catalysts which would precipitate out what we came finally to see as the human family. What was precipitated, in my opinion, was the hunter-gatherer way of life.

The male baboon is a control animal within a baboon society. An adult male does not tolerate instability in the group and he will give warning grunts toward a group of fighting juveniles. He will intervene frequently when any disturbance occurs. If the approach or exposure of the canines accompanied with a grunt is not sufficient, the male will attempt to pull

---

[3] With the interesting and instructive exception of the Patas monkey, in this species, protection from predators is sought by a combination of speed, stealth, and decoy maneuvers by the single adult male in the group (Hall 1965).

the combatants apart; thus, there is a constant stabilizing influence on the part of these males who actively interfere when fights break out. The dominant male baboon within a group makes a significant contribution to the total number of progeny born into that troop. As is well known, the sexual skin of the female baboon undergoes swelling at the time of estrus. The female goes through eight to ten days of partial swelling and then through five to ten days of maximum swelling. Young juvenile males and older juveniles all copulate with females during the period of partial swelling; however, during the period of maximum swelling when the female is ovulating, only the dominant males within the troop copulate. In the case of the troop that I analyzed, the three most dominant males confined their mating entirely to the time when the female was ovulating and therefore, of course, when pregnancy was most likely. This sort of mating situation sets up a kind of positive feed-back system in which every generation constantly selects the most egocentric, most vicious, dominant, striving animals. Here, as in the central hierarchy, there must be a modicum of cooperation with at least some other adult males before effective breeding is possible.

THE ROLE OF THE PRIMATE FEMALE   The role of the female within the primate troop has been underestimated in the past. In truth, the female-young unit is the essentially most cohesive subgrouping within a primate troop. Indeed, a given female's offspring of various ages will still seek to gather around her when she rests or feeds. The mother, we have found, helps determine the final status of the young male—her son, that is—when he grows up. When groups split up, all evidence that we have at hand indicates that they divide along mother-family lines.

THE ROLE OF THE SUBADULT MALE   In leaving the primates, a final word should be said about the role of the young male. In the savanna baboon, the young juvenile male, as he matures, must fight his way up through the female-dominant hierarchy until he reaches a kind of limbo above all the females but still below any of the adult males, much less the ones in the central hierarchy. There is, in other words, a kind of delayed social maturity in the young male baboon which is, I submit, the classic opportunity for frustration and, indeed, we find in such groups that the most aggressive animals are these young subadult males constantly quarrelling with the females and constantly being put down by the adult males. In some respects they are totally disruptive—the juvenile delinquents of the primate world. Not only are they unable to get into the establishment, they are literally in the hair of all the adults in the baboon group.

This kind of behavior is absolutely functional for the young subadult

305

male baboon if he is going to be an effective adult. If he is going to be able to fight effectively as an adult, he has to learn how to fight while he is growing up. On the other hand, from a certain point of view, he is expendable. He is the most expendable animal in the group—the baboon equivalent of cannon fodder. During this period of life, he often becomes spatially quite peripheral to the group. In some species of macaque, the young males simply leave. They go off into young all-male groups together. In species like the savanna baboon where no animal leaves the group at any time during his lifetime unless he is changing groups, they become socially peripheral (see Chapter 6 by Hans Kummer).

This kind of basis for behavior has persisted historically in human societies. Within human societies there is honor and respect for the young men who were most eager to fight to protect society or who were eager to raid the neighbors in the next valley. The young male has continued to be selected for his enjoyment of violent exercise, violent activity, sports, etc., which are in many ways thinly disguised preparations—psychologically and physically—for the more sober pursuits of war. This illustrates the sort of feed-back one gets between biology and behavior and refers also to the remarks of Dr. Wilson in talking about the persistence of behavior patterns if they continue to be selected for. Otherwise, such behavior patterns may be dropped out rather rapidly. That is to say, because man is a slow-breeding species, culture will take advantage of the biological potential of the material it has to work with and will tend to reinforce the trend that was started perhaps at a much earlier period. Today with certain secular trends like the age of puberty becoming younger and the length of education becoming longer and longer, we have completely maximized our opportunities for frustrating our young people. If you take the female point of view for a moment and contrast the female at the turn of the century who reached puberty at the age of 15 and was married at 17 and compare her with the girl today who reaches puberty at 11 or 12 and is expected to be in college until the age of 22, you can see what I mean by the period of frustration. Young men today are adult in many ways for the last ten years that they spend in college or school.

A CONSIDERATION OF HUNTER-GATHERER SOCIETY Now for some brief comments about the Bushmen[4] and other hunter-gatherers. When we first went to the Bushmen, we were surprised that they were nothing like what we had been led to believe. They were described in the textbooks as leading a hand-to-mouth existence—eating witchetty grubs and all sorts of

---

[4] *Editor's note:* The author refers to the !Kung Bushmen of Botswana. (J.F.E.)

things—during a life that was nasty, brutish, and short. In economic texts, they are always made to play the bad example, that is, the subsistence economy. We have been trying to collect, not only data on social organization and social anthropology but the same kinds of ecological and demographic data that we have been doing in our primate studies with some rather surprising results. The Bushmen have discovered a work pattern involving only about twenty hours of effort per week; something that our very best unions have not managed yet. Only the most able adults work at all. The youngsters and the old people do not. On this twenty-hour work-week, they are able to provide for themselves about 135 percent of the UNESCO-recognized minimum standards of fats, carbohydrates, and proteins which puts them ahead of a substantial portion of Americans. And, indeed, the demographers who are on our staff now assure me that you have to go to Western Europe and the United States to find life expectancy tables that compare with the Bushmen; that is, many Bushmen live into their eighties. It is no problem at all to find Bushmen who are over sixty.

In the sense of modern economic theory or in the opinion of J. K. Galbraith, human needs or desires are great and perhaps infinite and our means of production are inadequate or at least perfectable. On the other hand, the hunter-gatherers of the Old World tropics—the Bushmen among them—have a more Zen solution. In their point of view, man's needs are finite and his means of production are unchanging, but on the whole adequate.[5] The women, gathering fruits and nuts, are responsible for assembling 80 percent of the subsistence of the Bushmen. The collection of mango nuts permits a relatively stable way of life. Bushmen do not in other words primarily depend on hunting to eat. The nut itself is high in vitamin C. They occur in unharvested billions in the Bushmen area and, in fact, this tribe of Bushmen call themselves the "mango people." In other parts of the Kalihari Desert where the mango nut is not available, the basic staple of the diet for other tribes may be a bean which grows in great abundance and which is also very rich in protein.

One of the points that I am trying to make by showing these photographs is that we have not taken sufficient account of what the women

---

[5] *Editor's note:* Dr. DeVore showed several slides of Bushmen life illustrating that the men who decide to work for the day generally go as a group to carry out their hunting efforts whereas the mothers and women carry out collecting duties. He also showed slides of the trance dance for which they are quite famous. Something like half of all men over thirty go into spontaneous trances during these communal dances. During the trance state, special individuals can go from one person to another healing, laying on hands, etc. (J.F.E.)

are doing. Gathering is a sure way of making a living but hunting is risky. Anthropology has been largely written by men concerning men's activities, especially hunting, and furthermore I think we have been misled by the bias of the hunters themselves. The hunters value meat above all else; they pay no attention in terms of value to the fact that 80 percent of their diet is derived from vegetable foods. This is well illustrated, I think, in the problem of interpreting the archeological records. Women in the Bushmen society are producing 80 percent of the diet. Their tools include a digging stick and a leather bag. When she comes back to camp, she has a mortar and pestle made of wood and a pair of cracking stones. The men, in setting out, are equipped for anything. They have knives, arrows, and spears. Now, if you assume that these tools are buried and years later dug up and all the perishable material has gone, you will be more likely to find the vast array of hunting materials and you would come to the conclusion that these people were living a hunting way of life and perhaps doing a little gathering. Indeed, you would probably and quite justifiably classify the cracking stones for cracking bones for marrow rather than for cracking the very hard nuts for which they were devised.

In looking at people like the Bushmen and other Old World gatherers, one of the things that is immediately important is sharing. They never stored goods like all of their descendants afterward—particularly the agriculturalists—but they shared. This is a thing that the primates do not do very well; that is, it is quite clear that already in the primate social organization level it is relatively easy for the female baboon or chimpanzee to gather plenty in a day to feed not only herself and her offspring and any males that happen to be around but she does not share this. There is a bit of sharing in the chimpanzees but it is not very frequent. Now sharing is one of the most important of human attributes. One of the earliest and most important of all. Unfortunately, it is very hard to find evidence in the archeological record of sharing but we find evidence for what Washburn and I call the home base; that is, an area where you can go out in the morning in two different directions, the man in one direction and the woman and the juveniles in another, and come back in the evening to share at that home base. This is something strangely enough that no non-human prime has; that is, when a primate group leaves in the morning, all must stay with the group. There is no assurance that they will come back to the same sleeping place although this again is subject to some exception. But certainly there can obviously be no discussion about the strategy of the day. Now there must have been a time in human history when there was a catalyst which precipitated the family out of these patterns which were floating already in the primate social groups. It was not just hunting as we have tended to call it in the past but a hunting-gathering way of life. It was not just men hunting and feeding the women but it was a sharing in the real sense.

Partly on the basis of local evidence of the Paleolithic in Europe, it seems that man came from a vegetarian ancestry, went through a long period in which he was almost exclusively a hunter, and then returned to an omnivorous and highly vegetable diet. In the primate data we find virtually every pattern associated with the small human face-to-face group except—and most importantly—those patterns which are associated with language. I still see this as by far the major difference between ourselves and the nonhuman primates. It was at this time in the early to middle Pleistocene that language became ecologically and economically important for the first time.

In closing, let me speak on a matter which has concerned many speakers at this symposium, that is the business of aggression, of spacing apart, and of territory. As we have gathered data from the hunter-gatherers, it became increasingly clear that hunter-gatherers do not have a territory in the classic sense of the word. They do defend certain spots like water holes but then some non-territorial primates defend the trees they are in. As for aggression, Bushmen solved the problem of aggression by what is called fission. They just move off from the group for they can go to any other group in the area. For example, in the population that we were considering, there are 400 people in twenty groups of twenty but the constituents in those twenty groups of twenty change almost weekly, certainly every month; so that, at any one time, you find twenty groups of twenty but families have moved back and forth. Now the families usually give a good sound ecological reason for this arrangement. They say that they are going to go on a visit; but what you notice, if you are living at the camp, is that in fact a certain amount of social stress has developed between two families and it has reached a point where they want to separate.

Looking at subsequent human history, we realize that in ways the Bushmen are extraordinarily lucky. They can put all of their goods on their backs and move to the next group. Once you have fixed assets, once you have herds and inheritance, and once you own property this is something you cannot do. You must defend it and then the peculiarly human aspects of territoriality and human aspects of aggression and aggression over aspects of inheritance matters come into force. It is really a mistake to see these kinds of patterns as deriving from a more distant past. Although they are based on the same kinds of motivations and impulses—and I do

309

not deny that—I still think that what we see in human territoriality is really of quite a different order from what we see in the other animals. The Bushmen and the hunter-gatherers generally have what in the modern idiom might be called the "flower child solution." You put your goods on your back and you go. You do not have to stay and defend any piece of territory or defend fixed assets. It is interesting to observe then that for 99 percent of our history we have been hunter-gatherers, and pastoralists for only the last 10,000 years. The extent to which we can see carry-overs from these earlier ways of life to the present time are instructive. I submit that these changes will take place most rapidly in those aspects of behavior which are most maleable. Territoriality, a most complex kind of behavior, is clearly quite maleable in the nonhuman primates as well as in ourselves; hence it may show little carry-over from previous times in its present expression. On the other hand, one has the feeling that there are deep-seated reactions to the feelings of stress, rage, and affection which are much older and which I feel are quite persistent.

It is actually easier to illustrate the preceding conclusion with a medical example than with behavior which is more complex and difficult. Bushmen for example eat all of the honey and all of the animal fats that they can find. This makes a great deal of sense, if you are a Bushman, to get in these highly caloric packages; and presumably this made sense for ourselves as well through the Pleistocene. One gets calories where one can. Today we have perhaps inherited this liking for sweets, this liking for animal fats, but now we can satisfy this with chocolate bars and corn-fed cattle. One of the results is what we have come to call the degenerative disease in mankind. The biologists on our project reported that the Bushmen have the lowest cholesterol ever reported in any human population—it is roughly half of what we have. They have so little salt excretion that it compares with our being fed a salt-free diet. The point is that within the context of a hunter-gatherer life, eating sweets and fats is adaptive and beneficial. Within our own stress-filled, urbanized world, similar feeding patterns promote degenerative diseases.

REFERENCES

Editor's note: For the reader's convenience, the six citations offered below should lead to a wider acquaintance with some of the material discussed by Dr. DeVore. (J.F.E.)

Carpenter, C. R.
  1940. "A Field Study in Siam of the Behavior and Social Relations of the Gibbon." *Comparative Psychology Monograph* 16 (5). Baltimore: Johns Hopkins Press.
DeVore, I., and K. R. L. Hall.
  1965. "Baboon Ecology." In *Primate Behavior*, I. DeVore, editor. New York: Holt, Rinehart & Winston.
Hall, K. R. L.
  1965. "Behavior and Ecology of the Wild Patas Monkey, *Erythrocebus patas*, in Uganda." *Journal of Zoology*, 148:15–87.
Hall, K. R. L., and I. DeVore.
  1965. "Baboon Social Behavior." In *Primate Behavior*, I. DeVore, editor. New York: Holt, Rinehart & Winston.
Lee, E. B., and I. DeVore, editors.
  1968. *Man the Hunter*. Chicago: Aldine.
Washburn, S. L., editor.
  1961. *The Social Life of Early Man*. Chicago: Aldine.

311

CHAPTER 10

THE GREAT SHIFT:
INSTINCT TO INTUITION

SUSANNE K. LANGER

CONNECTICUT COLLEGE

In the discussion of the comparable aspects of animal communities and human society, emphasis has usually fallen on their similarities rather than on their differences. Their similarities, moreover, are often regarded as indications of basic identities in motivation, purpose, and value. But similar appearances, whether of form or action, are as often convergent evolutionary products as generic common traits. Think only of the hummingbird's flight, which looks for all the world like an insect's—a sphynx moth's, for instance, or a dragonfly's. Yet the mechanism of the hummingbird's movement is entirely avian, and quite unrelated to insect flight. Their similarity is a result of convergent developments, not of common heredity (Gregory 1951).

If you want to find the true relationships of taxonomic groups, a good method is to study the differences that set them apart. By pursuing their specializations backward as far as they go, you come to limits beyond which no distinctions can be made; then you have found the fundamental similarities of all animals of the phylum or phyla you are dealing with.

Bodily traits, both anatomical and physiological, may be hard to study *in vivo* because the observer has to disturb the fluid structures and the processes he would like to observe in an undisturbed state; but technological progress is making more and more of them accessible. In our genuine laboratory sciences of biochemistry, physiology, and embryology we are doing fairly well, and have every hope of solving the problems which at present still elude us, such as, what happens in the thinking and perceiving brain, or pragmatically vital issues like the cause of cancer formation, of cerebral palsy, and of others we all could think of. In genetics we have reached the point of checking mathematically formulated hypotheses against empirical facts. But the same cannot be said of the aspects of life— and, specifically, the life of higher animals, say the vertebrates—which interest us in the context of the present symposium: the causes of animal behavior, especially group behavior, and their relation to our own communal life, that is, to human society.

It is an interesting fact that all our advanced biological theory does not lead systematically into an equally advanced psychology. When an inquiry does not go on, but balks at perfectly relevant questions of some particular sort, the trouble is usually deep seated and conceptual. The basic concepts with which we are operating successfully in a limited field are not capable of extension to a wider one. But scientific fields do expand, and as they do, new questions arise, as for instance psychological questions from biological facts. Then a new conceptual vocabulary—not a metaphorical use of old vocabulary—has to make a new frame (Langer 1967), capable of housing the original field of research in a wider one. Let me introduce a couple of new basic concepts in terms of which we can talk adequately about the three phenomena mentioned in the title of this lecture—instinct, intuition, and the shift from one to the other which made the great divergence of genus *Homo* from the rest of the primate stock (or stocks, our line may be polyphyletic).

The key concept with which I have been operating for the past decade is the concept of "the act" as the unit of vital process. As an abstract concept, this term is used not in any of its several popular senses in which it commonly means a moral act, a conscious act, or at least an overt act, but technically; it is used here to designate any event of a particular form occurring in a particular sort of context, both of which can be physically defined. This concept of "act," though not popularly understood, is already current in physiological and psychological discourse; and it really goes far back in scientific language. Sir Henry Head, at a symposium of the Aristolelian Society fifty years ago, spoke of a "complete sensory act" (Head 1919, p. 79); E. von Holst (1957, p. 237) speaks of a direct perception as "ein ganz unmittelbarer Wahrnehmungsakt"[1] and of the cause of continuity in vision as "ein höherer integrationsakt"[2] (op. cit., p. 241); Paul Weiss (1959, p. 16) has called "conditioning" "a non-overt act" and refers to "the mitotic act" (Weiss 1958, p. 19). This usage is highly general, but in no respect vague. The act is a form that all vital events take, from metabolism to human thinking, from putting out a pseudopodium to visiting the moon. It is marked by a formative phase, the impulse, which may be very short or quite long; a phase of development, the buildup of the act; a phase of consummation, and finally a declining phase for which I can find no good English word except the musical term *cadence*. Cadence means "fall." It denotes the closing passage of a piece of music, in which an overall tension is finally resolved.

---

[1] A completely direct perception act.
[2] A higher act of integration.

316

Similarly, I think it applies naturally enough to the final spending of the impetus built up in the impulse, rise, and consummation of an act.

The reason why the concept of "act" also involves a special sort of context is that the act form, in itself, is not entirely peculiar to vital processes. It is exemplified in some nonliving processes, especially chemical reactions. A very simple illustration is what happens if you put a spoonful of soda into a glass of lemonade. After a few milliseconds the liquid foams up, climbs to a maximum head, then the reaction subsides, and the substance resumes its resting form in a new chemical state, as a salt. More than fifty years ago D'Arcy Thompson (1951, vol. 1, p. 258) pointed out the difference between such a chemical reaction and an act occurring in an organism: the chemical reaction ends with the appearance of a new compound, but the vital act goes on, engendering other acts (often repetitions of itself) or breaking up into subacts which are drawn into other acts in rising phases (Thompson 1951). This, as you can guess, is a long and intricate story. The upshot of it is that every "true act," as I would call it, arises from a matrix of other, concomitant acts, and spends itself in this same stream of act-engendered acts as part of the self-propagating process.

Such a matrix of activities is a physiological continuum, a living system, presented as a whole by reason of the involvement of its act with each other. It is an organism, and in regard to each of its acts it is the "agent." An agent is a product and producer of acts; a living being.

As acts, which are the units of vital process, have a complicated form, so the basic operation that produces new acts from an old one and creates the continuously growing matrix is a special operation. It is peculiar only in its complexity. This complexity, however, strains human powers of conception (Platt 1961, Schmitt 1963). Every act begins as an impulse caused by the occurrence of an energy pattern in the matrix. No single event is *the* cause. Any influence that may loosely be said to cause an act has to exert its influence on the matrix, the living system. The operation which really produces the act involves a special causal relationship between the matrix and the act; this constantly exemplified operation may be called motivation. Again, the word is commonly used in a more restricted sense, namely the influence of needs, fears, or desires on the overt acts of an agent. But that is a special case of the broader sense. As P. T. Young (1955), commenting on a symposium paper, said: "If motivation is a contemporary process of energizing, then all behavior is motivated since all behavior is determined by energy transformations within the tissues. If the process of motivation is revealed only in goal-directed behavior, then we can distinguish between motivated (purposive) and unmotivated (random) behavior. I prefer the broader concept . . ." I am following Dr. Young's usage. A word for the causation of impulses is needed, and the use of "motivation" for it is in the literature (Delgado, Roberts, and Miller 1954; Twitty and Niu 1954), so that is what "motivation" means here.

We have, then, these notions to work with: acts, having the variable but basically characteristic form of impulse, rise, consummation, and cadence; the operation of motivation whereby past and current acts engender new impulses; the dense system or matrix of acts, most of which are metabolic and trophic, microscopic acts in endless rhythmic trains. Imposed on such minuscule activities are the larger physiological activities that have larger cycles, and the whole system is a living organism.

So now, at last, we come to the problem of instinct. Let me say, first of all—categorically, for want of time to explain and justify the statement —that I do not think there are any specific "instincts," functions of special mechanisms, like reflexes and perhaps tropisms. But there are instinctive acts. That is, I will accept "instinctive" as an adjective without subscribing to the hypothetical units designated by the noun, "instinct." On this subject I find myself in complete agreement with J. B. S. Haldane (1956, p. 451) who said at a symposium on instinct in Paris: "Biffons si vous voulez, le substantif 'instinct,' mais pas l'adjectif 'instinctif.' "[3] The term "instinct" in the title of this paper is shorthand for "instinctive behavior."

Instinctive action is usually understood to be behavioral—that is, to be overt action rather than intraorganic or covert. But behavioral acts of such organisms as we are considering—vertebrates, especially the higher forms—arise before birth from somatic activities. Those muscular acts which develop *in utero* or *in ovo* belong to what embryologists call the "motor action system," which is a dynamic pattern of nervously generated, species-characteristic acts such as head turning, finger movements, flexions of arms and legs and trunk, chewing or sucking movements, eye movements (yes, *in utero*), and so on (Hamburger 1963, Ebert 1965). All these movements are unaimed yet typically formed acts. Unlike reflexes, which belong to another system that appears somewhat after the start of the motor-action phenomena, the latter gain in articulation in the course of gestation, so many of them are quite distinct and complete at term. These acts are the animal's basic repertoire, overt expressions of hereditary, systematically maturing behavioral impulses. They are not yet

---

[3] Reject, if you will, the noun "instinct" but not the adjective "instinctive."

instinctive acts (for reasons we are just coming to), but they are *instinctual elements*. The basic repertoire consists of such instinctual elements.

Instinctive behavior involves another factor besides native impulse, in that most acts of the organism as a whole become effective only if they are met by some extrinsic material in which they make a change. Eating requires something to eat. Digging requires something to dig into. That is, most behavioral acts presume a substrate to implement them. This part of any situation in which animals are able to act develops only after birth, and with it their instinctive life really begins. It is at this juncture that the organs of perception come into play, and are used in support of the internal feelings of desire and aversion, enticement and fear, to guide the agent in its constant search for opportunities to enact its impulses.

All animal reaction is instinctive. Animal intelligence is capability to find implementation for acts developed from the physiologically engendered instinctual repertoire. One may say that animal intelligence, where it exists, is exhibited in the pursuit of instinctive action. But instinctive behavior may also be quite devoid of intelligence; a rat with an urgent impulse to retrieve a pup when there was none outside the nest has been known to carry its own tail (Eibl-Eibesfeldt 1963). Perhaps we should credit it with the intelligence to help itself. Equally unadaptive is the spawning procedure of some large neotropical toads, which "will spawn in any kind of standing water, including narrow and shallow ditches . . . The eggs . . . contain very inadequate yolk reserves. Hatching occurs in a very rudimentary condition . . . which must result in heavy mortality" (Lutz 1948, p. 37). Yet no "natural selection" has bred toads too wise to lay in ditches and puddles that are about to dry up. Peter and Gertraud Krott, in a long first-hand study of the European bear in the wild, observed that bears neither learn to accept or ignore the presence of nonhostile human agents (such as road workers and foresters) nor learn to avoid danger when they are hungry (Krott and Krott 1963, p. 198). Dozens of further instances of such instinctual inadequacy could be added here, from bird, crustacean, and insect life.

The lengths to which the elaboration of instinctive behavior, practical or impractical, can go are astounding, especially in birds. But it is interesting that communal acts—which are the most complex in human life—among beasts and even birds remain relatively simple. The perfectly timed and coordinated movements of a rising, wheeling flock of blackbirds, and the much less perfect "V" formation of geese in flight, are about as cooperative as general group behavior becomes in birds and mammals. The "mobbing behavior" of birds jointly attacking a predator has no collaborative strategy (Hinde 1954). Tschanz, in a very thorough study of the colonial habits of the Atlantic Murre, found that the closely settled ledges where these birds nest are not cooperatively defended against predators, but as each nest site is defended by its owners and the nests are so close that the birds sit almost shoulder to shoulder, the effect of their individual actions is that of a closed front (Tschanz 1959, p. 94).

The most elaborate performances of birds occur in their reproductive cycles, which comprise courtship, coition, nestbuilding, egglaying, incubation, feeding and brooding the young in the nest or guarding them as chicks, and sometimes defending territory, nest, mate, or the clutch. In this cycle one finds not only great variations on the single, clearly identical theme, but the most improbable variants: consider the mound-building birds in which the male, with or without help from the female, builds an enormous mound of decaying vegetable matter, digs holes in it where the female then lays her eggs; whereupon he, generally alone, tends this incubator for weeks or even months, opening and closing it to keep the temperature steady (Kendeigh 1952, Frith 1959); or the strange development of behavior in the hornbills, where the female enters her tree-hole nest before the first egg is laid and the male brings clay to wall up the entrance (at which she helps him), leaving only a small window through which he feeds her for six to eight weeks (Kendeigh 1952); or the exaggerated courtship behavior of the bower birds which build walled display grounds and decorate them with colored leaves, shells, and man-made objects like bottle caps (Marshall 1954).

Yet in spite of such extreme elaboration of individual and mutual acts, the colonial nesting of seabirds, sand martins, herons, and some other species leads to no cooperative behavior, and even the communal nesting of some weaver birds has no interesting behavioral results; nothing like the division of labor in colonial insects, which we are not here considering, because their development has diverged too far from the vertebrates to be comparable to our own, and such comparisons are what we are aiming at. The same thing holds for mammals that live in herds or in territorial communities: any apparent joint action—like the group formation of a bison herd under attack—where the bulls are said to surround the cows and calves, results from the momentary impulse of each animal, most of the bulls being aggressive and forging to the fronts while the calves push to the center for protection and the cows are caught between the two movements. In the colonial life of the highly specialized mammals such as the beavers, there is no division of labor;[4] any number may be working together on a dam, yet the work of each beaver is exactly what it would be if he were building alone. In a prairie-dog town there is no plan except the automatic spacing-out of burrows, no urban life but the fright reaction of many at the alarm call of one, and the use of common runways (King 1959).

Elaborate instinctive practices develop predominantly, if not solely, from individual or sexual activities. Since they reach their highest evolution in birds,[5] I return to that order to consider the essential nature of instinct, which accounts to a great extent for this limitation.

Every instinctive act is roughly preformed in the impulse which it expresses. For the sake of brevity, I can only ask you to accept that assertion at present. I have given the factual grounds for it elsewhere (Langer 1967). Impulses can be very complex, so their expressions are not simple discharges of energy, but large acts with various phases, sub-acts, and often with both physiological and behavioral aspects. The marvel of their teleology, especially in cases where the agent could not possibly foresee the situation its behavior is to meet or to bring about, is comprehensible if you consider that every impulse spends itself if and as it can, as Konrad Lorenz pointed out long ago (Tinbergen 1951). The animal is not seeking the effect of its act, but the conditions that will implement its continuance and consummation. The goal of the act is simply its completion, and its completion involves the change it makes in the external world. The performance is guided by organic feeling and the perception of substrates, means, and obstacles. Such perceived conditions appear as enticements, lures, threats, blocks, openings; the internal needs arise and change partly by intrinsic timing and partly in hastened response to stimuli from the progressive, implementing situation.

In birds and beasts, unlike human beings, the procreative cycle—from mating to the final abandonment of the reared brood—is one act. This single act undergoes all the developments it possibly can in the confines of the situation and the hereditary potential of the stock. The influences which encourage the elaboration of particular elements are too diverse for

---

[4] *Editor's note*: Some division of labor is achieved through the classical division of activities into male and female sexual roles or through the serial role differentiation during the processes of extended maturation. (J.F.E.)

[5] *Editor's note:* While not detracting from Dr. Langer's statement, it may be fairly stated that Teleost fishes equal the birds in the elaboration of "instinctive practices." (J.F.E.)

discussion here, so I shall just give you one example: the fantastic court-ship preparations and antics of the bower birds can be traced to a great discrepancy between the onset of sex interest in the male and in the female. He has to wait six to ten weeks for her to attain the state and the mood for actual mating. All that time she watches him, but he has to express and also maintain his excitement until she is receptive. In the course of evolu-tion, the increase of the temporal gap has not been checked because his courtship activities have overdeveloped progressively to hold the pair-bond for a longer and longer stretch (Marshall 1954).

This unity of instinctive acts, which permits the development of their highly articulated sub-acts, is what makes it possible for animals to per-form feats that seem to aim at practical consequences. The agent lives from one impulse to another in the expression of a total act engendered by hereditary organic dispositions, implemented by ambient conditions, and enlisting the native repertoire of the species. It is not hard to see that such activity would be largely individual, sexual, or parental, rather than com-munal, though there are some (still relatively simple) exceptions.

A notable one is the behavior of the African hunting dogs studied on their range by Wolfdietrich Kühme (1965). These animals hunt in a pack that consists of adults of both sexes and such juveniles as can keep up with them. Puppies, nursing bitches, and other individuals unable to hunt stay behind; the returning hunters vomit almost-fresh meat for them. Kühme makes no mention of castes, clubs, or leaders and says explicitly that in spite of the closest observation he was unable to detect anything like a social hierarchy.

The tendency of acts to become more and more detailed and involved in the course of evolution can lead to a point where they become too intri-cate to be altogether practicable. Since numberless impulses are always pushing for actualization in an organism, any blocking of one mechanism allows some other to go into operation; then there is competition between two (or even more) systems to control the effectors to the same end. It may also happen that a primitive mechanism is no longer equal to its task because the organism is developing rapidly in other ways and throws too much of a burden on it. Again, some entirely different impulse pat-tern, working through different physiological channels, may achieve the instinctive end in a new way and gradually take over from the old one. That is known as *functional shift*. Whole sequences of functional shifts go on in the prenatal history of the higher animals. The greatest im-portance of functional shift, however, is in evolutionary progress, where anatomic, physiologic, and behavioral functions shift from primitive to

322

higher and higher anatomical mechanisms as these mechanisms become ready to assume the functions (Bock 1959).

Before we can discuss the promised key concept of this lecture, which I think of as "The Great Shift"—the shift from animal to human life—one other principle of biological existence must be recalled: namely, that every organism is always enacting all the impulses it can. Behaviorally this means that it tries to respond to all the perceptions and other stimulations its nervous system receives. This fact underlies the final synthesis of all the nervous developments in the Hominidae that made them depart so radically from the other advancing primate stocks.

It has been said that man owes his biological success to the fact that he has remained unspecialized, meaning that he is not closely and particularly adapted to any special environment, having remained plastic and unfixed, like an embryonic form. This proposition, on which Arnold Gehlen based his widely read book *Der Mensch* (1940), has been used by several animal psychologists to explain the biological success of cowbirds, crows, gulls, rats, and mice as unspecialized animals not limited by adaptation to a special habitat. (The originator of this idea with respect to man, according to Gehlen, was Bolk [1926].)

The human stock, in fact, has undergone several pronounced specializations. The upright posture is only partly available to other primates; it is natural to man because of anatomical modifications of the pelvis, femur, knee joint, and the development of his abductor and extensor muscles. The evolution of the hand involves more than the famous opposable thumb; its finger play and high innervation make it as much a sense organ as an effector. That may have been part and parcel of the fateful advance, which was the extreme overdevelopment of the central nervous system, including the sense organs. Epicritical vision and hearing, the sensibility of a naked skin, and probably a comparable broadening of the creature's range of interest and attention tended to overwhelm its capacity for overt responses. Yet animal acts arise from immediate conditions and normally terminate in behavior.[6] If we, in our present human state, responded to all the sensory stimuli that impinge on us, we would all have St. Vitus' dance.

This discrepancy between impression and possible expression must have

---

[6] *Editor's note:* Yet animals do not respond immediately to impinging stimuli and indeed a given animal may have a predisposition to respond to certain key stimuli which is completely tied to the current, predominating motivational state (see also E. von Holst and U. von St. Paul, *Naturwissenschaften*, 18:409–422). (J.F.E.)

begun millions of years ago in the hominid line, when the stock was still entirely animal (though perhaps always parallel, not identical, with ape and monkey stocks), and behaved only instinctively. But the strain of excessive awareness forced some of the cerebrally initiated acts to fall short of complete expression; the effect was a great intensification of nervous action that rose to the level of sensation as an image, and spent itself that way. Perhaps this happens in beasts, too, but is just a passing occurrence. In the human strain, however, it became habitual and constant, so that it influenced the evergrowing brain which provided the great outward receptivity, so the phenomenal forebrain development snowballed on its phylogenetic way. Images became cathected so that they attained an emotional value quite separate from the emotional value of percepts (sense data) as practical indicators. But actual percepts, too, became deeply affected by autogenic images, and were often distorted by their merger with such phantasms.

Products of imagination are probably not hereditary like instinctual elements of behavior, though I would not be too dogmatic in rejecting hereditary tendencies. (C. G. Jung's "archetypes" are supposed—on romantic rather than scientific grounds—to have some sort of hereditary status. Since this has not been investigated, I would not deny the possibility of inherited natural symbols.) All that is in the human gene pool, I believe, is the image-making tendency itself. But every normal individual soon acquires a repertoire of cathectic images, and these products operate in mental activity much as the elements of the instinctual repertoire function in overt behavior; that is, images are variable, combinable, and, above all, evocable by all sorts of involuntary acts and some voluntary ones. A direct perception may set off a train of quite different imaginal experiences; the stimulus need not be in the same sensory mode as the phantasy it motivates; for instance, a nonvisual experience, like a sound, may evoke a visual image.

Now, human beings are, and probably always were, gregarious and vociferous. Under the same pressure that motivated the consummation of many neural processes in the brain, their instinctive vocalizations not only increased but became articulated like the sexual antics of other creatures; but instead of evoking instinctive practical responses they evoked imagery. Repetition of vocal sequences standardized the diverse emotive and ideational responses and inspired animal posturing and bodily movements with a new driving force—participation in a communal expression —felt by each agent, and seen by him in all the others. That is celebration, and its fixed forms are ritual. What the earliest dances and rites expressed may have been very vague, personal phantasies, but every individual enacted the excitement of something imagined. Above all, even snatches of recurrent articulate sounds would activate images with all their terror and excitement and serve as *pars pro toto,* representing the whole habitual experience.

As soon as a purely imaginary object is conjured up by the familiar sound heard or made by the agent, symbol and meaning are born. The symbol evokes a mental act—conception—without any pointing and directing function. At once the two belong together, and the perception of each through and in the other is an act of intuition.

The word "intuition" has suffered many abuses, so we had better establish at once what it means. Certainly nothing mystical or irrational, such as "woman's intuition" and "moral intuition." I am using it in the sense given to it by John Locke in his very sober *Essay Concerning Human Understanding* (1690). Locke meant by it the kind of direct perception that may go through any available avenue of sense: the perception of relations, such as greater than, before, after, between, richer than; to the right of, like, different, same, and so forth. Also, the perception of form, pattern, unity of form, wholeness, gestalt; and the generally neglected, but all-important recognition of *exemplification*—that is, the recognition that *here is a case* of such-and-such a form, connection, or structure. Besides these logical data of intuition, there are the basic semantical ones of meaning and symbolic significance. Locke did not include semantical functions, but tacitly took them for granted, and he added one which I cannot accept as intuitive: knowledge of the existence of God, which must be classed with factual knowledge or belief.

Throughout most of the *Essay* Locke avoided the term "intuition," because of its frequent wrong uses, and spoke instead of "natural light." Only in the fourth book, where he felt sure that he had made clear what he meant and what he did not mean, he used the term "intuition," and I find it a good word for *logical or semantical perception.*

Unfortunately one cannot expound a whole theory of symbolism in so little space, so I shall have to simply skip the most intriguing part, namely how I think language began. All I can say is that I do not think it began with names for ordinary objects, as children's language learning begins in a speaking society. But it began with symbolic utterance, which motivated acts that terminated in the brain as emotionally charged inward visions, conceptions; and as the long, formalized utterances were communal, they could be started anywhere, by anyone, with the same sort of meaning for all hearers, until they broke up into bits with more and more

325

definite conceptual meanings. The main point is that true language is essentially conceptual, as no animal expression—vocal or gestic—is. Speech is not derived from animal communication; its communicative and directive functions, though all-important today, are secondary; its primary function is the symbolic expression of intuitive cognition (Langer 1960).

Meaning and relations among meanings are impossible to perceive without symbols, because they have no independent physical existence. Intuition, therefore, is momentary and implicit and unnegotiable without words, if it exists at all. But once the symbolic function has occurred, the shift from animal mentality to human mentality has begun. In a gregarious species, the easy production of vocal symbols makes the expression of symbolic impulses at once personal and public, and an entirely new form of interaction between individuals is created—exchange of ideas, or true communication. In this sense, animals do not communicate. They automatically stimulate each other and use each other's reactions, but they do not share or oppose opinions. They cannot express, and therefore cannot conceive, aspects of situations as *facts*.

But facts, opinions, and conceptions of causal relationship (often imaginary) have become the basis of human life; and therewith human community is no longer a matter of instinctive interaction and generic group cohesion, but is always—on every level of subsequent development —society. The greatest change, however, is not pragmatic, but a change of value feeling. Animal values are felt in good and bad situations, temporarily cathecting whatever objects function as aids or obstacles to acts in progress. Like relations or familiar patterns, they are implicitly given and instinctively dealt with. Consequently, the most elaborately stereotyped animal colony is not a society. To the human mind, however, values are permanent characters that mark classes of things, and especially classes of acts. Society is organized and upheld by value symbols. It is not essentially an aggregate of beings in which a natural "pecking order" develops; that does take place all the time, but in the confines of a more stable conceptual framework, the moral structure of human social life. Society is institutional; whether it is regulated by unwritten tradition or by a formal code, it has some system of prohibitions and prescriptions, and recognized classes of acts to which they apply. Specific acts are seen as exemplifications of the recognized classes, and valued as good or evil accordingly.

The power of institutions lies in that they are not simply actual, like instinctive animal ways, but that they can survive many lapses from behavioral realization. The law, the church, the army continue to exist

326

though many persons break the law, sin against the church, or evade military service. They are not so-called "ethological" patterns, but *ethnological* institutions, upheld by symbols that mean large, emotionally charged ideas. Such ideas are not possible without semantic intuition, and their construction is unthinkable without the logical intuition elicited by the structure of language, and the word-making tendency that has resulted from the specialization of the human forebrain.

The stamp of language is on everything we know and do, on every behavioral response we make to things in the human ambient; and because even our vaguest concepts can be verbally related to others, the human ambient is not a loose tangle of paths, places, lures, terrors, expectations —like an animal's—but is a world. It does not arise as we go into action and collapse as we go to sleep, but holds over from day to day and season to season. World, society, and self are conceptual products. The most spectacular effect of language is, of course, interpersonal communication; and in this process the moral structure becomes deeply articulated, because words have many functions, and the most ubiquitous is that they impute emotive values—good or bad, in all possible degrees—to the concepts they convey. That is why a clever speaker can publicly make black look white; it is also why each individual cares what others think of him, and has a so-called superego and a self-image.

The upshot of the shift from instinctive action to intuitive rationality (the derivation of reasoning from direct intuition being another story we have to skip) is that human beings probably do nothing exactly like animals. They have the same basic impulses to eat, sleep, chase, procreate, and (more than most other animals) make noise; but conception alters even our most direct enactments of such impulses. The main alteration is that sub-acts contained in larger total acts become distinct and more and more independent, so the big instinctive acts of animals, preformed in their vital impulses and (originally no doubt) in ours, fall to pieces under the catalytic influence of thought. Every new power is bought at a price; in the great shift from animal mentality to mind, in the development of imagery, intuition, and social communication, we have lost our elaborate instinctive patterns, such as guide birds in sequential, procreative acts from pairing to the independence of the new generation, and guide beavers in their architecture and home life. Our instinctive behavior has degenerated to very simple forms, so that what we mean by "sex," for instance, has shrunk to little more than coitus. We have to work along other lines. And I think one may say that we can afford to lose our guiding animal faith just to the extent that we can replace instinctive by symbolic

327

processes. We can sacrifice natural hierarchies and pecking orders as we institute authority and rule, and bear the change from the progressive specious present of animals to our past and future and the predestined end of each life by conceiving gods, souls, and an eternal state. Such concepts, of course, can be formed and maintained only by symbolic means; and those means are our holy symbols, rites and liturgies, and magical objects.

It is the fashion today to speak of formalized animal behavior, such as courtship posturing or even the nodding and displaying of two lizards that happen to meet, as "ceremonies" and "rituals," of animal interactions as "communication," and of inherited animal ways as "traditions," lately even as "cultural traditions." I think that is a pernicious source of scientific confusion. Clearly it is intended to bridge the gap between animal and human life, as an older generation tried to do by treating man as a super-rat or a not-very-super-ape; well, if the mountain won't come to Mohammed, Mohammed will go to the mountain. First we anthropomorphize the animals and then we discover that we are just like them!

The most serious harm to science that I see in the present fashion of applying ethnological terms metaphorically to animals is that—odd as it may seem—it is really based on the assumption that the two studies, ethnology and what is called "ethology" (the slightest possible variant of "ethnology"), will never become true integral parts of biological science. If they should ever do so, the use of words literally in one context and fancifully in another would cause havoc; we would always have to say "caste, I mean caste" or "caste, I mean status," because, as Dr. McBride points out, the essential property of caste in its original, ethnological sense is that one is born into a caste and normally cannot change it, whereas in his sense an animal can pass from one caste to another. That is not a properly generalized sense of the word, but a new sense which will not even subsume the literal meaning. Of course someone may say that I have done the same with the words "act" and "motivation," but if you view my generalized use of them more closely you will find that it is really "generalized" from the restricted use, and subsumes the latter as a specialty.

The use of a word in quotation marks does not make it a technical term, as all too many writers seem to think, who introduce a borrowed word as a metaphor—a literary florish—and then drop the quotation marks; as John A. King, in his articles on prairie dogs (King 1959, p. 131), calls their naso-nasal contacts upon meeting "the identification kiss," speaks once or twice of the "kiss" in quotation marks, then drops the marks and simply says that the animals kiss; although he points out that the "kiss" is exchanged with bared teeth, and—in his own words— "the open mouth which characterizes the kiss [no marks] probably serves as a threat rather than an expression of affection." Why, then, call that "kissing?" In view of the fact that—according to the Yerkes (1929, p. 296) and the Kelloggs (1933, p. 121), and most recently Jane Goodall, who made her observations in the wild (1965, 1967)—chimpanzee mothers really kiss their young ones. King's misuse of the word makes for confusion even in the field of ethology itself. Similarly, when Fox claims that monkeys born of high-caste mothers have a social advantage, he uses caste meaning status (a transient high status when the son was born but might not last until he grew up). The worst practice, however, is the use of "ritual," "rite," and "ceremony" for formalized animal acts; rites and ceremonies are expressive acts, symbolizing vague but highly imaginative ideas, and are characteristically human. To obliterate the distinction between typical expression of excitement and social ritual is scientific malpractice. Bierens de Haan (1940) is the only animal psychologist I have encountered who realizes and explicitly warns against the use of beguiling metaphors. So I shall here reiterate what I said at the outset: if you want to find true identities or precise relationships among biological phenomena, study their differences and guard the distinctions.

Now, how does this discussion of the "Great Shift" serve to answer the question of what we can learn from animal communities that could be applied to human society? I think the answer, though implicit, is clear: practically nothing that could be applied directly. Our problems of group life and self-realization, of involvement with our kind, and of the development of individual lives, are not like those of any other animal species. We cannot trust our instincts to see us through the most solitary and simple existence, let alone a normal human social life; they are too degraded and fragmented, their sub-acts reduced again to primitive impulses without any fitting hereditary forms. From that point of view, man is indeed unspecialized. He has specialized in symbolic activity to the evolutionary attainment of intellect, and his intellect has invaded and disrupted what he may have had by way of the marvelous adjustments of animals. Many animals are intelligent about finding the necessary external conditions for their instinctive ways of life; but no animal except man is intellectual. Our problems of handling ourselves as a society are intellectual, and as they arise—chiefly by incursions of formless instinctive "drives"—they have to be countered and steered by rational principles, formulated in tradition or, in extremity, by vigorous conception and consistent thinking.

But all this does not mean that there is nothing of human value to be learned from the study of animal behavior. We are all born as little creatures of pure instinct. A comparison of the development of instinctive behavior in babies and in animals which have a dependent babyhood shows at what early stages human impulses are no longer realizable by animal methods, and require thoughtful provisions for their socially safe and individually adequate expression. Many of our social problems, of course, begin in the crib. Thus, the point in every individual life is to learn what basic impulses we really have, and what instinctive methods of living we have lost forever and have to replace by conceptual ones. What I have tried to show is how deep the division between beasts and men goes. Very deep, indeed; but when we touch bottom, when we glimpse the beginning of man's great biological departure, we come upon the ultimate unity—the common source of his and all other animals' impulses pressing for expression, the basic vital needs he still shares with the field mouse and the crow.

REFERENCES

Bierens de Haan, J. A.
  1940. *Die tierischen Instinkte und ihr Umbau durch Erfahrung.* Leiden: E. J. Brill.
Bock, W. J.
  1959. "Preadaptation and Multiple Evolutionary Pathways." *Evolution,* 13:194–211.
Bolk, L.
  1926. *Das Problem der Menschwerdung.* Jena: Gustav Fischer.
Delgado, J. M. R., W. W. Roberts, and N. E. Miller.
  1954. "Learning Motivated by Electrical Stimulation of the Brain." *American Journal of Physiology,* 176:587–593.
Ebert, J. D.
  1965. *Interacting Systems in Development.* New York: Holt, Rinehart & Winston.
Eibl-Eibesfeldt, I.
  1963. "Angeborenes und Erworbenes im Verhalten einiger Säuger." *Zeitschrift für Tierpsychologie,* 20:705–754.
Frith, H. J.
  1959. "Breeding Habits of the Family Megapodidae." *The Ibis,* 98.
Gehlen, A.
  1940. *Der Mensch, seine Natur und seine Stellung in der Welt.* Bonn: Athenäum-Verlag.
Goodall, J. van L.
  1965. "Chimpanzees of the Gombe Stream Reserve." Pages 425–473, in

Primate Behavior, I. DeVore, editor. New York: Holt, Rinehart & Winston.

1967. *My Friends the Wild Chimpanzees.* Washington, D.C.: The National Geographic Society.

Gregory, W. K.
1951. *Evolution Emerging: A Survey of Changing Patterns from Primeval Life to Man.* Volume 1. New York: Macmillan.

Haldane, J. B. S.
1955. *L'Instinct dans le comportement des animaux et de l'homme,* P. P. Grassé, editor. Paris: Masson et cie.

Hamburger, V.
1963. "Some Aspects of the Embryology of Behavior." *Quarterly Review of Biology,* 38:349–352.

Head, H.
1919. "The Physiological Basis of the Spatial and Temporal Aspects of Sensation." *Proceedings of the Aristotelian Society,* supplementary volume 2 (Problems of Science and Philosophy): 77–86.

Hinde, R. A.
1954. "Factors Governing the Changes in Strength of a Partially Inborn Response, as Shown by the Mobbing Behavior of the Chaffinch (*Fringilla coelebs*), I: The Nature of the Response, and an Examination of its Course." *Proceedings of the Royal Society,* series B, 142:306–331.

Kellogg, W. N., and L. A. Kellogg.
1933. *The Ape and the Child.* New York: McGraw-Hill, and London: Whittelsey House.

Kendeigh, S. C.
1952. *Parental Care and Its Evolution in Birds.* Urbana: The University of Illinois Press.

King, J. A.
1959. "The Social Behavior of Prairie Dogs." *Scientific American,* 201:128–140.

Krott, P., and G. Krott.
1963. "Zum Verhalten des Braunbären (*Ursus arctos* L.) in den Alpen." *Zeitschrift für Tierpsychologie,* 20:160–206.

Kühme, W.
1965. "Freilandstudien zur Soziologie des Hyänenhundes (*Lycaon pictus lupinus* Thomas 1902)." *Zeitschrift für Tierpsychologie,* 22:495–541. [See especially pages 505 ff. and 515.]

Langer, S. K.
1960. "Speculations on the Origin of Speech and Its Communicative Function." *The Quarterly Journal of Speech,* 46:121–134. Reprinted 1962 in *Philosophical Sketches.* Baltimore: Johns Hopkins Press.

1967. *Mind: An Essay on Human Feeling.* Baltimore: The Johns Hopkins Press. [For a discussion of the differnce between a new conceptual structure and a metaphorical extension of current terms, see volume 1, pages 44–46, and pages 301 ff.]

Locke, J.
 1690. *An Essay Concerning Human Understanding*. London.
Lutz, B.
 1948. "Ontogenetic Evolution in Frogs." *Evolution*, 2:29–39.
Marshall, A. J.
 1954. *Bower Birds: Their Displays and Breeding Cycles*. The Clarendon Press. New York: Oxford University Press.
Platt, J. R.
 1961. "Properties of Large Molecules that Go Beyond the Properties of Their Chemical Subgroups." *Journal of Theoretical Biology*, 342–358.
Schmitt, F. O.
 1963. "The Macromolecular Assembly—a Hierarchical Entity in Cellular Organization." *Developmental Biology*, 7:549–559.
Thompson, D'Arcy W.
 1951. *On Growth and Form*. Third edition. New York: Cambridge University Press.
Tinbergen, N.
 1951. *The Study of Instinct*. New York: Oxford University Press.
Tschanz, B.
 1959. "Zur Brutbiologie der Trottellumme (*Uria aalge aalge* Pont.)." *Behaviour*, 14:1–100.
Twitty, V. C., and M. C. Niu.
 1954. "The Motivation of Cell Migration, Studied by Isolation of Embryonic Pigment Cells Singly and in Small Groups *in Vitro*." *Journal of Experimental Zoology*, 125:541–573.
VonHolst, E.
 1957. "Aktive Leistungen der menschlichen Gesichtswahrnehmung." *Studium Generale X*, 231–243.
Weiss, P.
 1958. [Discussion]. In *Conference on Dynamics of Proliferating Tissues*, D. Price, editor. Chicago: University of Chicago Press.
 1959. [Discussion]. In *Symposium on Endocrines in Development*, R. L. Watterson, editor. Chicago: University of Chicago Press.
Yerkes, R. M., and A. W. Yerkes.
 1929. *The Great Apes: A Study in Anthropoid Life*. New Haven: Yale University Press.
Young, P. T.
 1955. "Comments on Professor Rotter's Paper." Pages 271–274, in *Nebraska Symposium on Motivation*, M. R. Jones, editor. Lincoln: University of Nebraska Press.

CHAPTER 11

EVOLUTIONARY UNIVERSALS, CONTINUITIES, AND ALTERNATIVES

JULIAN JAYNES AND MARVIN BRESSLER

PRINCETON UNIVERSITY

The expansion of knowledge which has made scientific specialization a necessity has generated specialized loyalties, promoted accidental domains into jealously guarded academic departments, and elevated self-sufficiency into an ideal. This academic parochialism has often been defended by pointing to the errors which occur when intruders from one discipline invade the boundaries of another without taking the precaution of noting the hazards of the terrain.

Speculations on the relevance of animal behavior for the study of human societies furnish what are perhaps the most flagrant examples of such oversights. If the manic extrapolation of selected aspects of early evolutionary theory could yield the foolish excesses of social Darwinism, it is no wonder that a later and more skeptical generation of social scientists despaired that it was at all profitable to inquire what significance the "lower orders" held for men. Nor was this revulsion of great consequence. Neither the study of beasts nor men was well advanced and it would have been inappropriate to wonder too much about the implication of evolutionary studies for human societies. But now that the quality of the formidable output of ethology and the behavior sciences testifies that each has achieved a certain measure of maturity it seems permissible, almost mandatory, to inquire once again in what sense, if any, the study of animals is also the study of man. It is convenient to begin by identifying the extreme and antithetical perspectives of evolutionary determinism and human uniqueness.

THE EVOLUTIONARY PERSPECTIVE   To understand man and human society from the point of view of evolution is to speak chiefly of behavior patterns which have been anatomically built into the organism by eons of selective pressures acting upon chance mutations of genes involved in behavior. While this brief is sometimes argued from evidence obtained by riffling through the data on lower animals, the strongest argument rests on primate evolution. Since man and the other primates have evolved from a common Oligocene ancestor, he shares with them certain specific biologically fixed characteristics; and these, in various combinations and instances, and in response to various situations and crises which are also more or less innately determined, explain observed behavior. Nor does learning fall outside this determinism. Our capacity to learn particular items, to form characteristic social bonds, to acquire specific sentiments and loyalties—and not others—is the inexorable outcome of natural selection just as is our anatomy. Therefore, since evolutionary imperatives impose iron constraints on any conceivable human society, all social philosophy is a synonym for biological necessity.

THE PERSPECTIVE OF HUMAN UNIQUENESS   The alternative view is just as clear in its pronouncements and as ominous in its warnings. It is impressed by the unique properties of man and his liberation from his animal heritage. With his brain-body ratio twice that of his closest phylo-genetic relative, his digital dexterity equally superior, his relative freedom from hormonal control in such behaviors as mating, and his upright pos-ture—which frees his hands for carrying, holding, throwing, or gesturing —man is even in physique much more than a hairless ape. And if we add to this his syntactic language—a tool which allows him to build civilizations by creating concepts that act as behavioral controls and by placing the cumulative experience of the past at the service of the future —then we become aware how awesome is the distance between himself and all other animals. His world is not defined by innate imperatives but rather by history and belief, purpose and strategy. It follows, then, that for all intents and purposes the study of animal behavior is irrelevant for understanding the human condition. Moreover, to give credence to rival evolutionary hypotheses is to court the predatory ethics with which such beliefs have been associated in the past, and to support political doctrines based on inheritance and control instead of on education and reform. Animal studies promote misleading metaphors. The study of man must be based on man alone.

THE PROBLEM OF COMPARATIVE INFERENCE   How are we to decide between these two views? Evolution is a long-range process spanning mil-lions of years and even its shortest relevant time intervals are much too long to be studied directly. We are thus obliged to draw plausible infer-ences about evolutionary processes by observing the concordant and dis-cordant behavior patterns of men and animals at the same point in time.

Our analysis takes the form of asking what is implied in statements of the form that a behavior x is evolved from a behavior y. In our judgment this may be reduced to (1) the specification of x and y, or the problem of behavioral universals, (2) the nature of their relationship, or the problem of evolutionary continuities, and (3) the degree of "coercion" implied by these connections, or the problem of evolutionary imperatives.

BEHAVIORAL UNIVERSALS   Since evolution refers to the process by which a chance variation with survival value becomes permanent and subsequently universal, it seems appropriate to begin a discussion of the common elements of behavior shared by all members of any given species. Such universals are at once units of individual and social behavior, as well as behavioral evolution, and they are the major point of contact between the various disciplines that study behavior. The quest for common denominators of human behavior has, of course, been a durable preoccupation of modern anthropology since Clark Wissler. They are assumed in the concept of "human nature," are implied in functional analysis—the dominant school of contemporary sociology—and are one of the primary interests of structural linguists.

In the absence of satisfactory taxonomics based on reliable empirical data, classifications of behavioral universals may be generated logically by an array of cells in a dimensional space defined by as many important variables as we wish to consider. These might include, for example, a common psychological basis, a common function, or time or space relationships. As a more immediate task it may be useful to identify universals according to their content and in the process point to some distinctions which are too often neglected in most discussions of animal and human behavior.

Simple Behavioral Universals.—These are single actions, recognizable by all observers as elementary entities, that are observed in all groups of the same species. Examples are facial expressions, the startle pattern, fighting, aspects of courtship, and mating and maternal behavior.

There is no very precise way to distinguish simple behavioral universals from the items included in the next category. In general, the proportion of universals that are of this class grow fewer as the phyletic level increases. This is particularly evident in primates and men.

Variform Universals.—When two or more overt behaviors that are clearly different have the same functional significance, are aroused in the same situations, appear to share a like emotional tone, are similarly linked to a specific common subsystem of the brain, and are not concomitant, we call this a variform universal. The term refers, in short, to a set of behaviors which seem to the competent observer to have common elements.

Serious difficulties rise in trying to decide whether to classify particular items under this rubric. For example, although maternal behavior may be perceived as a variform universal, all of its manifestations in primates exhibit a coherent unity, and since we have evidence that in some species centers in the hypothalamus influence all branches of this pattern, we could infer that we are dealing with a single behavioral universal. Similarly, adornment in human cultures and play are in all mammalian family groups subject to similar perplexities.

"Aggression," a concept that has been used so blithely by writers of many persuasions, is an especially slippery term. It is doubtless a variform universal comprising a remarkably large repertory of behavioral items, particularly in humans. Everything from punching and kicking to pulling a trigger or verbal vituperation might be included. But it is not clear that the concept can be stretched to embrace teasing, aggressive humor, and so cooperative and "rational" an enterprise as war. The admissibility of subsuming these diverse behaviors under a single classification depends on the task at hand, particularly the degree of rigor to which we aspire. We can be certain, however, that almost all social behavioral universals in men are variform. Greeting ceremonies, for example, differ markedly across and within cultures, and between individuals although all greetings have underlying similarities.

Functional Universals.—When two or more behavioral configurations have no discernible common physiological basis, but have similar social consequences (e.g., speculations that team sports, ceremonies of allegiance, and rites of passage all foster group cohesion), we may refer to these as functional universals. In such instances evolutionary processes may help to explain the persistence and emergence of the fundamental social requirements to which otherwise disparate behaviors are a response, but they cannot be construed as the common source of these equivalent functional alternatives.

Diachronic Universals.—These are universals of behavior changed through time. All universals are in some sense diachronic either because they may be in the process of change or have already completed the transformation. It follows that no diachronic universal can lead to a violation of a valid universal of another kind. Examples of such universals, are, of course, the laws of learning and socialization when properly stated, and possibly such social processes as cultural replacement and diffusion. Unfortunately little is known about what might be called the *modification structure* of various species, or those parts, aspects, or links of behavioral sequences which are the favorite targets on which environmental influences operate. These, when ascertained, would themselves be universals and of great importance to many disciplines.

338

Relational Universals.—Universals are not necessarily confined to a single species; they may also be identified in an order or even an entire phylum. Moreover, within several related species, relations between nonuniversals may themselves be universal. We may, for example, identify *conditional universals* where the occurrence of one behavior implies another (e.g., if a species has a repertory of vocal signals, then it will have a warning cry, but not vice versa). Or *disjunctive universals,* where either one or another behavior occurs but not both (e.g., hierarchy or territory). These are, of course, interspecies behavioral relationships which are currently a major object of inquiry.

These, then, are the materials with which evolution works. In statements that a behavior x is evolved from a behavior y, x and y are universals from any of the categories above and others as well. Only by realizing that the material on which natural selection has operated is of such complexity and capable of such distinctions as we have suggested can we escape the kind of simplism that has characterized many recent formulations.

EVOLUTIONARY CONTINUITIES   Statements of the form that a behavior x has evolved from a behavior y, where x and y are both observed either in the same or different species, is actually a shorthand way of saying that behavior y is similar to a behavior z exhibited by a common ancestor in a previous era. All behavior in all species may be said to reflect evolutionary continuity; the perplexing problem is to establish the linkage between relevant types of extant behavior in existing species. Obviously, the first target of inquiry should be closely related species, and since our present discussion is specifically concerned with the evolutionary continuity of human universals, we shall here consider only primates. We are justified in this course because it is highly unlikely that an evolutionary continuity linking subprimates and men would not likewise be present in primates.

We may assume that any observed specialized behavior pattern would necessarily have evolved fairly recently, and that the separation in ancestral lines between the primates and other mammalian orders would therefore be considerably older. Thus it would be preposterous to claim that man's mastery of agriculture, which is nowhere observed in primates is evidence of an evolutionary continuity from, let us say, the nut-burying behavior of squirrels. It is far more likely that nut burying evolved too recently to be part of a common ancestry.

The proper study of animal-human continuities, then, should be confined to those which exist between primates and men. It is very often assumed that the discovery of a humanoid behavior in a primate indicates an evolutionary continuity. But at the risk of being excessively zealous, we feel it might be illuminating to consider all the possibilities of concomitance.

Table 1 shows all possible combinations of incidence in primates as a group and in races and tribes of man. Using "U" to mean universally present, "S" to mean present in some instances, and "O" to mean universally absent, we derive the eight possibilities listed. Beside each concordant or discordant combination we have listed several examples, and then in the last column the probability of evolutionary continuity. Thus the first row refers to human universals that are also found in all primates. It is obvious that the probability of evolutionary continuity under these conditions is very high. The second-row combination includes human universals that appear in only some primate groups, the probability of evolutionary continuity being only medium. The third row lists unique human universals that are not present in primates and therefore evolved in the hominids after they branched off from the common primate stock.

It is deplorable that some of the most familiar and extravagant claims for evolutionary continuity have been advanced in the popular and, alas, the professional literature in behalf of combinations which include neither a primate nor a human universal.

Limitations of This Analysis.—Aside from the fact that our examples are neither exhaustive nor exclusive, nor exist even on the same level, and are meant as suggestive for the sake of this discussion, the table only hints at the complicated analysis that is required. To lump all primate data together is to weaken the evidence. A proper table of coincidence would include entries for each of the primate species in order of their neurological position. When this is done, a behavioral item which shows an increasing incidence in the neurological sequence of primates is much more likely to be continued into human behavior and to be a real continuity, as perhaps is the use of tools by chimpanzees. A decreasing incidence, such as olfactory marking in several primitive primates—a favorite proof, incidentally, for establishing territory as a continuity—would have the opposite prediction.

A further reservation is that the table excludes everything except recognizable behavior universals. Evolution, unfortunately for scientists, who are frequently beguiled by simplicity, does not proceed by the discrete addition of new all-or-none patterns or capacities, but from the emergence out of past behaviors of new potentialities and variations of

TABLE 1.—Behavioral continuities of anthropoids and man.

Row	Primate groups	Human groups	Behavioral examples	Probability of evolutionary continuity
1	U	U	Mating, infant rearing, play, vocal signals, postural signals, fighting.	High
2	S	U	Tools, facial signals, hierarchical grouping.	Medium
3	O	U	Language, adornment, music, marriage and burial ceremonies, dancing, hunting, artificial locomotion, gift-giving.	0
4	U	S	Nomadism.	Medium
5	S	S	Nest building, group fighting, group stability, territoriality.	Low
6	O	S	Mathematics, seed-planting and harvesting, writing, animal domestication.	0
7	U	O	Social grooming, female behavioral periodicity.	0
8	S	O	Marking, arboreality.	0

U = universally present; S = present in some instances; O = universally absent.

older patterns. And since mutation is a random process, this is accomplished in many ways including partialization, ritualization, accretion, overt inhibition (perhaps involved in the evolution of thinking), changes in the modifiability of structure, in degrees of anticipatoriness, etc. The complexity and interconnectedness of the mammalian brain is evidence enough of the complexity of evolutionary changes in behavior. A table of coincidence, therefore, perhaps attaches undue significance to the major and most obvious similarities between species. In other words, there is far more evolutionary commonality between species than is exhibited by mutually shared universals. Nevertheless, as we shall see, even crude systematic efforts to examine the structure of inference may yield considerable benefits.

Clarifications Resulting from the Table.—The examples included in the table of coincidence clearly reveal that for the establishment of human universals, the presence or absence of an analogous item in primates is irrelevant to the demonstration. Language, no less than mating, has evolved.

If this caveat were to be taken seriously neither folk wisdom, nor serious scholars would be so eager to reclassify "U S" and "S S" items as a "U U" combination (see Table 1). It does not improve the case for continuity, or for that matter for "imperatives." Even if, for example, counter to all evidence, group fighting were universal in primates, we could not from this fact alone derive the evolutionary continuity, let alone the necessity of human warfare.

We are thus forcibly reminded that the presence or absence of human universals in other primates is useful in telling us not if, but rather when a behavior item evolved. Examples classified as "U U" probably evolved under selective pressures during the Oligocene period, and so on. A behavioral universal found in man alone, insofar as it originated in evolution, probably evolved after the hominid separation had occurred. The entries under "Probability of Evolutionary Continuity" are thus identical with the probability that a common ancestor in the Oligocene period exhibited the particular behavior.

The table also alerts us to the danger of substituting poetic metaphor for physiological substrate as a principle of classification, or of mixing behavioral analogy with homology. Thus the olfactory marking behavior, that occupies so much of the time of lemurs has, as far as we know, no common or even derived parallel in human behavior. It is possible, however, if strained, to extend marking behavior to include flag-raising, claim-staking, or stone-wall building, protection of the ghetto "turf," or even war in humans. Taken together these extrapolations conceived of as a single behavior, would elevate it from an "S O" pattern to an "S U" combination and thus deceive us into believing that we have evidence for a genuine human universal with a probable evolutionary continuity.

IMPERATIVES OR ALTERNATIVES? Several recent treatises on animal behavior imply that proof that a human activity has an evolutionary history is tantamount to demonstrating that men are at the mercy of evolutionary imperatives. This conception is in part a translation from non-behavioral evolution. Anatomy, its maturation, physiological functions, aging, and so on, are all inevitable. If we define evolutionary imperatives as universal characteristics for which evolution is the necessary and sufficient explanation, these aspects of man clearly fall within this definition. Once we demonstrate the existence of neurologically based behavioral universals which no less than any anatomical feature in man are the products of evolution, and particularly when we can point to their evolutionary continuity with related species, the conclusion that there are similar degrees of coercion becomes difficult to resist.

Another basis for the concept of behavioral evolutionary imperatives lies in the history of ideas. That our behavior is or can be forced out of us by primordial entities within us—whether such entities be demons, drives, or action-specific energies—has always had a poetic appeal to the romantic imagination. Such inevitability excuses us both from the difficulties of rational reflection and from the responsibilities for unwise decisions. From Greek gods and biblical demons, to Hegel's Spirit, Schopenhauer's Will, and Freud's Id, the idea of a necessity in behavior has brought some relief to intellectuals weary of choice. The notion of evolutionary imperatives is in this same tradition and continues to bring ancient comforts to new crises.

Apart from the impossibility of proving a social "must," the greatest difficulty with such a notion is that it is not in accord with the very facts of evolution from which it is supposedly derived. To be sure, in lower organisms behavior is the hostage of evolutionary imperatives. Behavior of a reflexive nature in simpler species can be as inevitable as anatomy. But the whole course of evolution in mammals has been the gradual release from stereotyped behavior and a consequent increase in the variance in any behavioral characteristic both in a species and an individual. And with this has gone the evolution of variform universals accounting for this increased variance. If a variform universal has n ways of expression, the statement that such a universal is an evolutionary imperative and must be expressed in at least one of n different ways is a very weak statement. It is, we feel, the only way in which an evolutionary imperative can be true of man, and as such leaves a world alive with choice, options, and alternatives.

CONCLUSION Human behavior is governed by evolutionary laws to the extent that there exist variform behavioral universals behind the idiosyncracies of individual lives. Of course there are genetic constraints on human behavior. These, however, do not define the specific social acts that men must perform; they are, rather, limitations on the range of their alternatives. Stating this differently, there is nothing that man by reason of his genes must do; but there is much that man by reason of his genes can do. In fact there is buried in the very question and the use of such words as "governed" and "laws," a metaphor which answers the question incorrectly as it is asked. Evolution does not govern behavior; it makes behavior possible.

We have tried to show in this paper that statements of the sort that a particular behavior is evolved from animal behavior break down into statements about universals, continuities, and suggested imperatives. We have tried to show that within each of these three domains, there is much to see and ponder, and that only by making careful distinctions of meaning can we be free from false implications and proceed with an assured step.

And what of the two alternatives with which we began? Academic territoriality has resulted in two partial views. The biotropic disciplines view man as engaged in patterns of behavior whose resemblance to other animals demands the hypothesis of continuity, and often assumes that evolutionary processes are the enemy of man's effort to control his own destiny. The sociotropes, on the other hand, view man from a radically different perspective; the dazzle of multivariate ethnography blots out the possibility of evolved universals, and the mysteries of linguistically based cultures make the simple antagonisms and affiliations of animal groups an impertinence to their considerations, as they chart the growth of culture and society through eras too short to be the theater of biologic evolution.

We must defer judgment as to whether these diverse perspectives can be reconciled until we have further refined the logic and the evidence that purportedly sustains trans-specific inferences. This process will ultimately require nothing less than a systematic inventory of *all* animate behavior. Ideally, this cross-species catalog should satisfy the formal criteria of any adequate categorical system, e.g., exhaustiveness, parsimony, clarity, and comparability. Its propositions should distinguish the ephemeral from relatively permanent, and idiosyncratic from universal behavioral items within and between animal and human populations. An aspiration of this magnitude will require a revision in the modus operandi of the social sciences: sociologists who are more receptive to cross-societal analysis, anthropologists who are more attentive to complex civilizations, and historians who can discern common patterns in discrete events. For their part ethologists will be obliged to show more respect for the subtlety and complexity of evolutionary processes.

The prospect of developing a unified science of social behavior is not tomorrow's. From the reptiles, through the egg-laying mammals of the Triassic era, the placental insectivores, tree shrews, tarsiods, and pro-anthropoids to man the course of evolution has resisted confident interpretation. At present, despite the emergence of a considerable body of research, there exists no wholly adequate classification of human universals, much less of their evolutionary origins. Social and biological scientists who jointly approach this problem will thereby signal their surrender of academic territoriality. We might then discover with much greater precision to what extent universals, continuities, and alternatives explain the lives of men.

PART IV

CAN MAN CONTROL HIMSELF?

INTRODUCTION

J. F. EISENBERG

It should be apparent from the preceding sections, that we can no longer consider man a potentially nonaggressive animal and that by applying such simple methods as appropriate conditioning techniques or rearing patterns we can produce an adult human being not prone to aggression. Rather, we must accept the view that man has the potential to express a great deal of aggressive behavior under a variety of circumstances. If we assume that man's aggressive tendencies have their roots in his neuro-anatomical constitution and that there is no way to eradicate the potential for expressing aggression, then we must consider the possibility of aggression control in human behavior by looking at the many alternative mechanisms for the expression of aggressive behavior that man has latent within him.

Man can affiliate with others and discharge a significant amount of latent aggressive behavior in group-condoned activities, such as organized sports or organized but innocuous demonstrations. He can sublimate aggressive impulses in controlled work habits and he can, of course, express raw aggression against a partner or against an unknown fellow human. It is only by considering the many alternatives open to man that we can then plan effectively for the controlled expression of aggression within societies and between them.

In the previous section, Langer, Jaynes, and Bressler discussed the primacy of symbolic communication and the necessity in human decision-making to weigh all possible courses of action. Even if man is in part subject to impulses and drives, he is not necessarily a slave to one option or course of action in achieving a new equilibrium.

Aggression control may be accomplished by brain stimulation, brain lesions, hormone administration, and by appropriate drug dosages. Current research is only beginning to explore these possibilities, especially where they are applicable to extreme pathological cases in human behavior (Moyer 1969, Garattini and Sigg 1969). The two contributions in the last section do not consider the more medically oriented proposals for the control of aggression in extreme cases, but rather consider the prospects

349

for more broadly based control and canalization of human aggressive behavior.

Halle concerns himself with human survival and points out that the population explosion, the increased utilization of energy, the rise of technology, etc., are all tied to the increase in world population. By any measure we have reached a critical stage of growth. He believes that total extinction of humankind is not an immediate danger from either nuclear war or starvation but the survival of a hopeful, civilized world is in peril. Halle suggests that man has plasticity with respect to his social organization and its many forms. Granted man's plasticity with respect to the modes by which he expresses his behavior patterns, we still cannot answer the question: How plastic is man's behavior? He proposes that man is capable of self education through his culturally imposed methods of training and, although he can transmit information, it seems that an equally valid question is: Can he alter his basic value systems; can he indeed change his needs? What we have missed in this essay is a consideration of the relationship between biological drives and the construction of human value systems and, to this end, the contribution by S. Pepper (1958) can be read with much profit. Furthermore, the basic question of What are universals with respect to human aspirations? has not been properly explored (see Cantril 1965, for an attempt to delineate cross-cultural needs and values).

Halle submits that the time left for humans to resolve some of their current critical problems is too short to even think of there being time for genetically based behavioral tendencies to manifest themselves through the agencies of selection; rather, any solutions we can arrive at will have to be culturally imposed. He disregards so-called miracle solutions to our problems—such as universal legal systems and universal political systems—and states that legal and political sanctions are rarely primary; they are secondary, arising out of cultural trends that have reached a maturity to demand symbolic national or supernational expression. Instead, Halle places his emphasis on the potential that humans have to readapt and accept new symbolic expressions. Cultural shifts in attitude are not only possible but apparently going on on a wide scale today. He draws on his experiences in Switzerland as an example, indicating that mutual self-limitation at the international level is essential to human survival and may be achieved in the same manner that the Swiss federation was achieved after a series of disastrous civil wars in the nineteenth century.

Normative conceptions, i.e., the created, abstract classification of objects or attributes is the rule for human conceptualization. Such normative conceptions as nations, states, and races are given a symbolic reality and reach at the symbolic level the status of myth. Normative conceptions can be and must be replaced. For example, the nation-state is an anachronism and yet is a normative conception which has some stock in Western Europe. He believes that at the grassroots level of the European populations, behavior has already altered to the point where the nation-state as a myth is in reality waning. That such trends can occur in Western Europe and have occurred in places such as the confederation of Switzerland gives him reason to believe that, unless a disaster strikes, a loose world organization of men will develop. The trends are already apparent. For Halle, then, the discussions at the political and legal level of world government are in the nature of derivative phenomena and not necessarily related. to the shift in attitudes already underway which promise to eventually express themselves in a more universal attitude toward a stability among the nations of men.

Mead in her chapter poses the question: Can we escape dependency on biological mechanisms and create new forms of human relationships based upon our collective experience? She implies that we depend too much upon speculations derived from the studies of infrahuman primates; rather than speculate too much on the past, today we more than ever need to evolve new concepts for expressing our position relative to nature. Today, we have a broader ecological view and see man in a contextual situation, not man versus nature but man in relationship to an environment upon which he depends; an environment composed of animate and inanimate objects; an environment within which we must survive.

Mead traces the results of the application of behavioral research from the 20s to the present and indicates how many of our attitudes and rearing practices were dominated by the conception that through appropriate conditioning and manipulation human behavior could be directed toward whatever ends were deemed desirable. Today, as recent literature suggests, the tide has turned. More and more we are coming to the view that man is dominated by physiological predispositions rather than the view that man is open to appropriate forms of authoritarian-imposed conditioning and propaganda. Recent popularizations, however, have tended to be pessimistic in the sense that current arguments favor the view that man is predisposed to war and aggression. Even given such a consideration, many of the books including Lorenz' *On Aggression* suggest alternatives to the aggressive impetus and cannot be classed as totally pessimistic. Lorenz himself states that one of the keys to the control of aggression is not to deny its existence but to accept its existence and strive to redirect aggressive impulses into group-coordinated activities and sublimates.

Mead acknowledges the continuing feedback between studies on animals and humans and insists that it should be fostered; but she sounds the same warnings as noted in the chapter by Jaynes and Bressler, that although the feedback is important we should not be too ready to reduce human potentiality to mere physiological drives nor, on the other hand, should we extend human potentiality too far into realms for which humans may be ill adapted to cope.

The interchange between animal-oriented studies and human studies has had a long history—a history in which Dr. Mead has participated. She acknowledges that one of the major contributions from ethologists has been to emphasize what animals *do* and, now with the emergent discipline of human ethology on the horizon, there is an increasing tendency to look at the actual activities of humans and to de-emphasize the study of words or symbolic communication. This is a necessary trend to compensate for the lopsided tendencies of earlier investigators.

In concluding, Mead stresses the theme that man is more and more becoming concerned with his whole environment and its limits. We are concerned with the conservation of resources, recycling of materials, de-emphasis of waste and pollution, and concerned with regulating the modes of economic expansion. These facets of endeavor have become primary in the minds of the urbanized peoples. She points out that we have many choices in controlling and regulating the directions in which our behavior patterns will manifest themselves. We can, on the one hand, cater to an evolutionary past which we are beginning to dimly perceive or we can promote divergence and independence from this evolutionary past by furthering our independence from biological constraints. We should give further thought, much more thought, to what goals we wish to achieve in the kind of world in which we wish to live.

REFERENCES

Cantril, H.
  1965. *The Pattern of Human Concerns.* New Brunswick, New Jersey: Rutgers University Press.
Garattini, S., and E. B. Sigg, editors.
  1969. *Aggressive Behavior.* Amsterdam: Excerpta Medica Foundation.
Moyer, K. E.
  1969. "Internal Impulses to Aggression." *Transactions of the New York Academy of Science,* 31(2):104–114.
Pepper, S.
  1958. *The Sources of Value.* Berkeley: University of California Press.

CHAPTER 12

INTERNATIONAL BEHAVIOR AND THE PROSPECTS FOR HUMAN SURVIVAL

LOUIS J. HALLE

GRADUATE INSTITUTE OF INTERNATIONAL STUDIES

GENEVA, SWITZERLAND

The question to which I have been asked to address myself assumes that our species may fail to survive—that, like so many others in the past, it may become extinct. If only as a remote possibility, this seems to me a fair assumption.

Although our species has been uniquely successful up to this point, its very success could prove its undoing. It could be like other species that— liberated from the environmental factors by which their numbers had previously been limited—proliferated to such an extent as to engender, by their proliferation, new problems of survival that they could not overcome. It has happened repeatedly that a population, by its sudden expansion, has exerted such pressure on the sources of its food as to destroy them, thereby condemning itself to mass starvation. Population explosions generally end in population crashes. The present population explosion of mankind could, conceivably, represent a fatal finality.

The possibility of man's total extinction, however, seems to me so uncertain and remote as not to constitute, in itself, a practical problem for the present. In a detached view, there can be no doubt that, if the nuclear holocaust we all have in mind as the most immediate threat should occur, our species would still survive. Perhaps its numbers would have been substantially reduced, perhaps it would have disappeared in large part from the north temperate zone, and perhaps those of its members who survived would be condemned to savagery. It is conceivable that it would have been so weakened, genetically and culturally, and its environment so damaged, that it would decline like other species in the past to ultimate extinction. In a practical sense, however, the more immediate problems of a crash must concern us more than its remote possible consequences.

It is even more unlikely that a failure to solve the problem of feeding our growing numbers would mean that our species did not survive. The death by starvation of nine tenths of mankind would still leave an ample seed stock. I am sorry to talk in such cold-blooded terms, but in a scientific context I must make it clear that, in truth, the extinction of our species is not among the immediate dangers we face.

Whether the terms of its survival would be worth it is the real question. The question is that of a tolerable future for our species—which means the survival of our developing civilization and the avoidance of such horrors as would make the living envy the dead. It is to the survival of a civilized and hopeful human world that I shall be addressing myself, and it is in this sense that I shall be using the term.

Man differs from all other species that have faced great crises in two related respects. First, he has not become committed to one established pattern of social organization and behavior, which evolving circumstances might render obsolete. No form of human society, whether at the level of the family or of the empire, has as yet been more than tentative and, in effect, on trial. The social organization and behavior of the honeybee are still the same today as fifty thousand years ago, and the same in China as in North America. By contrast, the social organization and behavior of man varies widely in time and in space. This means that man, uncommitted as he still is, has a plasticity, a capacity for adapting his behavior to changing circumstances, that the bee and every other nonhuman species has lost.

The second element that makes our species unique is the possession of intelligence at the level of self-conscious thought, expressing itself through language spoken and written. The result is that our species is self-educable, as no other is.

This is the basis on which human culture has developed and continues to develop—to evolve, if you will. Today man's evolution is as much cultural as it is genetic or Darwinian. It is, in fact, a combination of cultural and genetic, since the two elements do not operate independently of each other. Our cultural evolution, however, is by far the more rapid, so that today it both sets the direction and forces the pace of our genetic evolution.

The problems that threaten our survival, and that consequently call for behavioral adaptations on our part, are those that have arisen out of our conquest of nature—to use the rather crude traditional term for it. We have overcome natural limitations on the proliferation of our numbers, with consequences that, if otherwise unchecked, will lead to mass starvation or standing room only on this planet. We have overcome the natural limitations of communication, travel, and transport to such an extent that today a crisis of human society anywhere on this planet may be immediately upsetting to human society virtually anywhere else on it; we have overcome them to such an extent that we can deliver destruction to any point on the planet from any other point in a matter of minutes. Finally, we have brought into our service the practically unlimited destructive power that has hitherto been locked away, beyond our reach, within the nucleus of the atom.

So much for a general statement of what the position of our species appears to be today, in the second half of the twentieth century, after a million years of evolution.

We are, I am sure, agreed that the radical changes occurring in our circumstances present a challenge to our powers of intelligent adaptation. But adaptation generally takes time, and the challenge is immensely aggravated by the fact that the changing circumstances now allow us so little time. They do not, for example, allow us the time that is needed for primitive genetic adaptation, which cannot, even theoretically, occur in less than one generation, and which in practice would require many. (I exclude, here, the possibility of operating directly on the genes, which is still no more than a possibility that can be envisaged for some distant future.)

Man's so-called conquest of nature, in all its forms, has been taking place at an accelerating rate over the million years that he has inhabited the earth. If, on a graph in which the horizontal coordinate represented time, one drew the curve that showed the increase of his population over the past million years, or the curve that represented the increasing speed at which he has been able to travel and communicate, or the curve that represented the amount of natural energy he has been able to harness—if one drew any of these curves one would find them to be exponential curves rising sharply toward the vertical in our present. This is what identifies our present with the greatest crisis in the history of mankind—the greatest crisis, probably, in the history of life on earth—and makes such unparalleled demands on our powers of adaptation. I need only mention that, if present trends continue, a world population of some three thousand million today will be twice as great in another thirty years—that is to say, in another generation. It is evident that, in the adaptation required of our species, it cannot rely on genetic evolution.

If genetic evolution is excluded, so are the miracle solutions that have not been without their advocates over the past years. There is no use pretending that we are going to be able, at one stroke, to excise the old Adam from our human nature. What we basically are in our ambiguous animal nature we shall continue to be—which is to say, quarrelsome, competitive, and less than reasonable in our dealings with one another. It is conceivable that, at any time, some drug that alters our personalities will be invented and brought into general use, making us better fit to cope

357

with the problems presented by modern civilization, but there are no grounds for taking this into serious consideration at the moment.

Under the heading of miracle solutions I also exclude world government now, a United States of the World. The cultural conditions for it hardly begin to exist, and their instantaneous production is no more possible than is the instantaneous excision of the old Adam from our nature.

On the same grounds I exclude a pledge by all mankind to abide by some factitious body of international law. Even if all the nations of the world joined together today to outlaw war, the situation tomorrow would not be different from what it is today. This would not even be a miracle solution. It would be a nominal solution, a solution in words that was not a solution in deeds, and would therefore be merely illusory—in fact, no solution at all.

Having, perhaps, alienated some of my readers by what I have just said, I must now alienate more by excluding disarmament as, in itself, a solution for the problem of survival. It is certainly not true that the fewer arms nations have, or the less terrible the arms they retain in their arsenals, the less likely they are to fight. I should think it obvious that this would make them more likely to fight. And once they began fighting with their reduced armament, they would quickly restore the weapons they had discarded, especially those that were the most terrible. This, however, could hardly be in any case, simply because there is no way in which nuclear weapons, for example, could be deliberately abolished by international agreement in the world as we know it. Nuclear weapons could be hidden where even unlimited international inspection could not find them, and since no nation could trust its rivals to live up to such an agreement, no nation would live up to it itself.

It is not true, either, that the arms race is necessarily destabilizing to international relations and a cause of war. At the beginning of the present decade, in fact, the arms race was notably stabilizing and tended to make war less likely by reducing the vulnerability of the great nuclear armaments, in the United States and Russia, that had previously tempted each side to resort to surprise attack in time of crisis. I do not advocate the continuing arms race and, in fact, I fear what some of its effects might be, but what it produces is always a mixture of good with bad, and the bad does not always predominate. I share the general reluctance to admit how much mankind's constructive technological development owes to military competition, to the arms race, but the fact is there. There may be some whom I offend by these observations but we must liberate ourselves from the cant that dominates so many of these discussions, and that takes the place of thought.

In sum, I have little faith in legal and institutional devices of salvation by themselves. Law and political institutions, it seems to me, are rarely primary. They are necessary, but they are generally secondary in that they register changes of a more basic cultural character, once such changes have gone far enough to make such registration possible. When an aggregate of individuals achieves a sufficient sense of community, that sense of community tends to find institutional and juridical expression, which may in turn foster and secure the sense of community. It is because we lack the cultural foundations for a world government that there is no use trying to get one promulgated and adopted today.

Again, many features of the arms race undoubtedly are unnecessary, wasteful, and dangerous. But the race itself is the product of an international insecurity that represents, in large part, deep-seated cultural factors. As insecurity is lessened by the development of more favorable factors, military budgets will shrink automatically, and so the arms race will slow down.

I have now drawn what seem to me to be the limits of possibility within which our species has to meet the present problems of survival. I have excluded changes in our basic human nature and I have reduced to a secondary role all purely institutional devices, all paper undertakings, and all legal formulations.

What is left?

What is left, I think, are all the possibilities of cultural change within the terms of our basic human nature as it is. Here I rest my hopes on the fact that men's attitudes in society, and their consequent ways of dealing with one another, are open to wide variation and rapid change in response to changing circumstances.

This protean quality is almost ludicrous at times, as a few crude examples may show. Up through the spring of 1945 American soldiers were fighting the Germans as hated enemies; but when they moved in to occupy Germany they began to fraternize with them, and suddenly the whole relationship was transformed. I dare say that, a month after the atomic bombs were dropped on Hiroshima and Nagasaki, many of those who had applauded the deed, now living among the Japanese in Japan, would have fought to prevent a hair of any Japanese child's head from being harmed.

From 1936 to 1939 the Spanish people, with a long tradition of violence behind them, tore each other to pieces over their ideological differences.

Since then, they have been willing to endure almost any ill rather than again suffer the horrors of fighting among themselves that they experienced during those terrible years.

During the 1950s, the students in American universities showed themselves politically indifferent and inert to a remarkable degree. In the second half of the 1960s, however, important numbers of them suddenly began rampaging against virtually every aspect of established society. It was the same biological stock in both cases, but there had been a sudden shift from one attitude of mind to an opposite attitude, entailing a radical change in social behavior.

These cases show what I mean when I say that the attitudes and manners of people, unlike their biological heritage, can change radically overnight. It is in this that I find what grounds of hope I do for our ability, as a species, to meet the problem of survival. Here, in the domain of social attitudes and manners, we are nothing if not changeable—and therefore adaptable.

It is, if you will, in the superficial aspects of human behavior that I find my hope. There are men for whom I have the greatest respect, as individuals, who say that we should all learn to love one another, and that by so doing we shall find the way to salvation. Leaving considerations of religion aside, this seems to me impractical in that it asks too much too immediately of our human nature. What seems to me more practical, in the immediate crisis, is to accept the fact that we shall continue to dislike one another, and to ask merely that we take the sting out of that dislike by adopting good manners in dealing with one another.

I live, today, in what may well be the happiest country in the world— or the least unhappy. Soundings of opinion have shown that there is probably less dissatisfaction with their circumstances among the Swiss than among any other people. They are, very likely, more at peace with one another (as well as with the rest of the world) than any other people. This, however, represents an extraordinary paradox, for the Swiss constitute a nation that, culturally and politically, is deeply divided. Having now lived among them for over a dozen years, I have at last become familiar with what does not usually show on the surface of the national life, the bitter antipathies, often amounting to hatred, among the various subcommunities that make up what is, after all, a very artificial nation. There is an ingrained hostility of the French-speaking Swiss toward the German-speaking Swiss, which is reciprocated by the German-speaking Swiss. There is no love lost between the half of the Swiss population that is Protestant and the half that is Roman Catholic. There is bitter antagonism between Geneva and Lausanne, and similar antagonisms between the various cantons. Yet it is the rule that, in direct dealings between these mutually hostile groups, the greatest courtesy and consideration are shown. Good manners are a substitute for love. They take the curse out of mutual dislike and make Switzerland the relatively happy nation it is. In fact, it is the consciousness of how easily the nation could fall apart that makes the Swiss so moderate, so considerate, and so courteous in their dealings with one another.

The Swiss were not always this way. Warfare among the cantons was common up to 1847, when the last intercantonal war took place. By that time, the price the Swiss were paying for expressing their mutual antipathies or conflicting interests in such violent terms had impressed itself on them so thoroughly that they then and there developed the self-disciplined manner of dealing with one another that has happily characterized their association ever since. That association was finally institutionalized in the constitution of 1848, establishing the present Swiss Confederation.

I see something like this happening, as well, in the association of West European states generally. The cost of two European civil wars in this century has impressed itself on the European peoples, and while it has not caused them to love one another, it has brought about a moderation and mutual consideration in their behavior toward one another that was not evident in the years leading up to 1914.

It is possible that racial antagonism in the United States will, in the near future, produce such horrors as, by a common revulsion, will cause a new sobriety to prevail, impressing on both races the need of moderation and good manners in dealing with each other, whether they like each other or not. What else will enable us to live with the racial problem over the long decades until the secular evolution of human society has brought some solution, whatever it may be, that is hardly foreseeable as yet? We often do better with problems if we concentrate on how to live with them rather than on how to solve them completely at one stroke.

All this has its obvious application to the international relations of our times. The great peace-keeping art, traditionally, has been diplomacy, when properly exercised; and diplomacy, when properly exercised, has always entailed the most formalized good manners between antagonists, including a use of language distinguished by its courtesy and moderation.

Elsewhere I have argued that the intensity of the Cold War, and the consequent danger to all mankind, was notably heightened by the resort of the Russians, beginning in 1947, to a language of wild abusiveness, in which they accused the Western governments of the most outrageous intentions and vicious practices, referring to their leaders in terms so offensive that they were bound to arouse an implacable anger throughout the Western societies.[1] This immensely heightened the tension between East and West, and made any accommodation between them virtually impossible. Inevitably, it also provoked a certain violence of retort on the Western side, which added to the dangerous intractability of the situation. Under the circumstances, the moderating role of diplomacy was virtually excluded, all meaningful communication between the antagonists being broken off for a period of years—a situation that still exists between the United States and China. With the great nuclear armaments on both sides kept in a state of instant alert, nothing could be more dangerous than such a complete severance of effective diplomatic contact. It can be argued (and I have done so elsewhere)[2] that the Korean War might never have taken place except for this severance; and the Korean War, in turn, would surely have erupted into World War III if new councils of self-restraint had not prevailed in the nick of time.

The great change in the Cold War situation came after the Cuban missile crisis of 1962, when the importance of maintaining diplomatic communication was at last recognized by Russia and the United States alike, the recognition being registered in the establishment of the so-called hot line between Washington and Moscow. The revulsion from the horrors implicit in the situation that had prevailed up to then led to a new moderation, at least in relative terms, and the consequent development of certain mutual understandings between those who continued to be enemies. One might say that tacitly, if not explicitly, the two sides came to agree on certain "rules of the game" by which their contest would be limited. In the same way, the Swiss cantons, after the extremes of their previous rivalry, agreed on the rules of the game in 1848.

The point I have been making, summed up in a sentence, is that a degree of self-limitation in human behavior at the international level— mutual self-limitation which represents at least tacit agreement on the rules of the game—is essential to the survival of our species, and is also, as experience has shown, quite within the bounds of practical possibility.

We shall continue to live in a world of bitter conflict. We must expect that such conflict will occasionally take the form of warfare, of organized

---

[1] Halle, L. J., *The Cold War as History,* pages 151–152. New York: Harper and Row, 1967.

[2] Ibid, Chapter XXI; also *Encounter* (March 1968), 30(3):23–25.

military violence between opposed national communities. But we can realistically expect that such warfare, when it breaks out in spite of everything, will be kept limited. The two superpowers already agree on certain rules of the game in this respect. The Russian military forces have not been directly involved in any war since 1945, for Moscow has drawn back wherever conflict has brought it too close to the brink of such involvement—as in Berlin, as in Cuba. And certainly it is a radical change in our own traditional attitude that has made us Americans willing to forego victory in Korea and in Vietnam rather than transcend certain limitations in our conduct of warfare

I began by saying that man, because his social attitudes and consequent behavior have not become frozen, is capable of cultural adaptations that are startling in their rapidity. At one point a whole nation may appear completely committed to the attitude toward the conduct of war that General MacArthur summed up in his dictum, "In war there is no substitute for victory." A few years later, however, it may have been accepted as the rule in warfare that wars must be kept limited even at the price of victory.

What we are dealing with here is normative thinking. It is normative conceptions that govern the attitudes and behavior of all men and of all societies. Over the countless millenia during which secular changes in man's environment were so slow as to be imperceptible from generation to generation, normative conceptions commonly had a certain stability. They were passed on through successive generations in philosophy, in literature, in art, in the education of the young. Human societies—whether in the form of civilizations, of nations, or of lesser communities—were able to live by traditional attitudes and traditional concepts that had developed slowly to fit their relatively stable circumstances. Men found their intellectual security, even their mental health, in the assurance provided by tradition and its counterpart, custom. To the extent that custom told them how to behave, it spared them the agonies of doubt, indecision, inner conflict, and conflict among themselves that would otherwise have been their lot.

The malaise of our present is attributable to the fact that these old certainties are largely gone. This has produced a cultural crisis which afflicts authoritarian as well as free societies, and is vividly represented by the revolts of today's students against the generation of their fathers. Its implications are cultural anarchy, for human societies are based on custom, but it is easier to destroy old customs, when they become obsolete, than to create new ones for their replacement—and today's changes in basic circumstances may be so rapid that there is no time to meet them by the development of new customs in any case.

Faced with the challenge, nevertheless, we must look at the anatomy of normative thinking, which has hitherto been so closely related to tradition and custom.

Normative thinking is of necessity based on notional abstractions, conceptions engendered in the mind by its myth-making proclivities, conceptions that are not tied, in any immediate sense, to direct observation or to firsthand knowledge of what can be apprehended by the five senses. To take a simple example—I have never been to Australia, so that the concept of "Australia" is a nominal abstraction in my mind. So is the concept of "the Australian people" (as distinct from individual Australians). The disjunction between the idea and the existential reality, however, would be almost as great if I actually had been in Australia. I live within ten minutes of France and am constantly in and out of the country, but I cannot know the putative entity called "the French people" through my five senses any more than I can photograph it. For what the term denotes is not an existential reality at all but a nominal abstraction. You cannot see or touch a nominal abstraction. As a collective noun, "the French people" is notional merely. When I spoke of the "French-speaking Swiss and the German-speaking Swiss" I was merely translating a multitude of individual experiences in the realm of the existential into an enormously simplified notional abstraction that, as such, belonged to an entirely different order of phenomena. I was making a myth surrogate for a multifarious and fragmentary reality that it might represent more or less well, more or less badly. Normative thinking is, of necessity, mythological.

Here in America, our mythological notion of "the Japanese people" was one thing from 1941 to 1945—when we regarded them as vicious, cruel, and conspiratorial aggressors by nature—but quite another after 1945, when they became our friends and allies. A sudden change of circumstances induced us to replace one myth with another, and the fact that we were able to accomplish this so quickly is the basis of such hope as I have in our ability to meet the challenge of the future, to solve the problem of survival in the explosive circumstances of our day.

The organization of our political societies is based entirely on normative models that are subject to the same kind of alteration or replacement as all normative models, although it is our tendency always to attach the value of eternity to them. A famous example is Aristotle's statement that "the city-state belongs to the class of things that exist by nature, and that man

364

is by nature an animal intended to live in a city-state."[3] At the moment when he said that, the city-state was already obsolete in the world he knew, and his pupil, Alexander of Macedon, was about to replace it with the prototype of the universal empire, later realized by Rome. For many centuries thereafter men would think of the universal empire, rather than the city-state, as belonging to "the class of things that exist by nature."

The nation-state, too, is merely notional in its basis, a normative concept that replaced the normative concept of the dynastic state after the French Revolution. Like the city-state, it is a temporary artifice. It had its heyday in the second half of the nineteenth century, and I suggest to you that circumstances have rendered it increasingly obsolete in our own century. But normative models have a stubborn persistence in men's minds, representing as they do customary thinking of tradition, so that the institutions based on them tend to persist for a time even after they have become unsuited to the changing secular circumstances, as the dead tree remains standing in the forest.

Especially to one who lives in present-day Europe, it seems evident that the nineteenth century nation-state has become an anachronism. It no longer responds to the increasing mobility of populations, the increasing speed of communications and transport, the radically changed requirements of military security, the expanding scale of economic enterprise, the proliferation of cultural interchange, or the increasing interdependence of men over an area that at last embraces the whole world. A great transformation is consequently taking place that is not, however, altogether apparent to those whose training has taught them to think only in formal terms—in terms of formal institutions, constitutional instruments, and so forth.

The changes take place first at the grassroots. An example is the widespread and rapid disappearance of the peasantry in Europe. Having been attached to the soil for perhaps two thousand years, within a decade the erstwhile peasants have acquired first motor bicycles and at last small automobiles in which they now travel far and wide, crossing national boundaries. At the same time they are abandoning their cattle and their hayfields for employment in towns and cities. The result of this sudden mobility of populations is that international frontiers are losing their conspicuousness, are fading away. Where one still had to go through rather rigid formalities when one crossed a European frontier a dozen years ago, it is now common to do no more than slow down. The frontier between

---

[3] Aristotle, *Politics,* Chapter 2.

Switzerland and France begins to seem like the frontier between Maryland and Virginia.

It is this kind of continuous transformation of the circumstances and conditions of life, which never makes the headlines, that is fundamental. Only at the last stage is it belatedly registered in the formal institutional or constitutional changes that are the primary preoccupation of lawyers and political scientists.

A historical model for the transformation that is going on in Europe and all over the world is to be found in the increasing interdependence, in past centuries, of the separate and sovereign Swiss cantons, an interdependence that made their separate sovereignties and their warfare among themselves increasingly anachronistic, until the transformation of basic circumstances was at last registered in the Constitution of 1848, which formally established the present Swiss Confederation.

Viewing the rapid transformations that are going on today at the grassroots, I allow myself to predict that General de Gaulle will prove to have been the last great spokesman for the normative idea of the nation-state as it reached its apogee in Bismarck's day, and that many of us in our own lifetimes will see it increasingly replaced by the normative idea of a worldwide organization of man, however loose that organization may for a long time be in its conception and its realization alike.

In predicting this, however, I do so with one great qualification, which is that there will not occur, before it can be realized, a general crash of civilization and a worldwide collapse into anarchy. This is an alternative possibility, and not an implausible one. I am, therefore, in the same position as one who predicts of a boy that he will someday be a man—but has to add that this will be so only if the boy is not killed in an accident before the prediction can be realized.

My basic thesis is that human behavior has a notional basis. It has its basis in the normative ideas or mythological conceptions that inhabit the minds of men. In the past, these ideas or conceptions have generally had the persistent quality of tradition or custom. Under the stress of changing circumstances, however, they are susceptible of remarkably rapid transformation or replacement.

My final observations bear on one notional pattern that has always dominated our minds, a pattern that may have been vital for the survival of particular societies in the past, but that seems to me to be losing this value in our time and, increasingly, to be endangering the survival of civilization. I refer to what may properly be called *the fallacy of the two species*.

We are all of us brought up to think in terms of two opposed species:

the "good people," with whom we identify ourselves, and another kind of beings that, although they appear in human guise, do not share our common humanity but are distinguished, rather, by diabolical attributes with which we endow them in our imagination. In the fictional literature on which we are brought up the two species may be the young prince and his wicked elder brothers, or they may be the cowboys and the Indians, or they may be the cops and the robbers. In the mythical world of ideology they may be the Christians and the Saracens, or the Proletarians and the Capitalists, or the freedom-lovers and the Communists. The repeated identification of the Jews as a separate and innately vicious species engaged in a secret conspiracy against humankind is a classic example of the fallacy of the two species.

Closely associated with the fallacy of the two species is the abhorrent doctrine of collective guilt, with its implications of genocide. If the Jews, or the Germans, or the Capitalists, or the Mohammedans are wicked by their fundamental nature, then the only way to eliminate the wickedness they represent is—to use that peculiar term—by liquidating them.

Wherever there is conflict at the popular level, demagogy promotes the fallacy of the two species and the associated doctrine of collective guilt. During 1968, violent confrontations occurred at universities all over the world between students and police. On some of these occasions the students behaved badly, on some the police behaved badly, so that no responsible judgment could attribute all innocence or all guilt to either side. Many intellectuals, however, their minds inhabiting the world of ideological abstractions, automatically identified the students as the good species, the police as the villainous. To virtually no one did it occur that, stripped naked, there was no fundamental difference between the students and the police, that both alike had all the good and bad attributes of humanity, that both alike were capable of affection and of anger, of love and of hatred, that when either a student or a policeman was cut he felt the same pain, bled the same blood.

At one of these confrontations, however, a remarkable and significant thing happened quite unexpectedly. On the 27th of October 1968, masses of students marched into London's Grosvenor Square in an assault on the American Embassy, and there they came up against cordons of policemen blocking their way. Some of the policemen had stones flung at them, some had their helmets knocked off, many were subjected to verbal abuse and provocation. The policemen, however, managed for the most part to suppress such impulses to react violently as they must have felt. The movement of the students, which had also been kept within limits in response to the policy of their leadership, soon lost its momentum. Tension began to relax. At last all ended in a spectacle that was comical in the Gilbert and Sullivan tradition, but that was also touched with a certain pathos and nobility. Students and police concluded the conflict by all joining together to sing "Auld Lang Syne." What this represented was a sudden awareness that they were not two separate and opposed species, a sudden recognition of their common humanity.

In World War II, President Roosevelt, speaking for the Western Allies and the Soviet Union, proclaimed that the contest was between the "peace-loving nations" and the "aggressor nations" into which all mankind was divided. He asserted that the German, Japanese, and Italian peoples, regardless of what kinds of regime were governing them at any particular time, were aggressors by their very nature. The American soldiers I referred to before had bemonstered the Germans in imagination up to the moment of entering and occupying German towns and cities, whereupon they began to fraternize with them. These soldiers changed their attitude so radically and suddenly because, face-to-face with the actual German people, they found that these people belonged to the same species as themselves, that German individuals were essentially like American individuals in their common humanity.

Now that technology and crowding have brought all the races and nations of the earth face to face, so to speak, it seems to me both essential and possible for us to transcend the fairytale world in which our own virtuous humanity has always been represented as under challenge by some monster species bent on our enslavement or extermination. For this mythological conception, more than anything else, tends to make men desperate with fear—or with the hatred that is the sublimation of fear—to the point where the limitation of conflict becomes impossible.

What distinguishes our species from all the others is its cultural adaptability and its educability, which is only one aspect of its cultural adaptability. That adaptability is increasingly challenged, today, by the increasingly rapid transformation of our environment. Our basic biological nature—our gene complex—cannot be transformed in time to meet the challenge. Although our formal institutions—our legal and political arrangements—will have to be adjusted, such adjustment is secondary. The primary adaptation, now as always, can be only in the normative conceptions that inhabit our minds, that govern our behavior, and that ultimately shape our institutions. The great hope for our survival is that our normative conceptions will continue to develop, as they are developing today, so as to set new limits, and to set them in time, on the behavior of human societies in conflict.

CHAPTER 13

INNATE BEHAVIOR AND BUILDING NEW CULTURES: A COMMENTARY

MARGARET MEAD

AMERICAN MUSEUM OF NATURAL HISTORY

Whereas moralists of the Western world once asked if man is endowed with free will or is his fate predestined, scientists today have rephrased the question and now ask: To what extent is human behavior dependent on biological mechanisms that cannot be easily modified and how far can man go in making new adaptations? Are we humans free to learn from experience? Can we create new forms of human relationships and control our environment by using knowledge gained from that experience?

Finding answers to such questions about the biological bases of behavior is aided by a growing knowledge of the social life of wild primate groups described earlier in this book. Because of scanty fossil evidence, our poor knowledge of early human development makes us all the more dependent on speculations about early man based on what we can infer from recent studies of baboons, chimpanzees, gorillas, and others whose ancestors and ours sprang from the same stock. Their social life, by analogy, gives us clues with which we can speculate about early man, the contemporary human condition, and emerging patterns of social life ahead. In order to appreciate more fully the individually fascinating research and speculation already presented, we need to look further at recent intellectual history and the current trend of studying man as part of a world ecosystem. We need also to be aware of the rewards and limitations of how we extrapolate across species.

We anthropologists and other students of behavior have been attempting recently to apply the principles of ecology to our discussion of man and the creatures to whom he relates. Until very recently it was customary for specialists in animal behavior to discuss the animals, while the specialists in human behavior discussed the human beings. So we had people who knew about sheep, and people who knew about shepherds. But their knowledge was not integrated. And this was, of course, equally evident in our discussions of hunting peoples. The specialist who knew about the kangaroo seldom knew anything about the marriage classes of the Australian aborigine. Fortunately, we are now developing anthropologists and animal behaviorists who put it all together to give us a new

371

perspective on man as part of the whole ecosystem. This new perspective takes into account the species-characteristic behavior of relevant creatures, whether they be hunted, herded, used as work animals, or kept as pets. (This fresh, holistic view, incidentally, I think is characteristic of the last stage of urbanization.)

We are also beginning to use what we learn in experimentation on and observation of animals, birds, and fish to interpret and shape our attitudes toward human beings. This new, all-inclusive or ecological approach is the result of human beings trying to understand what is happening to their planetary habitat in terms of urbanization, war, pollution, and the population explosion. It draws extensively and importantly upon work being done on a great variety of species, from iguanas to primates and from sticklebacks to bees.

If we go back to the 1920s, we find that experiments on rats had a tremendous influence on our notions of education and child-rearing. As a result of this thirty years of research—during which the susceptibility of rats to their experimenters' whims and man-made mazes was tested—we gained a view of human beings which, on the whole, was linear. What the experimenter wanted, he got; the rat obliged. Then we began getting a few studies of the species-characteristic behavior of rats, which produced some rather disastrous changes in some of the conclusions that had been drawn.

Nevertheless, these linear, primarily authoritarian notions of education, child-rearing, and social manipulation persisted. One of these notions was that adults or people in power in any population were capable of manipulating that population as they wished. And theories of propaganda in totalitarian states were associated with types of conditioning experiments. In the application of Pavlov's experiments, for example, his recognition of the constitutional differences between his animal subjects was ignored; only the power elements were picked up and used.

At present, we are bombarded by a great variety of extrapolations from animal experiments. It seems we can pick and choose from the entire living world to find the creature whose characteristics reflect the moral wanted at the moment. We know, for example, that using one group of primates to explain human behavior almost always misleads us, and that additional field work or research on the next group of primates upsets the basic generalizations that have just been made. Nevertheless, we continue to draw at random on material from a great number of species.

Although this procedure can be exceedingly interesting, we have had a good many instances of its being overdone. In the late 1930s and early

1940s we discovered man was a mammal, and we had quite a long dose of that. This discovery meant a rather heavy emphasis on certain parallels that were to be drawn between mammals and ourselves, a tremendous emphasis on breast-feeding human infants, and an emphasis on removing constraints on sexuality. The Lorenz-Ardrey type of interpretation, which again draws on the characteristics of a variety of creatures, is being used at present to justify our feelings of despair, attitudes of helplessness, and pessimism. If man is a creature with ineradicable traits that make him murderous, carnivorous, continually prone to war, and, in the extreme, cannibalistic, then there is no need to do anything about him at all.[1] We are stuck with him. We are going to continue to have a world that is unmanageable, whose inhabitants may destroy it.

Curiously enough, on the other side of the coin, the geneticist comes forward and discusses the possibilities of modification through assortive matings, or through a preference for certain genetic combinations. And we are told by Dr. Edward O. Wilson in Chapter 5 that it is possible, even within ten generations, to make a considerable change in a population. This also tends to lead people into a kind of passive despair. In many cases it emphasizes our dependence upon specific genetic traits of one sort or another and tends to deprecate the possible results of improved nutrition, education, and environment.

In the contemporary world many proposals for needed social change are conducted with an intense preoccupation with the practical implications of conclusions from such ethological studies. This has implications for our assessment of the achievement potential of different parts of the population. There are fears that the present unmanageable bureaucratic structure with which we are struggling may permit genetic manipulation

---

[1] *Editor's note:* Senator J. William Fulbright, Regent of the Smithsonian, and a participant in two discussions related to the Man and Beast Symposium, reflected such concern when he questioned Dr. Karl Menninger, the psychiatrist, about whether man has an inherent aggressive tendency: "What is important to those of us who happen to be in the Senate, in the Congress, is to feel that it is possible, or even probable, that we can influence the decisions which affect the future of this country. . . . If we assume that men generally are inherently aggressive in their tendency, evidenced by the historical experience of using military force, physical force, to solve problems, if this is inherent and man cannot be educated away from it, it certainly makes a great deal of difference in one's attitude toward current problems. . . . If we are inherently committed by nature to this aggressive tendency to fight, well then, I certainly would not be bothering about all this business of arms limitations or talks with the Russians." See "Psychological Aspects of Foreign Policy." *Hearings before the Committee on Foreign Relations United States Senate,* page 67. Washington, D.C.: U.S. Government Printing Office, 19 June 1969. (W.D.)

to produce genetic changes and alterations not by waiting ten generations, but in the immediate present.

I think that everything discussed in the foregoing chapters has to be placed in the context of man's new relationship to the living world, his new relationship to the whole of the world within which he lives. We are attempting to learn from experiment, from observation, and from careful genetic studies, something more to be said about our genetic constitution in relation to our hopes for the kind of society we may be able to build. One of the important aspects, I think, of looking at these man-animal linked systems—whether they are men and kangaroos or men and detailed ecological experiments—is the feedback between the two. If we emphasize the relationship between human studies made by anthropologists and sociologists and ethological studies, if we continue to draw on the human studies to inform the animal studies, and the animal studies to inform the human studies, we get rid of some of the one-way linear manipulative elements present in earlier animal experimentation and in the conclusions we drew from them.

In anthropomorphizing the behavior of sticklebacks or graylag geese, or other creatures, we run the risks of the parallel position: zoomorphizing man.[2] The chapters in this volume can be divided pretty well between these two categories. Definite and purposive attempts have been made to use the findings of sociologists who have been working with small groups as a basis for discussing concepts of such humanly derived categories as status, role, and information in relation to the study of animal groups. On the other hand, we have the tendency to find constants in the organization of group-living animals and state them as valid for human organization. These constants will then guide our view of human behavior, very often limit it, and make it reductionist and myopic. Thus, we will

---

[2] *Editor's note:* Geoffrey Gorer, the British anthropologist, in his comments on Desmond Morris' *The Human Zoo,* observed: "In former days writers of edifying and instructive fables and sermons used to ascribe to animals all sorts of human behavior and point to them as examplars of human virtues and vices. This anthropomorphism and its practitioners range from Aesop to Rudyard Kipling and even more recent authors. In the last twenty years the reverse practice has suddenly achieved great popularity, the claim that we can only understand human beings by studying other animals, which might be called zoomorphism. The anthropologists did not feel that they had to know anything more about animals than could be gathered by casual observation and some desultory reading; similarly the zoomorphists feel that they need no more information about human beings than what they can gather from their own experience and reading; by considering the ways of the ant, or the ape, they have all that is needful for wisdom. Desmond Morris is one of the most popular of contemporary zoomorphists." (Geoffrey Gorer, personal communication, 9 September 1969.) (W.D.)

regard as predetermined constants those things we can think of and see as universals in whatever kinds of gregarious creatures we decide to study.

But if we go both ways, then danger of reductionism on the one hand and extensive and complicated anthropomorphism on the other is somewhat decreased. This is equally true of observation. Probably one of the greatest contributions that ethology has made to the study of human behavior is the effect it has had on observation. Most social scientists were bemused with words, either words actually heard (that was a speciality of the anthropologists in the field) or words put on pieces of paper as answers to questionnaires, then coded, reduced to numbers, and finally reduced to statistics. In various social sciences, there was a tremendous neglect of all the other aspects of human communication, whether it was between mother and child, between members of a group, or between a single leadership figure on television and the millions watching him. The social science of the first quarter of this century emphasized words almost exclusively, and a great deal of it still does.

A good number of social scientists still have not discovered either the camera or the tape recorder, to say nothing of the videotape or the interaction chronograph.[3] Meanwhile, the field observations of the experimental ethologists stimulated those observers to look at the nonverbal aspects of behavior.[4] I think that if we could go through the chapters in this book and throw out every "non" ("nonhuman primates," I think is a fascinating phrase) including "nonverbal behavior" and all the words with which we categorize part of behavior as not being something else, it would be a good thing. Our observations were refocusing at a time when instrumentation was being developed to make it possible to observe the multisensory communication of human beings in face-to-face situations—confrontations characteristic of animals who cannot normally affect each other or exchange messages at a distance.

This interaction between students of human behavior and ethology has been going on for quite a long time. Just before his death in the early

---

[3] *Editor's note:* Perhaps the leading exception to this statement is Dr. Eliot D. Chapple, a collaborator with Dr. Mead in the Society for Applied Anthropology, whose new book (*Culture and Biological Man,* New York: Holt, Rinehart & Winston, 1970) summarizes his several decades of investigations making use of the interaction chronograph. (W.D.)

[4] *Editor's note:* Dr. Ray L. Birdwhistell, a pioneer in the study of nonverbal communication processes and recording body movements (kinesics) with his conferences on group processes in 1954 and 1955 at which leading ethologists, including Konrad Lorenz, helped stimulate American social scientists to pay attention to wordless behavior of humans and other animals. (W.D.)

40s, Dr. Kingsley Noble, my herpetology colleague at the American Museum of Natural History, and I had a research plan. I was going to make out a schedule based on human babies in different cultures, and he was going to make one on primate infants. Then we were going to cross-reference our observations. Today, of course, many people are doing this.

In the mid-1950s, we first began to put together the studies of people who were working with children and those who were doing ethological studies. Dr. Frank Fremont-Smith, then of the Josiah Macy Foundation, persuaded Dr. Konrad Lorenz of the Max Planck Institute to do psychiatric-type case studies of graylag geese. No one had ever done this before, and it produced, as you all know, fascinating studies of graylag geese whose maturation had gone wrong in one way or another. At the same time, we persuaded Dr. Helen Blauvelt, then teaching in pediatrics at Syracuse, to look at human babies from her perspective of studying kids and lambs. She found behavior that had not been suspected, especially the ability of the neonate to move along on a flat surface for quite a long distance. We have been holding babies down, pinning them down, packing them up, putting them on cradle boards, and swaddling them. For thousands of years, the ability of a human baby to move upward, unassisted was simply not known.[5]

This cross-fertilization has been tremendously valuable. It stimulates a great freedom of observation. By putting all of the creatures of the living world into one framework, and then saying anything that we have learned about one may be relevant to another, we can sharpen our perceptions and clarify previously unclear issues. Dr. Robert Zajonc, for example, covers an enormous variety of creatures in the experiments he reported in Chapter 4. The result is to treat attraction, affiliation, and attachment in the abstract, with scarcely any identification of the creatures whose behavior has been observed.

Such comparisons, however, as well as cross-fertilization, must be done responsibly. In the present-day climate of opinion, extrapolating from a single species, no matter how closely they may relate to man, is exceedingly dangerous. We end up with "matriarchal" families or "patriarchal" families or some other construct that is utterly meaningless. Instead, we

---

[5] *Editor's note:* A detailed account of Dr. Blauvelt's comparative experiments with feeding patterns of human infants and goats is found in a published account of her discussions with other participants in the second Josiah Macy conference on group processes at Princeton. See "Neonate-Mother Relationship in Goat and Man," pages 94–140 in *Group Processes,* B. Schaffner, editor, New York: Josiah Macy, Jr. Foundation, 1956. (W.D.)

must realize that it is essential to man's survival today for him to under-stand the nature of the entire natural world as it was once essential for him to be able to think about evolution. Man must think consistently and continuously about the constraints on his behavior as a member of one component of the living world. Thus he can realize what is his "floor" and how high is his "ceiling." Under what conditions of human life will he keep safe? Nutrition, water, rest, sleep, and freedom from noise are some of the conditions which make up his "floor." Others are social interactions and parent-child stimulation. And for his relationships to the natural world, which are so peculiarly part of his inheritance as man, we must remember man's ability and desire to speculate and understand his universe. Unless we permit and provide for the basic conditions of our humanity—a part distinct to humans and another part which is the evolu-tionary inheritance we share with other living creatures—we run into very serious danger. At the same time, we have to guard against any extrapolation from existing materials that places too rigid a ceiling on where man can go. For example, let us not yet accept the suggestion that human beings are incapable of acquiring a tolerance for crowding or high-density living.

We have to deal continually with our extraordinary jealousy of our humanity. We must not emphasize so sharply the differences between man and other creatures that we ignore the continuum of all creature behavior. If so, we lose the chance to keep our self-knowledge constantly renewed by studying our ties with the rest of the animal kingdom.

I had an extraordinary experience recently when I reported, at a seminar of eminent people, almost all over sixty, on the "Frontiers of Science" lecture given in Dallas by Dr. John Calhoun of the National In-stitutes of Mental Health. Speaking before the American Association for the Advancement of Science, Dr. Calhoun discussed the whole human population explosion partly in the light of his research on rats. He declared his hope that the human population growth would level off, and then ac-tually decrease. Inasmuch as the capacity to multiply and multiply has been a characteristic of *Homo sapiens,* he observed, we should call man by a different name at the moment when he is able to take control of his reproduction rate. We will call him *Homo leo.*[6] And then the room blew

---

[6] *Editor's note:* The allusion here is to the vision of Leo Szilard in his parable of the lion in "Calling All Stars," a story in the collection, *The Voice of the Dolphin and Other Stories.* Dr. Calhoun's lecture, "Space and the Strategy of Life," appears in *The Uses of Space by Animals and Man,* Aristide Esser, editor, Bloomington: Indiana University Press, in press. (W.D.)

up without the slightest warning. People began to say, "But that isn't the only characteristic of man, and even if the population goes down, he'll still be man." I realized that he had struck something very deep and very highly entrenched in the definition of what man is; I detected a deep unwillingness to learn from all the experiments and studies we are making of other creatures, an aversion to thinking about what man might possibly have to be in the future, and how this could be worked out.

In the past, where change for most of the human population has been relatively slow and a great proportion of mankind lived on the land and grew up where their parents and grandparents and great-grandparents grew up, the resemblance between an animal colony of some sort—a troop of baboons or a group of langurs and a small group of humans— was very close. It was extraordinarily difficult, without comparative evidence, to say what was innate, heritable biologically, in their behavior, and what was heritable culturally. Why? The two had been blended and held stable for a considerable time.

We are now, however, facing a world in which none of these conditions is going to hold. We will not have consistency in child-rearing practices. We will not have homogeneous groups of juveniles who play together and teach each other how to handle whatever the social standards are. We will not have grandparents who will teach grandchildren what the end of life is like. We are approaching the point where we have no adult models at all for any of the young people growing up in the world.[7] The relatively smooth transmission of human cultures has been shattered. The shattering holds true whether we see ourselves as relying primarily on heritable characteristics modulated and developed, amplified and elaborated by culture, or for those people who feel that cultural systems are relatively independent of any particular group of human beings who will spend different periods of their lives with different groups of people who have had different experiences. All the traditional cues, whether they are communicable across cultural barriers or highly stylized, are disappearing. Dominance and submission or affiliation and separation have been modulated in the past by both animal and human societies, by cues that were taught to the young or learned and developed as they matured. This is no longer so. We are going to have to face the problem of discriminating between exploring the innate characteristics of man as man and exploring special types of men.

---

[7] *Editor's note:* Dr. Mead has amplified this point in her "Man and Nature" lectures given in March 1969 at the American Museum of Natural History and published as *Culture and Communications,* Garden City: Natural History Press, Doubleday, 1970. (W.D.)

I have been impressed, incidentally, with the assumption in the preceding chapters that there is general variation on any trait discussed, whether it is selfishness or neurosis. Assuming a general variation within a population, with no attention to a constellation of traits, or to physical constitution and somatotyping, may cause us to ignore one of the ways in which mediations between innate, heritable behavior and particular cultures occur. We should consider at least two ways of analyzing the processes and components of new human societies and stating our preferences. Do we want to foster those traits that have a larger heritable component—paying more attention to those procedures between mother and child, or affiliation within groups, or types of courtship behavior—which can be related more precisely to our evolutionary past? Or do we want to move away from such close fits between biologically given behaviors and social institutions?

Breast-feeding illustrates this as well as any other biological and social trait we have been working with, (or should I say "monkeying with" in this context?). Biologically, it seemed "natural" that all mothers could breast-feed their babies before bottle-feeding became possible in Western, industrial societies. Then when travelers and anthropologists brought back the word from primitive societies that breast-feeding was the *only* technique, it became important for some modern mothers to think about reverting to the breast. That all mothers *could* breast-feed their children became a principle in infant care. It took us quite a long time to realize that all children in primitive societies who survived were breast-fed—a totally different statement. It was not until Dr. Helen Blauvelt discussed the biological adequacy of a mother's losing her milk so that a child who did not flourish on it could die and she could have another child who would live, that we began to realize the limitations of the statement that breast-feeding was natural.

True, it gave infants a wonderful beginning in life. A breast-fed baby was pretty well guaranteed the sort of security and warmth we knew was necessary for human babies, and for many other primate babies as well. But babies who did not fit their mothers died.

We can now say that moving from breast-feeding to bottle-feeding means that a society saves a great many more children. If it then moves back to breast-feeding for a limited number of cases, it saves more still, because in those cases, after bottle-feeding is introduced, breast-feeding is used only where there is a good mother-and-baby fit. The good mother-and-baby fit probably draws on evolutionary strength in the way that no bottle or formula ever will. It keeps the child and mother inevitably together, and it establishes a very firm base. But it also reduces enormously the chances for the infant's survival, and of course does not permit that other social invention: the inclusion of the father as a continual baby-sitter, an innovation that may have tremendous evolutionary significance.

Now a child that is not breast-fed can be brought up by a mother with whom it is biologically uncongenial. This means a relationship between mother and child of a very different order from that which we had when we were drawing only on our biological and evolutionary relationships. But it may be that—in the new kind of world into which we are moving —some denial of the strength of such evolutionary development may be the wisest thing we can do. I refer to the world of mobility, of separation, of loss of cues, of sensory bombardment, and of the substitution of television events for the events that were once a part of the face-to-face group.

Finally, I wish to discuss briefly one of the aspects of human evolution that has tremendous behavioral and social consequences, but about which investigators and educators are doing very little at present. It is exceedingly important to know under what circumstances man's maturational style developed. Why is apparently precocious sexuality followed by a long period of growth with a very limited interest in sex before the adolescent bursts into puberty? We need further to know about the menopause and the hymen. How can we explain the development of these particular biological changes which made it possible to shorten and limit human reproductivity and to give the growing child a longer period to learn? What was the function of maturational styles for early man, and what do they mean now?

These questions are important not only for theoretical reasons. The age of puberty—especially evidenced in females—is dropping four months a decade, creating a change in the population that is having enormous—and potentially drastic—effects. It is steadily shortening the learning period for children before the onset of puberty, when the disturbances that are introduced by the endocrines begin to interfere with the learning process, at a time when education is becoming more important than it has ever been before. (A longer learning period means more time to learn to survive.)[8] I think it can be taken as a paradigm of the way in which a better knowledge of early man—from paleontology and

---

[8] *Editor's note:* In discussions of this point with other participants in the symposium, Dr. Mead heard Dr. E. O. Wilson point out that in genetic studies of the *Drosophila* (fruit fly), if you expand the population, the maturation period is also shortened. Is there, he asked, a possible correlation with our expanding human population? (W.D.)

archeology, and comparative studies of living animal groups—can be tied into contemporary problems. As we draw reciprocally on human and animal studies, we can reach a better understanding of the problems that face us today.[9]

---

[9] *Editor's note:* Perhaps stimulated in part by the Man and Beast Symposium discussions on early man at a hunter-stage, emphasized by Dr. Irven DeVore, and also by Dr. Lionel Tiger's book, *Men in Groups,* Dr. Mead wrote recently that women should not be overlooked in life-conserving and resource-conserving activities. Women, by providing staple foods, saw to it that no one need starve, irrespective of the success of the hunt. In today's world, society must take the direction of encouraging greater participation by women in public life devoted to enlightening men and women both about the necessity of conserving human life and natural resources. (W.D.)

EPILOG

ALEX A. KWAPONG

UNIVERSITY OF GHANA

We have come to the end of the Third International Symposium of the Smithsonian Institution on Man and Beast and have had our rich feast of comparative social behavior. On this occasion, as a man trained in the classics, my mind naturally—or should I rather say instinctively? —goes back to the most accomplished of Plato's dramatic dialogues, the *Symposium*. As you will recall, in this intellectual banquet or dinner party, Plato has immortalized, with as much artistry and poetry as with philosophy, the nature and origins of love. That *Symposium* was, of course, not like our own, "scientific" or international, but an all-Athenian party given by the tragic poet Agathon in his house to his eight guests, of whom Socrates was the most important. I recall the *Symposium* not only because of its relevance as a literary genre or because like our own it was characterized by wit, friendliness, and intellectual integrity; but also because of the brilliant fantasy or jeu d'esprit on human evolution which Plato has put into the mouth of the comic poet, Aristophanes. Man today, says Aristophanes, has evolved from the first human creatures who were originally of three sexes: male, female, and hermaphrodite. When these rebelled against the gods, Zeus bisected them as a punishment for their pride. Man today is therefore but a mere half of his original tripartite whole and "Love is the desire and pursuit of the whole," that is, man's endeavor to reunite himself to his former lost half.

It is a beautiful and humorous fantasy and Plato does not, of course, expect us to take it too literally or seriously.

Every generation and every people have their own mythology on the origins and nature of man. And in all these, man's kinship with and origin from the beasts have been a recurrent theme. This is, for example, particularly true of the view of life of the Akan people in Ghana to whom I belong, in whose language and culture, through proverbs and folklore, man's interconnection with beast is richly portrayed. And in all this, the tendency to anthropomorphize, that is, to cast beast in the mold of man, is no less strong than the tendency to zoomorphize or make a beast out of man.

As I contemplate the relations between man and beast, it is obvious that we must keep the tendencies to anthropomorphize and zoomorphize clearly in mind and be conscious of their limitations as well as their possibilities. In our enthusiasm to embrace the new discipline of ethology —the biological study of behavior—it is essential for us to heed one of the points on which there has been a clear consensus: We need to bring man and beast together, but we must also keep them apart.

Every educated man of today, whatever his hue or nationality, now accepts without question the fact that man has evolved, slowly and gradually, from ancestors which were far more similar to other mammals than man is now. This means that everything man is and does must have evolved, through a long series of minute evolutionary steps, from what his animal ancestors were and did. Man has diverged very gradually from monkey or ape-like stock to what he is now, just as modern, closely-related animal species have diverged from common stock.[1]

This process of divergent gradual evolution has produced man— *Homo sapiens*—who, until the recent advances of ethology, was often said to be "unique," that is to say, so essentially different from animals, that he was something altogether new, and that he was divided from animals by a deep and unbridgeable chasm.

To the layman like myself, one of the salient conclusions which has emerged from the various presentations during the symposium—each based upon different premises—is that man is unique only in the sense that he is "strikingly different" from the other animals. Man is unique all right, but he is an animal of a kind, as in Tinbergen's paraphrase of George Orwell's dictum, "all animals are unique, but man is more unique than others."

In body and functions, man is very similar to other mammals; his uniqueness lies, however, in the matter of behavior, and it is his brain that is unique and functions in a unique way and has produced his language, culture, and his civilization. But this culture is as much rooted in man's biology as in his environment. This insight into the importance of biological factors in cultural evolution is one of the crucial contributions made recently by the science of ethology to human understanding.

Man, as a result, possesses the unparalleled ability of handing on his experience from one generation to the next, and thereby radically

---

[1] Tinbergen, N. "On War and Peace in Animals and Men." *Science* (1968), 160:1411–1418; and "Aggression and Fear in the Normal Sexual Behaviour of Some Animals," pages 3–23 in *The Pathology and Treatment of Sexual Deviation,* I. Rosen, editor, London: Oxford University Press, 1964.

changing his environment, both physical and social. This cultural evolution is, of course, much faster than genetic evolution. Witness, for example, the landing of astronauts on the moon. Yet these astronauts have not genetically diverged very differently from Cro-Magnon man. However much we may individually adapt to these technological changes, the fact remains, nevertheless, that there are limits imposed by our hereditary animal constitutions on the rate at which human behavior can be adjusted and modified and that we are all conditioned by the much slower speed of genetic evolution. I have recently learned that man's limited behavioral adjustability has been outpaced by the culturally determined changes in his social environment and that is why man is now a misfit in his own society.

It is in this context that I have found particularly illuminating and rewarding the discussion on aggression during this symposium. The nature and scope of aggression in animals have, I think, been placed in reasonable perspective, and shown to be a complex process of interaction between factors, both internal and external, both genetic and environmental. Aggression is not a simplistic, mechanistic process nor is it the only pebble on the animal behavioral beach (if I may be allowed this mixed metaphor). Competition and aggression in the world of nonhuman primates is also accompanied by fear and withdrawal and, as John Crook has so vividly shown, by cooperation within the group. "Men, like monkeys," and I quote him, "appear to cooperate best when at their most competitive." Nevertheless, human beings, again like monkeys, are socially mobile and may change the frame of reference from a narrow sectarian concern to broader avenues of wider significance. An understanding of the forces controlling the maintenance of social position in relation to human needs in terms of identity, in-group membership, and role transfer in relation to self-esteem would much improve our chances of social control.

It is from this perspective that we may view the issue of war and peace and international cooperation. Far from giving way to despair and defeatism, I am encouraged by the results of this symposium. The development of behavior is very complex; so far, much progress has been made in analyzing it in animals, but with respect to men only a small beginning has been made.

I would like to suggest in all humility, being a classical scholar from a continent which is the home of the Australopithecine ancestors of man, the hamadryas baboon which has been so extensively studied, and the Bushmen of the Kalahari Desert, of whom we have heard and seen so much during this symposium, that what is needed very much today is also a serious and "truly scientific and powerful anthropology" of "Homo Industrialis" or "Technology Man," whether in America, Europe, or elsewhere. Man, the cultural animal, should once more take the center of the modern stage, instead of technology and the impersonal computer. That, it seems to me, is what the restless youth in their violent gropings and fumblings, appear to be saying today. The problem "moves back to an economic and educational level," again in John Crook's words, "with a focus on the needs of humanity as a whole."

Education and scientific research, human understanding and coopera- tion, these are among the means by which man has risen above the beasts. It is by these means that we can hope to bridge the dangerous gap which now divides the rich nations from the poor. The difference, how- ever, between now and the previous centuries, is that the world has been knit together by instantaneous communications, and we are all each our brother's keeper. That is the final point I would like to make and, of course, I am Socratic enough to believe that the "increase and diffusion of knowledge" is one of the highest ends of man; and for this, we are grate- ful and indebted to Smithson and all of you who have labored so success- fully to bring Smithson's ideal into fruition.

We have been reminded by Marvin Bressler that to achieve this syn- thesis, social biology and sociology must come together in sympathy as a "unified life science that would define the nature and limits of human variability."[2] That is a proposition which, I am sure, we all very much share.

And here I may be permitted, in concluding these brief remarks, to end as I began by going back to ancient Athens. Let me remind you of Sophocles' great hymn in his *Antigone* which the chorus sings to the ingenuity and limitations of man:

> Wonders are many on earth, and the greatest of these
> Is man, who rides the ocean and takes his way
> Through the deeps, through wind-swept valleys of perilous seas
>> That surge and sway.
>> He is master of ageless Earth, to his own will bending
> The immortal mother of gods by the sweat of his brow,
> As year succeeds to year, with toil unending
>> Of mule and plough.
>> He is lord of all things living; birds of the air,

---

[2] *Editor's note:* This quotation comes from Bressler's "Sociology, Biology, and Ideology," in *Genetics,* David Glass, editor, New York: The Rockefeller University Press and Russell Sage Foundation, 1968. *Genetics* was a background paper for symposium participants. (W.D.)

Beasts of the field, all creatures of sea and land
He takes, cunning to capture and ensnare
    With sleight of hand;
    Hunting the savage beast from the upland rocks,
Taming the mountain monarch in his lair,
Teaching the wild horse and the roaming ox
    His yoke to bear.
    The use of language, the wind-swift motion of brain
He learnt; found out the laws of living together
In cities, building him shelter against the rain
    And wintry weather.
    There is nothing beyond his power. His subtlety
Meets all chance, all danger conquers.
For every ill he has found its remedy,
    Save only death.
O wondrous subtlety of man, that draws
To good or evil ways! Great honor is given
And power to him who upholds his country's laws
    And the justice of heaven.
    But he that too rashly daring, walks in sin
In solitary pride to his life's end,
At door of mine shall never enter in
    To call me friend.

AUTHOR INDEX

Adams, O. S. See Alluisi, E. A.
Adams, R. McC., 287
Adorno, T. W., 201
Alexander, B. K., 74, 83
Alexander, R. D., 80, 83, 195, 211
Allee, W. C., 238, 255, 256
Alluisi, E. A., 162, 174
Altmann, M., 148, 174
Altmann, S. A., 197, 211
Anderson, L. E. See Pinckney, G. A.
Anderson, P. K., 29, 32
Andrewartha, H. G., 198, 211
Ardrey, R., 7, 78, 81, 83, 183, 210, 211
Aristotle, 365
Ashmole, N. P., 198, 211
Auchincloss, L., 255
Autrum, H., 229, 233
Ayala, F. J., 206, 211
Baerends, G. P., 67, 83
Baerends-van Roon, J. M. See Baerends, G. P.
Bakker, K., 198. See also Miller, R. S.
Barlow, G. W., 45, 55
Barnett, S. A., 73, 83, 183, 202, 211
Bartholomew, G. A., 241, 257
Bastock, M., 204, 212
Bateson, P. P. G., 148, 171, 174
Beg, M. A., 78, 241, 243, 260. See also Southwick, C. H.
Bernstein, I. L., 247, 251, 257
Bierens de Haan, J. A., 329, 330
Birch, L. C. See Andrewartha, H. G.
Birdwhistell, R. L., 32, 375
Blair, W. F., 195, 212

Bleibtreu, J., 7
Blitz, J., 104, 105. See also Ploog, D.
Blurton-Jones, N. G., 295
Bock, W. J., 323, 330
Bohannan, P., 18
Bolk, L., 323, 330
Bowden, D. P., 106, 122
Bowers, J. M., 74, 83
Boyd, H. See Fabricius, E.
Brain, C. K., 232, 234. See also Gartlan, J. S.
Breder, C. M., Jr., 145, 175
Bressler, M., 7, 388
Brian, M. V., 188, 189, 190, 212
Broca, P., 101, 122
Brodbeck, D. J., 147, 175
Bronson, F. H., 193, 212
Bruce, H. M., 193, 212
Bucy, P. See Kluver, H.
Buechner, H. K., 83, 91
Bugental, J. F. T., 256
Burghardt, G. M., 148, 151, 175
Busnel, R. G., 30
Butterfield, P. A., 246, 257. See also Crook, J. H.
Byers, P., 17. See also Mead, M.
Cairns, R. B., 148, 149, 150, 171, 175
Calhoun, J. B., 200, 212, 229, 233, 249, 257, 377
Calving, A. D. See Igel, G. J.
Candland, D. K., 148, 149, 175
Cantril, H., 350, 352
Carpenter, C. R., 221, 233, 241, 257, 304, 310
Castell, R., 98, 122

391

Cazaly, W. H., 81, 83
Chance, M. R. A., 55, 227, 233, 248, 257, 289, 296
Chapple, E. D., 375
Cherry, C., 30
Chitty, D., 188, 198, 212
Chomsky, N., 282, 296
Christian, J. J., 145, 175, 229, 234
Clark, L. R., 185, 187, 212
Clark, S. L. See Ranson, S. W.
Clark, W. E. LeGros, 277, 296
Clausen, C. P., 192, 212
Clements, F. E., 184, 212
Cloar, J. F. See Melvin, K. B.
Coates, C. W. See Breder, C. M., Jr.
Cole, H. A., 168, 175
Collias, N. E., 148, 175
Connell, J. H., 188, 212
Coombs, C. J. F., 188. See also Crook, J. H.
Corbet, P. S., 78, 83
Cornell, J. M., 172, 177. See also Salzen, E. A.
Coulson, J. C., 67, 83
Counter, S. A. See Grier, J. B.
Crevecoeur, A., 66, 83
Crook, J. H., 9, 67, 78, 84, 195, 213, 240, 241, 244, 246, 248, 252, 255, 257
Cross, H. A., 148, 152, 154, 175
Darling, F. F., 67, 84
Dart, R. A., 201, 208, 213
Darwin, C. R., 59, 84, 255, 257, 277
Darwin, E., 59, 84
Davis, D. E., 229, 234, 241, 257. See also Christian, J. J.
Deag, J., 244, 257
Delafresnaye, J. F., 31
Delgado, J. M. R., 318, 330
Dennenberg, V. H., 149, 175
Descy, A., 66, 84
DeVore, I., 241, 246, 248, 257, 258, 304, 311. See also Hall, K. R. L.; Lee, E. B.
Dillon, W., 17
Dobzhansky, T., 206, 208, 209, 213

Dumas, P. C., 188, 213
Dunn, L. C., 207, 213
Durrell, G., 7
Ebert, J. D., 318, 330
Eckman, J., 148, 175
Ehrlich, P. R., 29, 33
Ehrman, L., 206, 213
Eibl-Eibesfeldt, I., 32, 60, 84, 319, 330
Eisenberg, J. F., 33, 134, 137, 138, 139, 240, 242, 255, 257, 303
Elmes, G., 189, 212. See also Brian, M. V.
Emlen, J. M., 80, 84
Espmark, Y., 68, 84
Fabre, J. H., 64, 84
Fabricius, E., 155, 175
Falconer, D. S., 38, 56, 203, 205, 213
Fischer, H., 132, 139
Fisher, A. E., 147, 175
Fisher, R. A., 28, 33
Foenander, F., 38, 56. See also James, J. W.
Ford, E. B., 206, 213
Foster, W. A., 84, 91
Freeman, D., 80, 84
Friedman, H., 64, 84
Friedrich II, F. von Stauffen, 112, 123
Frincke, G. See Johnson, R. C.
Frith, H. J., 320, 330
Fulbright, J. W., 373
Fuller, J. L., 28, 33
Galbraith, J. K., 10
Galton, F., 67, 68, 70, 84
Garattini, S., 349, 352
Gardner, B. T., 117, 123. See also Kellogg, W. N.
Gardner, R. A., 117, 123. See also Kellogg, W. N.
Gartlan, J. S., 232, 234, 241, 246, 247, 251, 255, 257, 258. See also Crook, J. H.
Geddes, P., 255, 257
Gehlen, A., 323, 330
Geier, P. W. See Clark, L. R.

Geist, V., 59, 84
Gibb, L. M. See Gibb, T. R.
Gibb, T. R., 256
Gibson, J. B., 206, 213
Gifford, D. P., 243, 244, 258
Glass, D. C., 149, 177, 388. See also Latane, B.
Goodall, J. van L., 7, 255, 258, 329, 330
Gorer, G., 374
Gottlieb, G., 151, 155, 168, 176
Gould, E., 138, 139. See also Eisenberg, J. F.
Grant, E. C., 44, 56
Gray, P. H., 148, 176
Greenberg, B., 148, 176
Greenewalt, C., 10
Gregory, W. K., 315, 331
Grier, J. B., 152, 176
Griffiths, A. See Corbet, P. S.
Grünbaum, A., 114, 123
Guiton, P., 152, 155, 171, 176. See also Taylor, A. W.
Haldane, J. B. S., 84, 90, 318, 331
Hall, E. T., 234
Hall, K. R. L., 199, 209, 213, 230, 246
Halle, L. J., 7, 10, 362
Hamburger, V., 318, 331
Hamilton, W. D., 29, 33, 63, 64, 70, 74, 78, 84–85, 90, 199, 213, 242, 250, 258
Hamilton, W. J., 30. See also Marler, P. R.
Hamilton, W. J., III, 64, 85. See also Orians, G. H.
Harlow, H. F., 147, 176
Harris, V. T., 207, 213
Harrison, A. A., 166, 176
Hartley, P. H. T., 188, 213
Haskins, C. P., 189, 214
Haskins, E. F. See Haskins, C. P.
Hayes, C. See Hayes, K. J.
Hayes, K. J., 117, 123
Head, H., 316, 331
Hebb, D. O., 269, 272
Hediger, H., 56, 148, 176

Heinroth, O., 8
Hess, E. E., 147, 148, 151, 175, 176. See also Burghardt, G. M.
Hewitt, R., 152. See also Taylor, A. W.
Hinde, R. A., 132, 139, 155, 177, 195, 214, 242, 243, 258, 259, 320, 331. See also Kaufman, I. C.; Rowell, T. E.
Hirsch, J., 203, 206, 214
Hobby, B. M., 64, 66, 85
Hoffman, H. S., 152, 153, 176
Holcomb, A., 148, 152, 154, 175
Holst, E. von, 229, 233, 316, 323. See also Autrum, H.
Hooker, B. I., 195, 214
Hopf, S., 106, 107, 123, 125. See also Ploog, D.
Horn, H. S., 194, 214
Hornocker, M. G., 137, 139
Hostmann, E., 67, 85
Hudgens, G. A. See Dennenberg, V. H.
Hudleston, J. A., 67, 85
Hughes, R. D. See Clark, L. R.
Hutchinson, G. E., 187, 199, 214
Huxley, J. S., 7, 96, 123
Igel, G. J., 147, 176
Imanishi, K., 242, 258
Itani, J., 243, 244, 255, 258
James, J. W., 38, 56, 221, 234. See also McBride, G.
Jaynes, J., 148, 176
Johnson, R. C., 165, 176
Jolly, A., 241, 258
Jürgens, U., 110, 111, 123
Kanner, L., 117, 123
Kaufman, I. C., 155, 177
Keith, Sir A., 278, 296
Kelley, A. F., 189, 212. See also Brian, M. V.
Kellogg, L. A., 331. See also Kellogg, W. N.
Kellogg, W. N., 117, 123, 329, 331
Kendeigh, S. C., 320, 331
Kimura, M., 74, 85
King, J. A., 241, 258, 321, 328, 331

Kleiman, D. G., 137, 139, 303
Klinghammer, E., 132, 139
Klopfer, P. H., 183, 214
Kluver, H., 101, 123
Knight-Jones, E. W., 168, 175, 177
Koestler, A., 7
Kozma, F., Jr. See Hoffman, H. S.
Krohn, H. See Castell, R.
Kropotkin, P., 255, 258
Krott, G. See Krott, P.
Krott, P., 319, 331
Kruuk, H., 67, 85
Kuehn, R., 137, 138, 139. See also Eisenberg, J. F.
Kühme, von W., 241, 258, 322, 331
Kummer, H., 7, 60, 78, 85, 221, 222, 225, 228, 234, 245, 247, 248, 259
Kuo, Z. Y., 151, 177
Kurt, F., 137, 139
LaBarre, W., 292, 296
Labine, P. A., 85, 91
Lack, D., 67, 74, 78, 80, 85, 146, 188, 198, 214, 240, 241, 259
Lahiri, R. K., 244, 259
Langer, B. See Spiess, E. B.
Langer, S. K., 8, 316, 321, 326, 331
Latane, B., 148, 149, 177
Latta, J., 109, 110, 125. See also Winter, P.
Latyszewski, M., 38, 56. See also Falconer, D. S.
Laws, R. M., 303
Leach, E., 183, 214
Lee, E. B., 311
LeGros Clark. See Clark, W. E. LeGros
Lenneberg, E. H., 113, 114, 120, 123, 282, 296
Lerner, I. M., 203, 214
Levins, R., 184, 193, 214
Leuthold, W. See Buechner, H. K.
Leyhausen, P., 195, 200, 214, 224, 234
Locke, J., 325, 332
Loconti, J. D., 193, 214

Lorenz, K., 7, 8, 60, 74, 77, 85, 96, 123, 131, 132, 139, 155, 171, 177, 183, 190, 214, 288, 296, 351
Lorge, I., 156. See also Thorndike, E. L.
Lovaas, I. O., 119, 124
Luce, R. D., 63, 85
Lutz, B., 319, 332
MacArthur, R. H., 199, 214. See also Hutchinson, G. E.
MacLean, P., 98, 100, 101, 102, 103, 104, 124, 125. See also Ploog, D.
Mainardi, M., 148, 177
Malyshev, S. I., 78, 85
Mandelbaum, D. G., 6
Manning, A., 204, 212
Marler, P. R., 30, 33
Marshall, A. J., 320, 322, 332
Martin, P. S., 11
Mason, W. A., 224, 234
Massingill, L. S. 150. See also Melvin, K. B.
Matlin, M. A. W., 166, 168, 177
Matter, C. G. See Cross, H. A.
Maurus, M., 105, 110, 111, 123, 124
Mayr, E., 207, 215
McBride, G., 55, 56, 221, 234
McCook, H. C., 189, 215
Mead, M., 8, 17, 378
Mech, L. D., 137, 139
Meltzer, J. D., 149, 175
Melvin, K. B., 150, 177
Merrell, D. J., 205, 215
Meyer, C. C., 151, 152, 174, 178. See also Salzen, E. A.
Meyerriecks, A. J., 188
Michener, C. D., 78, 85
Miller, N. E. See Delgado, J. M. R.
Miller, R. S., 184, 194, 198, 215
Milliron, H. E., 66, 85
Milne, D. See Candland, D. K.
Mitra, J., 105, 124. See also Maurus, M.

Moltz, H., 155, 171, 177
Montagu, A., 7, 183, 215, 255
Moore, N. W., 194, 215
Moore, W. G., 67, 85
Morris, D., 7, 183, 215, 241, 259, 374
Morris, R. F. See Clark, L. R.
Morrison, J. A. See Buechner, H. K.
Moyer, K. E., 272, 349, 352
Mykytowycz, R., 197, 215, 241, 259
Nadel, S. F., 251, 259
Napier, J., 7
Naylor, A. F., 193, 215
Nelson, J. B., 198, 215
Nicholson, A. J., 197, 215
Nietzsche, F., 59, 86
Niu, M. C. See Twitty, V. C.
Noble, G. K., 194, 215
Oliver, D. R. See Milliron, H. E.
Orians, G. H., 64, 85, 194, 215, 240, 259
Paget, Sir R., 156
Paine, R. T., 188, 215
Parker, I. C. See Laws, R. M.
Parsons, P. A., 203, 206, 215
Payne, R. S., 16
Penfield, W., 114, 115, 116, 117, 124
Pepper, S., 269, 272, 350, 352
Peterson, N., 152, 153, 177
Petras, N. L., 77, 86
Pfeiffer, J., 7, 255, 267, 272
Pinckney, G. A., 148, 177
Pitelka, F. A., 194, 199, 215
Pitz, C. L., 151, 177
Plateaux-Quenu, C., 66, 86
Plato, 388, 389
Platt, J. R., 317, 332
Ploog, D., 98, 102, 103, 104, 105, 106, 107, 109, 110, 111, 122, 123, 124, 125. See also Bowden, D. P.; Castell, R.; Jürgens, U.; MacLean, P.; Maurus, M.; Winter, P.
Ploog, F., 104, 105, 125

Pontin, A. J., 189, 216
Pratt, C. L., 172, 177
Pryer, H., 67, 86
Rabinowitch, V. E., 151, 178
Raiffa, H., 63. See also Luce, R. D.
Ranson, S. W., 116, 125
Rapoport, A., 63, 86
Rasmussen, Th., 114, 115, 116. See also Penfield, W.
Raven, P. H. See Ehrlich, P. R.
Reynolds, F., 255, 259. See also Reynolds, V.
Reynolds, V., 232, 234, 255, 259
Ribbands, C. R., 73, 86
Richards, O. W., 66, 86
Ripley, S. D., 198, 199, 216
Ritter, W. E., 241, 259
Roberts, L., 117, 124. See also Penfield, W.
Roberts, W. W. See Delgado, J. M. R.
Robinson, B. W., 103, 117, 124, 125. See also MacLean, P.
Ropartz, P., 193, 216
Ross, R. B. See Pitz, C. L.
Roth, L. M., 193. See also Loconti, J. D.
Rowell, T. E., 242, 246, 247, 259
Russell, C., 68, 86
Russell, W. M. S. See Russell, C.
Rutter, M., 120, 125
Ryder, S. R., 241, 259
Sackett, G. P. See Pratt, C. L.
Sakagami, S. R., 78, 86
Salt, G., 193, 216
Salzen, E. A., 151, 152, 155, 168, 171, 172, 174, 178
Sarbin, T. R., 251, 259
Schaffner, B., 17, 376
Schaller, G., 137, 139
Schenkel, R., 197, 216
Scheven, J., 66, 86
Schmitt, F. O., 317, 332
Schoener, T. W., 188, 199, 216
Schooland, J. B., 171, 178

Scott, J. P., 28, 33, 68, 86, 147, 148, 155, 168, 171, 178
Sessions, R., 15
Sharpe, L. F. See Bernstein, I. L.
Shearer, W. M. See Grier, J. B.
Shelford, V. E., 184, 212
Sherif, C. W. See Sherif, M.
Sherif, M., 256, 259
Sherrington, C. S. See Grünbaum, A.
Shipley, W. U., 148, 178
Shoffner, R. N., 221, 234. See also McBride, G.
Siddiqi, M. R., 78, 241, 243. See also Southwick, C. H.
Sigg, E. B., 349, 352
Skutch, A., 241, 260
Sluckin, W., 148, 152, 155, 168, 171, 178. See also Salzen, E. A.
Sommer, R., 230, 231, 234
Southwick, C. H., 78, 86, 229, 234, 241, 243, 244, 259, 260
Spassky, B., 206, 213. See also Dobzhansky, T.
Spencer-Booth, Y., 242, 243, 258, 259, 260. See also Hinde, R. A.; Rowell, T. E.
Spiess, E. B., 206, 216
Spuhler, J. N., 207, 216
Starck, D., 97, 125
Stebbins, G. L., 95, 96, 125
Stern, C., 207, 216
Stettner, L. J. See Moltz, H.
Stevenson, J. P., 168, 177. See also Knight-Jones, E. W.
Storr, A., 7, 183, 216
St. Paul, U. von, 323. See also Holst, E. von
Suzuki, A., 255, 258. See also Itani, J.
Szilard, L., 377
Tajfel, H., 256, 260
Talbot, M., 189, 216
Taylor, A. W., 152, 178
Thiessen, D. D., 145, 178
Thoday, J. M., 206, 213, 216

Thomson, C. W. See Johnson, R. C.
Thompson, D. W., 317, 332
Thompson, J. A. See Geddes, P.
Thompson, W. R., 28, 33
Thorndike, E. L., 156, 178
Thorpe, W. H., 148, 178, 285
Tiger, L., 7, 281, 381
Tinbergen, N., 7, 67, 86, 96, 125, 198, 217, 296, 321, 332, 386
Tinkle, D. W., 80, 83. See also Alexander, R. D.
Tolman, E. C., 148, 179
Tschanz, B., 320, 332
Twitty, V. C., 318, 332
Vandenbergh, J. G., 248, 260
Verheyen, R., 199, 217
Verner, J., 63, 86
Von Haartman, L., 188, 217
von Holst. See Holst, E. von
Waddington, C. H., 53, 56
Wallace, B., 202, 217
Washburn, S. L., 311
Way, M. J., 191, 217
Wecker, S. C., 207, 217
Weiss, G. H., 74. See Kimura, M.
Weiss, P., 316, 332
Wheeler, W. M., 66, 87
Wickler, W., 222, 234, 271, 272
Williams, G. C., 67, 80, 87
Willson, M. F. See Verner, J.
Wilson, A. P., 241, 247, 260
Wilson, D. P., 168, 179
Wilson, E. O., 9, 193, 197, 217
Winter, P., 106, 107, 109, 110, 111, 123, 125. See also Bowden, D. P.; Jürgens, U.; Ploog, D.
Woodring, J. P., 78, 87
Wright, H. E. See Martin, P. S.
Wright, S., 87, 90, 91
Wynne-Edwards, V. C., 145, 179, 221, 234, 240, 260, 289, 296
Yasuno, M., 189, 217
Yerkes, A. W. See Yerkes, R. M.
Yerkes, R. M., 329, 332

Yoshiba, Y., 230, 234
Yoshikawa, K., 66, 87
Young, P. T., 317, 332
Zajonc, R. B., 146, 156, 158, 162,
    166, 168, 170, 179

Zarrow, M. X., 149, 175
Ziman, J., 17
Zipf, G., 156
Zolman, J. F., 145. See also Thies-
    sen, D. D.

SUBJECT INDEX

Act, the, as the unit of vital process, 316, 317
Activity rhythms (see Circadian rhythms)
Adaptation, 52
Aesthetic sense in birds, 8
Affiliation, 147–155 (see also Pairing)
  Individual recognition, 70
  Kinship, 72
Aggregation, 39
Aggression (see Agonistic behavior; Dominance; Spacing mechanisms; Submissive behavior; Territory)
Aggressive neglect, 133
Agonistic behavior, 183–202 (see also Warfare)
  Aggression, 183–187, 188–193, 201–202
  Competitive behavior, 184–197, 249
  Intergroup, 177, 187–188
  Intragroup, 69, 187–188
  Scramble competition, 197–198
Altruism, 29, 59, 65, 69, 71, 72 (see also Cooperation)
  Heritability of, 72, 78, 91
Anthropomorphism, 374–375, 385
Appeasement postures (see Submissive behavior)
Attachment, 146
Attraction, 146
Australopithecines, 301
Autistic children, 117–120
Behavior patterns
  Computer analogy for, 47–48

Behavior patterns (*continued*)
  Organization, 41
  Temporal, 41
  Functional, 45
  Regulation of, 45–50
Bonding, 54–55 (see also Affiliation; Pairing)
Brain and behavior, 98–103
Brain stimulation, 110
Breast feeding, 379
Breeding season, 46–47
  Hormones, 46
  Photoperiodic effects on, 46
Cannibalism, 190
Caste, 42
Circadian rhythms, 41, 43, 49
Communication, 96–98 (see also Speech)
  Auditory, 108–112
  Brain mechanisms, 103–111
  Distance and communication, 223
Competition (see Agonistic behavior)
Conflict behavior, 48 (see also Display)
Cooperation, 238–239, 240–241 (see also Altruism)
  Contingent cooperation, 249–255
  Heritable basis, 78, 91
  Male-male, 247–249
Conservation, 10–11
Crowding, 145–146, 200–201, 229–233
Cruelty, 80–81
Culture, 278–280
  Cultural differentials, 279

Density dependent controls, 184–185, 226–227 (see also Crowding)
Diplomacy, 361–362
Disarmament, 358
Dispersal, 74
  Panmictic, 74
  Stepping stone, 74
  Viscous, 74
Displacement activities, 50 (see also Conflict behavior)
Display
  Genital, 103–108
  Lizards, 98
Dominance, 43, 194, 246
  Hierarchy, 246
Drive (see Motivation)
Endogenous rhythms (see Circadian rhythms)
Evolution of human society, 299–310
Evolutionary continuities, 336–337
Evolutionary trends of social behavior, 95–98
Fallacy of the two species, 366–367
Fitness, 29
  Inclusive, 72, 76
Genetic assimilation, 52–54, 202
Genetic drift, 89–90
Genetics of behavior (see Heritability of behavior)
Gregarious behavior, 30, 67 (see also Social behavior)
Heritability of behavior, 27
  Behavior traits, 61
  Character evolution, 202–210
  Definition, 38, 202
  Factors of population size, 74, 77, 89–91
  Fitness of traits, 72
  Inheritance and coding, 51–52
Hierarchy (see Dominance)
Hormones and behavior, 42–43, 45–49
Hostile behavior (see Agonistic behavior)

Human behavior, 54–55, 255–256, 277
  Attributes, 277–279
  Uniqueness, 295, 329, 336, 356
  Violence, 6
Human survival, 355–368
Hunter-gatherer society, 306–310
Imprinting, 131–132 (see also Pairing)
  Exposure effects, 147–154
  Exposures effects in humans, 155–174
Individual distance, 44, 222–223 (see also Spacing mechanisms)
Inheritance of behavior (see Heritability of behavior)
Innate and learned behavior, 27
Instinct, 27, 318
Instinctive behavior, 318–320
Institutions, cultural, 326–327
Interaction, 44 (see also Caste; Role)
Intuition, 324–352
Kinship, 281 (see also Relatives)
!Kung Bushmen, 306
Language, human, 55, 282–283, 325
Leadership, 247, 303–305
Learning, 51
Male associations, 281 (see also Cooperation)
Mating systems (see also Monogamy; Polygamy)
  Assortative, 65
  Dissortative, 66
  Random, 60, 61
Mobbing behavior, 319–320
Monogamy, 63
Motivation, 317–318, 322
Nature-nurture controversy, 37, 52 (see also Innate and learned behavior)
Neurological correlates of behavior, 95–122
Normative thinking, 363, 364
Pain, 78
Pair bond, 132 (see also Pairing)

Pairing
  Affiliation, 147
  Assortative (see Mating systems, assortative)
  Bonding, 54–55
  Dissortative (see Mating systems, dissortative)
  Selective, 65
Panmixia, 61
Parasitism, 64, 66 (see also Selfish behavior)
Parental behavior, 240–245
  "Auntie" phenomena, 243
Peripheral males, 248 (see also Submissive behavior; Dominance)
Polygamy, 63
Population control, 185 (see also Crowding)
Prisoner's dilemma, 63, 81
Psychic unity, 287
Rank order (see Dominance)
Reductionism, 374
Relatives, 70–74 (see also Kinship; Parental behavior)
  Coefficient of inclusive relationship, 70
  Formation of inbreeding groups, 74, 77
  Recognition of, 71, 73
Roles, 42, 43, 54, 251–254 (see also Kinship)
  Primates, 303–306
    Adult female, 305
    Adult male, 303–305
    Subadult male, 305–306
Selection, 202–210 (see also Heritability of behavior)
  Experimental, 38–39
  Natural, 202–204
  Dysgenic, 62
Selfish behavior, 30, 59, 60

Social control mechanisms, 245–249 (see also Dominance; Submissive behavior; Social privacy)
Social Darwinism, 6
Social distance, 194, 222–223
Social organization, 39–45
  Aggregate, 39
  Caste, 42
  Division of labor, 42
  Roles, 43, 251–254
  Subsystems, 41
  Territorial (see Territory)
Social privacy, 227–229
Spacing mechanisms, 43, 193–194, 221–233 (see also Territory)
Species-specific behavior, 32
Speech, 114–117 (see also Autistic children; Language)
  Brain mechanisms, 112–120
Spiteful behavior, 30, 60, 91
Submissive behavior, 224–226
Survival, human, 355–368
Swiss Confederation, 361, 366
Symbolism, 281, 325, 326
  Inherited natural symbolisms, 324
Tabula rasa, 280, 286, 295
Territory, 41, 194, 223
  Rhinoceroses, 9
Tradition in birds, 8–9
Universal grammar, 292
Universals, behavioral, 279, 337–340
Warfare
  Arms race, 358, 359
  Human, 77–78, 361
  Insect, 79, 189
  Limitations on, 358, 362
Zoomorphism, 374, 385